Culture and Economy

Culture and Economy

The Shaping of Capitalism in Eastern Asia

edited by Timothy Brook and Hy V. Luong

Ann Arbor

THE UNIVERSITY OF MICHIGAN PRESS

First paperback edition 1999
Copyright © by the University of Michigan 1997
All rights reserved
Published in the United States of America by
The University of Michigan Press
Manufactured in the United States of America
⊗ Printed on acid-free paper

2002   2001   2000   1999   4   3   2   1

A CIP catalog record for this book is available from the British Library

Library of Congress Cataloging-in-Publication Data

Culture and economy : the shaping of capitalism in eastern Asia /
    edited by Timothy Brook and Hy V. Luong.
        p.   cm.
    Includes bibliographical references and index.
    ISBN 0-472-10776-3 (cloth)
    1. Capitalism—East Asia.   2. Capitalism—Asia, Southeastern.
3. East Asia—Economic conditions.   4. Asia, Southeastern—Economic
conditions.   5. East Asia—Social life and customs.   6. Asia,
Southeastern—Social life and customs.   7. National characteristics.
I. Brook, Timothy, 1951–   .   II. Luong, Hy V.
HC460.5.C85   1997
330.12'2'095—dc21   97-3281
                                                             CIP

ISBN 0-472-08598-0 (pbk. : alk. paper)

Acknowledgments

This volume of essays arises from a conference organized under the auspices of the University of Toronto—York University Joint Centre for Asia Pacific Studies in May 1994 to celebrate the twentieth anniversary of the founding of the Joint Centre. Paul Evans, the director of the Joint Centre, played a seminal role in directing us to mark the occasion in this way. The conference became the first in a series of annual conferences by which the Joint Centre strives to bring together specialists in Canada and beyond to think through issues of current relevance to the study and understanding of Eastern Asia.

In addition to the authors represented in this volume, Claude Comtois, Michael Donnelly, Victor Falkenheim, Takeshi Hamashita, Thomas Rawski, André Schmid, Patcharee Siroros, Richard Stubbs, Wei-ming Tu, and Jialin Xie presented papers at the conference. Mitchell Bernard, Gregory Blue, Donald Brean, Charles Burton, Ping-Chun Hsiung, Janet Landa, Ruth Hayhoe, and Janet Salaff served as commentators. We are grateful to all these scholars for contributing their expertise to the project, and we wish to acknowledge their combined influence in shaping our thinking on the subject of culture and economy in Eastern Asia.

Principal funding for the project was generously provided by the Chiang Ching-kuo Foundation and the Social Sciences and Humanities Research Council of Canada. Additional support was furnished by the Consulate-General of Korea in Toronto and the Canada-ASEAN Centre. Within the University of Toronto, we are grateful to the Office of the Vice-President for Research and International Relations, the School of Graduate Studies, and the departments of Anthropology and History for their financial support. From York University, assistance was generously provided by the offices of the Vice-President (Academic), the Associate Vice-President (Research), and the Dean of Arts.

It would not have been possible to organize the conference or produce a volume without the interest and commitment of Carol Irving, the administrator of the Joint Centre, and we acknowledge all her work to support this project. Lynne Russell edited portions of the manuscript, compiled the bibliography, and otherwise attended to the details that eluded us. At the University of Michigan Press, we thank Susan Whitlock for never wavering in her enthusiasm for this book and Michael Landauer, Kevin Rennells, and Jillian Downey for seeing it through to publication.

Contents

Introduction: Culture and Economy in the Postcolonial World

Timothy Brook and Hy V. Luong

Capitalism may have erupted in sixteenth-century Europe, but since that time it has urgently remade economy, society, and politics not just in Europe but throughout the world. The dominant model for explaining how capitalism came about, and how it has interacted with other socioeconomic formations, argues from internal causes and sees capitalism as intrinsic to the character and quality of European life. By extension, its effective adoption outside the European West is regarded as contingent upon the degree to which the norms of "local" social and economic life can be made to adapt—or, better still, conform—to the "universal" norms governing the conduct of human and material relations in the West. The record of the colonial era seemed to confirm the truth that capitalism was a characteristically European—and rational—response to the challenges of economic growth and material change and that other cultures had "failed" to generate capitalism. From this perspective, capitalism at its origin was specific to its Western cultural context, but as the world system grew it developed into a universal "set of social rules by which people try to increase the value of capital through market competition" (Shimada 1993, 17). Capitalism late in the twentieth century can now be applied anywhere, in this view, and will transform the cultural contexts into which it comes in whatever ways it needs so as to encourage the free accumulation and movement of capital.

This book has been compiled to explore these claims in the context of the remarkable expansion of capitalism in Eastern Asia (as we shall designate in one unit the conventionally distinguished East and Southeast Asia). Is capitalism as one finds it in Eastern Asia the same system of production and consumption as one finds in the West? If it differs, are those differences in form or in substance and does this matter? Does the notion of difference go to the heart of culturally based changes in the world system or does it merely reflect an ideologically distorted view of Western capitalism (e.g., Rutten 1994)? Capitalism is indubitably shaping Eastern Asia, and being shaped by it, yet the flows of influence are far from unproblematic. Has capitalism's shaping involved a fundamental reordering of how Asians work within the global system or has it simply required the reregistering of certain habits and practices long established in the West but entirely familiar in Asian contexts as well? Is capitalism in Eastern Asia mutating into uniquely Eastern Asian forms or has it simply dressed itself in systems of cultural reference that camouflage its fundamental incompatibility with, and hegemony over, indigenous cultural forms? More simply: what does it mean to say that the countries of Eastern Asia are either capitalist or becoming so?

Culture and Modernization

The questions arise in part because of the split within Western social science between economistic and culturalistic ways of thinking about the presence of "Western" systems in an Asian context. The economistic explanation, which Karl Marx favored, regards culture as superstructural and having a derivative relationship with economic relations: the economy sets the conditions for culture, and when the economy changes culture changes to accommodate it. A culturalistic explanation turns the relationship between economy and culture around, as Max Weber did, to argue that culture is the formative influence on the development of the market economy. According to this view, capitalism can be understood only by panning out to the larger field of values and relationships that predispose individuals to act in ways conducive to capitalist accumulation. The economic actor is seen first as a cultural being who acts from "the capacity and the will to take a definite attitude toward the world and to lend it significance" (Weber 1949, 81). Weber found that Europeans, notably Protestants, had the right "capacity and will" for capitalism, acting to enhance their store of capital through certain types of business practices that conformed to a notion about the getting of wealth he characterized as the "Protestant ethic." This ethic he felt was expressive of "the specific and peculiar rationalism of Western culture" (1958a, 25). To corroborate his findings, Weber turned to Hinduism (1958b) and Confucianism (1964) to examine the ethics of Indian and Chinese civilization in relation to his thinking on Protestant European culture—and found both Asian cultures wanting as enablers of capitalism. Weber's view of China and capitalism thus involves a double determination, first about the sufficient cultural conditions for the generation of capitalism and second about the failure of Chinese culture to nurture the appropriate "capacity and will" for generating capitalism.

The idealism inherent in the Weberian view of capitalism was passed down to modern social theory through the work of Talcott Parsons and the postwar modernizationists. Parsons interpreted Weber as reducing "the major conditions of existence of the capitalist economy . . . to the regulation or freedom of an *orientation* of individual actors." This specific orientation was "the rational pursuit of self-interest on the basis of monetary (marginal) calculation, i.e., economic rationality" (Savage 1977, 13). What determined this rational orientation were cultural values. Yet this assertion involved a circular logic in two senses: historically, in the sense that the cultural values that produced this rationality preexisted it; and, conceptually, in the sense that capitalist subjectivity is viewed as having been generated autonomously within the sphere of culture and not from the conditions created by markets, capital, or labor (Jones 1977, 48–49, 60–61). But Parsons accepted this circular explanation that value orientation was the basis for action, and to connect value to action he conceived of culture as a system that controlled all other systems within a society. It was the source of final sanction or legitimation for all institutions and practices. In giving meaning to social acts, culture served to unify—even dominate—all explanations of the social by grounding all aspects of social existence in ideal, as opposed to material, conditions of life. All meaning resided in culture (1972, 255). By implication, a social system could evolve only when propelled by a transforming and transformative culture. This conclusion was imported into modernization theory, which has tended to interrogate culture in terms of whether its value orientation hinders or facilitates the application of rational business and investment practices. This interrogation has often been reduced simply to asking whether the value orientations that have been deemed to drive Western capitalism are present or absent. In Asia, Weber, Parsons, and many others have found them to be absent.

The Parsonian use of culture—which is vulnerable to the charge of crediting culture with too much explanatory power while failing to assign it any material basis—provided the theoretical foundation for the "scientific" analysis of cultures in American sociology and anthropology in the 1930s and 1940s (Dower 1986, 118–20) and thereafter for postwar area studies, notably of East Asia. Parsons's junior colleagues at Harvard University, John Fairbank and Edwin Reischauer, applied his systems analysis to China and Japan. They accepted culture as the irreducible base from which the peculiarity of these two cultures could be identified and explained (Farquhar and Hevia 1993, 492–94). In an essentially Orientalizing move, China was deemed "bureaucractic" and Japan "aesthetic": both were forms of excess that had to be overthrown to establish the reign of rationalism that Western culture represented and desired to disseminate as the core of the modernist project through which "they" would become more like "us." This confidence Fairbank and Reischauer took directly from Parsons, who declared, "I believe that the United States is a model for other countries in structural innovations central to modern societal development." Convinced that his own country was moving in the direction of the ideals of individualism, decentralization, and free association, he concluded that "other societies will necessarily adopt these features as they move toward modernity" (1977, 215). American political and economic supremacy after World War II seemed only to confirm his, as well as neoclassical economists', theoretical premises about the postwar transformation of the world into a Western mold.[1]

Capitalist Growth in Eastern Asia

The recent growth spurts that many parts of Eastern Asia have experienced as they have adapted their economies to take advantage of the global economy—which could not have been predicted from the vantage point of Fairbank's Chinese particularism or Reischauer's Japanese exceptionalism—have obliged Western social science to reconsider what it thinks it knows about both capitalism and the cultural context appropriate to it.

In the 1965–90 period, the average rate of capitalist economic growth in Japan, the "Four Tigers" (South Korea, Taiwan, Hong Kong, and Singapore), and the stronger economies in Southeast Asia (Malaysia, Thailand, and Indonesia) was more than double the rate in the OECD countries. Real per capita income more than quadrupled in Japan and the Four Tigers and more than doubled in the three Southeast Asian countries (World Bank 1993, 1–3). This economic transformation is widely heralded as "miraculous." The rapid expansion and consolidation of capitalism in Eastern Asia since postwar decolonization and the widespread reproduction of many precolonial cultural forms in contemporary Asian economies constitute the greatest challenge to Western social theory since the concept of capitalism was first theorized. The explanations of Eastern Asian economic growth have ranged from the emphasis on context-neutral economic policies at one end to cultural analyses at the other.

A World Bank study published in 1993, while not dismissing culture, emphasized the importance of setting right economic policy fundamentals: macroeconomic stability with limited price distortion in the market and the promotion of accumulation, efficient allocation, and rapid technological catch-up. World Bank economists stressed that selective state interventions are effective only to the extent that these measures are carefully chosen to address market failures. This study suggested that, contingent upon policy flexibility, the Eastern Asian model can be adopted by other developing economies elsewhere in the world. Against the conventional wisdom of modernization theory, but still grounded in the premise of culture as constituting the economy, a diametrically opposite perspective argues that economic growth in Eastern Asia has been favored and promoted precisely because the cultural environment there has nurtured economic habits conducive to the operation of a modern economy. Such habits include devotion to assigned tasks, respect for superiors, high rates of savings, and repression of personal need or claims. Eastern Asian cultures, it is argued, reward entrepreneurial initiative, monitor investment costs and benefits efficiently, discipline workers through differences of status and gender, mobilize domestic labor as capital, and dampen the alienation that accompanies urban wage labor. These habits and cultural predispositions have been assembled into the notion of an "Asian way"—whether of capitalism, ethnic identity, or governance.

Theoretical divergence notwithstanding, both of the aforementioned perspectives share a triumphalist view of capitalist transformation in Eastern Asia. While properly emphasizing such positive impacts of economic growth as the reduction in absolute poverty, in our opinion they have not fully examined the heavy costs that have been exacted on people living under the new economic regimes in Eastern Asia in order to gain entrance into the global economy. If our task is to understand how capitalism has been shaped in Eastern Asia, it behooves us as well to reflect on the costs—social, environmental, and health—that Eastern Asia's inbrication with global capitalism has bequeathed. Global capitalism has brought about an increasing mobility of capital, which escapes wherever possible from the high labor costs, labor militancy, and environmental regulations in the capitalist core to various peripheries. For these reasons, multinational corporations have set up factories in export-processing zones in South Korea, Taiwan, Malaysia, the Philippines, and more recently in China and Vietnam. In addition, throughout Eastern Asia, in the name of flexible production and global competitiveness, international and domestic capital have both made extensive use of subcontracting and home production in order to reduce labor costs (including social benefits) and pollution control expenditures. The environmental degradation of Eastern Asia that has followed from these capital movements has been underestimated, and we consider it important to reflect on these costs as a way of suggesting the wider scale of the burden that the global economy has placed on the local populations of Eastern Asia.

Industrialization and higher consumption levels have led to a marked increase in industrial and vehicular pollution, as well as pollution from hazardous and ordinary wastes, which affects both personal health and the sustainability of development. Although these burdens can be reduced if local governments and populations are willing to address them early on in the process of industrial development, this has rarely been the case. Even in Japan, where environmental regulations became quite vigorous as early as a quarter-century ago, despite progress in the disposal of toxic substances, there was either no or only slight improvement in water quality, and only mixed results in air quality, between 1979 and 1990 (O'Connor 1994, 104–5). In Taiwan, air quality hardly improved in the 1980s, while the unpolluted portions of twenty-one major rivers declined from three-quarters to two-thirds in the 1983–90 period. The heavily polluted areas increased from 5.7 percent to 11.3 percent of the total areas (107). According to government sources in the late 1980s, industrial waste had contaminated 20 percent of farmland (Bello and Rosenfeld 1990, 201). In Hong Kong, it is estimated that industrial factories dump approximately 100,000 tons of untreated toxic waste into the soil and water every year (O'Connor 1994, 168).[2] In Thailand, the sulphur dioxide and nitrous oxide emissions into the air increased 2.5 to 3 times in the decade from 1981 to 1991 (11). Water quality declined markedly as the industrial release of biological oxygen demand substances almost doubled over the period from 1978 to 1989 (to 800,000 metric tons), threatening or killing aquatic life in many areas. Over the decade from 1979 to 1989, water-polluting firms in Thailand increased in number from 5,393 to 20,221, and toxic-waste-generating enterprises from 7,183 to 17,057 (168).[3] In China and Vietnam, where environmental regulation has hardly begun and any popular expression of concern about pollution is kept tightly in check by highly authoritarian political systems, industrial waste is regularly dumped into the nearest body of water and untreated sewage into rivers and canals.

Increases in air, soil, and water pollution threaten the sustainability of economic growth, but their direct impact is borne by local populations. Japan has had a number of well-publicized cases: mercury poisoning from wastewater released from chemical plants; cadmium poisoning in Toyama Prefecture due to toxic waste dumped by a lead and zinc mining and processing operation; an increase in asthma and respiratory diseases in Yokkaichi city as a result of the sulphur dioxide emission from oil refineries, chemical plants, and power stations (O'Connor 1994, 28). The health costs associated with industrial development are not evenly distributed but are borne most heavily by the poor, who live closer to industrial plants and do not always have access to clean water.

Other things being equal, industrialization in Eastern Asia has placed its heaviest burdens on women. Given the possible impact of pollution on fetuses, women suffer most heavily the long-term effects of air, soil, and water pollution. In the short term, they also face the health dangers associated with participating in the unprotected sector of the work force. Poor females face the additional health threat posed by burgeoning sex tourism in Eastern Asia. In the extreme case of Thailand, where female (as well as male) bodies, including those of minors, have become open commodities in a capitalist sex market, it is estimated that the number of HIV-positive cases reached 700,000 in 1994 and might soon exceed 1 million in a country with a population soon to surpass 60 million. Even where sociocultural norms and governmental policy are less tolerant of the sexual commodification of the local population, women workers bear a higher cost of capitalist growth. In export-processing zones, foreign firms frequently subject young female workers to long hours, lower wages, limited employment security, and few opportunities for advancement as supervisors are mostly male (Ong 1991, 286–89; Lim 1983; Phongpaichit 1995). As Kim points out in her chapter in this volume, in the South Korean export-processing zone of Masan, female workers found no stability working in electronics firms, driven out after less than a decade by managers who believed that women above the age of twenty-two did not have the requisite manual dexterity. Throughout the region, female workers in export-processing zones are regularly discarded after their most productive years in their twenties. They must turn to work in local subcontracting firms where wages and benefits are even lower. Those who engage in home work with the help of their elderly relatives and children receive no labor protection or benefits whatsoever (see Nonini 1993). In all these ways, as Aihwa Ong has perceptively noted of many countries in East and Southeast Asia, "industrial discourses 'disassemble' the female worker into eyes and fingers adapted for assembly work, at the same time reassembling other parts of their bodies according to commodified sexual images" (1991, 291). All this must be factored into the costs that Eastern Asian "cultures" have rung up in the course of working their various adaptations to the demands of global capitalism.

The Reinvention of Culture in Eastern Asia

In the context of the unequal share of the costs of capitalist growth, Eastern Asian elites have found culture useful in providing a repertoire of plausible meanings serving ideologies celebrating an indigenous "capacity and will" to participate in capitalist modernity. In the search for local correlatives to the Protestant ethic, Eastern Asian elites have constructed nativizing genealogies that seek to explain in indigenous (frequently Confucian) terms the values of hard work and thrift—values that are deemed to underpin personal and national economic success anywhere within world capitalism but may have little to do with what motivates Asians to take up the economic options presented by modernizing states. In this process, "culture" serves either to generate or reinforce a shared identity among the members of the indigenous population and to render more acceptable the tight engagement with global capitalism.

The political capital that comes from reinventing local cultures to make local participation in capitalism appear as a natural outgrowth of indigenous traditions can be considerable (see also Hobsbawm and Ranger 1983). Rather than picturing capitalism as an imposition from above or—and this move is particularly appealing for formerly colonized peoples—from the outside, it is seen as coming from within and therefore adhering to a higher moral legitimacy. This strategy not only reaffirms the legitimacy of the state that claims to represent the honored tradition, but it makes elements of the reclaimed tradition available for persuading people whose standards of living are rising to accept whatever controls the state regards as necessary for scaling the global ladder and ensuring the dominance of its elites. By instrumentalizing regional cultures—by highlighting the market-oriented aspects of Asian cultural heritages, praising native values of thrift and hard work, and showing a natural fit between local habits and the requirements of international markets—Asian elites can install programs for modernization and labor discipline that assist capitalist market economies to grow profitably and without political opposition.

Reinvented culture on its own is usually not enough to push this project through. Modernizing states still have to provide material incentives—as well as institutional opportunities and coercive disciplines—to carry out marketization. Nonetheless, culture makes values available through invention/construction as resources on which states and elites can draw to foster a compliant subjectivity among subjects and promote integration into the capitalist world-system, while doing so on ostentatiously non-Western terms. This course not only is attractive but may be politically necessary. To ignore popular subjectivity is to leave an opening for moral challenges to modernization programs, whether from Marxist fundamentalists (in China and Vietnam) or from Islamic fundamentalists (in Malaysia), based explicitly on appeals to cultural/ethnic identity.

In China and the Chinese diaspora in Southeast Asia, and particularly in Singapore, the reinvention of culture to provide a native genealogy for capitalist engagement has involved the resurrection of Confucianism to bear the burden of explaining economic success. This is a novel role for Confucianism to play. Through most of the twentieth century, Confucianism has been periodically credited with the retardation or failure of the modernizing project. It was pilloried in the second decade of the century in China and Korea for having played this role and was scourged in China as late as the 1970s as an impediment to the state economy.

If Confucianism is now available for explaining Asian capitalism, this may be in part because of the enlarged role of the state in late-twentieth-century capitalism, for Confucianism has had a long and close relationship to the state in China, Korea, and Vietnam and to a lesser extent in Japan as well. A philosophy of moral being extending from the individual in the family to the individual in the cosmos, it has also been translated from the domestic to the political field to serve as an ideology informing the relationship between the state-as-father and subjects-as-children. Its careful registration of a naturalized hierarchy extending from the lowest positionings (female, junior, bonded) to the highest (male, senior, enfranchised) placed the emperor, impersonating the state, at the apex of political and moral authority. The installation of backwardness in Eastern Asia with the spread of the capitalist world-system obliged states to build strong regimes to carry out modernization or else perish. The emperor, who had provided the authority needed to direct the political order, had to be superseded by the state, which now serves as the authority necessary to direct the economic order. This translation made good sense to the East Asian political imagination, and once the new state was secure Confucianism could be rendered as an ideology of productive subordination—enunciating the values of hard work, labor discipline, and high rates of saving—that binds subjects effectively to the economic authority of the modernizing state and its elite.

Arguments in favor of a modernizing Confucianism are seen to be specific to that particular Sinic worldview when Confucianism is contrasted with the other great cultural tradition of Eastern Asia, Buddhism. When Weber contemplated Buddhism, he was struck with its concern with directing this-worldly effort to other-worldly goals and so tended to disqualify it as a motivating factor for this-worldly transformation. On the other hand, it was just this sort of eye to other-worldly accounts that inspired Protestants to hard work and thrift. While Buddhism is not cited frequently for contributing to the recent economic growth in Asia, Charles Keyes (1993, 389) has argued that Buddhism contributes to capitalist development of Thailand through compromise, ambiguity, and silence. Christine Gray suggests further that through the royal patronage and sanction of capitalist patronage of Buddhist merit-making ceremonies, "economic power is converted into religious prestige, and religious prestige entails symbolic and linguistic capital: the ability to assign authoritative names or meanings to words and events and hence to make legitimate moral judgments on behalf of the collectivity" (1991, 47). Through this process, the largest commercial bank in Thailand increased the efficacy of its words in texts extolling diligence and energy in the pursuit of profit (59). Keyes also suggests that the discipline to forgo immediate gratification, acquired through widespread pagoda internship, has contributed to entrepreneurship in rural northeastern Thailand and possibly elsewhere. Furthermore, among the Sino-Thai, the worldview of establishment Buddhism in combination with an entrenched pragmatism has fostered an ethic of tolerance conducive to laissez-faire capitalism (Keyes 1993, 390). The notable difference between Buddhism and Confucianism is that Buddhism opens up no obvious or direct opportunities for enhancing the power of the state. By contrast, Islam, despite its rules against usury and its strictures against contact with non-Muslims, has proven to be an adaptable vehicle for mobilizing people for capitalism precisely because it has historically been amenable to functioning as a totalizing state ideology.

From an outsider's perspective, Eastern Asia's tight engagements with Western-originated communication technologies and financial systems make appeals to any sort of primordial Asian identity—Islamic, Buddhist, or Confucian—seems beside the point. Indeed, to cast culture anywhere in Eastern Asia as "native" or "indigenous" (read: non-Western) obscures its historical construction via the colonial experience.

Culture and Postcolonialism

The difficulty of sorting out culture's relationship with the economy in Eastern Asia is a postcolonial matter, for it is colonialism that precipitated the crisis that has led to this rethinking. When European trade found toeholds outside Europe, it came as an external set of economic relations and cultural technologies that had to interact with indigenous political and social structures. This interaction between new economic interests and existing power structures occurred abruptly, unlike the more gradual interaction that characterized the formation of capitalism in early modern Europe. To the extent that capitalism is thought of as a European system (as Weber did), it bore a cultural definition that may have inhibited its transfer to a different setting. A European identity for early capitalism is not to deny the considerable cultural differences within Europe that contributed in divergent ways to the making of European capitalism. But these differences were more easily absorbed (and dominated) in the process of capitalism's formation in Europe than were the differences with cultures outside Europe.

Indigenous cultures in Eastern Asia entered historical relationships with an externally induced economic system against a background of preexisting understandings of economic activity. Long-standing habits regarding the getting of wealth influenced how people responded to the opportunities that the Europe-centered trading system brought, particularly as the noncapitalist sectors of the economy continued to function around or alongside imperialism. What is interesting to explore here are the cultural formations that took shape during the colonial period. Although many parts of Asia were not directly absorbed into colonial empires, if we think of colonialism as a category that can include not just the familiar political regime of the colony but also the regime under which indigenous sovereignty is constrained without being directly infringed (what Chinese in their self-historiography have called "semicolonialism"), then no part of Asia escaped the influence of the European colonial project (Barlow 1993).

Colonialism did not simply override the cultural patterns it encountered but generated unique cultural formations. Writing in the context of colonial Indian history, Nicholas Dirks has advised that we consider colonialism not simply a system of conquest that had cultural effects but "a cultural project of control." The colonial encounter produced its own culture; at the same time, certain cultural formations, once observed by the colonizers, were isolated and conceptualized as something that could be termed "culture." In other words, "the concept itself was in part invented" because of the colonial encounter (Dirks 1992, 3–4). Of particular concern to the colonial project was the identification of cultural differences among the groups that colonizers encountered. Indeed, the project of identification led them to conceive of such groups precisely as "cultures" bound by seemingly irreducible rules of language and action rather than as the "societies" or "states" that one found in Europe. These differences, once generalized onto categories of gender and race, allowed the colonizers to create national identities for these cultures, thereby setting up a system of states in Asia that was familiar to them by virtue of seeming to approximate the multiple-state system of Europe. These identities, being "cultural," were inferior to the fully developed national identities in Europe and often remained dependent on the identities of the colonial states that ruled them. This way of reading the world resulted in a Hegelian hierarchy of nations that peaked in Europe, sloped through Asia, and dwindled to nothing in Africa and the Pacific.

Assessing the impact of the colonial experience on Asian cultures is not a purely academic exercise, given that the contemporary economic upsurge of Eastern Asia states is not only chronologically postcolonial but logically as well, in the sense that it could not have occurred without the colonial experience. While indigenous elites have argued that imperialist control had to be removed in order for indigenous values to play their role, it is also possible that the colonial encounter generated the space within which these values could be reconstructed and without which the advent of capitalism would have been inconceivable. Thus, when we speak of culture (and of cultures) in contemporary Eastern Asia, we are dealing to some extent with modes of knowledge generated through the encounter with imperialism. To ask about the sources of Eastern Asian dynamism is therefore to pose a post- rather than precolonial question, however ostentatiously precolonial the invented traditions offered in answer appear to be.

Singapore provides a good case study for considering the problems that postcoloniality raises for culture. Singapore is perhaps unique in having crafted in the 1960s a state ideology that acknowledged the multiple genealogies of its cultural makeup and conceded value to all the contributing ethnicities that it chose to recognize, including even British colonialism. This recognition was not simply a matter of acknowledging Singapore's past as a British colony but of using the disruption of colonialism as a basis for blocking any attempt by the member "nationalities" in Singapore to appeal to a primordial ethnic identity that could break up the state. Cultural difference thus served as the signifier of Singapore culture and served as a base for constructing Singapore's version of a modern society (Wee 1993, 720). The Singaporean ideology of modernity underwent a major reconfiguring in the 1980s and early 1990s in coordination with the reform and growth of the Chinese economy. The government has chosen to shift the basis of Singapore culture from cultural difference to

> a generalized Asian identity which allows scope for distinct Southeast and South Asian identities (i.e., Malay and various Indian identities) while yet elevating a pan–East Asian and Confucian identity as the basis for an *Asian* (as opposed to an Asianized *Western*) logic of modernity that is to have underwritten (if not exactly caused) the success not only of Singapore but of the other Pacific Rim "Little Tigers." (738)

Although ostensibly rejecting the colonial element of Singapore's cultural formation in favor of something exclusively Asian, this reconfiguration, in aggressively positing the Asian, underlines the colonial lineage by straining to exclude it.

The case of Singapore is particularly interesting because the construction of a national ideology for Singaporean culture has been a transparent process, openly discussed and promoted by top leaders, including Lee Kwan Yew. The transparency allows us to see not only how culture is invented but how the colonial encounter has set the context for culture creation in the first place—and continues to do so as long as Singapore participates in the global (in addition to regional) economy. Singapore of course experienced the colonial project in a fashion far more direct than did most other parts of Eastern Asia; yet the cultural aura of the West, whether ostentatiously absorbed, as in Japan, or defensively challenged, as in Malaysia, emanates from all versions of urban culture throughout Eastern Asia.

In general, the postcolonial reinvention of culture in Eastern Asia can have a powerful impact, as many Asians, among the elites and beyond, have come to speak of their success at enlarging their wealth in Asian terms, in clear distinction from—and rejection of—the cultural forms that have accompanied Euro-American capitalism into the region. In the final analysis, nothing much changes whether one argues that native cultural value systems have "really" enabled Asians to work effectively inside capitalism or whether one observes that Asians have simply internalized state-promoted ideologies telling them that this is so. If Asians (as well as non-Asians) believe that indigenous value systems are responsible for an increase in personal or national wealth, then it becomes nearly impossible to disengage values from the persuasive genealogies they have been given and ask people to account for why they are able to produce, consume, and save.

Bringing Culture Back In

The theme we have chosen for our collective inquiry in this volume—the influences on or uses of culture in the economy—was selected to address this problem of considering the cultural framing of Eastern Asian economies and to ask to what extent culture "matters" in the process of capitalist transformation and economic growth and how the ways in which it matters might best be conceptualized.[4] Rethinking capitalism in the light of the Eastern Asian experience is an important historical topic given the hegemony that Europe established early on in the formation of the world capitalist system. But it is also a fully contemporary project, occurring at a time when international trade and capital markets are eroding entrenched assumptions on both sides of the Pacific about the getting of wealth. Nor is this an isolated project, for it rests within the broad rethinking of the contemporary world order currently under way with regard to such issues as trade boundaries, regional security, ethnic identity, and human rights. Because of its imbrication with these other issues, the question of what capitalism has become is tied to contemporary debates regarding the institutions and values appropriate to guaranteeing stability and prosperity under conditions of increasing global interdependence. The culture-economy relationship thus sets broad but reasonably precise terms within which to consider what capitalism has become, what it is presently doing, and how it is being both accommodated and resisted by everyone from international financiers like Robert Kuok to young female weavers in the villages of Shandong Province.

Within the social sciences, the question of to what extent culture "matters" in the process of capitalist transformation and economic growth is no longer being raised in isolated circles, as even some economists now acknowledge a need to bring culture back in, at the very least at the microeconomic level. In the paper he presented at the conference out which this volume arises, Thomas Rawski turned to the cultural realm of popular values to find "aspects of traditional Chinese culture and society that contribute to the production of individuals who seem particularly well prepared to function successfully in a modern market system" (1994).[5] If Rawski recognizes the need to understand the importance of culturally constituted human resources in contributing to market development and the nurturing of entrepreneurship among Chinese, it is because China's recent economic performance appears to contradict strongly what economists for decades regarded as the absence of suitable conditions for modern economic growth in China. Fellow economist Kunio Yoshihara has argued similarly for the need for economists to bring culture back in, though he recognizes that what gets designated as culture varies greatly depending on whether the economist is neoclassical or institutional. He also stresses that culture is never unchanging:

> We have to realize that people are the agents of economic development and that they react differently to government policy or behave differently even under the same institutional arrangement. Culture shapes the pattern of their behavior. Culture is not, however, something given. It changes, and is dependent to some extent on the working of institutions. But culture has some autonomy, and, to this extent, it can be an independent factor. (1994, 266)

The contributors to this volume do not approach the concept of culture in a uniform way, but all argue that culture, however theorized, must be incorporated into our understanding of the shaping of capitalism in Eastern Asia, although not necessarily in a formative sense. Meaning systems are of great importance in relation to the material and political circumstances of daily economic life, both in the microscopic analysis of human action and in the macroscopic examination of system transformation.[6] At the same time, all the contributors recognize that, however influential local or national culture may be on the forms that Asian capitalism is taking, the global political economy is powerfully shaping the changes in Eastern Asia. Although states and elites may choose to represent cultural meaning as static and coherent, they are constantly being reconstructed through moments of contest. This approach has been cogently argued by Ruth McVey. In her analysis of the growth of Southeast

Asian capitalism, McVey emphasizes the linkages among the state and capital-ist entrepreneurs, as well as the roles of foreign capital and markets, to argue against the determinative role of culture. She suggests that, when we accept, for example, that the culture of Chinese entrepreneurs in Southeast Asia is explanatory of the dynamism of Southeast Asian capitalism,

> we rather tend to forget that the overseas Chinese economic role is rela-tively recent and was determined by historical-political factors which had little to do with Chinese culture. There was nothing particularly entrepre-neurial about the China from which the immigrants to Southeast Asia came. . . . This does not mean we should cease to take cultural characteris-tics seriously: values *are* important, but they must be observed in social and historical context. (1992, 18)

The historicity of culture, and its vulnerability to change, are the givens that are too often forgotten in the rush to explain merely the present. Again, as McVey points out, "people are not always the way they were. Any cultural tradition has many strands of meaning, which may be emphasized, forgotten, and reinter-preted over time, providing legitimacy for quite contrary modes of behavior" (18). Rather than a system or set of fixed predispositions, culture is an arena of discourse and action in which claims against others are raised and conflicts acted out through the articulation of meanings and values.

The authors in the present volume, varying with their theoretical perspec-tives, focus on different ways in which culture is shaping and being shaped by the contemporary economy of Eastern Asia. Tae-Kyu Park, Farid Harianto, and Heng Pek Koon adopt a theoretical perspective close to McVey's approach, emphasizing how meanings and values are selectively invoked in the construc-tion of political-economic institutions for capitalist growth and how, due to its essential mediation by larger institutions, the same set of invoked values may have different impacts in diverse spatio-temporal contexts. In this approach, the class dimension of cultural construction does not loom saliently, in con-trast to the (neo-)Marxist approach discussed subsequently. In his chapter on Korean economic development after 1961, Park examines in depth how both state and business leaders selectively invoked Confucian values during Korea's rapid industrialization through the 1960s and 1970s, thereby contributing to the creation of the unique structure of an authoritarian regime with compliant firms. He hypothesizes, however, that the extensive use of Confucian ideology by the state, business, and the family may not prove to have positive impact after an initial period of strong growth. In his analysis of Sino-entrepreneurs' reliance on family ties and trust-based personal networks, fellow economist

Farid Harianto emphasizes that these historically conditioned cultural features function well only when institutions are underdeveloped in order to support the market, as in the case of Southeast Asia. Sino-capitalists with the same culturally rooted practice do not thrive as well in North America, where the structural and economic conditions are different. Outside this volume, Jamie Mackie shares this perspective when he argues that certain cultural characteristics of Southeast Asian Chinese that facilitated economic success in the early stage before the 1960s are not necessarily appropriate in the context of large-scale business today (1992a, 162). Along the same lines, Ruth McVey is not confident that Chinese entrepreneurship, shaped by business networks that Chinese merchants established on the basis of a political pariah status and their cosmopolitan linkages with both Western business and local economies, can be sustained. The need to act in an increasingly internationalized business world imposes forms of behavior that erode Chinese exclusivity. Both business interests and cultural forces bring together Chinese and indigenous elites into a common, cosmopolitan, nouveau-riche consumer style, which offers itself as the high culture model for modern capitalist Southeast Asia (McVey 1992, 26). In her chapter on the Chinese-Malaysian entrepreneur Robert Kuok, Heng notes the extent to which Kuok uses Confucian values and cultural styles in his business dealings, and she regards his invocation of these values as having contributed to his success in building a commercial empire to date. Like Harianto, Park, Mackie, and McVey, Heng questions whether the Kuok group can survive the founder's demise, given the probable incompatibility among heirs and the difficulty for such a culturally rooted organization to survive in the modern international capitalist environment.

In a more Marxist approach, culture is examined in terms of its impact on class and gender relations, especially the appropriation of labor for capital accumulation by the dominant class. Culture is conceived as a historically situated ideology and analyzed in terms of "its role in social reproduction: legitimating the existing order, mediating contradictions in the base, and mystifying the sources of exploitation and inequality in the system" (Ortner 1984, 140). In this volume, Ellen Judd and Seung-Keung Kim adopt this approach to culture and economy, focusing particularly on the structure of gender relations of village enterprises in rural China and export-oriented industries in Korea, respectively. The appropriation of women's labor is a general and widely noted feature of capital accumulation in emergent (as well as mature) capitalist economies. While not embracing a Marxist approach, Diana Lary in her chapter argues in a similar vein that preexisting organizational arrangements used in the presocialist economy have survived to serve the current development of "market socialism" in China to the benefit especially of the state, employers, and families but not individual workers. She sees this not as a result of ideological shaping or persuasion, however, but as a matter of quickly adapting culturally acceptable mechanisms to mediate the relationship between capital and labor that the new economic system requires. Among all three chapters, culture is examined in terms of social practices sited within a structure of class relations and the larger system of political economy.

In the past two decades, under the influence of Raymond Williams and Antonio Gramsci, neo-Marxists have analyzed in depth the powerful role of ideologies in shaping class relations. Neo-Marxists view ideology as constituting a dynamic field whose relation to the class system is not readily read as determination and is far from mechanical. Working in the wake of that tradition, poststructuralists and postmodernists have also articulated a conception of culture as a discursively constructed and contested domain. Neo-Marxism, poststructuralism, and postmodernism all share the theoretical emphasis on the actual or potential conflict over meanings and values as well as their historical construction and reconstruction.

In this volume, Hy V. Luong examines the interplay of multiple ideologies in shaping the organization of ceramics firms in northern Vietnam and how the relative positions of different ideological strands are inextricably linked to the larger political-economic framework. Roger L. Janelli and Dawnhee Yim offer an original extension of Michel Foucault's poststructuralist framework that rejects the idea that culture is constitutive of the economy. They note how certain ideas held by Korean white-collar workers may be genealogized in relation to Confucianism, but they attend more closely to the material conditions within which economic life takes place. While noting that some Koreans identify Confucianism as constitutive in the sense of blocking economic development, as Park does in his chapter, they advise that Confucian ideas be viewed not as fixed but as involved in an ongoing dialectic with material interests: both Confucianism and capitalism are thus constantly refashioned and to some extent reconciled in a process of a continual mutual revision.

The chapters by Timothy Brook, Alexander Woodside, and Judith Nagata in the opening section of this book examine ideological uses to which culture has been put as China, Vietnam, and Malaysia respectively attempt to induce economic practices favorable to the expansion of the market. All three are drawn to the ambiguities involved in such attempts and see the use of culture as a matter of reinvention, to use the term that Eric Hobsbawm introduced into the historical and social science literature. Brook explores Chinese attempts to rewrite Confucianism as an ideology of capital accumulation four centuries ago and again in the past decade as indeterminate responses to disruptive contradictions between status and wealth, and regards the contemporary outcome as inconsequential to China's interaction with the global economy. In her chapter on the manipulation of Islamic ideology by political factions in Malaysia to legitimize conflicting paths toward a modern capitalist economy, Nagata finds the attempts to refashion Islam as an ideology of economic modernization similarly anomalous. This anomaly parallels the Vietnamese use of Confucianism to aid a socialist market economy in Woodside's chapter: a state appealing to a premodern cultural identity to push an essentially anticommercial ideology in the direction of supporting economic growth.

Most contributors recognize that the state is playing a key role in inducing economic growth in Eastern Asia: promoting certain economic arrangements, enabling labor to be mobilized and disciplined in certain ways, sponsoring certain ideologies, staging certain contests, and refusing certain appeals against its authority. The direct role of the state is now accepted as a basic fact of East Asian development (Cotton 1994; Ozawa 1994). As Woodside nicely phrased it at the conference, the state is conspicuously "at the intersection of economics and culture, being the producer and the product of both." If the influence of the state is unmistakable, what precisely should be credited to its agency, and how that agency may change in the future, are open to debate. Park acknowledges that the military state in Korea in the 1960s was responsible for planning the capitalist transformation of the Korean economy but notes that it did so by an interventionism in markets and the private sector that he believes cannot be repeated in the future. Harianto and Heng note that close cooperation between states and business elites in Southeast Asia has benefited both sides, though Harianto doubts that this is a strategy that would work outside the region. Woodside's account of the Vietnamese state's attempts to indigenize market economics suggests that the Vietnamese state has realized that it must take the lead if economic growth is to happen. R. Bin Wong is more guarded in his assessment of the ability of the Chinese state to generate a capitalist economy of the sort developing elsewhere in Eastern Asia, for it works from within practices that have historically accommodated the need to impose limits on the concentration of private wealth. Culture matters to the extent that ideas from the imperial era about the operation of the economy, and about the state's role in that process, persist in ways that most observers tend to miss, focused as they (we) are on trajectories of Western modernization. However evaluated, the role of the state will be critical in shaping the marketization of Eastern Asia and the integration of national economies into global capitalism. Whether this role depends on a cultural construction of the state peculiar to Eastern Asia remains in question.[7]

There is also substantial agreement among the contributors that this development of capitalism in Eastern Asia will proceed with fewer obstacles if it is pursued in relation to already existing patterns of economic culture. Both Wong and Brook remind us, in different ways, that we must attend sympathetically to long-standing Chinese understandings of the economy if we hope to grasp what Chinese planners are currently trying to achieve rather than falling back on Western sensibilities that dismiss their efforts as "twisted and artificial."

What is indisputable is that the social life of capitalism in Eastern Asia does look rather different from its Euro-American manifestations. Preestablished economic practices as well as indigenous ideas about economic reciprocity and social morality have not only persisted but have shaped the economies that have grown up in response to the demands and opportunities that the global economy poses. Despite the adoption of international commercial practices, modes of industrial organization, and consumption styles from around the world, cultures outside the Euro-American sphere have not remade themselves entirely in the Euro-American image. It is tempting to look to that difference to find the key for understanding the high levels of dynamism and exploitation that characterize the recent growth of capitalism there; on the other hand, without global capitalism, little of what is overtaking Eastern Asians today would have been conceivable.

The Challenge

As the states of Eastern Asia expand their competitive advantage in the capitalist world system and yet continue to organize their polities and societies in ways that are not associable with the political and social categories of Western social science, the need to understand what is happening without recourse to old Western models becomes only more urgent. There are two possibilities, not equally compelling. One is that this irreducibility is transitional, that, as modernization theory has long held, world capitalism is bringing with it cultural technologies that will in the end overwhelm and push aside the habits of wealth generation and distribution in the regions that it has brought into the world economy: capitalism as a cultural system will triumph in a way that it could not merely as an economic system.

The other possibility is that, even as capitalism establishes itself in Eastern Asia, indigenous cultural practices and attitudes that preexisted capitalism's entry will continue to animate and direct the lives of those who are being drawn into the global economy. Although cultures are constantly reinvented, reinvention takes place not in a vacuum but in a meaningful, albeit contested, space. This contest goes on under the historical constraints of Western capitalism and colonialism but also in terms of the postcolonial sociocultural formations that are now in place. In this process, it seems inevitable that Eastern

Asian cultures will shape, even remake, capitalism into a system of production and consumption beyond its original definition, letting it become something that is more genuinely universal than the European version. At that point, what was capitalism as the nineteenth century understood it may not be what becomes the global economy of the twenty-first. The challenge for social science is not to retreat from this transformation back to the implied moralism of Weberian or even Confucian accounts but to think anew about the unanticipated reconfigurations of economic and political power that are being worked in Eastern Asia and about the strategies that ordinary people will have to develop to survive in the presence of that power.

NOTES

1. By insisting on the causative function of culture, Parsonian structural functionalism proved to be more sensitive to cultural variation than neoclassical economics. The two approaches are compatible to the extent that the latter accepts that preferences are given variables shaping economic choices, though neoclassical economics has tended to gloss over variations between cultures in the search for general quantitative models of behavioral choices at the microscopic level and of systemic changes at the macroscopic level. By contrast, one can see from the great volume of painstaking research of Fairbank, Reischauer, and their students at Harvard that Parsonian analysis was favorable to the close observation of foreign cultures, even if it did sometimes confirm mistaken assumptions about "them" or school students in wrong lessons about "us."

2. In South Korea, another Asian Tiger, air quality has increased due to environmental regulations in the 1980s, but water pollution, although reduced for the Han River near Seoul, has deteriorated for some other areas (O'Connor 1994, 106). In the late 1980s, in some areas water sources were so heavily polluted that at nine out of forty-six water purification plants in South Korea bacteria were at a level five times higher than the acceptable standard (Bello and Rosenfeld 1990, 101). In the 1985–90 period, while South Korean GDP rose by 63 percent, industrial waste increased by 84 percent (O'Connor 1984, 26).

3. The coliform count in Thailand's Chao Phraya River in 1990 was roughly six times higher than the acceptable standard, and in Indonesia, in a sample of fish caught in Jakarta Bay, "44% exceeded WHO guidelines for lead, 38% for mercury, and 76% for cadmium" (O'Connor 1994, 107–8).

4. An analogous project at an earlier phase of the postwar period, which dealt with the globalization of the Japanese economy, was directed to rethinking what was identified more broadly as modernization rather than capitalism; this project is surveyed in Hall 1965. On the recent revitalization of the concept of modernization in the study of Japan, see Garon 1994.

5. Rawski's interest was complemented at the conference by Wei-Ming Tu, who argued that the bourgeois or low Confucianism of the people, as opposed to the high Confu-

cianism of the elite, has supplied a value system that has enabled some to participate effectively in a capitalist market (1994).

6. Within anthropology, Clifford Geertz and Marshall Sahlins, among others, extended the Weberian/Parsonian approach to understand culture as a system of meanings that shapes "material rationality" far more than do biological, economic, or ecological advantages. Sahlins suggests, for example, that American preferences for beef and pork and the taboos on eating horse and dog meat relate not to any techno-economic, biological, or ecological benefits but to the meaningful and structural relations of cattle, pigs, horses, and dogs to one another and to human beings. More specifically, cattle and pigs are more distant from human beings than are horses and dogs. The higher valuation of beef is rooted in what Sahlins has identified, using a now suspect term of cultural inclusion, as "the Indo-European identification of cattle or increasing wealth with virility" (1976, 171). In other words, "edibility is inversely related to humanity" (175). More generally, "goods stand as an object for the signfiication and valuation of persons and occasions, functions and situations. Operating on a specific logic of correspondence between material and social contrasts, production is thus the reproduction of the culture in a system of objects" (178). In this way, culture defines social life, and "the finalities as well as the modalities of production come from the cultural side" (207). Sahlins's view of culture as the constitutive framework subsuming economic choices has been critiqued from both materialist and poststructuralist perspectives.

7. The role of the state in directing economic transformation in Eastern Asia was first argued persuasively by Chalmers Johnson in his study of Japan's Ministry of International Trade and Investment (1977). Significantly, while he highlighted the signal importance of the "developmental state" in shaping Japanese capitalism, Johnson did not recur to the concept of culture to explain why the Japanese state acted as it did or why its strategies were successful.

Part 1
CULTURE AND POWER

The past three decades have witnessed not only strong economic growth in many parts of Eastern Asia but also their structural transformation from a peripheral position to a more central one in the world capitalist system. Even the command economies of China, Vietnam, Mongolia, Cambodia, and Laos have moved in the direction of market reforms and capitalist development. In parallel with this development is the greater incorporation of these economies into the global capitalist system. Many social scientists have hypothesized that globalization and capitalist development not only threaten state power but exert considerable pressure toward sociocultural homogenization in East and Southeast Asia.

The four essays in this part of the volume examine the cultural shaping of market and capitalist development in three states in the region: China, Vietnam, and Malaysia. They analyze how culture constitutes an integral part of the economic transformation in the region, both as capitalist development is shaped by the local sociocultural configuration and as culture is reinvented to provide a logic for market and capitalism.

Pointing to cultural anxieties in the face of profit-driven commercialization in China, Timothy Brook focuses on the construction of cultural meanings for economic practice and commercialization, meanings that he suggests cannot be directly deduced from the Western conception of capitalism. He examines in depth two polar Chinese conceptions of economic morality in the sixteenth century that still constitute the chief moral judgment on economic practice in China in the past few decades. On the one hand was the mainstream Confucian emphasis on "agrarian self-sufficiency, price stability, social harmony/hierarchy, and the restriction of commerce to the circulation of basic necessities." On the other was the merchant ideology, which accepted "accumulation, commodity circulation, social mobility, and the beneficial redistribution of wealth through exchange." In one moral reformulation in the sixteenth century, for example, the good became rich and loss was a sign of moral failure. However, "the moralizing of profit taking imposes limits on profit. Unlimited profit was still unacceptable within this Confucian merchant ideology." Confucianism is currently being promoted as the prime candidate to supply an ethic for contemporary capitalism in Eastern Asia. To overcome its traditional bias against commerce, advocates of a revived Confucianism face the task of reinventing it in a postcommercial guise or at least of selectively abstracting certain moral values and placing them in the altogether different context of capitalism and deeming the outcome to be Confucian. Success will depend on the commitment that states and elites bring to this task.

Yet culturally specific patterns of economic activity can persist over time in the absence of ideological manipulation, as R. Bin Wong shows when he argues cogently for continuity in the dominant Chinese conception of commerce over the past few centuries, even while recognizing the process of ideological negotiation and transformation in the twentieth century. It is an ideology that is rooted in a millennium-old and twofold concern of the state with: (a) developing reasonable and effective revenue-raising measures in order to pursue state policies, and (b) promoting and regulating the economy for the people's livelihood. In this context, from the Song dynasty onward, the state and its ideology have recognized the value of trade and market exchange. In the late imperial period, for example, the government generally allowed trade without much governmental oversight and with only modest taxation except when it was foreign trade or intended as a revenue maker for the government. Despite the Confucian anxiety about the unbridled pursuit of profit and wealth concentration, the dominant Chinese ideology of commerce does not oppose commercial exchange; yet it is wary of unbridled capitalism. Wong suggests that more than their Russian Communist counterparts post-1949 Chinese leaders have been able to conceive a positive role for market exchanges in contradistinction to capitalism, as manifested in their policy since 1978. More generally, Wong argues that:

> cultural factors help to explain the kinds of economic change that can take place, but by themselves can neither guarantee economic development nor prevent it. Other factors and conditions contribute to the growth and transformation of economies. A stress on cultural factors does remind us that when economic development takes place outside of Europe it will not necessarily replicate some set of European cultural logics.

Examining the interplay of ideology and economy in Vietnam in the past decade, Woodside too emphasizes the importance of the matrix of meanings within which the economy is embedded. As he argues in his chapter on Vietnam,

> no system of market economics has ever been successfully legitimized anywhere for a long time in a pure form just by itself, for all its technical efficiency. Economic orders based upon free market exchanges must, to survive, be embedded in a larger religious or ideological ethos.

In the search for a cultural logic for market economics and for state power in the market era, the Vietnamese intelligentsia has probed not only into "the precolonial Asian Confucian civilization" but also "the pre-Leninist past of Marxist and European thought." More specifically, the search for a cultural logic in Vietnam involves a neotraditional reinvention. Woodside suggests that the revival of village convenants in the northern Vietnamese province of Ha Bac, for example, is not "modernization inspired by Confucianism" but "Confucianism inspired (retrospectively) by modernization."

In the fourth chapter, Judith Nagata examines the role of Islamic ideology in the construction of Malaysian economic policy. She argues that the particular shape of Malaysian capitalism cannot be fully understood without reference to the reinvention of Islamic ideology (and more recently of Confucianism) as well as its historically conditioned socioeconomic conditions. This process of reinvention is historically embedded in the British colonial creation of an ethnically plural society in which Malays controlled the political system and Chinese dominated the business domain. In terms of specific events, it relates to the Chinese-Malay polarization with the 1969 riots as well as the intensification of religious and economic linkages to the Muslim world with the Islamic resurgence in the Middle East. Through the Institute of Islamic Understanding, the Malaysian government attempts to convince its citizens that its aggressive development policy (including receptiveness to Western technology but not to Western "decadence") is not incongruent with Islam. Economic development is promoted as a means of furthering social justice and assistance to the poor. "This represents an attempt to extract the essence of capitalism as economic practice from the Western culture in which it has historically been embedded and to transplant the seeds of a different, religious culture."

Regardless of whether culture is examined in terms of relatively stable ideological premises, as Wong does, or as a recurrent process of ideological reinvention in the context of global capitalist engagement, as Brook, Woodside, and Nagata do, the authors of the four chapters in part 1 work from the common understanding that culture shapes economic practices and does so in a power-laden process.

Profit and Righteousness in Chinese Economic Culture

Timothy Brook

Wealth signals abundance, but it also entails imbalance—in the distribution of material goods, in access to productive resources, in the concentration of social power. In most cultures prior to the installation of capitalism, people have used such simple public devices as envy, shame, and expropriation to critique the accumulation of wealth in individual hands and resist the power that it brings to some and denies to others. Capitalism, relying as it does on the accumulation of wealth to organize production and exchange, may like to see moral denunciations of wealth as excess or imbalance discouraged, but it has not brought the natural resistance to wealth to an end. Capitalist ideologies have nonetheless sought to ascribe to wealth meanings beyond the utterly selfish or merely hedonistic: to endow wealth with positive moral quality. Once constructed in such a fashion, wealth can be made to signify not imbalance but moral attainment.

Ascribing moral meaning to wealth occurs not just under capitalism, of course, but in all market cultures. This ascription is most energetically pursued under conditions of rapid economic growth, when some get rich and many more do not and social instability results. A positive moral justification for wealth helps reduce that instability by stimulating a subjective willingness to participate in the economy and otherwise minimizing resistance from those unable to take part or do so successfully. An ideology of economic growth combined with social discipline enables market growth by conceding to market forces the power to determine the allocation of resources and labor and overwhelm competing moral claims. To be convincing, the moral meaning ascribed to wealth has to be conceived in relation to established cultural norms, even if that meaning runs against the claims of older, moral-economy notions favoring subsistence for all over advantage for some. The substance of these claims varies from one culture to another; so, too, and in part for this reason, the modern cultures of capitalism that are developing in Eastern Asia are not uniform from one place to the next. It is in this sense, among many others, that culture matters to the economy.

The moral ambiguity of wealth is a theme over which Confucianism has long worried. This worry got expressed two millennia ago in a discourse that derided profit as lacking moral meaning. This discourse continues to resonate today for some Chinese, particularly the well educated. The purpose of this chapter is to show that, despite the shift to capitalist rationality imposed by the market reforms of Deng Xiaoping, Confucianism's negative evaluation of profit is still available to structure the calculations of educated Chinese as they strive to come to terms with living in the market. At the same time, though, some intellectuals are seeking to redefine Confucian attitudes toward economic activity in such a way as to forge positive links with the culture of work and gain in contemporary China. The importance of the Confucian tradition to economic growth is not fixed but, rather, amenable to considerable play of interpretation. If Confucian concerns continue to animate Chinese understandings of the economy as it undergoes rapid marketization, whether in support of it or against it, it is not because cultural tradition somehow "lives on" by force of inertia[1] but because its selective strategic reintroduction can provide a persuasive language for enunciating moral claims.

Contemporary language for entering the market in pursuit of wealth furnishes a simple demonstration of the ambivalence that some educated Chinese feel toward commerce. The common colloquial expression for this is *xia hai,* literally, "going out to sea." The term is used to mean going into business to make money, and it implies risk taking. It is in current use noticeably among those who are considering leaving safe, fixed-income jobs in government or academe for a life in business. As the rewards of the latter come severely to outweigh the former, this choice is becoming increasingly simple at the level of financial calculation. Still, choosing to "go out to sea" is not easy. In a culture of continental orientation like China's, the ocean has traditionally been viewed as more threat than opportunity, and only the most desperate urge for wealth could prompt someone to venture out into it. To *xia hai* is to "take the plunge," to turn one's back on secure and familiar ways of earning a living in the hope of getting rich. It is a term with a history of negative connotations. During Japan's wartime occupation of China, for example, *xia hai* was how one spoke of deciding to collaborate with the Japanese or, among women, of working as a prostitute. To "go out to sea" is thus to pursue the expedient if greatly profitable course and to do so while knowingly abandoning ethical standards of the culture. That this should be the signification for entry into the marketplace among intellectuals-turned-entrepreneurs in the 1990s signals the ambivalence attached to what the market would consider the sensible choice. Today the phrase may have little more than ironic force: a self-deprecating acknowledgment that going into business requires a certain adjustment in old habits and ways of thinking although it is the smart move (e.g., Guo Chuan et al. 1993). Yet the implication that this move involves giving up one's allegiance to the fundamental values of elite culture has not disappeared.

The reappearance of *xia hai* in the language of public choice in the late 1980s and 1990s signals that the lucrative market economy has been leading some Chinese to want to overthrow the established regime of values. In a precommercial economy, economic value tends to be quarantined from moral value and can be converted to moral value only under the narrow rules of transposition that charity or philanthropy make available. In a commercial economy, by contrast, economic value enjoys greater independence from moral norms. It can be identified and determined according to concrete, finite measures, and its importance for society—which cannot be reproduced without wealth—comes to appear relatively uncomplicated. The establishment of moral value, on the other hand, involves ongoing and indeterminate arbitrations of particular interests. Moral value is thus constantly open to dispute in commercialized societies, even among those who claim to adhere to the same value system. When economic value is regarded as setting standards, moral value loses force in affecting the conduct of social life.

The Confucian tradition, which has been elaborated from principles established in a precommercial context, does not permit economic value to set standards. Sensitive to the possibility that excessive profit taking involves an infringement of moral values, it provides almost no opportunity for transposing wealth into virtue. The virtuous may be wealthy, and may deserve the comfort and prestige of wealth, but the wealthy do not have easier access to virtue because of their wealth. Accordingly, at first glance, Confucianism does not to provide an obvious model for Chinese in a commercializing era who seek to construct a positive moral orientation to the expansion of the market. Yet, as we shall see, many in the past decade have attempted to revise Confucianism for this end.

In contrast to Confucianism, the "Protestant ethic" of Europe has been cited to provide such a model by virtue of endowing success in the market as appropriate reward for entrepreneurial initiative and intelligence. The history of this interpretation may be traced back most conveniently to the sociology of Max Weber, who felt that capitalism could not have arisen in the absence of the Protestant culture of redemption. Weber had no desire to argue that the pursuit of wealth was good in itself; indeed, he regarded the businessman's pursuit of ever greater profit at the expense of personal gratification as ultimately irrational (1958a, 70). Nonetheless, recognizing that the pursuit of profit could be morally validated within Protestantism, he argued that this validation contributed to the ceaseless expansion of capitalism in Europe.

As the market economy expanded in the mid-1980s, Chinese social theorists were drawn to Weber, previously anathema among them because of his opposition to Marx. Their first explorations of Weberian sociology examined his insights into rational bureaucracy in the hope of depatrimonializing China's bureaucratic apparatus and improving its ability to manage the new economy. But that interest soon broadened into considering the cultural factors conditioning the rise of capitalism, again with a practical concern in mind: to nurture something akin to Weber's "spirit of capitalism." While some scholars contented themselves with reducing Weber to the sort of caricature that Marx and Engels drew in *The Holy Family* of political economists caught in the irresolvable contradiction between private property and rationality (Su 1987, 207), others, notably Yü Ying-shih of Princeton University, have applied Weber's argument about European capitalism to the Chinese case (Yü 1987; see also Zhang Liwen 1990, 146–48). The attempt to mobilize Confucianism as a source for developing an ideology of the market is intended not just to rescue that tradition from the negative assessment it usually receives in modernization circles but to impart to it positive signification precisely in the sphere regarded as exerting that influence—the economy. Arguments about historical foundations for economic rationality might seem to have only academic interest at a time when the Chinese economy is shifting decisively to market principles. Most Chinese now recognize the economic value of extending the market into most spheres of production and consumption, and many are mobilizing their labor or capital to take advantage of the new opportunities for gaining wealth. In the face of this activity, it might seem trivial to argue, as I shall in this chapter, that indigenous ethical notions concerning the pursuit of profit are exerting a drag on the free operation of the market. Yet deep-seated anxieties about the moral value of expanding the market, and about the ascendancy of economic over moral values, continue to affect both popular attitudes and the policies of the Chinese state (Wang Gungwu 1991, 196–97). Only by recognizing the effects of these anxieties can we begin to come to terms with the economic culture of contemporary China and anticipate the future shape of what the Chinese government for the moment calls its "socialist market economy."

Profit as a Problem

Over the past four decades, and for the past two millennia as well, Chinese economic policy has oscillated between two poles. Around one pole have clustered the ideals of agrarian self-sufficiency, price stability, fixed residency, social har-mony/hierarchy, and the restriction of commerce to the circulation of basic necessities. At the other pole have gathered the ideals of accumulation, com-modity circulation, social mobility, market competition, and the benefits of redistributing wealth through exchange. During the imperial era, the policies at the first pole came largely to define what might be called the Confucian vision of the economy. The policies at the second pole were not able to find equally solid philosophical ground on which to stand. Until the sixteenth century, expediency rather than genealogy was the best argument in their favor: they delivered economic goods.

Chinese thinking about the economy in the last four decades has taken a place in this history. At the one pole stand the economic policies pursued under Mao Zedong through the third quarter of the twentieth century. Agricultural production was organized into communes, prices were set, distribution was centralized, and residential and occupational identities were fixed. These poli-cies stand directly in the wake of the Confucian commitment that the economy be put to the service of moral goals—that redness prevail over expertise, to use Mao Zedong's old polarity. By contrast, the policies of Deng Xiaoping during the last quarter of the century—commercialization of agriculture, free circula-tion of private commodities, removal of price and wage controls, and forma-tion of an unregulated labor market—cleave far more to the expedient pole of prizing expertise over redness. Put in extreme terms, Dengist policies accept the necessity of placing economic values ahead of moral values, which in ideologi-cal practice has meant rewriting economic values as moral values.

Although Confucius himself made comments in this direction in the "Liren" chapter of the *Analects,* the locus classicus of the view that moral value should be elevated over economic appears in the opening passage of *Mencius,* the second founding text of Confucianism:

> Mencius was received in audience by King Hui of Liang.
> "Sir," said the king. "You have not thought a thousand *li* too far to come, so surely you have some teaching that will profit my state."
> "Your Majesty," replied Mencius. "How can you talk of 'profit'? There is only 'benevolence' and 'righteousness' and nothing else."

King Hui clearly got off on the wrong foot in this now famous conversation with Mencius (372–289 B.C.), which occurred about the year 320. When the poor monarch used the word *profit,* he was unwittingly citing a concept that utilitarians of his day thought reasonable in calculating how to rule effectively. He did not anticipate the trouble Mencius would give him for following this fashion. In Mencius's view, the goal of the ruler was to be good, not merely effective. Efficacy would follow only when goodness was assured. Mencius was not against gaining advantages for the state. After all, his professional career was built on the claim that his advice could be used to improve the security of the ruler's position and the lot of his subjects' lives. But that improvement, in Mencius's view, could not be gained by thinking outside moral categories.

Mencius was sufficiently well pleased with his retort that this little polemical exchange is featured as the opening passage in his writings. His repartee not only punished King Hui for all time. It also—and, I think, quite inadvertently—imposed embargoes on the terms by which Confucian discourse has subsequently been able to speak about the economy. Mencius was not making a judgment on economic activity when he reduced the king's concern about improving his kingdom to a blind pursuit of selfish advantage. His comment was intended solely for application within the sphere of state administration. Yet, by polarizing the term "profit" with the twin concepts of "benevolence" and "righteousness" (using a polarity he inherited from Confucius), Mencius set up a distinction that has continued to affect the ways in which Chinese have thought about the economy ever since. This is not to say that good Confucians, or Chinese more generally, have pursued righteousness rather than profit over the last two thousand years, but it is to say that they have had to do so within a cultural framework that preferred to praise moral reciprocity over profit taking and to see in each the diminution of the other.

Historically, so long as the Confucian discourse of moral action could be extended comfortably over economic activity without inspiring a sense of dissonance between minimum ethical standards and the getting of wealth, the tension between moral reciprocity and profit taking remained manageable. Modest profits could be regarded as reasonable payments for the work of supplying otherwise unavailable necessities: as fees for labor service rather than as return on capital investment. But when scales of production increased and rates of profit rose above customary standards, as happened during periods of commercialization, this tension broke the surface. In times when the commercial economy expanded so rapidly that social relations were altered, Confucians resuscitated Mencius's warning against profit in an attempt to reimpose moral values without which they felt social stability could not be ensured. Against "profit" they mobilized its Mencian negation, "righteousness."

The Chinese term that gets translated as righteousness, *yi,* is awkward to put into English without recourse to archaisms: it might more felicitously be translated as "integrity" or "responsibility" in its later usage. One was deemed to have realized *yi* to the extent that one fulfilled duties to others. *Yi* signified the realization of moral standards in a public context, which contrasted with the essentially private accrual of wealth or other advantage expressed in the term *li* ("profit"). Among contemporary scholars, Qian Xun (1991, 52–54) has argued that *yi* and *li* in Mencius's time were viewed as quietly complementary, with the former understood as modifying or regulating the latter. Indeed, this is how imperial policymakers often related the two concepts, concerned as they were with adequately funding the state while maintaining social order under their dominance. And yet, as Qian notes, Confucian philosophers tended to place the two concepts in fundamental opposition, absolutizing righteousness and reducing profit to a position of moral indefensibility.

Although the Mencian dichotomy between righteousness and profit developed in such a way that the denunciation of commercial expansion as moral failure became a cliché of Confucian discourse, not all Chinese intellectuals have wanted to disparage commerce. Some have sought to rework the terms of the debate to realign profit and righteousness as noncontradictory values. Prior to the present, this attempt at reworking was most conspicuous in the sixteenth century, when commercialization pressed on established values to such an extent that some were moved to reevaluate the anticommercial bias within the Confucian normative order, even to rewrite Confucian values as buttresses for a procommercial ideology. In recent years, scholars of contemporary Chinese capitalism have been keen to recover these voices, appealing to this particular moment of revision to construct a Weberian logic that would allow modernization to be genealogized within the Confucian tradition.

Moralizing Profit in the Sixteenth Century

The Confucian discourse on commerce in the Ming dynasty (1368–1644) took Mencius's dictum against profit literally. As a fifteenth-century scholar complained about unscrupulous publishers in Beijing who were turning out spurious libretti, "fellows who aim for profit" were not to be trusted to maintain the ethical standards to which the book-buying elite self-consciously adhered (Ye 1991, 21.11a). Traders were permitted to circulate basic necessities but not to redistribute wealth, for it was the role of the Confucian state to guarantee the appropriate distribution of economic goods. Since profit in one place was understood as entailing an equivalent loss in another, the state had to resist the unchecked circulation of commodities. Commerce's offense against redistributive norms was read as an infraction of moral norms. To constrain merchants from committing these offenses, Confucian ideology lodged them in the lowest occupational category and sustained a discourse that in the early- to mid-Ming praised the noncommercial and thereafter bewailed its decline (Brook 1997).

To offer an example: the editor of the mid-Ming gazetteer of Dingan

County on Hainan Island in the far south happily declares that the local people "are hardworking and frugal and do not engage in commerce or the miscellaneous trades." This declaration is presented both as actual description and moral comment: good people do not go into trade. By the 1560s, according to the prefectural gazetteer, this laudable disinclination to engage in trade had evaporated. "The people by nature are quick in mind and good at argument. They compete with each other for wealth and try to outdo each other in boldness." Worse still, sumptuary distinctions were disappearing. "The delicacies they eat are far beyond grand," he regrets to note. In nearby Lingao County, the report of growing commercialization is even more desperate: "People in recent days are so driven by the pursuit of wealth that right and wrong have changed places. At the first sign of an argument they charge off to the nearest market town, confuse the officials, and get all their witnesses thrown into jail" (*Qiongzhou fuzhi* 1619, 3.85a–b). Clearly, commerce was expanding its corrosive presence in county life on Hainan Island in the sixteenth century, and this presence was read as a decline in restraint and moral reciprocity.

To the relief of some within the Confucian elite, not all Hainan islanders were sliding down the slippery slope of commerce. The prefectural gazetteer of 1619 was able to note that in Danzhou Subprefecture "the people by nature are simple and upright and value ritual and righteousness," code words for correct behavior. "They do not work as merchants but devote their efforts to plowing and weaving," the appropriate sex-specific activities for male and female peasants. Even better, among the gentry, "many families practice the recitation of Confucian texts." To this idyllic picture of a place uninfected by commercialization, the writer adds one potentially contrary element: "Also, many families practice the craft of weaving cowrie shells into the cloth they make. Since people don't have servants or tenants, the women carry it off to sell" (*Qiongzhou fuzhi* 1619, 89a). Danzhou peasants may not have yet been absorbed into the new culture of profit competition that would soon inundate Hainan Island, yet they were producing a commodity for the market, and in doing so were moving themselves onto the margin of the commercial world, although the gazetteer compiler appears not to have caught this drift.

The men who oversaw the compilation of local gazetteers tended to be conservative guardians of the Confucian moral vision who were ready to criticize local customs they did not like and highlight evidence of adherence to the best values of elite culture. The increasingly insistent presence of commerce in sixteenth-century life, however, prompted some scholars to consider the possibility that a commercialized economy could produce benefits in addition to hazards and to consider ways of incorporating profit taking into the Confucian framework. A good example is Zhang Han (1511–93), an official from a commercial family in Hangzhou who proposed some adjustment to the conventional denigration of trade in his now well-known essay "On Merchants." Zhang begins the essay by regretting the universal lust for profit but then turns to a defense of commerce by arguing that the exchange of surplus is not a matter of profit entailing loss but of profit bringing benefit to all parties. He does not go so far as to suggest a direct revision of Confucian ethical values, but he gets close to this notion when discussing profit as a reasonable standard for evaluating policy options regarding the management of the economy: if commerce generates wealth and contributes to state finances, then to promote it must be an exercise in "benevolence" (Brook 1981, 208).

The son of a family that got rich through the textile trade, Zhang Han was at the liberal end of the spectrum of gentry opinion in the sixteenth century. Among merchants, procommercial opinion found even stronger expression. In sixteenth-century texts by or about merchants, we begin to hear more sympathetic views of the morality of commercial gain (Lufrano 1996). The examples I give in this chapter are taken almost entirely from a collection of historical texts from Huizhou, the mountainous prefecture south of Nanjing that was the home of one of the most powerful merchant groups in late imperial society. The passages I have chosen are those in which writers comment on the term *profit,* which stood between them and Confucian grace. In these writings, *profit* is only one term in a broad and refreshing vocabulary that begins in the sixteenth century to speak of commerce in the language of "making" (*gong*), "living" (*sheng*), and "growing" (*zhi*). This language contrasts starkly with the anticommercial vocabulary of conventional Confucianism, which expressed the essence of its Way in the language of "reversion" (*fu*), "preservation" (*shou*), and "antiquity" (*gu*). This language signals that the Confucian goal was not gain over what existed before but maintenance of what already was.

Constrained to speak of profit, sixteenth-century writers of merchant biographies developed a new discourse of profit taking. Rather than designating it as the morally unfortunate aspect of commercial activity, they construed profit taking as necessary to commercial enterprise and thus as having moral validity. This construction is suggested in a text by the Huizhou scholar-official Wang Daokun (1523–93), himself the son of a salt merchant, regarding a local student named Cheng Fen. When Cheng's merchant-father wanted to punish Cheng's two brothers for failing in a business venture, the earnest student mobilized Confucian reasoning to come to their defense. "The merchant acts to obtain profit," Cheng reasoned to his father. Since his brothers had acted as merchants were supposed to—using their capital to make a profit—they should be judged on their willingness to take risks for the sake of business, not on their failure to gain profit. They may have made bad business decisions, but that result was secondary to the fact that they had acted according to the duty assigned to them by their calling.[2] In Cheng Fen's Confucianized version of commerce, the touchstone for judging merchants was duty, not performance.

This attempt to Confucianize the merchant's calling entailed that merchants who pursued profit energetically should be regarded as moral men. This attitude appears in the views of a merchant quoted in a Huizhou genealogy of about 1570: "What one does in the world shouldn't be judged in terms of his fixed occupation, but in terms solely of how well he follows what he should do." The merchant takes this a step further, however, to argue for ends as well as means. "Whether gentry, peasant, artisan, or merchant, the bold always get ahead. As for me, I am of the merchant's occupation. Were I to shrink from the difficulties involved in [the pursuit of] profit, my great enterprise would fail" (Zhang and Wang 1985, 232). As the "great enterprise" of the merchant was to make a profit, the merchant who devoted himself to doing just that was simply meeting his duty.

This proposition left the way open for working a moral equation between the Confucian and the merchant, each committing himself to meeting the moral obligation of his career to the best of his ability. From this perspective, profit could be related narratively as the reward for successful business. Thus, we read in the biography of a merchant that, though he was trusting to a fault, "yet his profit doubled and tripled, such that by his middle years he had accumulated thousands of ounces [of silver]."[3] Profit did not follow because he struggled for it; rather, it simply came to him because he was "sincere" and "honest." In this moral vision, the good become rich. Financial success absorbs the moral ambiguity of profit taking. With profit held hostage to this moral equation, its opposite, loss, came to stand as a sign of moral failure. To lose money in business in a big way was to fail to realize "the way of the skilled merchant," as another lineage genealogy puts it (Zhang and Wang 1985, 145). The concept of loss thus evolved under the pressure of sixteenth-century moralizing to signify that a merchant had fallen short of ethical duty. This simplification suited the project of turning profit into a positive moral sign, not only by counterexample but by outcome. A merchant who pursued profit without regard for any other consideration would then be punished with loss in such forms as heirlessness, illness, family squabbling, and financial ruin.[4] Profit as reward made possible loss as punishment; thus did success and failure round out commercial careers in Confucian morality tales.

This moralizing perspective did not wholly remove the ethical ambiguity surrounding profit. It was not simply a matter of the richer you were the better you were. The moralizing of profit taking imposed limits on profit; unlimited profit was still unacceptable within this Confucian merchant ideology. Willingness to aim for only a 10 percent return on investment is used in the genealogy biography of a filial bookseller as evidence of his moral character (Zhang and Wang 1985, 207). Correspondingly, when a grain merchant in Suzhou was not satisfied with the prospect of a fourfold profit during the drought of 1589 and sought out a diviner to ask the God of the Southern Ultimate how high the price would go, the deity was so disgusted with the man's greed that he caused his warehouse to burn to the ground.[5] Here loss serves the narrative purpose of assigning a moral evaluation to this merchant's covetousness.

The notion that profit taking had to stay within a reasonable range (okay at 10 percent, unacceptable at over 400 percent) indicates that even merchant culture was not free from anxiety regarding commercial exploitation. Profit taking remained vulnerable to the charge of being socially destabilizing in the absence of restraint. For this reason, merchant Xu Mingda (1478–1538) was praised by his lineage biographer in 1527 as "righteous" (*yi*) for refusing to force his debtors to sell their children when a disastrous harvest made repayment impossible. "How can I tear from someone those he most loves for the sake of profit," he is recorded as having declared (Zhang and Wang 1985, 164). His voice is made to stand out here presumably because others in the same position would not have shared his compunction. In the same vein, his Huizhou contemporary Cheng Ying (1471–1533) was praised for "not manipulating market knowledge to entrap others, nor so concentrating on profit as to cause resentment." According to his biography in the 1573 lineage genealogy, Cheng simply relied on his natural commercial talent and honest practices to become a very rich man (Zhang and Wang 1985, 275). By conducting business in certain ways, his success did not provoke resentment, thereby removing any ethical doubt tied to his vocation as a merchant.

The consistent vocabulary of these biographies and testimonials indicates that the good merchant had to be portrayed in certain terms. Hard work alone was not sufficient to redeem profit taking. It had to be accompanied by recognizably Confucian values about concern for the needs of others and reciprocity in the treatment of others' interests. We have already noted that "sincerity" and "honesty" were moral qualities associated with the good merchant. The lineage biographer of Xu Zhen (1503–33) says that he was so much more concerned with "trustworthiness" and "righteousness" than "profit" that no one could bear to cheat him (Zhang and Wang 1985, 273). The lineage biographer of Xu Wencai uses "righteousness" and "trustworthiness" to describe his commercial dealings but also introduces "closeness" to characterize Xu's conduct within his family: "Were going after profit to mean going against closeness, then even if he could have gained a thousand taels a day, he wouldn't have done it" (278). Of all these values, "righteousness" posed the greatest contrast, and the most potent corrective, to profit, as practically every merchant biography reminds us: "he took profit through righteous conduct"; "he treated profit lightly and valued righteousness"; "he frequented the places for making profit yet wouldn't take it if it meant going against righteousness" (287, 288, 445). Such phrasing was intended to close the difference between righteous conduct and profit taking.

This rhetorical strategy came about as a way of resolving the contradiction between status and wealth that mid-Ming commercialization was generating. With the expansion of commerce, some merchants became sufficiently secure in their wealth and social position to command Confucianized biographies (a redundancy, given that biography was a Confucian genre). But this explanation does not tell the whole story. These biographies may also be seen as the product of expanded commercial opportunity in another sense. That is, the opening up of the commercial sphere may have made possible not just the getting of great wealth but the getting of it by means other than deception, fraud, and market manipulation. In other words, the appearance of a morally righteous tone in mid-Ming merchant biographies may have come about not because of the greater clout that rich merchants commanded, nor because of a shift in the larger ethical environment, but because a more fully commercialized economy was providing merchants with opportunities to gain wealth by means that were popularly construed as ethically positive.

The effect of this realigning of Mencian righteousness and profit was to remake the image of the merchant in the mold of the Confucian scholar. The merchant who could "enrich himself without talking of profit" was one who "followed commerce using Confucian means" and deserved to be called "the merchant's Confucian" (Zhang and Wang 1985, 276). Thus, the biographer of Huang Jifang (d. 1559) could declare him to have been "merchant in name but Confucian in conduct." Huang so impressed the locals in Confucius's home region, his lineage biographer insists, that he was regarded as embodying "the essence of the Duke of Zhou," Confucius's model of the perfect ruler (441).

The rhetorical quality of this language is exposed by the continuing voicing of the opposite rhetoric of profit taking as socially destabilizing, even in merchant circles. The genealogy of a Huizhou merchant family (ca. 1570) was willing to admit that those who become "powerful merchants and large traders, by transporting their great capital vast distances, dupe the common people and take advantage of every opportunity to fish for profit: only then do they become wealthy" (Zhang and Wang 1985, 289). One could read a statement like this as nothing more than a simpleminded parroting of hegemonic ideology rather than as evidence of how merchants actually thought of themselves. Yet the positive self-representations we find in other merchant texts are equally eloquent of the same thing: the pressure for merchants to continue struggling against the negative evaluation of commerce within elite culture and to create for themselves a recognizably Confucian identity. After all, Huizhou merchants had notorious reputations for usurious pawnbroking, exorbitant luxury, sexual voracity, and litigation (Wang Zhenzhong 1993). These were exactly the sorts of economic activities from which the Ming elite insisted on distancing themselves (Brokaw 1991, 136) and against which the image of the righteous merchant was set up in the first place. What the merchant biographies signal then is not that this concern had been overturned but that, under the pressure of an expanding market, two ideologies were contending—and together formed the organic culture characteristic of late-Ming China.

Virtuous Profit, Profitable Virtue

Does the moralism of commerce that found expression in the sixteenth century mean that "profit" had successfully entered the Confucian lexicon desensitized of its Mencian coding? Was profit taking henceforth valorized as righteous and commerce regarded as not only necessary but laudable? Had commerce at last come up equal to gentility? Was profit taking now legitimate within Confucian discourse? Within the last decade, this is precisely the argument that some Chinese scholars have made. By rethinking the Mencian rupture between profit and righteousness, they have sought variously to challenge the assumptions that Confucianism was, or remained, hostile to economic development. Zhang Liwen, in a study of the Chinese tradition completed in 1988, sought to downplay Confucianism's anticommercial orientation by arguing that it recognized profit as a natural motive for economic activity. Profit was problematic only to the extent that it served the narrow advantage of the individual rather than yielding benefits for all society. Confucianism, Zhang argued, placed righteousness before profit in order to regulate profit taking, not to discourage it (Zhang Liwen 1990, 151–53; see also Liu Yunbo 1990, 228). Qian Xun has read the Confucian relationship between righteousness and profit in a similarly nonpolarizing way by arguing for balance between the rights and benefits of the profit-seeking individual and those of the state (Qian Xun 1991, 58–59). These arguments feel forced, as though they were written (as indeed they were) against the pressure of the opposite and widely held view, which is that China's cultural heritage did in fact denigrate profit and promote an overly high minded concept of the good and that such attitudes are inappropriate to the "socialist market economy" (cf. Hayhoe 1993, 39).

Other scholars have taken a bolder, less apologetic stance. In a long essay on the commercial spirit in Chinese culture published the year before Zhang Liwen completed his study, Yü Ying-shih argued that late-Ming Confucians were coming to accept commerce as a necessary form of economic activity and that commerce had a fully legitimate place within the Confucian worldview. Using the same compilation of sources on Huizhou merchants that I have used in this chapter, Yü pointed out that the status of merchants was rising through the sixteenth to eighteenth centuries, not just within their own circles but in elite society as well. He attested to this transformation by quoting several late-Ming scholars to the effect that they regarded merchants and scholars as following the "same Way," bearing the "same commitment," and sharing the "same mind" (Yü 1987: 525, 529). Reading sameness as identity, Yü concluded that the traditional exclusion of merchants from the Confucian mainstream was disappearing. This conclusion potentially misreads the Chinese term for "same" (*tong*), which can signify a relationship among things that are not identical but are equal yet distinct (Brook 1993, 22–23). To say that merchants and scholars followed the "same Way" could mean that the distinction between them had paled to insignificance, but it could also mean that merchants were an accepted but distinct group within the Confucian condominium of power: not scholars themselves but fellow travelers. The latter reading would require that the original Confucian gap between commerce and gentility—between profit and righteousness—be left open. Profit could serve righteousness, but righteousness could not be collapsed into profit.

But Yü Ying-shih's view rests on an even bolder proposition: that the elevation of the status of merchants came about, not in spite of Confucianism, but because of it. He has argued that neo-Confucianism since the Song dynasty has fostered an ethic of thrift, honesty, and effort—core values that, being conducive to commercial activity, have contributed to the formation of a new merchant consciousness. To make that argument, Yü invokes Weber's account of the spirit of capitalism in Europe and applies it to Confucianism, arguing that a new merchant consciousness was transforming the Confucian value system. Yü had started building his Weberian explanation of Chinese economic rationality in 1984 in an extended essay on the impact of modernization on the Chinese value system. He noted that the value systems of China and the West vary but insisted that the Western system did not necessarily provide the only environment in which economic modernization can occur. Yü accepted Weber's distinction in *The Religion of China* (1964) between the Protestant ethic as externally motivated and the Confucian ethic as internally driven, yet he challenged Weber's claim that the latter was ill suited to the rational enterprise of constructing the modern world. Arguing for the importance of the individual in neo-Confucianism, Yü could challenge the conventional notion that Chinese culture does not reward individual initiative. To the contrary: central Mencian concepts like righteousness elevate the reciprocity of relations between individuals as the truest realization of the Confucian ethic-in-the-world (Yü 1984).

By means of this bold reinterpretation of Confucianism, it became possible to assemble a genealogy that locates the development of a commercial spirit in China within the Confucian tradition. Yet a historical problem remains: whatever Confucianism's potential for encouraging commercial enterprise, it did not generate capitalism in China (Chen Shaoming 1992, 186). The attempt to call up a hoary Confucian genealogy for contemporary economic rationality in the absence of a historical effect thus seems forced. Even so, the appeal to an indigenous cultural foundation for the contemporary economy, which is the argument that Yü Ying-shih is tacitly making, is compelling for those having to readjust their assumptions about China's place in the world capitalist economy, whether that appeal is constructed via Confucianism or some other recognizably indigenous form. From the state and elite points of view, naturalizing the acceptance of capitalist relations is a good ideological strategy, for it obscures any question of compulsion. When individuals are seen to function well within the reformed Chinese economy, their success is made to appear as entirely to be expected rather than explained once the master explanation of Confucian capitalism is in place.

From a contrary point of view, however, participation in the market economy in China today seems for most to be a matter of economic compulsion, not of moral self-realization. The new entrepreneurs wish to be thought well of, and an ideology that extols their efforts and protects their profits now assists their ascent into a ruling class of changing composition. Yet it is doubtful whether one can interpret their psychology in the language of Weberian calling—and even more doubtful that it can be applied to the mass of wage workers and unemployed who are struggling to survive within what for many has become a brutal and cynical environment, as Diana Lary describes it in her chapter in this volume. With wealth validated as its own end, it is difficult to find a logic for a Weberian-style argument suggesting that the acquisition of wealth in Chinese capitalism has undergone a cultural reconstruction that endows it with intense religious or ethical meaning. Historically, the fitting of commerce to Confucianism in the sixteenth century was too brief, and occurred within too narrow a social realm, to transform Confucianism into a discourse of personal salvation for the entrepreneur.

This conclusion does not imply that Confucianism cannot be used to generate an ideology of moral meaning for capital accumulation. After all, Confucianism today is invoked constantly throughout the Sinic world to construct systems of production and distribution favorable to capitalism, and values that Weber recognized as conducive to hard work and reinvestment are being regularly discerned in indigenous traditions in Eastern Asia and labeled Confucian. Whether Confucianism "does" any of this is impossible to prove or disprove. Confucian understandings may well animate the subjective assessments that individuals make of their economic choices; at the same time, though, the amenability of cultural explanations to invention and reinvention, whether by sixteenth-century merchant biographers or late-twentieth-century intellectuals, means that genealogical ties can be construed between present practices and past values to justify authority, motivate action, and urge compliance. Still, once certain narratives of moral value have gained status as public traditions, they provide widely agreed upon repertoires of keywords and symbols that are difficult to ignore.

A problematic fault line in the contemporary logic of invoking Confucianism as a work ethic is its reliance on an explicit analogizing of a European discourse. Yü intended the citation of Weber as an appeal to a general logic regarding the impact of value systems on economic performance; yet the point of reference is clearly Western, and the unstated handicap therefore remains the problem of why China has only recently produced capitalism. From a May Fourth perspective, the challenge of the twentieth century for China lies less in China's competition with the West than in the struggle between Chinese tradition and Chinese modernity (Gan 1987; Chen Shaoming 1992; for a contrary view, see Tu 1988a, 116–19). By yoking Confucianism for present service, the tension between earlier and contemporary modes of livelihood is deemed to have been done away with and the distinctiveness of the Chinese way reaffirmed. This sleight may serve a useful ideological function for promoting economic modernization in China and throughout Eastern Asia, but it generates ultimately an ideology rather than an explanation: a tailoring that fits Confucian ("Chinese") values to the economy without actually expecting them to play a significant role in leading economic modernization (Wang Xun 1993). A significant element within the intellectual mainstream in China remains unenthusiastic about embracing a Confucian version of the modern market economy, seeing the link between Confucianism and capitalism as a retreat from general theory to ethnic particularism (Xie Xialing 1994, 38).

In any case, as economic values overwhelm values of other types, it seems almost inevitable that profit will displace the more diffuse, and increasingly archaistic, concept of righteousness in Chinese livelihood strategies. Short of becoming the rallying cry of a significant sector that has been left out of the modernization program (though note that the term for "uprising" is *qiyi*, "to rise in righteousness"), lingering anxiety about the moral inadequacy of profit taking should erode as economic gain is assured. At best, the Mencian caution will linger on in the repertoire of concepts capable of expressing small resistances to the state's imposition of a market-based economy and the hegemony of pure wealth. On the other hand, it is possible that the Mencian denigration of profit has not yet run its full course. Most cultures, capitalist and noncapitalist alike, build restraining concepts into their discourses about the acquisition of wealth, as was noted at the beginning of this chapter. These restraining concepts—duty, disinterest, public spiritedness, self-sacrifice (all of which can find room under the umbrella of *yi* [Rankin 1990, 38–42])—help to impart a sense of stability and continuity to social life and serve to encourage some diversion of resources into family or community reproduction. From a critical perspective, such restraining concepts disguise the exercise of power by inducing a misrecognition of profit accumulation as public service. The power of those deemed to act in the public interest disappears behind a rhetoric of disinterested generosity, generating symbolic capital that may be used elsewhere in the economy. Such concepts are the language of what Pierre Bourdieu (1990a, 127) has called "symbolic violence": a sort of "gentle, invisible violence, unrecognized as such, chosen as much as undergone, that of trust, obligation, personal loyalty, hospitality, gifts, debts, piety, in a word, of all the virtues honored by the ethic of honour." *Yi* expresses that very ethic of honor in Chinese.

From this point of view, the Confucian discourse of righteousness over profit has for two millennia served the need to sustain the priority of political over commercial power in China. The disabling of "profit" in the Confucian lexicon aided the dominance of the imperial state over competitors from the realm of profit taking; so, too, one could argue, the revival of an anticommercial bias under Mao Zedong (in the guise of a ban on private marketing) served the same purpose. Mao's moral condemnation of commerce, enhanced by giving it the foreign label of "capitalism," created ideological scaffolding for sustaining state-socialist economic policies and enforcing the Communist Party's monopoly on political power. Yet even then the state did not act unilaterally, for Mao was able to sustain this anticommercial bias because it chimed with peasant attitudes favoring egalitarian redistribution, attitudes that continue to resonate today (Anagnost 1989). The reforms of Deng Xiaoping require a different ideological course: one that lauds surplus over subsistence, enterprise over maintenance, entrepreneurial initiative over fulfillment of duty. Neither Deng nor his planners would go so far as to say that there is profit and nothing else— though the slogan "to get rich is glorious" proved popular in the 1980s. The enunciation of moral values still has a role in state ideology. Yet the architects of the new economy may find in the future that they need the symbolic violence of Mencian moralism as much as they need capitalist economic motivation to construct a vision of the economy that most Chinese find comfortable to inhabit.

Appealing to the Protestant ethic and the spirit of Western capitalism may ultimately prove ineffective in generating this ideology. The foreign aura of these terms will only serve to remind Chinese, at least of this generation, that the legitimacy of the People's Republic of China was built on the rejection of capitalism as imperialist. The irony of calling up Confucianism for present service is that both sides can appeal to this tradition as a source for constructing narratives of meaning: those who resist capitulation to an amoral capitalism as much as those who seek to install the labor discipline and consumption patterns needed to maintain profitable linkages to the global economy. Confucianism's availability to both sides may well be construed as attesting to the power that culture can have in shaping the economy. On the other hand, it may signal its ultimate insignificance in the face of more powerful forces.

NOTES

An earlier version of this essay was published under the title "Weber, Mencius, and the History of Chinese Capitalism" in *Asian Perspective* 19, no. 1 (Spring-Summer 1995): 79–97.

1. Claims about the "force" of cultural traditions tend to rely on a reification of culture into a fixed inventory of permanently accessible ideas that are available to "members" of that culture without mediation. When Wei-ming Tu (Tu 1988b, 85) tells a Chinese audience that "American culture is very young, having a present but no past," he reveals his view of culture as a closed body of established ideas and identities, which in turn allows him to stage his particular argument that Chinese culture cannot evade its Confucian heritage. From a contrary perspective, one might suggest that the terrific pressures on Chinese cultural traditions exerted by both the Maoist and the Dengist dispensations have reduced the lived culture of Chinese to an even more limited range of ideas and commitments, with state-appointed elites carefully controlling access to habits of heart and thought associated with life before the People's Republic.

2. Wang Daokun, *Taihan ji* (Collected writings of Wang Taihan), *juan* 40, quoted in Zhang and Wang 1985, 232.

3. Li Weishen, *Dami fangshan ji* (Collected writings from Dami Mountain Hut), *juan* 73, quoted in Zhang and Wang 1985, 278.

4. All four are combined in the biography of Merchant Wang in Dong Han, *Sangang shilüe* (Brief history of the Three Bonds), *juan* 8, quoted in Zhang and Wang 1985, 291.

5. Zhu Jiaxuan, *Jianhu wuji* (The hard calabash, fifth collection), *juan* 1, quoted in Zhang and Wang 1985, 195.

Chinese Understandings of Economic Change: From Agrarian Empire to Industrial Society

R. Bin Wong

We usually look to the individual when we analyze the relationship between economic behavior and culture, and research on microeconomic behavior scrutinizes private economic actors rather than public ones. Beyond the possible links between individual behavior and culture, though, questions must be asked about how culturally specific forms of economic understanding shape the preferences and behavior of larger collective actors like states or social classes. This chapter explores the ways in which Chinese officials and elites have perceived agrarian and industrial economic activities in imperial and postimperial times. It considers the ways in which understandings of economic behavior directly shape policy preferences and more generally influence possibilities for economic change, and thus it highlights culturally constructed visions of economic behavior. But to focus upon how people thought the economy worked and the purposes they attributed to various economic activities does not mean that the material world is irrelevant to determining what is economically possible. It simply suggests that an analysis of economic activity that does not include some assessment of the intentions and understandings of the actors themselves is limited. This chapter also outlines briefly some important features of economic activity in late imperial China within analytical categories that propose some basic contrasts between developments in Chinese economic history and those in European economic history. Together, the following remarks on culturally determined perceptions of economic activity, organizational structures of economic activity, and dynamic processes of economic change offer a brief sketch of how Chinese economic development can be related to history, culture, and global context.

Economic Change and Cultural Knowledge

As analysts of human behavior across the humanities and social sciences commonly recognize, human intentions and results do not always match. One kind of gap between intentions and results occurs when people do not achieve what they want. This gap is created by two large clusters of factors: first, incompleteness of knowledge, not knowing what one needs to know in order to gain intended results; and, second, limitations of power, not having the capacities to make happen what one desires. Sometimes, however, people are pleasantly surprised when a second kind of gap emerges, which is when results outstrip expectations. Through no conscious efforts of their own, people's activities create unanticipated results in moments of major historical change. An obvious example of this effect in economic history is the Industrial Revolution; no one consciously set out to make an industrial revolution in order to transform radically production possibilities that have made possible standards of living far in excess of those conceivable in agrarian economies. But once people apprehended that something dramatic had occurred in England, there was a rush to figure out how such changes could be promoted elsewhere. In many nineteenth-century instances, largely confined to the European area, these efforts were crowned with success. In the twentieth century, creating economic development has proven more difficult. The shift in production possibilities initiated by the Industrial Revolution made possible efforts to create these opportunities across ever wider areas but could not guarantee their success.

The gap between what people thought they could create and their results was troubling and puzzling. The technologies of economic development were widely understood by the 1950s and with their mastery came an optimism that economic transformations could be achieved at will. Some other set of factors must account for failures. Some observers turned their gaze upon culturally based customs and habits to explain economic change and its absence. Explanations of economic success in one country encouraged scholars to identify what was missing when another failed to achieve economic development. In the 1950s one common family of explanations meant to explain the *failure* of East Asian countries to develop modern industrial economies were cultural explanations stressing the absence of an aggressive and acquisitive individualism in Confucian cultures. Based at least loosely on Weberian arguments, some scholars of the post–World War II world argued that a country like Japan lacked the entrepreneurial spirit of daring and innovation necessary for a modern industrialized economy.[1] More recently a very different story has been told in which Confucian virtues, such as respect for authority, including the submerging of individual desire to group goals in a spirit of self-sacrifice, are promoted to explain the Japanese economic miracle.[2]

The juxtaposition of these polar assessments of "culture" suggests a contradiction. How can cultural attitudes be simultaneously a barrier and a promoter of economic change? Together these polar views suggest that cultural factors help to explain the kinds of economic change that can take place, but by themselves they can neither guarantee economic development nor prevent it. Other factors and conditions contribute to the growth and transformation of economies. A stress on cultural factors does remind us that when economic development takes place outside of Europe, it will not necessarily replicate some set of European cultural logics. Keeping this notion in mind encourages us to be wary of explanations of economic failures in terms of any particular "lack." Typically, when explanations of failure focus on what is absent, they have in mind a particular idealized path of change. Certainly Japanese culture lacks an Anglo-American individualism, but this absence hardly precludes economic growth.

The search for what is missing in order to explain what has not happened exacts other costs. First, it tends to diminish the value we assign to the intentions of native actors and, as a consequence, to their more general understanding of the economy. Second, because the results of their efforts do not accord with notions of what was important in European economic development, we tend to discount the significance of their results. To see this, consider how the Chinese political economy in imperial times is both well studied and poorly understood. It is well studied in the sense that much research has reconstructed policy principles and actual practices. But the Chinese political economy remains poorly understood in terms of what it achieved; when we think of Chinese economic policies in an evaluative sense we tend to note what they did *not* do that would have promoted economic change according to one or another interpretation of what we, as outside observers with historical hindsight on success stories, choose to label a sensible path of economic change.

Based on what we can tell about Chinese policies and practices toward economic activities, I propose to review briefly the manner in which Chinese political economy in late imperial and postimperial times conceived agrarian and, later, industrial changes without imposing, I hope, criteria for what they should have thought in order to promote economic development. Since there are multiple ways to imagine economic development, each of which entails a different set of policies, it is in fact very difficult to make general judgments about the best choices. My task here is considerably easier. I will consider Chinese economic activity within Chinese categories of understanding and offer a very brief interpretive sketch of what has happened in late imperial and postimperial Chinese economic history. After assessing views of agrarian and industrial economic change, I will hazard some suggestions about how understandings of economic activity in late imperial times continue to be relevant today.

Visions of the Agrarian Economy

Chinese political economy is part of a long-standing tradition of governing, which like so many other basic themes in Chinese culture is traced back by Chinese thinkers to texts of the Zhou dynasty. Some of the principal concerns of Chinese political economy have a clear continuity through the centuries. They fall into two main clusters. On the one hand are the efforts to define reasonable and effective measures by which the government can secure adequate revenues to pursue its state-making projects. On the other hand are the efforts that officials and elites make to promote and regulate the economy for the benefit of the people. These two concerns overlap in important ways, but to the extent that they can be distinguished I will focus on the second set of concerns because policies regarding agrarian production and distribution reveal Chinese understandings of economic change most directly.

Two qualifications should immediately be made. First, the presence of perduring priorities in Chinese political economy does not mean that Chinese understandings of the economy did not change over time; as the economy became more monetized and commercialized in the eleventh and twelfth centuries and again over a wider area beginning in the sixteenth century, for example, new understandings of what the government's role(s) with respect to the economy should be were also articulated. In general the state reduced its measures of direct control and aimed to take advantage of commercialization through monetizing its tax collection. The strategies and policies conceived and implemented by the government were hardly frozen in a classical moment of creative insight; institutions of political economy changed over the centuries. Second, to highlight certain views basic to Chinese political economy in a short essay like this does not preclude major policy debates and differences of opinion; Chinese officials and elites disagreed on policies regarding money, mining, famine relief, and frontier development, to name just a few subjects. More generally, officials and elites disagreed strongly in different times and different parts of China over what roles each should play in maintaining a stable social order, but all agreed that at the base of a stable social order were secure livelihoods providing dependable material resources for as many people as possible.

As all students of Chinese history learn, Chinese political economy awarded a salient position to the land. This can hardly be considered surprising since in an agrarian society the principal source of production is the land, but we do well to remember that a preoccupation with land systems is not typical of most states in world history. Governments certainly cared about how to extract resources to meet their own needs, but they did not develop a Chinese level of concern for land distribution schemes as a means not only of gaining state revenue but also of promoting social stability. From the well-field system (*jingtian*), with its division of an area into nine squares with eight families who each work one square and together labor on the ninth for the ruler, to the "equal-field" system (*juntian*) proclaimed in the Sui (581–617) and Tang (618–907) dynasties, which in principle allotted all able-bodied men a plot of land to work during their lifetimes, Chinese writers have imagined ideal systems of land distribution to assure the government its revenue and the people equal access to a simple but adequate living. Institutional historians of China are fond, like Chinese officials themselves, of criticizing the shortcomings of bureaucratic practice and thus stress repeatedly the failures of institutional practices to conform to ideal regulations. But an exclusive focus on shortcomings can obscure the commitments, efforts, and results of Sui and Tang officials. Moreover, the ideal of providing land to peasants as a means of securing them a livelihood continued to be a theme in Chinese political economy after the Tang dynasty. Thus, we see in the Ming (1368–1644) and Qing (1644–1911) dynasties the promotion of land clearance as a principal means of keeping people settled on the land. The government at times distributed free land, tools, animals, and housing to settlers who cultivated new fields (Peng 1990; Wang et al. 1991). To reproduce agrarian empire with a settled population meant encouraging migrations from regions where poor peasants lacked adequate land. Moving people to areas with resource bases awaiting development and exploitation reduced the pressures on densely populated areas. While the vision of equal plots of land for all peasants was not directly pursued, the underlying commitment to seeing peasant households work their own plots of land was affirmed.

A second general set of strategies to keep populations settled on the land was to make their current holdings more productive. One important way to do this was to raise the agricultural productivity of already cultivated land through expanded irrigation, increased fertilizer use, and improved seed varieties; in addition, nearby land previously considered too poor to merit cultivation became arable and was often planted in inferior food grains. Chinese officials promoted the dissemination of agricultural knowledge as part of a larger responsibility to promote production.[3]

A third cluster of strategies to keep people firmly rooted in an agrarian economy involved official promotion of handicraft production, the most important case being cotton textile production by women. As Susan Mann has shown, official and elite promotion of household handicrafts fostered a gendered division of labor that kept women at home (1992). In economic terms, rural industry created a source of income to supplement agricultural income, thus enhancing the viability of small-scale peasant agriculture as the unprecedented population expansion of the eighteenth century doubled the population (B. Wong 1988a).

Promoting Commerce without Capitalism

Chinese stress on the importance of the agrarian economy has often led people to assume that the principles of Chinese political economy decried commercial activity. The modest measure of truth in this view distorts the overall context within which commercial activity was generally seen by Chinese thinkers from the Song dynasty forward when the economy became increasingly commercialized. The commercial revolution of the Song dynasty has been well examined, especially by Japanese scholars (Shiba 1968). While there appears to have been some decline in commercial activity in at least some parts of China during the Yuan dynasty (1272–1368) and the early Ming, an expansion of commercial activity in the sixteenth century is generally recognized by economic historians and dubbed by mainland Chinese scholars as "incipient capitalism" (*zibenzhuyi mengya*) (Nanjing daxue lishixi 1981, 1983). Chinese officials and elites of the time were aware of these changes and, contrary to conventional textbook assertions, recognized a useful role for trade. Indeed, the promotion of cash crops and rural industry would have made no sense without a simultaneous acceptance of market exchange as a means of distributing goods.

When trade moved goods from areas of low prices to those with high prices, market principles of supply and demand played a positive social function in Chinese official eyes. By volume, weight, and value, the most important good in late imperial long-distance commerce was grain; Wu Chengming has estimated grain to account for more than 40 percent of all long-distance trade in the eighteenth century (1985, 251). As the commodity most important to survival, the government took a special interest in the grain trade. Officials generally approved of long-distance shipments that moved grain from areas of surplus to those depending on commercial imports. But they were simultaneously against merchants holding grain off markets to drive up prices. They considered this to be hoarding to garner profits illegal and quite distinct from profits that came from moving grain from areas of surplus to those of deficit. A potential contradiction surfaced when merchants bought large amounts of grain in surplus areas to export elsewhere. Such activities could be interpreted as hoarding, yet, since the intent was not to sell the grain on the same market after prices rose, this was not the activity about which officials were most concerned (Wong 1982, 1983).

Officials generally favored market exchanges, except when shipments beyond an official's jurisdiction might cause hardship for his subject population. Officials understood the basic ideas of market supply and demand, consistent with Adam Smith's notions of how markets promote specialization and exchange. But at the same time they opposed the monopoly behavior of merchants who held grain off local markets to push prices upward. Government policies toward food supply included, in the eighteenth century, the maintenance of more than one million tons of grain for sale and loans in the lean spring season and in years of especially poor harvest (Will and Wong 1991). Subsistence issues made grain commerce of particular interest to the state. Where markets failed to provision people adequately, officials were more likely to take an active role. Government efforts at stabilizing grain distribution complemented elite efforts at making grain available at the local level. These efforts of both officials and elites to influence grain circulation flanked the efforts made by officials to expand production through clearance of new lands and better seed selection and water control.

Grain was a special case because of its fundamental importance to survival. More generally, the late imperial government allowed trade to be carried on without much official oversight and with modest taxation. Most cash crops and handicrafts—fruits, vegetables, medicinal herbs, paper, leather goods, textiles, and so on—circulated across different parts of the country through a well-developed marketing system analyzed by many authors since G. William Skinner's classic work of over three decades ago (1964–65).

In certain situations, however, officials departed from their support for markets and commerce with many buyers and sellers in favor of regulated exchange through a small number of merchants. The foremost example of commodity regulation was the salt monopoly. Salt was a revenue source for the state; licensing distribution made the state money, and it made a small number of merchants extremely wealthy. Second, foreign exchange was often regulated. Some foreign trade was framed within the tribute system, which offered a political as well as economic rationale for exchanges between foreign governments and merchants. Other foreign trade was controlled because the goods desired were of strategic importance. The tea and horse trade with the northwest, for instance, was regulated because of the crucial importance of horses to the military and secondarily because revenue could be made on the tea sales. But when trade was neither foreign nor intended primarily as a revenue maker for the government, it was generally given free rein by the state as long as officials believed that no small number of merchants was able to manipulate supplies and hence prices to the detriment of the consuming public at large.[4] Officials thereby supported commercial exchange without promoting concentrations of merchant wealth. The famous eleventh-century official Wang Anshi (1021–86), a reformer responsible for promoting an activist set of government policies intended to raise revenues and order society, went so far as to help small-scale merchants with government credit to make them more competitive with large merchants. More generally, by late imperial times officials simply cared about whether the markets were running smoothly.

While they believed markets to be socially useful, late imperial officials did worry about people leaving the land to take to the road in search of profit. There were two concerns at stake. First, there was a social concern that people who were in perpetual or periodic movement were potentially dangerous to social order, which was defined in terms of an ideal sedentary agrarian society in which men worked the fields and women wove cloth and tended the home. Late Ming literature often counseled its readers against the dangers of men taking to the road for months or even years at a time.[5] Second, and more directly related to the economy, some official and elite writers despaired over what they perceived to be a growing taste for luxury and extravagance acquired by people who pursued profits from trade. The superior man was not swayed by the pursuit of advantage or profit; instead he was guided by his quest for Confucian virtues of benevolence and righteousness. The merchant pursuing profit (and not virtue) needed some external constraints on his behavior so that lust for luxury did not overcome Confucian sensibilities of restraint and moderation. Chinese Confucianism may well have afforded resources for merchants to construct a positive view of their activities similar to the example of the Osaka merchants, studied by Tetsuo Najita, who promoted a self-justification of their activities in Confucian terms (Najita 1987). But differences in social structure between the two countries, specifically the contrast between Japanese merchants, who formed a social class distinct from warrior and noble elites, and those in China, who remained more closely tied to large landowners and officials, appears to have limited Chinese possibilities for a distinctly merchant vision of their properly Confucian social role to gain an independent base from which to compete with the ideals expressed by agrarian and official elites.

The Confucian anxieties of officials and elites over the unbridled pursuit of profit qualified Chinese understandings of the market's social usefulness. Chinese officials recognized the virtues of market principles of supply and demand and yet abhorred the aggressive pursuit of wealth and prominent displays of extravagance. Within the late imperial Chinese political economy, officials could comfortably promote market exchange on the understanding that an expanding commercial economy could afford peasants additional opportunities to make a living. But official support for a market economy the benefits of which reached the many peasants who bought and sold goods did not mean that the government therefore favored concentrations of wealth gained through market manipulation. Chinese official support for commerce did not mean promotion of a commercial capitalism like the one that developed in Europe.

The political context for Europe's development of capitalism was fundamentally different from the political context of China's late imperial economy. Commercial capitalism in Europe produced merchant houses of extraordinary wealth beginning in the sixteenth century. This in itself is not so very different from what happened in China, where sizable merchant fortunes were also created, especially from the salt monopoly. What is, however, fundamentally different are the relationships that emerged between European states and their rich merchant classes. Much of European commercial wealth was tapped by needy governments anxious to expand their revenue bases to meet the ever escalating expenses of war making. Centralizing territorial states accordingly extracted revenues from growing European commerce. From the fourteenth through the eighteenth century, the Chinese government, in contrast, lightly taxed commerce, except for brief moments when extraordinary extractions took place. Amid the mercantilist competition among European merchants and their governments for wealth and power, maritime expansion played a role of particular importance. Both European merchants and their governments benefited from their many-stranded relationship, the former by gaining monopolies or other favorable conditions under which to amass fabulous profits, the latter by securing dearly desired revenues.[6] The late imperial state did not develop the same kind of mutual dependence on rich merchants. Lacking the scale of fiscal difficulties encountered in Europe between the sixteenth and eighteenth centuries, Chinese officials had less reason to imagine new forms of finance, huge merchant loans, and the concept of public as well as private debt. Not only did they have little dependence on mercantile wealth to support the state, but they also feared the potentially disruptive consequences of both concentrations of wealth and the *pursuit* of such wealth. This opposition to what might have become a kind of commercial capitalism, had the government needed the merchants more and thus been supportive of them, does not mean that officials opposed markets and commerce more generally.

I wish to argue for a distinction between a market economy and commercial capitalism in a manner somewhat similar to Fernand Braudel's discussion of the two concepts.[7] Market exchange among many buyers and sellers at prices determined by supply and demand conditions is economically and socially very different from the transactions masterminded by a small number of very rich merchants who can set the terms of exchange with producers and consumers to gain dramatic profits, often minimizing competition through monopoly and force. What I would like to stress here is the crucial political component of capitalism. European governments created the conditions for commercial capitalism to work both within Europe and across the globe. In contrast, the Chinese state had no incentive to promote any sort of capitalism. My claim is quite a separate statement from the common complaint that the Chinese state somehow blocked market activities and commerce.[8] The Chinese state, I argue, supported a market economy in an agrarian society but did not promote much commercial capitalism, with the qualified exception of those merchants engaged in the monopolies of salt and foreign trade. Chinese officials created conditions for the formation of considerable merchant wealth for two kinds of reasons, first, as in Europe, when they were tapping merchant wealth for resources, as with the salt monopoly; and, second, when they were controlling access by foreigners to China. In general, Chinese rulers had no reason to imagine, let alone promote, the mercantilist policies invented by European rulers.[9]

Chinese political economy envisioned an agrarian commercial economy in which expansion came from opening new lands and improving productivity on already cultivated fields. Rural industry was clearly conceived as complementary to cash crops—giving women more work to do to supplement income from the fields was one way to keep the household economy going amid population expansion—and market exchange helped to balance supply and demand. Chinese political economy tied production and distribution together through its commitment to reducing or ameliorating relative inequalities and guaranteeing some absolute minimal standards for survival. When China was exposed to new kinds of industrial production possibilities in the late nineteenth century, how did this political economy of agrarian empire change?

Perceptions of Industrialization: Problems and Possibilities

Our expectations for industrialized economies are derived principally from Western European and North American success stories. Within this frame of reference, some features of post-1949 Chinese industrialization, including backyard steel furnaces and local fertilizer plants, seem strange. But these traits are neither accidental nor a simple product of Communist ideology. Indeed, at least some of the features of Chinese industrialization are shaped by their placement within a larger vision of social order that carries forward an unac-knowledged connection to a Confucian vision of an agrarian world.[10]

For much of the twentieth century, many people have thought of indus-trializing as synonymous with developing a modern economy. But before the late nineteenth century, the conventional identification of industrialization with modernization was not so obvious to rulers, elites, or people in general. In China, the example of foreign industries first inspired official efforts to estab-lish factories, usually with foreign advisers. These endeavors aimed to strengthen the state in its relations with foreign governments. It would be anachronistic to attribute to the nineteenth-century Chinese government a desire to industrialize the economy.[11] Even if the government were to have made this a conscious commitment, we must wonder what kind of differences these efforts might have made to the trajectory of industrialization in the first half of the twentieth century. Mere conceptual commitment to industrialization does not mean the government could have created the institutions to channel larger quantities of resources and products in more efficient ways, formulated more sophisticated managerial organizations, or more swiftly adopted techni-cal innovations. Nor does it tell us how the Chinese economy would have found demand for its new industrial products either domestically or internationally. In any case, this grand counterfactual predicated upon aggressive state-led growth becomes even more unlikely after the collapse of the Qing dynasty in 1911. With the absence of any strong national government for at least three of the next four decades, industrialization could not easily become a widespread process guided by any broad vision of national political economy.

Industrialization in pre-1949 China was basically a private sector phe-nomenon. Urban factory industry developed principally at treaty port sites, often with foreign capital and foreign management. Numerous studies have affirmed the rapid growth of the modern industrial sector; with a small base, its proportional growth was, not surprisingly, quite swift, even if its overall impor-tance in the economy grew far more slowly. Centered in two areas, Shanghai and Manchuria, China's modern industry was guided by an emerging class of urban industrialists and financiers. Rawski estimates that the Shanghai region and Manchuria accounted for two-thirds of China's modern industrial output with only one-seventh of the population in 1933 (1989, 73).

China's industrializing areas likely experienced growth rates well within the range of growth rates common in European regions during their periods of rapid industrialization. Rawski argues that China would have continued to experience modern growth in the 1930s had the Japanese invasion not dis-rupted the economy. He bases this argument on a comparison with growth rates achieved by Japan when it initiated a process of modern growth. One problem with his logic is the assumption that spatially specific patterns of industrialization will be able to transform ever larger areas of the country over time. This perspective fails to account for the challenges of creating economic integration across an area as vast as China. Growth rates in China's industrially advanced areas drive Rawski's national estimates of per capita output increase of 1.2 to 1.3 percent annually and per capita consumption increase of 0.5 percent annually. This means, as Rawski points out, that "other regions experienced below average, and possibly negative, growth" (1989, 271). How the areas with little, if any, growth were to become integrated with successful regions is not clear.

If we think of the problem of industrializing Europe as a whole, we realize immediately how much of Europe remained nonindustrialized for decades, stretching well beyond a century since the late-eighteenth-century origins of England's Industrial Revolution. In European cases, governments often played an important role in mobilizing investment and making industrialization decisions. Governments from France to Russia helped to mobilize funds for large-scale investments by creating financial institutions through which capital was amassed and, in some cases, by directly extracting funds through taxes. European strategies for development ranged from protective measures to develop domestic industry for domestic markets to specialization in products for international markets. Chinese governments between 1912 and 1949 were unable to mount comparable programs to industrialize the country's economy. Research remains to be done to show how effectively the largely private process of Chinese industrialization was moving to displace rural industry as a source of goods and how completely modern industrial production was becoming integrated into China's well-developed agrarian market economy, which spanned much of the country's landscape before 1949. Certainly there was no equivalent transformation of China's market economy by industrialization to the one that had occurred in parts of nineteenth-century Europe.[12]

The establishment of the People's Republic returned China to rule by a state with an agenda of creating strong centralized government. Industrialization became a principal component of the regime's program for transformation of the country into a socialist success story. Following the Soviet model of industrialization, the first Chinese Five Year Plan (1953–57) concentrated investment in heavy industries, machine-building, and energy, which were responsible for producing the goods required to create an urban industrial base. Just as China's late-nineteenth-century factories were developed by officials as part of a program to create wealth and power, so the First Five Year Plan aimed to develop the economic infrastructure of a strong state in charge of an independent country. The expansion of heavy industry in the 1950s did little to change the spatial concentration of industries in those areas where an industrial base had been created before 1949. Subject to central planning, industrialization had little need for market institutions to decide how industrial products should be produced or distributed. To the extent that Chinese industrialization during the 1950s was geared toward producer goods, public goods, and the military, regional disparities in standards of living that could have attended an industrialization stressing consumer industries did not occur. Furthermore, the government's decision to keep the agrarian sector politically and economically separate from the urban industrial sector meant that the vast majority of China's peasants would be little affected by improvements in consumption patterns that attended urban industrialization. The First Five Year Plan extracted resources from agrarian China to capitalize urban industry, but a socialist version of a dual economy with institutionally separate modern and traditional sectors meant that the challenge of imagining an economic future in which urban and rural or industrial and agricultural were closely integrated had yet to be faced squarely.

A radically different kind of decentralized industrialization after 1957 was prompted in part by the intention explicitly to benefit the vast majority of the population, many of whom had not been much affected by heavy industrialization. Though its positive impacts were far smaller than anticipated by policymakers and its logic has earned the ridicule and disdain of analysts inside and outside China, the Great Leap Forward (1957–59) retains its significance for its intentions and achievements. The aim of setting up small-scale rural industries across agrarian China so that peasants could gain access to modern industrial goods like steel that had reached them infrequently and in limited quantities was conceived in the spirit of self-sufficiency that also marked concerns for food supplies in agricultural production. This logic of industrialization recognized the constraints on spreading the benefits of modern industry if they remain located in a few urban centers. In order to avoid the inequities of access to the benefits of industrialization that obtain spatially from industrial concentration, the Great Leap Forward promoted a strategy for bringing industrialization to the countryside. While backyard steel furnaces may not have produced much usable output, fertilizer and tool-making plants were more successful. Note that under this strategy as well markets played very little role in deciding how products were to be produced or distributed. More generally, as Dorothy Solinger has shown in her study of domestic commerce in China between 1949 and 1980, Chinese planners have been ambivalent about assigning markets much role in determining production and distribution decisions (1984). Neither centrally planned industrial production nor commune-level production for local people made much use of markets.

Conventional Western assessments of the market economy and capitalism in the contemporary world view markets as a basic component of the larger institutional structures of capitalism. Communist assessments in both the former Soviet Union and China have generally accepted this identification. But, where Western analyses promoted the virtues of markets and capitalism, Russian and Chinese economic policies generally avoided what they considered to be dangerous vices. Recall that late imperial Chinese thinkers could distinguish between the beneficial impacts of markets allocating products and services according to supply and demand and the manipulative power of rich merchants who made huge profits by controlling prices. Confucian ideology supported one and decried the other. Though post-1949 Chinese leaders have not consciously called upon this Confucian distinction, they have proven more able than their Soviet Communist counterparts to conceive positive roles for commercial exchange.

Economic Knowledge and Cultural Change

Since the reform period began in 1978, Chinese policymakers and theorists have repeatedly asserted a basic distinction between a commercial or market economy and capitalism. Chinese capacities to make what seems to current Western sensibilities such a twisted and artificial distinction may well derive, at least in part, from an earlier tradition of understanding economic change. The transmission is not consciously articulated, but it is culturally determined. Even if Chinese policymakers can only recognize their categories of analysis as twentieth-century principles imported from the West, what they can imagine and desire connects them with their own culture and history.

Given their culture and history, what might constitute a Chinese ideology of a market system that does not promote or even accept the apparent problems of capitalism? Can a country industrialize with market institutions playing a key role without the pitfalls of capitalism? Late imperial ideology accepted markets and understood how they could promote economic welfare. The same ideology also aimed to control degrees of inequality and guarantee minimal subsistence to all. But late imperial ideology never completely accepted the profit motive, as Brook argues in the preceding chapter; virtue always lay beyond the pursuit of material advantage. Communist ideology has also had difficulties accepting the pursuit of profit. Like Confucian understandings, Communist visions aimed to reduce inequality and provide for the material security of everyone in society. With a double rejection of at least some Confucian and Communist sensibilities, what will guide future Chinese understandings of economic change? Now that industrialization clearly offers new producer and consumer opportunities and markets are understood to be a power-ful instrument for allocating capital, labor, and products, in what ways will Chinese economic leaders take advantage of these possibilities and surmount the many problems that span the gap between economic goals and realities? Current Chinese understandings of economic change are uncertain. The strongest conclusion we can make is that they leave open possibilities for both revolutionary successes and failures.

NOTES

1. Of course, even in the 1950s, as the Japanese economy recovered from the catastrophe of World War II, the long-term base for economic development was firmly placed, but this did not resolve the challenge of embracing Japanese cultural traits in a concept of "modernization"; see, for example, Hall 1965.

2. A range of interpretations locates Japanese economic success in its particular history and culture. They include works as different as Morishima 1982 and Dore 1987.

3. A recent survey of agricultural treatises that aimed to promote agricultural productivity underscores the role of officials in writing and disseminating these works (Deng 1993, 126–30).

4. On salt, see Xu 1972 and Chen 1988. Overseas foreign trade in the late imperial period is reviewed in detail in Li 1990 and Lin 1987. For the horse and tea trade and northwestern trade more generally, see Lin and Wang 1991.

5. One famous example of this sort of literature is "The Pearl Sewn Shirt" in which the opportunities for amorous misadventures depend upon husbands being away from home on commercial ventures; see Birch 1958, 37–96.

6. The developments of capitalism and modern European states are closely entwined processes, which I am comparing at considerable length with Chinese dynamics of political and economic change in Wong (forthcoming).

7. Fernand Braudel's three-volume *Civilization and Capitalism, 15th-18th Century* (1981–84) develops a basic distinction between a market economy and capitalism. Braudel, especially in volume 2, argues for the widespread presence of market exchange in Eurasia in the early modern period. He suggests that capitalism, however, is more a distinctly European phenomenon. While not all scholars agree with Braudel's arguments about the uniquely European character of commercial capitalism or his ideas of how capitalism builds on a market economy, the basic distinction between a market economy and capitalism is an important one. A more concise presentation of Braudel's idea of the differences between a market economy and capitalism can be found in Braudel 1977, 39–78.

8. Many authors within and without the Chinese history field have fingered the Chinese government's failure to promote conditions for economic development. Many suggest that economic development is its own self-propelled process, which can only be derailed by the deliberate and perverse efforts of governments. This perspective is shared by authors who otherwise are very different, including champions of free markets and Marxism (see Balasz 1964; Hall 1985; Hong 1983; and Jones 1981, 1988).

9. There are scholars who have characterized some Chinese policies as "mercantilist." Paul Smith's study of the Song dynasty Tea and Horse Agency characterizes Wang Anshi's policies as such (1991). In a large and as yet unpublished project of translations and commentaries on selected essays from the *Huangchao jingshi wenbian* (Writings on statecraft from our august dynasty), Helen Dunstan has identified one general concern of Qing officials with wealth as "mercantilist." These scholars have good reasons for employing the term, though the policies they review do not closely parallel in logic or effect the kinds of European policies I've briefly mentioned. When comparing European and Chinese policies, it would seem to me preferable to avoid the term *mercantilist* for both, even though there are certain, albeit very general, ways in which the term might apply to both.

10. For arguments about the similarities, usually not explicitly acknowledged, between late imperial and post-1949 agrarian policies, see R. B. Wong 1988a.

11. Dwight Perkins (1967) implicitly does this when he discusses the failure of the Chinese government in the nineteenth century to mobilize fiscal resources or develop modern education in order to support industrialization. Without such an intention, it is difficult to see why the government should have wanted to make these efforts.

12. The counterfactual of whether or not such a set of changes would have taken place in the absence of the establishment of the People's Republic is large and complex. I caution against expecting this outcome in Wong 1992a, 1992b.

The Struggle to Rethink the Vietnamese State in the Era of Market Economics

Alexander Woodside

One of the ironies of an age that is hostile to Marx and Marxism is that one of Marx's most embattled beliefs—that the state is a secondary and illusionary form due for eventual retirement—has begun to be echoed by non-Marxist theorists of the new capitalist globalization. In his 1992 Massey Lectures for Canadian Broadcasting Corporation, Robert Heilbroner asserts that "the increasingly globalized pattern of production" is an unprecedented challenge to state power, the "defensive capability" of which remains "largely static." The economic reach of capital has become immeasurably larger than the political reach of the state. The transnational accumulation of capital now occurs "above" the state realm (1992, 58–60). Other analysts agree but believe that such state fragility is most true of the Western welfare states, leaving more open the futures of the more mysterious states in the non-Western beyond. Jürgen Habermas writes that such welfare states have proved to have "too narrow a framework to . . . guarantee Keynesian economic policies against external factors—against the imperatives of the world market and the investment policies of business enterprises operating on a worldwide scale" (1990, 56).

The counterpoint to all the anxiety about capitalist globalization overpowering the state is that both Eastern Asia and the Western world itself at the end of the twentieth century share a renewed interest in the theorization of the state. Capitalist globalization may threaten state power. But it also requires organization to manage it and to mobilize the capital itself, and states remain the world's most powerful managers. Chinese researchers now meditate on what they see as the postwar cycles of interest or noninterest in the state by

Western thinkers. One such Chinese observer recently noted that in the immediate postwar period Western thinkers adopted "society-centered theories" to explain political behavior, reducing the state to such "dependent" activities as legislative procedures and the distribution of tax advantages among big corporations. By an odd symmetry, such Western "society-centered" theories of development were matched in Eastern Asia by local revolutionaries' revolution-centered biases, which were equally inclined to marginalize the problem of the theorization of state power. But the end of a Cold War whose Asian Marxist ideologues were more interested in revolutions, and whose Western anti-Marxist ideologues were more interested in social structural functionalism, has allowed a rebirth of interest in thinking about the capacities of the state. The decisive emergence of successful non-Western states in which organization and policy making are clearly not simple duplications of Western models has only magnified such interest. Japanese capitalism suggests that there is a good deal more to states than those characteristics that haunted agenda-setting German thinkers like Max Weber and Otto Hintze at the beginning of this century: their monopolization of force and their attempted achievement of an impersonal, rational, legal, and administrative order (Zhang Jing 1992).

The rebirth of theoretical interest in the state, by forcing us to confront states' particular embodiments of the eternal human frailties, has probably contributed to the pessimism about their future every bit as much as has the intensification of worldwide transfers of capital. Even in Eastern Asia, the premonition that no known form of state, Eastern or Western, is adequate to human needs had become a subject for playwrights as well as futurologists. In the prologue to his brilliant 1992 satire "The Lady of Soul and Her Ultimate 'S' Machine," about an unnamed Southeast Asian city-state's search for its soul, the Singapore Chinese writer Tan Tarn How has a shopper go to a store called a "Nations Boutique" and ask to look at the different brands of states on offer. The sales girl first shows him what she calls the "Western brand," which is "solid and reliable and popular among the libertines but very expensive." Then she unveils the "Middle East model," with Jerusalem and Mecca thrown in free of charge, conceding its unreliability but recommending it to customers who crave excitement. Finally, after mentioning that the boutique is having a clearance sale on the Communist brand, she offers him the "Asian Dragon model." At that point she whispers nervously: "To be very honest with you, sir, these Asian Dragons work very well . . . but you know sometimes when you wrap up a present in nice, fancy paper in a big box, but inside there is really nothing? Our Friends upstairs keep on adding more layers of even more fanciful paper, but inside there's still nothing. . . . Our Friends say not to worry, if we have enough layers, people will take a lifetime to unravel it and they will not notice that it's empty" (How 1993, 2–5).

Contemporary capitalist globalization does not fatally threaten state power. But it obviously does require, for its success, that that state power be based, if not upon democracy, at least upon sophisticated forms of popular trust in the state's exercise of a growing multiplicity of abstract economic capacities, particularly those involving banks and currencies and markets. Whether successful short-term elite mystification campaigns such as Tan Tarn How describes in his play can be converted into general long-term trust is problematic. In any event, no major Asian state faces a greater challenge of trust creation than does the modern state in the ancient country that pioneered the use of paper money in Southeast Asia at the end of the 1300s and now has one of the fifteen biggest national populations in the world: Vietnam.

As the American investment banker Felix Rohatyn recently observed, in an indirect tribute to the lack of economic obsolescence of nation-states, the amount of capital required to finance the continued growth of "the developing world" is now "beyond the capacities of the West, either from private or public sources." Global growth, therefore, in the presently accepted capitalist mode must be based not only on direct foreign investment in "developing countries" but on "large-scale domestic investment by those countries themselves" (1994, 50). Of all the epitaphs for the old Leninist state in Vietnam that declined in the 1980s, few were more instructive that one published in 1991 by a senior Hanoi economist, Hoang Kim Giao. He suggested that pre-1986 Vietnam was a mobilizational state whose rulers were so lacking in popular trust (*dan tin*) that they not only could not mobilize but could not even discover the significant quantities of private domestic capital that still existed among the Vietnamese people. He himself estimated in 1991 that the capital hidden in private hands in Vietnam was "many times bigger" than the state budget and that if the state could only mobilize, for its "renovation" purposes, one-third of all the private domestic capital that existed in concealment it would have a sum of capital equal to its entire official budget. He then contrasted the Vietnamese government's inability to know how much private capital there was in Vietnam with the capacity of other world governments—such as the French—to know how much capital there was in their countries (Hoang Kim Giao 1991, 27–29).

This complaint was not about mere economics. More than economic analysis is needed to understand just how popular habits of trust are constructed historically so as to permit domestic investment mobilization of the sort that Felix Rohatyn says is indispensable to the world's future but that the old Leninist dictatorship in Hanoi found beyond its reach. No issue involving

Eastern Asia calls out more strongly for a combination of cultural and economic analysis, though the answers are still far from obvious. Professor Hoang demanded in 1991 that future Vietnamese governments try to understand more fully what he called the popular, orally transmitted, economic cultures of the Vietnamese people and, rather than problematizing them, draw up a state economic development strategy that would be compatible with them (1991, 27). But his criticism of a dictatorship that had conscripted its subjects into the Weberian "iron cage" of planned material production after 1975 without enough dynamic grassroots consent has to be understood against the background of the earlier gestation of that dictatorship. Only then can we appreciate the contrast between its earlier practices and the limited flirtations with cultural neotraditionalism in political management—but still not a full acceptance of unwritten popular economic cultures, as Hoang Kim Giao requests—in the present.

The present Socialist Republic of Vietnam originated in the ramshackle guerrilla republic, known then as the Democratic Republic of Vietnam, that Ho Chi Minh and his communist associates founded at the end of World War II in Hanoi and the northern Vietnamese hill country. Back in 1923, when he was a young communist journalist distributing propaganda in Paris, Ho had called for the creation of a "genuine world republic" that would abolish the "capitalist boundaries" of existing nation-states (1980, 1:116). Ironically, his own Vietnamese republic followed the example of other postcolonial Southeast Asian states, such as Indonesia, in undergoing a gigantic bureaucratic inflation after independence in 1954 rather than abandoning bourgeois state worship. In 1954, the Hanoi republic had eleven ministries or their equivalents: by 1986, after eleven years of governing the south as well as the north and on the eve of its conversion to its "renovation" (*doi moi*) program of decollectivization and market economics, it had sixty government ministries or their equivalents (such as state commissions and "general offices" or agencies directly attached to the Council of Ministers). A similar expansion occurred at lower levels among 40 or so provinces and municipalities, 500 or so counties, and 9,500 or so administrative villages. Between 1976 and 1989 alone the total number of "state workers and functionaries" increased from 2.4 to 4.3 million; in contrast, all of French Indochina had only about 100,000 functionaries of all types, including postal clerks (Pham Xuan Nam et al. 1991, 437–50; Hoang Chi Bao et al. 1992, 184–85).

The state, as one critical insider wrote, had become "absolutized" (*tuyet doi hoa*) in Vietnam between the 1940s and the 1980s (Chu Van Thanh 1991, 99, 53–56). Its "absolutization" was accompanied by its partly self-willed aloofness from the noncommunist world around it. This aloofness was extraordinary even by the standards of the Soviet bloc—or of a country like Cuba, which was also subject to an American trade embargo. In 1980, one of the last years of the Soviet bloc, Poland allegedly participated in 81 international nongovernmental cultural organizations out of more than 900 identifiable ones; East Germany participated in 62, the Soviet Union in 55, and Cuba in 8, whereas Vietnam itself participated in just 1 (Tran Do 1989). As recently as the early 1980s, Vietnamese economists even studied the dynamic ethnic Chinese capitalism of their closest Southeast Asian neighbors by reading Russian books about the subject, such as Andreev's polemical 1975 work on overseas Chinese business as a "tool of the Beijing reactionaries in Southeast Asia" (Le Hong Phuc 1981).

Vietnam's "renovation" reforms since 1986 have ended the introversion of an autarkic state that was folding in upon itself. Imported Soviet prejudices about overseas Chinese capital have evaporated and Vietnamese economists no longer have to go to Moscow to study Singapore. Indeed, the intensity of the renovated Vietnamese state's positive recognition of the inescapable Chineseness of the first generation of Southeast Asian capitalists is reflected in its increasingly close-textured calculations about the capacities of the million or so ethnic Chinese who remain in Vietnam itself in the aftermath of the earlier organized terror directed against this community in the late 1970s, which diminished its numbers substantially. It is now publicly and happily asserted in Hanoi that 55 percent of the 80,000 ethnic Chinese households of Ho Chi Minh City have "relatives" (*than nhan*) in more than twenty foreign countries from whom they could raise investment capital; 10,600 of the 16,200 ethnic Chinese households in the fifth district of Ho Chi Minh City alone are counted upon as having this strategic international economic leverage (Vu Hanh Hien 1993).

But Vietnam's reforms since 1986 have not solved the riddles of how to think about state power, particularly the end of its primitive "absolutization" and its shift to the cultivation of more complex forms of popular trust. Four constitutions in less than fifty years (in 1946, 1959, 1980, and 1992) attest to the continuing Vietnamese Communist obsession with the definition and redefinition of the state's administrative powers. (Communist-ruled Laos, in contrast, with no mandarin traditions, got by without any public constitution at all before 1991.) But even four constitutions, and a government reorganization law of September 1992, have apparently still failed to achieve a tolerable simulation of a "federal" distribution of budgetary powers in Vietnam so as to allow localities enough real power, but not "anarchic freedom," over the management of revenues. The number of state-run business enterprises was reduced from 12,000 in 1990 to 7,050 by the summer of 1993. Yet the Vietnamese state in 1993 was still a formidable presence. It comprised about 100,000 "work units" not related to material production, and the state-run economy itself still accounted for most of Vietnam's production of a vast miscellany of consumer products such as soap, light bulbs, thermos bottles, cardboard paper, and canned goods (Vu Huy Tu 1993).

In one sense, the Vietnamese states limited shrinkage between 1986 and 1993 reflects the fact that it was originally "absolutized" in part as a substitute for private non-Chinese indigenous ownership of the economy. It was not "absolutized" as an alternative to a large native business class, which in fact never existed and cannot be constituted now. It is not always remembered that nominally Confucian political systems permitted a variety of relationships between the state and its commercial sector. As elsewhere in Southeast Asia, but in sharp contrast to the three other Asian Confucian societies of Japan, Korea, and China, Vietnam's national economic tradition was a partnership between indigenous royal courts and the nonindigenous overseas Chinese traders they patronized. The one legendary Vietnamese businessman of the French colonial period, Bach Thai Buoi, successfully competed with the ethnic Chinese merchants dominating Vietnam's inland commercial shipping routes only by placing collection boxes on his ferries and appealing to his Vietnamese passengers to make patriotic donations beyond their fares to his ships' success.

There were few people beyond the ambit of the state and its official culture to whom a "downsizing"Vietnamese state could transfer economic production. The great majority of the owners of private businesses in Vietnam in 1993 inevitably came from the ranks of present or former state officials, cadres, or "workers." Their efficient conversion into risk-taking capitalists within a short period would not be easy. Vietnamese surveys showed that only 15 percent of the private business owners in Hanoi in 1993 raised capital by borrowing it outside their own households and that only 31.5 percent of such private business owners generated their business capital outside their families in Ho Chi Minh City (Danh Son 1993). Their whole psychology predisposed them to think of economics in terms of either a national planned economy or a family business but as little in between.

Yet, in another sense, the limits of the Vietnamese state's shrinkage since 1986 betray the subterranean survival of the quasi-millenarian political consciousness that Ho Chi Minh and other revolutionaries created fifty years ago in addition to reflecting the historic absence of a native business class. Of the eleven languages in which the World Publishers Company in Hanoi as of early 1993 still published books about Vietnamese affairs for foreign readers, one remained Esperanto, the utopian language of hope of left-wing revolutionary cosmopolitans dreaming of the unity of humankind in the grimiest Asian port cities in the 1920s and 1930s. The Vietnamese state's most important political figure, Communist Party General Secretary Do Muoi, still feels compelled to strengthen his leadership by publishing collections of essays on culture and literary theory with such titles as "Realizing the Aspiration of the People for the True, the Good, and the Beautiful" (*The hien khat vong cua nhan dan ve chan-thien-my* [1993]). There is still a considerable spiritual distance, if not a geographic one, between Vietnam and such Southeast Asian neighbors as Brunei and Singapore.

The Vietnamese Communist state succeeded not just French colonialism but eight centuries of Confucian emperors who prayed for rain for their peasants and whose powers were both political and religious. One may surmise that the young Ho Chi Minh's faith in Enlightenment ideals like equality and universal literacy, as mediated rather grimly by Lenin, was all the more absolute when he founded the present Vietnamese state in 1945 because he had to make such a faith compensate for the revolutionaries' amputation of an ancient, semisacred (if in fact deeply debased) monarchy. The gospel of the renovation years since 1986—that Vietnamese leaders must pay special attention to the science and mystique of management—not only fails to challenge the preeminence of the Vietnamese state but merely transmutes or sublimates the quasi-millenarian political consciousness upon which that state was founded in 1945. The new evangelism about the potentialities of the proper administrative theory reconciles a newly acceptable market economics' assumption about the selfishness of human nature with the older revolutionary desire for the perfectibility of humankind, this time as much through rational organization that transcends people as through the most direct political mobilization of the people themselves.

But one must be fair about Vietnam's new context. Vietnamese thinkers since 1986, in searching for ways to reconceptualize state power in an era of market economics triumphalism, have faced challenges that a narrow "area studies" approach to Vietnamese politics cannot illuminate. The global triumph of market economics has not necessarily facilitated the development of equally powerful ideas in political theory. The "invisible hand" of the market may create certain economic efficiencies that were beyond the dreams of the repressive Stalinist Vietnam of the 1960s and 1970s. But the "invisible hand" is not adequate as a civic faith to compel social cooperation in more comprehensive terms. In a regime of market economics, politics is in jeopardy of being trivialized and reduced to a question of interests; as the philosopher George Grant used to warn eloquently, the principle of calculating individualism is unlikely to generate "a doctrine of the common good" broad enough to hold states, or the planet, together in the long run (1985, 40–41). Market economics, while requiring greater trust in the state, does not show theoretically how to create it.

Under such circumstances, it was perhaps inevitable that the Vietnamese, like everyone else, would be driven into a sympathetic reconsideration of the political and moral philosophies of the past before market economics fully triumphed—and into an acceptance as well of the possibility that such philosophies' potential has not been exhausted by the historic contexts in which they first arose. The "past," here, does not just imply the statecraft ideas of the precolonial Asian Confucian civilization to which Vietnam once belonged. Most ironically, it also includes the pre-Leninist past of Marxist and European thought. In the early 1990s, for example, the Vietnamese Community Party ordered the national government publishing house to publish the first Vietnamese translation—in twenty-six volumes between 1993 and 1995—of the complete works of Marx and Engels. Until the mid-1990s, it was not possible even for the most privileged state-supported researchers in Vietnam to read all these works systematically in their own language; during the war years, the most anticommunist American college students had better access to the whole range of nineteenth-century Marxist writings than Vietnamese party functionaries did. Now the members of a desperate Politburo in Hanoi clearly hope that their allowance of a belated Vietnamese discovery of the textural riches of pre-Leninist Marxism may save some of regime's legitimacy rather than threaten its stability.

But it is the limited relegitimization of the statecraft ideas of prerevolutionary Vietnam that is particularly interesting. One of Vietnam's establishment intellectuals wrote in the journal for party cadres in 1992 that there were many reasons for the "collapse" of states such as the Soviet Union but one of them had been the degeneration of such states' administrative machinery because of the failure to clarify systematically such machinery's tasks and objectives. The proper antidote to political collapse through such Leninist marginalization of the administrative superstructure, he implied, was a renewal of interest in precolonial Vietnamese administrative theory (Van Tao 1992).

To help this renewal, in 1993 Hanoi published, at great expense, a romanized Vietnamese translation (in fifteen volumes and almost eight thousand pages) of a work entitled "The Imperially Authorized Compendium of Institutions and Institutional Cases of the Great South" (*Kham dinh Dai Nam hoi dien su le*). (The Great South was the Vietnamese emperors' official name for Vietnam, adopted in the late 1830s.) The state translators of this vast work bragged of their determination to ensure that libraries, schools, cultural agencies, and even family libraries all over Vietnam obtained copies of their translation

(Nguyen Q. Thang 1993). The "Compendium of Institutions" had been compiled originally in classical Chinese by senior mandarins of the Vietnamese court at Hue in the 1840s. It was supposed to be an encyclopedic handbook of Vietnamese government in the first half of the nineteenth century. Its very organization reflected the structure of the Nguyen emperors' government, with the business of the dynastic family itself coming first. Consequently the whole weight of the text was not toward the differentiation of state from society so much as toward showing how a marriage of elite values and administrative authority could be perfected, through year by year challenges, so as to assimilate most historical possibilities. Its translation and popularization in the 1990s represent, so far, contemporary Vietnam's most ambitious effort to explore or at least consider the modernizing potentialities of the country's precolonial bureaucratic Confucianism. They also show how the globalization of market economics inspires the ironically contrapuntal theme of the reassertion of indigenous political theory. In the previous high noon of communism, Vietnamese leaders would have regarded such a work as obsolete and "feudal."

As I have tried to suggest, the crisis in the normative theorization of the state at the end of the twentieth century is worldwide. There is nothing exotically Vietnamese or Southeast Asian about the resumption of interest in premodern political theory that the crisis has provoked or about the willingness to increase dependence upon inherited theoretical capital from eras that preceded the triumphalism of market economics. In the Western world, for example, American philosophers like John Rawls have recently revived an interest in the ancient and supposedly defunct Western tradition of the social contract, despite what one critic calls social contract theory's "archaic assumptions about natural law and presocial man" (Shapiro 1990, 3). How much of this global neo-traditionalism is genuinely historical, and how much of it is merely a desperate "postmodern" archaeological plunder of a few seemingly useful monuments or pieces of monuments from a past more coherent than our own, is another question. It is a question that is particularly important in assessing the contemporary Vietnamese rediscovery of early-nineteenth-century Vietnam's single most significant Confucian political thinker, Phan Huy Chu (1782–1840). Phan Huy Chu's great work, "The Classified Survey of the Institutions of Successive Courts" (*Lich trieu hien chuong loai chi*), was first compiled in Chinese characters between 1809 and 1819. As part of Communist Vietnam's "renovation," it was reissued in a three-volume paperback translation (into romanized Vietnamese) in Hanoi in 1992.

The original "Classified Survey" appeared in 1819 in forty-nine volumes. It was divided into ten categories of statecraft: geography, people of talent, government offices, rituals, civil service examinations and tests (for Confucian mandarins in Vietnam between the eleventh century and the end of the eighteenth), state revenues, laws and punishments, military institutions, Vietnamese classical literature of various genres, and foreign relations. Translated into modern romanized Vietnamese, it runs to over 1,400 pages of fine print and would overshadow *War and Peace* on any bookshelf. This huge repository of history and at times daring political commentary is traditional Vietnam's textural equivalent of Angkor's great galleries of sculptures; some of its most imaginative passages are so far less well understood than are Angkor's galleries.

Nobody in Vietnam before Phan Huy Chu had ever documented the ideal and real forms of the premodern Vietnamese state with such systematic critical self-consciousness or had pictured dynastic politics so uncompromisingly as a panorama in which rational principles should govern rulers rather than the other way around. Modern Vietnamese Marxists, however time bound their prejudices, are probably right to admire the work for seeing politics in terms of an objective structure of offices, laws, rituals, and procedures for the management of wealth that should all be relatively independent of any particular dynasty. "The Classified Survey" also reflected the peak of influence, in premodern Southeast Asia, of the intense managerial principles of an ancient Asian text, the *Zhou li* (Rituals of Zhou), compiled in what later became "China" about the third or fourth century B.C. For reasons we cannot explore here this text probably had a greater direct political impact on premodern Vietnamese elite thought than it did on that of imperial Chinese elites—at least those above the educational levels of the Taiping rebels—after the Song dynasty.

Phan Huy Chu singled out for praise the *Zhou li*'s requirement that the ideal ruler use a network of registrars to take annual censuses of the numbers of every one of his subjects "who had sprouted teeth," regardless of their social status. Only through such a rigorous knowledge of a polity's economic assets could rulers "balance" tax burdens equitably between the weak and the strong and thus show their closeness to the people. No author has ever worked harder than Phan Huy Chu did to rationalize a morally responsible authoritarianism on the basis of mythic and historical precedents. The Vietnamese emperor to whom Phan Huy Chu presented "The Classified Survey" in 1821 rewarded him for it rather offhandedly with a silk shirt and thirty writing brushes and ultimately sent him away on a trade mission to Batavia in the Netherlands Indies. This emperor rightly construed the work as a criticism of his own government.

Contemporary Vietnamese state intellectuals, in the aftermath of decollectivization, show a nostalgia for the older, broader, Confucian notion of statecraft (more literally, the notion of "manage the age and help the people," *kinh the te dan* in Vietnamese) that Phan Huy Chu embodied; it seems to them more holistic (if less specialized) than borrowed Western administrative theories, which reflect the spirit of market economics more strongly. Indeed, Phan Huy Chu is even seen as a possible antidote to the more disintegrative effects of market economics on the world stage. His present-day Vietnamese apostles suggest that "The Classified Survey" taught that the territorial management of a state could never be separated from the knowledge-based control of its local natural resources. The imminent globalization of the exploitation of Vietnamese natural resources by foreign researchers and multinational businesses is said to require in response the more dynamic integration within Vietnam of different levels of domestic political power with rigorous intellectual surveillance of natural resources, something that the "geo-economic" (*dia-kinh te*) theory of Phan Huy Chu taught but Western Marxist-Leninist texts have overlooked (Van Tao 1992).

The background to this resurrection of premodern statecraft theory is conferences in Hanoi like the one on "Globalization and Its Influences on Vietnam-ASEAN Relations," sponsored jointly by the Central Economic Management Research Institute and the Friedrich Ebert Institute and held in August 1992. At this conference Singapore manufacturers' representatives recommended the economic "synergy" of such state-transcending economic zones as the Singapore-Johore-Riau "growth triangle," with Johore and Indonesia supplying the management and marketing. The psychological need for a balance in the rapid reconceptualizing of the economic space around them since 1986 encourages the Vietnamese to take a new look at the precolonial thought of Phan Huy Chu, not so much for reasons of pure traditionalism as to stabilize globalization's multiplication of the discontinuities involved in imagining the future. To put it another way, Leninist economics may have been disastrous but it had an understandable narrative. The new developmentalism conveys more hope (for the moment), but it comes with a confusing cluster of interactive narratives. This confusion invites a more elaborate neotraditionalism in response.

Just how much weight this attempted reconstruction of an authentically national genealogy for a more profound managerial politics will have in Vietnam's future remains to be seen. But the Vietnamese state, though less primitively "absolute" than it was before 1986, is clearly not about to surrender yet to the erosion of market economics. Cultural neotraditionalism is part of the renegotiation of authoritarianism in a postcollectivist era, not its abandonment. The trend is clear not just in the resuscitation of classical political theory but in the debates in Vietnam in the early 1990s that surrounded the country's proposed adoption of two of market economics' hallmark institutions: shareholding companies and a national stock market.

Vietnam's state-run companies in the late 1980s and early 1990s lost hundreds of billions of piasters through waste, bad expenditures, and misconceived forms of profit distribution. The losses mounted as percentages of their capital assets. Important government intellectuals such as the economist Vu Huy Tu argued that only such companies' conversion to shareholding ownership would end the waste and lead to an effective use of capital. The state Council of Ministers (for which Vu Huy Tu works) twice issued directives (in May 1990 and June 1992) requiring the experimental introduction of shareholding to state-run companies, including some companies directly controlled by the central government. The process was slow and was resisted. As Vu Huy Tu saw it, state companies should be divided into two categories: a minority of firms not based on shareholding, either because they were linked to national defense or because they required more capital than nongovernmental interests could supply; and a majority that ought to be converted in whole or in part to shareholding by individuals or by "groups" or organizations, domestic or foreign. As proper examples of the latter category, in early 1993 Vu Huy Tu suggested such industries as textiles; shoes; pottery, porcelain, and glass; construction materials; maritime transportation; and retail commerce (Vu Huy Tu 1993).

This vision did not imply the wholly unfettered creation of a society of property-owning individuals. Of course, it would be fair to say that shareholding and stock markets in Western capitalist countries do not imply pure property-owning individualism there either: the bulk of their equities are increasingly held by huge pension funds and life assurance companies. But Vu Huy Tu went on to propose that shareholding in Vietnam would solve the "problem of ownership" in such a way that workers' "motive force" would no longer be "annulled" and that workers as shareholders would no longer be inclined to steal from their companies or waste their assets. At this point, insider critics of the old state-run economy such as Vu Huy Tu stir their audiences by conjuring up pictures of the exciting new communitarian forms through which shareholding Vietnamese workers might shape their companies: elected "assemblies of shareholders" (*dai hoi co dong*), management councils, control boards, and the like. The trust creation problem would be solved through a decentralized communitarianism with a capitalist surface.

In this approach the shareholding principle remains part of the Enlightenment project of a design society, which we have been told by some collapsed with the recent demise of high communism (Bauman 1992, 221). For this approach to the shareholding principle has as its task the moral perfection of Vietnamese workers and the exorcism of their thievery and waste (despite the evidence to the contrary in capitalist countries) as orchestrated by the Vietnamese state through a new legal framework. The state does not really shrink.

It becomes more subtle. It strives for a new utopia. In this thought the theoretical exaltation of workers' councils and assemblies is particularly interesting because it can be seen to reflect both the prerevolutionary dynastic state's willing accommodation of such communitarian forms as village councils of elders and the early Leninist revolution's gospel (much abused) of the necessary gestation of local soviets.

Robert Heilbroner has suggested that contemporary capitalism masks the continued survival of older historical instincts. The drive to accumulate capital, he surmises, is a modern transformation of earlier human drives for military aggrandizement. The difference is that the drive to expand capital is open to more people than the premodern drives to accumulate military glory ever were. The ultimate unconscious source of both is (he thinks) infantile fantasies of omnipotence (1992, 31–33). In contemporary Vietnam, the idea of capital shareholding may not be a mask for anybody's unconscious, collective or individual. But it is absorbed into an older tradition of thought that searches for ways to harmonize, rather than demarcate absolutely, the interests of the central government and the interests of individual taxpayers. Shareholding becomes a sort of modern rhetorical replacement for the traditional village communal lands, through whose maintenance Vietnamese emperors tried to preserve stability by guaranteeing a material stake in the status quo to as many villagers as possible. There is little in Vu Huy Tu's scheme about shareholding as a destabilizing means of accelerating the turnover of capital between less successful firms and more successful ones. In other words, if one major function of shareholders in advanced Western capitalism is to legitimize the acceleration of capitalist production—in everything from assembly lines, to the deskilling and retraining of workers, to the introduction of robots—in early "renovation" Vietnamese thought the imagined function of shareholders appears to be rather one of state-directed popular mobilization of a postcollectivist, neotraditional kind.

The struggle to create a Vietnamese stock market, culminating in the preliminary establishment of a Negotiable Securities Trading Center in Ho Chi Minh City in April 1993, also tells us something about the local cultural indigenization of market economics. The initiative came from the State Bank of Vietnam, not from private traders. It was regarded as a notable venture in state-directed cultural borrowing. Delegations of Vietnamese government cadres were sent abroad to study stock markets in foreign countries. They publicly sounded warnings about the bad examples of the fledgling Thai stock market of the early 1970s, whose immaturities, and the "subjective desires" behind them, had required the intervention of a rescue team of American specialists soon after it was founded.

Vietnamese official advocates of a national stock market clearly see it not as European coffee house traders would have seen it in the dawn of the capitalist era but as a state-introduced laboratory of psychological and cultural change, rather like a miniature treaty port, whose intent is to redesign Vietnamese behavior where collectivism failed and make the Vietnamese people more economically "daring." Prerevolutionary Vietnamese dynastic politics featured a curious bilingual polarity between a controlling Sinicized elite language and a far less standardized, less Sinicized, village language; a hegemony of Sino-Vietnamese linguistic abstractions accompanied the importation of Chinese bureaucratic procedures into Vietnam. Even this feature from the past has been renewed in the era of capitalist globalization and is now pressed into service to dramatize the importance of stock markets to modern state formation. For, as one Vietnamese banking official put it in 1993, the native Vietnamese word for "market" (*cho*) implies the undesirable: disorderly and slow trading techniques, an insufficient volume of transactions, and an absence of government-imposed legality. Therefore, the Sino-Vietnamese term for market (*thi truong*) must be used for the negotiable securities trade because it alone embodies order and modernity, not to mention a sense of elite control (Nguyen Dong 1993). All of this suggests that global capitalism, far from simply threatening the Vietnamese state, is supplying an arsenal of techniques by which state-directed cultural borrowing will salvage and refine a managerial regime whose previous policies had seriously tarnished it.

But the salvage operation will not work without the cooperation of Vietnamese peasants. "Renovation" requires a complete rethinking of the state's relations with its villages. In the era of collectivism and autarky, before the full introduction of household contract farming and the return of private landholding in 1988, the state subjected the villages to heavy controls. Before 1988, the state's attempted appropriation of the peasants' rice harvest through taxes and at least sixteen sorts of secondary charges was so extreme that, as one Hanoi economist calculated, Vietnamese peasants could keep a mere fifteen or twenty kilograms out of every hundred kilograms of rice they grew. Between 1966 and 1988, the state also conscripted peasants for at least ten days of draconian unpaid labor each year and even meddled with the villages' religious festivals. In the north, traditional spring Dragon-Boat Day boat races once attracted thousands of peddlers, peasants, religious specialists, and actors; the Communist government tried to shrink the size of the boats and their crews and to make its new production cooperatives the owners of the boats, removing ownership from such traditional units of religious solidarity as hamlets (Woodside 1991, 190). As one Hanoi researcher warned, the result of this era of collectivism was that the villages had fallen into the hands of a "new caste structure" of village-based state functionaries and their relatives, who used the labor conscription law and other devices to exploit the majority of peasants (Woodside 1989).

The resentful peasants, being collectivized, were in effect tenured state employees. They were no longer the disposable tenants of private landlords. Thus, they could respond to oppression by simulating the work habits of other state employees—professors, for instance—if not actually subversively mixing the rice they delivered to tax collectors with sand and grit. Collectivized farming lasted as long as it did only because of the introduction into Vietnam between 1969 and 1989 of more than fifty new high-yield International Rice Research Institute strains, which permitted rises in rice-growing productivity despite all the peasant anger. Even so, the country came close to famine more than once before contractual land rights were transferred to peasant households. As of early 1993, about 80 percent of the farming cooperatives had disintegrated or survived only in form and subsidized food distribution had ended. By the end of the 1980s and the early 1990s, Vietnam had become, improbably, the third biggest rice exporter in the world, behind only Thailand and the United States. Rice exports, the foundation of colonial capitalism in French Indochina, are now paying for the renovation of the Socialist Republic of Vietnam.

But the village organizations through which the state deals with the peasants have withered. New forms of mobilization that both the peasants and the state will trust must be found to avoid a reconquest of the villages by kinship networks and religious beliefs that the state cannot trust; for the eternally managerial elite, the trust creation issue cuts both ways.

Apostles of a partial return to indigenous political theory, in Vietnam as elsewhere in Southeast Asia, are tempted to look for the key in the formula that the supremacy of the community over the individual is an eternal "Asian value." That the "rediscovery of Asia" means the reassertion of the community over the individual seems to be the message of new Southeast Asian elite organizations such as the recent Malaysian-sponsored Commission for a New Asia. The temptation is especially strong in Vietnam, where it has long been an article of faith that Vietnamese peasants are decently communalistic. One Hanoi historian recently assured Vietnam's legal cadres that, whereas all the farmland in China had been "privatized" by the end of the seventeenth century, in Vietnam as recently as the 1930s some 21 percent of all farmland remained village common land; the implication was that responsible rural communitarianism was an indestructible Vietnamese national characteristic, giving Vietnam an edge over China (Vu Minh Giang 1993).

The irony of this is that, whatever the historical facts, the actual concept of the "communal Eastern society" was something of an intellectual invention of the Western colonial period, albeit one with different rhetorical functions.

Before the Dutch departed Indonesia, professors of "Eastern economics" like J. H. Boeke at Leiden analyzed countries like Indonesia as "dual societies" where capitalism could not overcome a residual "communalism." Equally ironically, the largely Asian postcolonial rural economy specialists who meet at Asia-Pacific region "peasant organization and peasant poverty" conferences like the one held in Malaysia in July 1986 candidly recognize that the modern forms of Asia-Pacific village economic cooperation, such as credit associations in Malaysia itself, date only from the Western colonial period and continue to be managed by postcolonial governments from the top down; few of them reflect spontaneous peasant instincts (Du Xiaoshan 1988). The complexities of the construction of communitarianism in modern Eastern Asia were only underlined by the veteran Chinese social scientist Fei Xiaotong's recent recollection of how a modern Chinese term for "community" (*shequ*) had to be invented at Yenjing University in the 1930s in order to translate the "community study" theories of the Chicago sociologist Robert Park (Fei Xiaotong 1994, 3–4).

The practical danger of confusing elite theorizations with peasant cultural reality, in any attempted resurrections of more "communalistic" villages, is made obvious by the fact that most Asia-Pacific elites do not want merely obedient villagers; they want capital-subscribing ones. In Vietnam, domestic capital investment of the type Felix Rohatyn stresses increased by 1993 to about 10 to 15 percent of the size of the Gross National Product. That meant that it was still slightly below the level of Taiwan in the 1950s, according to one government statistician, and far below contemporary domestic capital investment rates of South Korea, let alone Singapore (Le Dinh Thu 1993).

To reorganize its villagers, the Vietnamese government has launched in some parts of Vietnam a movement to "restore rural community covenants" (*Tai lap huong uoc*). The "community covenants," in Vietnam as in China and Korea, were codebooks of village customary laws for the enforcement of proper moral behavior within the villages. They were most popular in the postaristocratic Vietnam of the seventeenth, eighteenth, and nineteenth centuries, when Vietnamese society was no longer run by a hereditary aristocracy but by a degree-holding scholarly gentry; the earliest surviving Vietnamese codebook (from Nghe An) dates back to 1600. The neotraditionalism of their revival in present-day Vietnam matches that of a campaign to revive them a decade ago in rural China (where such covenants, or *xiangyue*, emerged in the eleventh century).

The restoration of village covenants is not an example of modernization inspired by Confucianism. It is one of Confucianism inspired (retrospectively) by modernization. Far from the covenants being spontaneous emanations of the villagers' own consciousness, models of the right sort of covenants are drafted by the county governments first, in consultation with lawyers, anthropologists, and historians, and then passed down to the villages. Between 1990 and the summer of 1993, some 520 of the 3,011 hamlets of rural Ha Bac Province in the north acquired covenants (known by the slightly different title of *quy uoc*) in this way (Bui Xuan Dinh 1993). The state matches its market economics with managerial anthropology.

But the restoration is controversial among the Vietnamese elite. To some it looks like a partial abandonment of the ideal of a modern state based upon law and an open-ended acceptance of a half-modern, half-traditional state. There are also misgivings about whether the traditional formula of village codebooks can be stretched to cover the much larger, more complex villages of contemporary Vietnam, which may comprise ten thousand or more people, ten or more hamlets, and plentiful supplies of unlicensed video cassettes, even before market economics begins to generate millions of itinerant peasants outside the villages, as it has done in China. Beyond the immediate misgivings, it was never clear in traditional Vietnam itself whether village religious and social solidarity were sources of national political stability or instability. When political observation was rooted in a vague local communitarianism, and seen as the mere derivative of a village- and family-centered ethical system, it was not easy for rulers above the villagers to command villagers whose political obligations were such a dependent and weakly conceptualized part of a wider texture of local social relations from which the rulers were remote.

The problem is that no system of market economics has ever been successfully legitimized anywhere for a long time in a pure form just by itself, for all its technical efficiency. Economic orders based upon free market exchange must, to survive, be embedded in a larger religious or ideological ethos, even if it is a different ethos from what George Grant once memorably called "the intimate and yet ambiguous co-penetration between contractual liberalism and Protestantism" in the minds of English-speaking Westerners (1985, 58). What one can say in conclusion is that from the Southeast Asian angle, the state system of the modern world is still emerging. Talk of its eclipse by international capitalism is premature. But there is no single "Asian Dragon" model of an Eastern Asian state, contrary to the parody of ideal type analysis that the Singapore playwright Tan Tarn How puts in the mouth of his fictional "Nations Boutique" salesgirl. And the modernity of state power is still conditioned from within as well as from without by traditions that even the most self-confident elites may exploit but can hardly control. The dialectic between market economics and culturally ancient Asian political systems with large peasantries has only begun. Most of the Asian national success stories to date—Hong Kong, Singapore, Taiwan—are not representative enough, even in the most general sense, to foretell its future.

Religious Correctness and the Place of Islam in Malaysia's Economic Policies

Judith Nagata

By conventional measures, the past twenty years for Malaysia has been a period of stellar growth. A per capita GDP of $7,992, an annual GDP growth rate of 8.1 percent, life expectancy of seventy-one years, and a literacy rate of 78.5 percent (*Asiaweek* 12 January 1994) place Malaysia third in the ASEAN ranks, behind Brunei and Singapore, and well on the way to Newly Industrializing Countries (NIC) status. Malaysia is a popular recipient of foreign investment, and now a donor as well. The country is also a respected leader among nations of the "South," the Group of Fifteen (G-15), and the Non-Aligned Movement (NAM) as well as among the members of the Organization of Islamic Conference (OIC). The country's leadership is increasingly of the technocrat variety, explicitly committed to a national policy of full industrial development by the year 2020 through a program known as Vision 2020.

Yet Malaysia as a state is fraught with a number of discordant characteristics. Its managers have to steer a precarious path between the shoals of assorted ethnic, political, and religious interest groups and even economic strategies. Today, the most pressing issues revolve around what might be called "religious correctness," for Islam has now assumed central stage in most public and governmental discourse and policy. The problem is to accommodate within a common framework both Muslims and non-Muslims, at home and overseas.

In its career of over thirty-five years as an independent state, Malaya/Malaysia[1] has been preoccupied with nation building and self-transformation into a meaningful nation-state, with the Malay people forming the dominant national component. In comparison with most of the states described in the other chapters of this volume, except Singapore, Malaysia is

79

unusually complex culturally, being the product of multiple Asian traditions ranging from the Middle East to China. The construction of a new nation has been an exercise in the management not only of economic development but also of ethnic relations. Ethnic and religious cultures remain central to all economic planning, and in some instances, as will be shown, actually preempt the planning process.

For about a decade following independence in 1957, several styles of economic activity coexisted with what was generally a laissez-faire, transplanted colonial model of economic development. This model intersected with a vibrant Chinese entrepreneurial community (operating along the lines variously described by Harianto elsewhere in this volume) as well as with less tightly organized cohorts of Indian and Arab traders participating in networks linking the Malay Peninsula with South Asia and the Middle East. At this time, Malays were conspicuous by their absence from any significant economic activity beyond that of peasant subsistence production, the final component in the mosaic of the ethnic-cultural division of labor in this plural state.

Beginning in the late 1960s, a resurgence of Malay ethnic consciousness, combined with a "rediscovery" of Islam, became central preoccupations in Malaysian state policies, to the extent that state political legitimacy was defined, at least in part, by Islamic principles. Having already embarked upon a capitalist path, with links to the world economy, the Malay leadership now had to come to terms with the idea of "Islam as a way of life" and so engage in scriptural exegeses of economic ethics. In contrast with neighboring Indonesia, where Islam is depoliticized and its economic influence marginalized, as also originally envisaged in Jinnah's secular Pakistan, Islam in Malaysia is being reinvented in step with local perceptions of political and economic needs. This refashioning of Islam has led to contested interpretations of what constitutes "Islamic" behavior, even among Malay Muslims.

The other force propelling the Malaysian economy lies in the opposition between Malays-as-Muslims and non-Muslim Chinese, who provide the other ideological pillar of Malaysian economic policy, pushing Malaysia in the direction of state captialism through Malay patronage. As the alter egos of the Malays, the Chinese have been represented variously as an example to be emulated for their obvious efficiency and success and one to be excoriated for their alleged clannishness and (un-Islamic) unscrupulousness. For both reasons they are to be controlled or constrained. It is the economic adversarial relationship between Malays and Chinese, as much as the ethnic distance alone, that animates public policy, oscillating as it does between poles of a zero-sum perception of economic resources and appeals to cultural and religious incompatibility. Malaysian economic policy since 1970 has thus been infused with "noneconomic," even "nonrational," factors without reference to which Malaysian capitalism cannot be fully understood.

Prelude to Development

The evolution of Malaysia's current economic conditions and ideology has its immediate roots in the country's colonial legacy, which ended in 1957. During the colonial era, which began about the middle of the nineteenth century, the Malay Peninsula was divided into nine independent sultanates, plus the three Straits Settlements of Penang, Malacca, and Singapore, each having separate treaties and understandings with local British administrators. Cross-state economic integration was achieved nonetheless, particularly in the early twentieth century, through the medium of immigrant Chinese who were introduced to develop the basic infrastructure of commerce, mining, urban labor, and other services. Their work created linkages between rural and urban areas. Also in the early twentieth century, indentured labor was first brought from India to service the rubber plantations. It was this radical regrouping of peoples that shaped the postcolonial state. Meanwhile, the indigenous Malay populations (of all sultanates) were left largely intact by social class. The peasantry continued to form the backbone of the agricultural economy and rice production, the Malay elites were educated and groomed as minor civil servants and bureaucrats, and members of the royalty retained their religious and customary authority as Heads of Malay Religion and Custom (*adat*) within their own sultanates.

With the anticipation of independence following World War II, plans for a Malayan Union were drawn up in 1946. These plans raised debates over eligibility for full citizenship rights of the resident populations on the Malay Peninsula and pitted the "immigrant" Chinese and Indians against the indigenous Malays. Eventually, when the constitution was drawn up at independence in 1957, all permanent residents, regardless of race, religion, or origin, were given the option of citizenship in the new federation (Ratnam 1965). As a result of a vigorous Malay lobby protesting the equal sharing of civic privileges with "immigrants," the Malays were accorded "special rights," which included the entrenchment of their hereditary rulers as Heads of Religion and Custom in their domains and the designation of Islam as the official religion (Federation of Malaya Agreement 1948). This event marked the first mass mobilization of Malays beyond their original sultanates and with it the emergence of the first (and still dominant) Malay political party, the United Malays National Organisation (UMNO). It also marks the beginning of an affirmation of an identity and quality of Malayness distinct from the others in their midst. The distinctiveness of Malay identity has in one way or another been a persistent theme weaving through the subsequent history of modern Malaysia.

Malays devoted the first few years following independence to finding political and cultural expressions of their identity. The symbolic ascendancy enshrined in the constitution protected not only their rulers and religion, but also guaranteed for the UMNO party a senior role in the new triple-party coalition then called the Alliance. The other two were the ethnic-based Malayan Chinese Association (MCA) and the Malayan Indian Congress (MIC), both selected from among pro-British, English-educated, business and professional constituencies.

The Pan Malayan Islamic Party (PMIP), ancestor of today's Parti Islam Se-Malaysia (PAS), was another party of Malays that germinated a few years prior to independence. The PMIP espoused a vision of the new nation more solidly Malay and Muslim in character if not a full Islamic state. The contrast with UMNO, then as now, was a stark one, ideologically and politically. Whereas the PMIP espoused Islam as a "way of life" in which religion, society, and the polity merge, UMNO's approach to Islam under the first prime minister, Tunku Abdul Rahman, was essentially secular, consigning religion to the private domain or to a few highly ritualized and symbolic public and ceremonial occasions. From the standpoint of the state, religion would be limited to the celebration of Independence Day and royal occasions but would not be allowed to intrude upon daily life or economic pursuits (cf. Hamid Jusoh 1991, 99).

During its first decade of independence, Malaya/Malaysia's infrastructure was based largely on primary commodity production and import substitution. It was a period of laissez-faire market economics whose principal propellants and beneficiaries were members of the Chinese and colonial business sectors, giving rise to the enduring and pervasive stereotype of a society built on an ethnic division of labor, in which non-Malays held the purse strings. Already in place was a social environment in which the relative economic disadvantages of the Malays were assigned to historical and "structural" causes over which they had little control but whose remedy could be found in heavy doses of state intervention over which they could exercise substantial control. Ahead of his time on this matter was a certain Dr. Mahathir Mohamad, then a small country doctor in the northern state of Kedah, whose own prescription was published in 1970 in his now-celebrated book, *The Malay Dilemma*. In this book, Dr. Mohamad was highly critical of the Malays' lack of initiative and dependence on others in their own country, but, more heretically for the time, he also had the temerity to suggest that the Malays should take charge of their own future by emulating and using the entrepreneurial tactics of the Chinese and, if necessary, by learning their language to penetrate their networks. When first published, this provocative volume made Dr. Mahathir a political enfant terrible. He was expelled from membership in UMNO.

Until the early 1970s, the newly united Malays were preoccupied with articulating an identity based on popular ideas of "race" and language. The constitution also laid out more specific parameters of Malayness: Malay speakers, practitioners of Malay custom (*adat*), and followers of Islam. Although these formal criteria were all cultural and could in theory be acquired by any non-Malay,[2] what could not be acquired was the more intangible quality of Malay identity, and indeed there was never any attempt, nor the political will, to promote ethnic assimilation. A large minority, hovering around one-third of the population since independence, the Chinese have continued to enjoy substantial latitude in promoting their own schools, languages, associations, and religions, as have the Indians. Malaysia thus remains a resolutely plural society.

The lack of ethnic and political fusion was most devastatingly played out in the riots of 1969, which arose out of disputes over national election results. The disturbances, which initiated a new phase of Malay-Chinese polarization, were followed by a brief political interregnum in 1970–71, which was the gestation period for a more formal and assertive plan of affirmative action to promote Malay economic advancement under the label of the New Economic Policy (NEP). This plan guaranteed special access by Malays to certain key educational benefits, higher civil service positions, loans, and participation in special government-sponsored land schemes and urban resources. It set forth the explicit goal of attaining 30 percent Malay ownership and control of industrial and equity interests by the year 1990, from a low base of 2.4 percent in 1970. The NEP marked the beginning of a heightened level of state intervention in the Malaysian economy and of growing Malay hegemony. Not surprisingly, raising the economic stakes of being Malay intensified an obsession with Malay authenticity, ever vulnerable to the dangers of assimilation. Appeals were made to the unassailable claim of aboriginality, or status as "sons of the soil" (Bumiputra). Although this definition locked the Malays into the same category with the non-Muslim "tribal" populations of both West and East Malaysia, operationally it never eclipsed Malay dominance.

At about the same time, the quest for Malay identity took yet another turn, in the direction of Islam. This development symbolically reinforced the Malay component of the Bumiputra. In the early 1970s, events in the Middle East, especially in Iran, combined with the continuing uncertainty of their economic role at home, led many Malays of the younger generation to experiment with the latest wave of Islamic resurgence rippling across the world. This was the generation that, without any role models or precedents, was destined to shoulder the burden of Malay modernization. Thrust suddenly into intensive education programs at home and overseas, they encountered fellow students from other Muslim countries and ideas as to alternate ways of handling personal, role, and identity problems through the empowerment of religion. The peer pressures of student networks together with ethnic and occupational pressures at home provided fertile ground for religious experimentation, which swiftly spread among Malays in schools, colleges, and universities across the country. From this ferment, known generically in Malaysia as *dakwah*, emerged two movements in particular, whose names and effects continue to influence the Malaysian political and religious scene today. One, ABIM (Angkatan Belia Islam Malaysia, or the Muslim Youth League of Malaysia), arose out of the Malay Language Society at the University of Malaya in 1969, reflecting the transformation from linguistic to religious symbols of Malayness. Its leader and first president, then an antigovernment student rebel and even a suspected sympathizer of the Islamic party PAS, was Anwar Ibrahim, whose subsequent (1982) co-optation to UMNO by Dr. Mahathir stunned Malaysia and the world at the time. The resonance of this conversion has continued ever since, as Anwar has rocketed through several cabinet positions as far as the post of deputy prime minister and is a possible successor to the premiership. Since Anwar's departure, ABIM has lost its charismatic power and image of religious dissent, and today it functions as a more docile voice of religious legitimation for UMNO and the government.

A second *dakwah* movement, the shadow of which still falls over the government from the sidelines, is Darul Arqam, now Al Arqam. Also started in the late 1960s, Arqam is a more mystical, Sufi-like movement under the leadership of a more traditional rural religious teacher, Ustaz Asha'ari. Arqam is distinctive for its utopian-style communal settlements which attempt to achieve a level of economic self-sufficiency, production and redistribution of material needs (*ma'ash*) within the community through the manufacture and sale of basic commodities such as ritually pure (*halal*) foodstuffs and toiletries, enabling independence from "infidel" Chinese and foreign resources. Arqam community and family life is modeled after an idealized or "invented" version of seventh-century Islamic society in Arabia and includes polygyny and appropriate gender relations (Nagata 1984, 1992; Muhd Syukri 1992). Many of Arqam's approximately six thousand nonresident sympathizers are highly trained professionals and civil servants and graduates of the MARA Institute of Technology, whose computer, graphics, and other technical skills provide them with substantial incomes and experience that are turned to Arqam's profit. Other members contribute medical, legal, pharmacy, and accounting services to the movement, as well as a proportion of their income, to support its schools and medical clinics. To the official mind, the potent combination of these qualities with the members' undoubted zeal and commitment make them a potential political threat. This is compounded by the unknown identity of some sympathizers as "enemies in the blanket," and the perennial fear that Arqam could forge an alliance with Islamic opposition elements within or even outside Malaysia, notwithstanding Arqam's own declared apoliticism.[3] Membership in a formal Islamic political party on the other hand at least identifies the "enemy." One strategy toward minority religious groups adopted by the federal government, although it by no means removes the problem, is to destroy by defamation and to declare the movement deviant and heretical.[4] The intent here is to deter the more submissive faithful from venturing into "unorthodox" religious territory on pain of penalties transcending those of mere mortal politics.

Now that the rallying cry has switched to religion, Malays have also discovered a new identity, which situates them more prominently on the international scene, as members of the world Muslim community (*ummah*). This shift has brought with it eligibility for funds from such Islamic economic giants as Saudi Arabia and Libya, and from 1973 onward the volume of trade with the Middle East has expanded (Hussin Mutalib 1990, 129). These linkages have alienated Malays further from their fellow non-Muslim and Chinese citizens, who have become the epitome of the infidel (*kafir*).

While these events were unfolding, the orbit of the NEP widened to involve Malays in a range of state-sponsored enterprises, including state banks, the national petroleum company, urban development schemes, and entrepreneurial loans. The precipitous rush to create a solid class of Malay entrepreneurs in less than a generation with ownership of 30 percent of corporate assets by 1990 interrupted the laissez-faire tradition that had left the Chinese to their own resources. In the Industrial Co-ordination Act (ICA) of 1975, terms were specified by which a certain percentage of Malays were to be employed or taken into partnership with foreign and Chinese firms "in the national interest." Another consequence of such managed development was the encouragement of so-called ersatz capitalism, whereby, instead of more productive industries involving transfer of technology or skills, quick profits were sought through the farming out of privileges and licenses, flipping of stocks and property, and so on, while some loans were even diverted to consumption rather than investment.

Malaysia's Political Formation: Ethnic and Religious Politics

The Malays are not a monolithic community, and thus are also represented by parties other than UMNO. Undoubtedly the deepest intra-Malay cleavage, which has become irreversibly politicized, is religious. The rift can be traced back to the late 1940s, when a burgeoning Malay nationalism bifurcated into the secular core of UMNO and another movement that saw Islam as an essential component of Malay identity and inseparable from daily life. What began in 1951 as the Hizbul Muslimin was eventually transformed through the PMIP to the PAS (Parti Islam Se-Malaysia) of today. Historically, PAS and its predecessors were never in favor of the idea of Malaya/Malaysia as a secular state, especially when Singapore with its large Chinese population was still attached. PAS supporters are drawn principally from the more rural, monolingual, Malay northern and eastern states of the peninsula, where local leaders are often also the teachers in traditional religious schools (*pondok*). Through them, the pupils are inducted into the party's ideology. By contrast, UMNO supporters are often urban, more likely to be English speaking or exposed, and by PAS standards more "secular." During the frenetic *dakwah* period of the 1970s and 1980s, the appeal of the PAS in the wider Malay community expanded substantially beyond its heartland, although not sufficiently for it to win a federal election. Between 1974 and 1978, however, PAS felt confident enough to "join the enemy" in the Barisan coalition. Several PAS members were appointed to the cabinet and to diplomatic posts in Muslim countries, which increased their influence further. During this period, it was well known that many ABIM followers were sympathetic to, even members of, PAS. This suspicion extended to Anwar Ibrahim before his spectacular leap into the UMNO camp in 1982. A series of internal squabbles culminated with the withdrawal of PAS from UMNO in 1978 in an apparent loss of power that was actually a prelude to a party makeover under a new generation of leaders, many from the more youthful *dakwah* contingent.

After Anwar's defection to UMNO, ABIM lost impetus, but some of its exiles formed a core of agitation against the UMNO center, partly through PAS.[5] Others joined the ranks of the more independent but conservative Islamic scholars (*ulama*), whose pronouncements carry great weight and legitimacy in the daily decisions and lives of the faithful and who often serve as officials and judges in local religious (Shari'ah) courts. The consolidation of the new PAS also coincided with the Iranian revolution (1979), and more than ever Malay Muslims were exposed to alternate political visions from outside the country, notably a revival of the idea of the Islamic state. For the first time, Malay *ulama* seriously began to explore the possibility of implementing full Islamic law (*hudud*) in Malaysia, which would mean substituting the Shari'ah for the existing civil and criminal courts, for Muslims and non-Muslims alike. In Malaysia, such a move would contravene the constitution. Insofar as the constitution is the supreme law of the federation (Article 4 [1]), any law passed subsequently, if inconsistent with the constitution, shall be void, including all such state laws (Hamid Jusoh 1991, 33). This would require a federal constitutional amendment involving the vote of all members of Parliament, Malay and non-Malay, Muslim and non-Muslim. An Islamic state would also endanger the constitutional guarantee of freedom of religion for all citizens, including Muslims who could be accused of apostasy. In fact, there is no universal template for an Islamic state, as the Sudanese, Iranian, Saudi, and Pakistani variants attest.

PAS political statements are long on rhetoric but short on specifics. Even shorter are they on possible economic policies. Aside from the small-scale, but highly visible and contentious, experiments of Al Arqam, religious conservatives have engaged in little discussion, and have shown even less consensus, concerning the nature of "Islamic economics." PAS leaders have never clearly spelled out their formula were they ever to rule multiethnic, multireligious Malaysia, save for vague references to rule by popular consultation (*shura*), to the universality of "Islamic justice," and to the model of the multiethnic city of Medina at the time of the Prophet. Nor, as will be seen, have PAS leaders established a clear position on economic development, capitalist or other. In keeping with the occupation of the Prophet and his wives, trade and commercial profits and accumulation of wealth are acceptable as long as they do not contravene Islamic precepts and morals. Thus, it is the means as much as the ends that are at issue.

Since PAS won political control of the state of Kelantan in 1990, it has threatened to implement full Islamic law in that state, three times tabling it to the state legislature and sultan (between 1992 and 1993) and as many times withdrawing it "on technical grounds." While PAS leaders are aware of the constitutional impediments to their Islamic state designs, they take the moral high ground and constantly goad the federal government, especially UMNO and fellow Malays, with accusations of being irreligious, even infidels. Such challenges play well to the rural Malay constituencies as well as to some younger urban *dakwah* sympathizers of the post-1970 generation, who are also more likely to be aware of Islamic writings and ideas outside Malaysia.

Institute of Islamic Understanding (IKIM)

Since religious intepretations are now central to the process of political communication for most major policies and projects, PAS, UMNO, and other Malay interest groups regularly solicit the services of Islamic scholars and jurists, or *ulama*, who are courted by all sides as spokesmen and legitimators of their respective positions. Among the most useful to political leaders are religious court (Shari'ah) *ulama*, who are the legal gatekeepers of religious interpretations and are empowered to issue *fatwa,* or definitive rulings on the application of religious law in society. Such *ulama,* together with other hand-picked scholars from Islamic faculties of local universities and the International Islamic University, are regularly invoked as exegites whose judgments (*tafsiran*) are needed to vindicate official policies and carry weight with Malay voters. Some of these are employed on a permanent basis in the Islamic Centre (Pusat Islam), which is run from the Prime Minister's Office (PMO). Many other *ulama,* including some from other Muslim countries, are developing profitable new careers as government consultants, as counterpoints to the array of PAS *ulama* and indeed of every significant Muslim interest group in Malaysia. At many levels, religious metaphor infuses political rhetoric and lends weight to public arguments.

For the over 40 percent of non-Muslim Malaysians, and indeed for foreign and international audiences, Islam has to be presented in a more nuanced light. To this end, UMNO tries to present an image of a universalistic religion whose system of justice is generous enough to accommodate any civilized population, even of a different faith, and which does not discriminate along racial or ethnic lines. By way of reinforcement, the latest and most ambitious of UMNO's creations (in July 1992) is the Institute of Islamic Understanding (IKIM in its Malay acronym), a generously funded religious think tank accountable directly to the PMO that serves as a broker between different religious and other interest groups. To IKIM are seconded selected "senior fellows" from the ranks of the *ulama* and university religious commentators, whose task it is to make public pronouncements, publish papers, and organize seminars in Malay and English on topics of concern to all major constituencies, Muslim and non-Muslim, and even to foreigners, but especially to businessmen and investors.

For Muslim audiences, IKIM's agenda involves convincing voters that, contrary to PAS statements, the government's aggressive development policies (including Vision 2020) and its courting of Western technologies and agencies are not un-Islamic. For the success of its economic platform and its raison d'être as a government, UMNO must reconcile its policies to Muslims of all stripes and try to be all things to all people. One of IKIM's mandates is to represent Islam as consistent with development and the modern world, progressive yet spiritual, receptive to Western technologies yet immune to Western decadence. The Muslim public is now treated to a one-way flow of discourse, offering such maxims as: there is a correlation "between piety and productivity in Islam"; "the material and spiritual are interdependent"; "Muslims should pay as much attention to the world as to the afterlife"; "wealth must be put into circulation to create more economic activity"; and "creation of economic activity is a virtue" (*Star* 20 Apr. 1993). IKIM seminars publish edicts to the effect that

Islamic countries must develop strong and self-sufficient institutions parallel to those of the West (*Berita Minggu* 26 July 1992). IKIM also claims that, as a faith, Islam is unique in that it simultaneously "cultivates spiritual, rational and physical development in a single unity." Further, encouraging economic development and growth is justified as a means of helping the poor. This was the IKIM verdict to vindicate the annual federal budget brought down by Anwar Ibrahim as finance minister in November 1992.

Part of IKIM's approach and style is didactic and even corrective. A recurrent theme, and one of the prime minister's favorites, is to recall the glorious past, the scientific and artistic achievements of Muslims in the heyday of Islamic civilization, when Middle Eastern mathematicians, astronomers, doctors, and philosophers led the medieval world (*Dakwah* August 1992, 61ff.). This is contrasted starkly with the situation today, when Islam is lamentably equated with economic backwardness and fanaticism (*Utusan Malaysia* 22 Nov. 1992). Some daring IKIM commentators even claim that "nearly all Islamic thinking today is still based on tenth-century Persian and Arabic scholarship and observance of religious rituals" (*New Straits Times* 30 Dec. 1993) and assert that too much preoccupation with trivial details detracts from the broader spirit of Islam (*Al Islam* August 1992, 50ff.). The task today, as heard through the voice of IKIM *ulama*, is to upgrade the quality of both Islam and its practitioners as an example to the rest of the world, a different kind of religious revival, with a boost for morals and morale. *Ulama* are now advised, too, as in a speech by Anwar Ibrahim in 1993 at the International Islamic University near Kuala Lumpur, to be au courant with modern scientific and technical developments as well as with urgent social problems such as mass poverty, AIDS, and reproductive technology, not merely with the casuistry and arcane debates of the Shari'ah alone (*New Straits Times* 30 Aug. 1992). Now, too, Muslims are exhorted to be environmentally correct (*Star* 1 June 1993) and the Qur'an is cited to show that environmental sensibility is part of the divine message. IKIM's invited guests sometimes include Muslim intellectuals from neighboring countries, such as Indonesia and Singapore, to add credibility to more non-traditional messages. Many of these "progressive" arguments do double duty and help to reassure non-Muslims as to the government's breadth of vision and freedom from religious fanaticism. This is a theme periodically engaged by the prime minister, who in addressing conservative and opposition Muslim audiences is obliged to parade the Islamic content of his policies and government. IKIM also makes a point of inviting to its conferences many non-Muslims. Some seminars target them directly. In these meetings, efforts are made to convince leaders and members of other faiths of their shared values (*Utusan Malaysia* 17 Nov. 1992), to persuade non-Muslim businessmen of the govern-

ment's desire for full multiracial, multireligious cooperation in all its enterprises, and to "correct misconceptions" others may have about Islam (*New
Straits Times* 4 July 1992).

A third prong of IKIM's program is directed toward non-Malaysians,
especially those for whom Islamic policies or perceptions of such could be a
deterrent to investment. Several workshops on "Islam and Industrialization"
and appropriate business ethics, sponsored by IKIM, have been addressed to
representatives of German and Japanese multinationals, which the prime minister usually graces in person. In one address to a Japanese audience, an IKIM
scholar declared that, if the Japanese could "incorporate Shinto belief to its
work culture, there [was] no reason why Muslims could not do the same" (*New
Straits Times* 4 July 1992). IKIM is supported and aided in its task by a growing
assortment of other government-funded Islamic institutions for dissemination
of information about Islam and several religious journals directed toward the
special constituencies of women, youth, and schoolchildren, each of which has
its counterpart (and competitor) among PAS publications.

In promoting its development policies, the government, including
UMNO, is constantly on the defensive. On one front, it must outflank PAS by
appearing "holier than thou" by stressing the spiritual and "caring" and just
quality of its programs and by regular incantations against Western decadence
and excess. Here, the presence of Anwar is crucial, in view of his past ABIM cre-
dentials. Considerable attention and funds are conspicuously directed toward
building religious schools and mosques and toward national Qur'an-reading
competitions. By way of antidote, it must also emphasize its progressiveness
and distance from the "fanatical" fundamentalist *dakwah* fringe, for which purpose Arqam is most often symbolically targeted. Malay students overseas are
also regularly monitored for their religious activities by roving government
supervisors. These audiences are moving targets ideologically, for it is often
hard to gauge where to position a policy along a religious spectrum in issues of
concern to the growing Malay middle class, many of whom are successful products of the NEP and comparatively Westernized in matters of personal behavior, education, and consumer culture. Finally, and closer to the prime minister's
own policy goals, the non-Muslim and international business and investment
communities must be disarmed and reassured as to Malaysia's moderation,
even as Malaysia courts other Muslim countries when it is expedient to do so.

Domestic Economic Policy

Among its concessions to local religious sensibilities, UMNO has been responsible for launching a number of Islamic economic institutions. The first of

these was the Pilgrims' Savings Fund (Tabung Haji) to assist aspiring pilgrims to travel to Mecca, which uses "profit," not interest, accrued by the fund from its investments in housing and other schemes. In 1983, the Bank Islam was opened, where savers receive, in lieu of "interest," profits from its investments, while borrowers share the "costs." Subsequently, several other commercial banks opened Islamic counters, although it appears that most of the country's high-volume and international business continues to be transacted in conventional banks. By 1988, only 2 percent of commercial bank deposits, or 10 percent of total deposits by Muslims, were in the Islamic system (Mohd Ariff 1991, 249–50). In principle, the notion of insurance is seen by Muslims as either a form of gambling or as a sign of lack of trust in God; nevertheless, an Islamic insurance company (Takaful) was established in Malaysia in 1984, based on an ethic of "mutual aid and shared responsibility" (188ff.). To honor its Muslim commitments, the federal government is now making a systematic effort to collect the religious tax, *zakat*.[6] Until recently only enforced on farmers and agricultural produce, attempts have been made since the *dakwah* resurgence to exact *zakat* from urban professionals and businesspeople on the basis of their savings, property, and jewelry assets (*Dakwah*, March 1993, 48). Some urban middle-class Muslims, however, are voicing secular concerns over what they perceive to be double taxation (*New Straits Times* 21 June 1992), despite claims that *zakat* could be used as the basis of productive capital investment in the public sphere.

One zone of contested civil-religious jurisdiction revolves around land endowed for religious purposes (*wakaf*). Such land, usually intended for religious schools, cemeteries, mosques, and housing for indigent Muslims, currently occupies what is potentially valuable real estate in several Malaysian cities. Realization of its full market value for development is restricted by religious law, and this has become a source of frustration for municipal and state authorities and for potential developers. Today, however, it is the religious councils themselves, in conjunction with other Muslim entrepreneurs, that are pressing for changes in *wakaf* land use on the grounds that this would provide greater benefits to the Muslim community than do the present meager monthly yields. A recent case concerning the proposed building by the Penang Religious Council of a block of low-rent flats on *wakaf* land was taken by outraged Muslims to the (secular) Supreme Court. The court ruled that, whereas religious councils have jurisdiction over such land, they have no right to subvert the original intent of the donation (*New Straits Times* 3 Sept. 1992). In 1993, however, the picture changed again when Anwar Ibrahim, then minister of finance, who represents a Penang constituency, lent his support to the development of *wakaf* lands in the name of Vision 2020 and reputedly of his own financial interests. For this purpose, Anwar used personal and religious connections (the mufti of the Penang Religious Council being his old ABIM colleague), to form a development company, Shahadah. This issue has been taken up by PAS, which has mobilized its Penang constituents in religiously righteous opposition. It remains to be seen whether this is a portent of future policy under a possible Anwar premiership.

The situation confronting UMNO in its economic programs is one of maximizing foreign and domestic investment without offending local religious sensitivities and to achieve industrialization without excessive Westernization or moral decadence. This task is complicated by the spectrum of its voting constituencies, from poor, rural, and often fundamentalist Muslim Malays to the growing segment of "New Malays," the successful products and beneficiaries of the NEP, who are the base of the first solid Malay middle class. The prominence of Malays in the civil service bureaucracies and the professions is usually associated with a middle-class consumer lifestyle, but this does not invariably reflect a Western mind-set. There still remains a small but significant minority of *dakwah* sympathizers whose youth and college days coincided with the active 1970s and 1980s. Indeed, at one time some early zealots among the graduates were accused of deliberately rejecting modern jobs and opportunities (cf. Nagata 1984), which sharpened the acrimony between government and *dakwah* elements, but eventually most of the activists accepted NEP benefits and settled down to their careers. The same is true of many Al Arqam supporters who do not reside in its communities but instead contribute their professional skills and at least one-tenth of their incomes to the movement from outside.

For some middle-class Malays, consumption is directed in part symbolically toward a newly constructed "Malay culture industry" (cf. Kessler 1992). This encompasses not only elaborated versions of traditional crafts but also a vibrant women's fashion industry, producing unique assortments of modest Muslim yet stylishly "modern" combinations of headcoverings and dresses, which are promoted in women's magazines. PAS leaders, on the other hand, publicly advocate moderation in consumption. The chief minister of Kelantan occupies a conspicuously modest house but conveniently ignores the fact that most of this state's taxes are derived from tobacco production.

There is also evidence among middle-class Malays of a strong concern for the religious education of their children, and enrollment in double-stream (religious-secular) schools (*madrasah*) has increased over the past decade (*Mastika* July 1992, 17–19). Some of the best-known of these regularly achieve better results in the national promotional examinations than do many public schools. Most Malay parents are obsessed with secular educational achievement for their children, but they try to pursue the best of both worlds by sending them to daily Qur'an instruction. Meanwhile, the traditional religious schools still flourish in PAS territory, but they, too, increasingly offer more secular subjects and examinations, and many of their teachers now send their own sons to urban secular schools (Nagata 1984).

Finally, even the pilgrimage to Mecca (*haj*), obligatory for all Muslims with the financial means, has evolved into a touristlike venture, with specialized travel agencies offering special packages, including flights by Malaysia's national airline and prearranged accommodations in the Holy Land. The local (Malaysian) hotel industry has also begun to profit from elaborate "breaking the fast" buffets during the fasting month of Ramadhan, followed by a festive period during which middle-class expenditure, including the purchase of religious books and other items, is visibly on the increase.

Malay Business

One of the goals of the NEP was to create a class of Malay entrepreneurs largely through state sponsorship and patronage. Most of these are in the small business category, often as proprietors in such trades as woodworking, rice milling, printing, batik design and manufacture, and petty retail (Mohd Ariff 1991, 248). It is notable that Kelantan Malays, historically the most entrepreneurial on the peninsula, have been conspicuously neglected by federal programs since PAS came to power, although that party has launched some small projects of its own.

A growing class of larger Malay capitalists marks an unprecedented achievement on the surface for the NEP, and names such as Daim Zainuddin and Azman Hashim have become emblazoned on the public consciousness as lights to the Malay community. The percentage of Malays in the total business sector went from 14.2 percent in 1970 to 30.5 percent in 1986 (Jesudason 1989, 102), although only a minority reached the heights of these multimillionaires. Most of these made their mark in banking, property development, construction, and transport and owe their success largely to government contracts, political networks, and NEP affirmative action shares and loans policies. Members of several royal families are also among the beneficiaries, while Anwar himself is said to have substantial interest in the stock market. Other industries such as oil and petroleum (PERNAS) and energy (Tenaga Nasional) were taken over by the state under Malay management. UMNO itself manages its own conglomerate holding company, the National Equity Corporation (PNB), and each state has its own State Development Corporation. By the late 1980s, the success of these programs began to lose luster, as businesses failed or remained propped up or bailed out by unrepaid loans. Others, such as Perwaja Steel, were turned over to Chinese management. According to a review by Jesudason (1989), only about 15 to 20 percent of Malay businesses were soundly based and operated or could have stood independently of government support. In addition to this dependence, Jesudason attributes their weaknesses to lack of adequate experience and skills, quests for quick profits, and a tendency to use capital for consumption at the expense of investment. Malays, it is often argued, with their "feudal mentality" (Alatas 1968; Chandra 1979; Tham Seong Chee 1983), aspire to an aristocratic lifestyle, which may interfere with deferred gratification. This view places responsibility in the domain of culture as much as in dominance by Chinese and foreigners. Less charitably, they are accused of desiring the lifestyle of Chinese millionaires without preceding generations of sacrifice and commitment by means of what one Japanese commentator calls "ersatz capitalism" (Yoshihara 1988).

Although by 1990, when the NEP came to term, the Malays had not quite achieved their target of a full 30 percent share of the corporate pie (for the reasons already cited plus a serious recession in the mid-1980s), they had made the crucial psychological and symbolic leap of confidence from their initial fumbling search for economic power and autonomy in 1970. This comes with a fresh sense of cultural and religious assertiveness, which has produced the various types of "new Malay": more or less Islamic, UMNO or PAS, and bureaucrats or businessmen, although all possibly at the expense of economic efficiency at the state level. Since the New Development Policy (NDP) replaced the expired NEP in 1991, some of the emphasis has shifted from ethnicity to merit as qualification for economic support by the state. At the same time, however, Malays are reminded by their minister of trade and industry, Rafidah Aziz, that the key to Chinese success lies in their industriousness, not in state protection, and they are urged to "emulate that so-called overseas Chinese mentality . . . [to] be strong and competitive" (*Straits Times* 23 Jan. 1994).

The Public Role of Muslim Women

It is clear that in the Vision 2020 approach to Malaysian development Muslim women are expected to play a substantial role, and they are prominent in higher education, overseas training, and scholarship programs. Women are also being channeled into studies of architecture, medicine, physics, and other sciences alongside their male counterparts. Since 1970, women have noticeably moved into the public and private sectors, although their presence in "professional and higher management" occupations by 1990 still hovered around 1 to 2 percent. Two cabinet ministers are now women, including the minister of trade and industry, who despite criticism from conservative religious quarters, refuses to cover her hair in public. Across the board, women in Malaysia comprise 48 percent of the work force.

Only in Kelantan under PAS have women's public activities been curtailed, especially in matters of dress code, night shifts, and employment in "places of entertainment." Paradoxically, Kelantan women have historically been renowned as successful petty traders in local markets and as traveling batik sellers. Today, the PAS religious order persuades them that a Muslim woman's priority should be in the domestic domain. Nevertheless, women are still prominent sellers in the local Kelantan markets. Elsewhere, a growing number of success stories of Malay women entrepreneurs in such operations as upscale boutiques, interior design, and travel are featured in the popular media, although some of the latter are also politically, socially, and maritally well connected. Malay women are now visible in most public government offices as teachers, nurses, and university lecturers and also in voluntary and nongovernmental organizations.

By far the largest cohort of women employed outside the home, however, is in the factories of the free trade zones, especially in Penang and Malacca. To these are drawn many rural Malay women, most of them single. It is widely recognized that such work, especially when female employees are required to live away from home, can cast a cloud over their reputations, and such electronics workers are often popularly labeled with a term meaning "live wires" (*minah karan*), carrying a sexual innuendo. This represents another kind of "new Malay" for whom there was no role precedent in their rural Muslim familistic environment. These women had to chart for themselves a path between the seductions of unsupervised urban life and the duties of daughters making essential contributions to the family budget (cf. Ong 1987), and their labor is often a calculated tradeoff between potential loss of reputation, family pressures, and material gain. Generally, factory women are distinct from their middle-class and college-educated counterparts for their relative lack of exposure to the extremes of *dakwah* activity. Moving in entirely separate social networks, they seem to have avoided the principal channels of communication (including those of ABIM and Al Arqam), by which *dakwah* was carried, and their Islam is a less self-conscious, less obsessive variety more characteristic of (non-PAS) rural areas. For them, assuming a modest form of dress, with headscarf or other headcovering, represents conformity to a near-universal, nonextreme style of Malay national costume now current in female circles.

In addition to government encouragement, Malay women also enjoy the heritage of a bilateral kinship system, which historically avoided the extreme patriarchy of Chinese and Indian families, allowing women to inherit property in their own right. The patriarchal element is strengthened, however, at times of

Islamic revival (Karim 1992), and it is women most under influence of *dakwah* or PAS who are faced with difficult decisions over work and male authority. In the early *dakwah* days of the 1970s, stories abounded of women abandoning their studies to retreat from public life and of women doctors refusing to treat male patients or the reverse. In retrospect these appear to have been overblown by the media or to have quickly passed, for today many self-declared female *dakwah* followers are visible across the labor spectrum. One general observation, however, is that, where a direct choice has to be made, more Malay women place duties as wife and mother ahead of employment than would be customary in the West.

The many roles and faces of Malay women are portrayed in an assortment of journals targeted at their various interests: from the moralizing religious publications of PAS, ABIM and Al Arqam, respectively, to those on homemaking, children, and domesticity. One prominent feature in most of the magazines concerns profiles of working women in various occupations. Whereas more "secular" publications and the organ of the revisionist ABIM (*Risalah*) stress themes of equal opportunity and achievement for Muslim women, those of PAS and other religious groups counsel women to place priority on their wifely and maternal obligations, even to the point of some self-sacrifice and subordination to male leadership and authority. Interestingly, Arqam women are often highly qualified and competent graduates in technical subjects from the MARA Institute of Technology and other universities, and contribute their skills to the movement in its economic arm of petty manufacturing and craft enterprises. But they are also firmly committed to traditional Muslim family roles, including polygynous marriages, which they see as providing occupational freedom through the rotation of co-wives between domestic and external activities.

One of the more contentious issues of women in public life has revolved around dress codes. Since 1970, most Malay women have assumed some form of nonintimidating, generalized Muslim costume, which includes a nunlike headcovering (*tudung*), but without a face-veil, and a loose, two-piece dress obscuring all body contours. These are amenable to attractive variations in color, material, style, and accessories. Yet even Arqam women who restrict their attire to black (with a full face veil, gloves, and socks), are not thereby impeded from an active life when they so desire, and some religious magazines profile women who manage careers as anaesthetists, nurses, and technicians even while wearing full Islamic dress.

In keeping with official images of modernity and progress, however, female government employees are proscribed from "extreme" forms of Islamic attire, especially the face veil, in public offices, as are teachers, doctors, and university lecturers, and this has led to moral outrage in some religious circles, including those of PAS. The face veil is also officially banned on all campuses, including that of the International Islamic University, which has predictably prompted angry opposition from women offended for being unable to follow their religious obligations in a Muslim country (*Muslimah* April 1992, 7). One recent legal case reveals the complexity of the problem of women's dress code in public workplaces. A government clerk was fired in 1986 for appearing at work in full purdah, despite an official injunction forbidding it, and took her case to court. A committed *dakwah* follower, the woman chose a civil rather than a religious court, however, and a non-Muslim lawyer, on the grounds that her civil-occupational rights had been violated. Her avoidance of the Shari'ah court was allegedly because she wished to reduce the possibility of sullying the face of Islam in public through any association with backwardness or recalcitrance and for fear of raising political confrontations were PAS to take up the cause against UMNO, which could then be "exploited by non-Muslims." The plaintiff eventually lost her case, after an appeal to the Supreme Court, on a judgment of "insubordination" for disobeying government regulations (*Star* 10 Mar. 1993). But in her defeat she felt morally vindicated in having made an affirmation of her personal faith and shown the government to be less than Islamic (*Dunia Islam* April 1992, 66). This case encapsulates the loose ends and latent tensions still unresolved in the ad hoc character of state Islam in the economic domain.

The Economic Role of the Chinese

Since the advent of the NEP, the Chinese have had to make a number of creative adjustments to their economic activities and style in Malaysia. Serious limitations to the free market arose from Malay affirmative action, notably the Industrial Co-ordination Act (ICA) of 1975, which gave the state power to control most licenses and conditions of business (especially manufacturing) conduct. In practice, however, an older practice of "Ali Baba" alliances continued covertly throughout this period in which the Malay (Ali) obtained the license and remained a "sleeping partner" while the Chinese (Baba)[7] provided most of the capital, expertise, and operations. At higher levels, such partnerships were effected through the historically close ties of members of the MCA with their UMNO counterparts. They underlie the ceding of Perwaja Steel to a Chinese manager (Eric Chia) and many alliances between Chinese loggers on (Malay) royal lands. On balance, two and a half decades of the NEP do not appear to have eroded these special relationships: a 1995 assessment in the *Far Eastern Economic Review* (21 December) placed seven Chinese individuals or firms among the top ten Malaysian businesses in terms of net worth.

As long as the total economy was expanding, a zero-sum mentality was deferred. The recession of the mid-1980s made this fiction no longer tenable. At first, state enterprises expanded alongside those of the Chinese, but once the latter were threatened, a pervasive dissatisfaction developed. This marked the beginning of a loss of MCA credibility and a swing to the more radical opposition Democratic Action Party (DAP) by Chinese voters. It was also a period of growing Chinese emigration and redirection of Chinese capital investment offshore. Chinese investment declined from 66.9 percent in 1971 to below 30 percent in the late 1980s, even lower than the 40 percent ideal set by the NEP (Jesudason 1989, 142). The response of most Chinese businessmen was to maintain a high degree of liquidity and to engage in less productive "ersatz" activities such as property flipping and aggressive trading on an overheated local stock exchange. One Chinese institution, however, remains impenetrable by non-Chinese. The closed, family-based network, particularly strong in the Chinese-educated community, can always be turned outward to kin, clan, and compatriots overseas. Most Chinese economic activity in Malaysia has remained in this middle range, a familiar pattern documented by Harianto elsewhere in this volume whereby local Chinese have always made a virtue of their internal economic and organizational flexibility and their ability to keep moving into areas still not occupied or coveted by Malays (e.g., computers and telecommunications). Despite these constraints, as many as 90 percent of the 130 companies on the second board of the Kuala Lumpur Stock Exchange are Chinese owned.

Now that China itself has been opened to trade with Malaysia and is aggressively promoting its own modernization, its appeal to Chinese entrepreneurs in Southeast Asia has become irresistible. Already, Robert Kuok, one of Malaysia's richest Chinese entrepreneurs, is investing heavily in China, as Heng describes elsewhere in this volume. But here the Chinese are caught in a dilemma. Characterized for decades as permanent "sojourners" and "immigrants" *(kaum pendatang)* whose association with the "Communist" Emergency between 1948 and 1960 made their loyalty as citizens questionable, they have managed only recently to establish credibility as Malaysians in the country of their birth. It is just at this time that temptation in the form of direct appeals from China to invest in the land of their ancestors and home villages is intruding, adding a new pull factor after several generations. More than most Southeast Asian Chinese, save possibly for the Indonesians, the Malaysians are caught in a powerful dilemma, fearing that their status and trust as citizens may once again be compromised. Some Malaysian Chinese are prepared to be tempted to invest in China in the name of clan and cultural obligations. Others would do so only on the condition of solid material advantage and gain, putting business and profit ahead of kin and culture. In Malaysia as yet there is little attempt to relate business to Confucian ethics and obligations, unlike in Singapore, where the issue is debated with vigor, as for instance at the International Conference on Southeast Asian Chinese: Culture, Economy, and Society in January 1994. As China's future rule as a preeminent economic regional and even global power is recognized, with inevitable consequences for all of Southeast Asia, some rethinking of Malaysia's economic policies and the place of the Chinese in the economy would seem to be only a matter of time. Subtle symbolic hints are already in the air, as can be inferred from the changing style and content of recent speeches by Deputy Prime Minister Anwar in which he has introduced a few phrases in Mandarin and referred positively to "Confucian values." For Malaysia, the local Chinese may yet come to be regarded less as a liability than as an asset.

Conclusions

The construction of Malaysia's economic and political policies, domestic and international, is grounded in the unique character and mix of its populations and their histories and cultures. A long and uneasy accommodation between Malays and non-Malays, Muslims and non-Muslims, continues to function through cooperation and tradeoffs among political and business elites. These have undergone severe strain since 1970 and the implementation of the NEP. Although the transformation of the NEP into the NDP in 1990 now requires greater Malay accountability and demonstrated performance, it still leaves the basic props of affirmative action in place and with it a certain tension between the goals of maximum economic growth and ethnic equity. Meanwhile, the Chinese have not totally relinquished their distinct culture and identity within Malaysia and, far from undergoing assimilation along the lines of their Indonesian cousins, have possibly been moving farther from the Malays over the past two decades.

Much of Malaysia's economic ideology and policy over these same decades has been constrained by the quest for Malay identity and Malay nationalism, the girders of the Malaysian state. As Malay identity has become more tightly intertwined with Islam, the state has had to accommodate, though uncertainly given the role of religion in economic and political life. In the absence of a universal template, either of an Islamic state or more narrowly of an Islamic economics, incumbent Malay leaders have had to pick their way eclectically and reactively through multiple conflicting goals. In trying to appear suitably Islamic both to conservative PAS supporters and to more "secular" or "progressive" Muslims and overseas investors, the leadership risks satisfying no one. Under these conditions, Malaysian Islam is constantly being reinterpreted and "reinvented."

The other measure of Malay identity is its opposition to Chinese identity.

Historically this relationship has been marked by a chronic ambivalence: on the one hand, a grudging respect for Chinese economic prowess; on the other, a rejection of perceived Chinese personal and cultural abrasiveness and all that this implies in moral and religious terms. The tangible expression of these attitudes has been the maintenance of two largely separate and parallel economies, one fostered by the postcolonial Malay "trustee state," the other a marginalized small business sector of independent Chinese family firms linked to clan and ethnic networks elsewhere. By these strategies, direct competition has largely been avoided; where the two intersect in the form of Ali Baba alliances, the conditions are limited and controlled. The invocation of Confucian values in relation to business was rarely heard until recently, in stark contrast with the situation in Singapore, where it has been incorporated into that state's development ideology and strategy for nation building. Unofficially, debates continue as to the role of Malay pre-Islamic "feudal" values in accounting for their economic attitudes and performance as well as the degree to which maximum national economic efficiency has been compromised by culturally or ethnically directed programs.

It is ironic that the Malaysian state of the 1990s accords great recognition to business relations with China while relegating many Malaysian Chinese citizens to the economic periphery to make way for the burgeoning Malay bourgeoisie. Within the Malay community itself there remain internal differences between supporters of PAS and the various *dakwah* movements, factory workers, and middle-class professionals, save for the participation of all to some degree in capitalist consumer culture. As the prime minister ponders, like many before him, whether Muslim countries can modernize without compromising the faith (*Ummah* August, 1992, 41ff.), he faces the task of creating a style of capitalism acceptable to most Muslims without sacrificing Malaysia's economic credibility overseas. These differences keep alive a busy discourse over Muslim spirituality and Western decadence, made the more pressing in a climate of an expanding consumer culture in which the Malay middle class in some instances is demonstrating a unique or indigenized style of consumption of religious items, services, and educational options.

If Malaysia's immediate future lies with Anwar Ibrahim, as seems likely, the question is whether he will continue uninterrupted the aggressive industrialization policies of Vision 2020 or try to recultivate some of his fundamentalist ABIM roots. More liberal Muslims and some non-Muslims fear the latter, with more Islamicization to come. By contrast, the PAS opposition fears that he may steal from that party the support of marginal conservative Muslims for whom the present UMNO is too secular. Yet other evidence points to Anwar's personal commitment to development, from his activities over the *wakaf* land, to his insertions of Mandarin and Confucian references into recent speeches to local Chinese. But his personal record, like that of Dr. Mahathir, shows his essential pragmatism and flexibility. On Malaysia's behalf, in the future he will probably try to keep all the balls of Islam, ASEAN, Asian identity, NAM, G-15, the "South," and above all modernity in the air.

NOTES

The opportunity to engage in research in Malaysia during 1992–93 was afforded by a generous grant from the Social Sciences and Humanities Research Council of Canada, which, however, is in no way responsible for any of the statements or conclusions expressed in this essay.

1. From 1957 until 1963, Malaya consisted of the Malayan Peninsula plus Singapore. In 1963, the two Bornean states of Sarawak and Sabah were added as East Malaysia; two years later, Singapore seceded.

2. There were sporadic attempts by some Malay-speaking Chinese who were as familiar with Malay custom as many urban Malays, and who had converted to Islam, to claim Malay status and by the same token to apply for some of the perquisites of the New Economic Policy, though with little success (Nagata 1978).

3. Such assertions fail to convince the authorities, in view of the essentially political nature of Islam as a total way of life and Arqam's commitment to it. At least three political observers, S. H. Alatas, Mohd Sayuti Omar, and Yusof Harun, have separately noted Ustaz Asha'ari's potential as a possible future prime minister of Malaysia (Muhammad Syukri 1992, 259). In July 1994, more dramatic allegations about the training of Arqam "suicide" squads in Thailand were circulated, though without verification.

4. In order to make such declarations of heresy credible, the secular government has to convince the religious courts, whose views do not always accord with those of UMNO. Other Muslim scholars, however, are apprehensive over the messianic claims heard from Arqam's leader Asha'ari and prefer to restrict his preaching or even counter it with "official" sermons disseminated to mosques within their jurisdiction.

5. Ex-ABIM names still familiar on the PAS scene include Ustaz Abdul Hadi Awang and Ustaz Fadhil Nor. Another new leader, the current PAS president, is Nik Aziz, son and heir of a traditional religious scholar from Kelantan.

6. *Zakat*, one of the five pillars of Islam, is a mandatory tax based on a locally fixed percentage of economic assets to be distributed during the holy month of Ramadhan, to the poor and needy by religious authorities.

7. "Baba," used interchangeably with "Peranakan," refers to locally born male Chinese, some of whom have adopted local customs, personal networks, and even domestic use of the Malay language.

Part 2
CULTURES OF CAPITALISM

The four essays in part 2 analyze economic practice in Korea and among Southeast Asian Sino-capitalists and consider its implications for economic development in the region. Rooted in different theoretical traditions as these essays are, from both microscopic and macroscopic perspectives they share an emphasis on seeing how economic practice and capitalism have been shaped by Confucianism in particular, and by Sinic culture in general, in their specific historical contexts.

Adopting postmodernist and Foucauldian genealogical analyses, Janelli and Yim examine the mutual reformulation of capitalism and Confucianism in South Korea on the basis of their field data on one of South Korea's four largest *chaeböl* (conglomerates). They point out, for example, that the Korean term *injöng* is often invoked to contrast the self-perceived humane sympathy for the plight of the other with the strict legal and materialistic adherence to contracts in the West.

In their business practices, owners and managers in South Korea use the Confucian familial metaphor to legitimize their highly authoritarian rule. They also reinforce this metaphor through numerous fringe benefits and gifts of company products to employees at major holidays. This metaphor, however, disguises the conflict of material interests between owners and employees as well as the tension between managers and staff, who may eventually be promoted over the managers themselves. While not openly challenging the father-son and family analogies, many young workers use instead the metaphor of the army. Janelli and Yim emphasize that "transformations and reformulations of Confucian ideas have been informed by a sense of material interests while the pursuit of material advantage has simultaneously been informed and reshaped by understandings of Confucianism." In the global system, Janelli and Yim suggest that this dialectical transformation can extend beyond the South Korean context since Western capitalist practices have been transformed through the encounter with some Confucian-informed practices.

In his macroscopic analysis of Confucian ideology and South Korean economic transformation, Park focuses on how the state, the family, and business have made extensive use of the Confucian legacy to promote rapid economic growth. More specifically, Park examines how respect for the bureaucracy facilitates the role of the government in the development process, how the value families place on education and its material rewards strengthens the human resource base for economic development, and how, together with repressive labor laws and the abundance of unskilled labor, the authority-oriented patriarchical kinship system facilitates the use of the family metaphor in the economy and contributes to the formation of a docile cheap labor force for business and the state. However, Park emphasizes that South Korean economic development cannot be attributed directly to Confucianism. Instead, in their economic pursuit, the state, business, and the family have made extensive use of traditional social values formed under the influence of Confucianism as well as material incentives and disincentives (including preferential interest rates, the provision of crucial economic information by the government, and surveillance of business by the intelligence agency).

Park hypothesizes that after a certain period of strong growth, government intervention and an authoritarian labor regime may no longer contribute to market efficiency, competitiveness, innovation, and growth. From a macroscopic perspective, the economic growth in South Korea does not necessarily solve the equity problem, as considerable wealth differentiation exists among income earners as well as between urban and rural areas. From a microscopic one, neither the authoritarian organizational structure nor the educational system encourages the innovation and creativity needed to meet the demands of the changing environment. The extensive use of Confucian ideology by the state, business, and the family has shaped the development of South Korean capitalism, though this shaping may not prove so positive after an initial period of strong growth.

If Park examines the use of a tradition of a relatively settled population in the construction of an economy over an extended period, Harianto offers comparative insights on the role of historically constructed diasporic cultures among Sino-capitalists in spatially diverse institutional contexts. In his analysis of Sino-capitalists' practices and their role in the growth of many economies in Southeast Asia, Harianto focuses on the tradition of family- and network-structured firms as well as on their reliance on trust-based personal networks for economic exchange, access to information and capital, and potential sanctions in a breach of contract. This reliance on a personal network reduces the risk of failure and the costs of transaction. From his perspective as an economist, he sees that, due to market failures within the economy at large and "organizational failures" within firms or conglomerates in underdeveloped Southeast Asia, networks have gained a salient role in structuring business practice and economic growth. Harianto emphasizes that the historically conditioned cultural tradition among Sino-capitalists functions well wnen institutions to support the market are underdeveloped, as in the case of Southeast Asia. Sino-capitalists with the same culturally rooted practice do not thrive as well in North America, where the structural and economic conditions are different. While highlighting how capitalist practices among ethnic Chinese entrepreneurs are shaped by their diasporic cultural tradition, Harianto emphasizes that this historically constructed tradition constitutes only one among many factors in the development of a strong ethnic capitalism in Southeast Asia: "no overseas Chinese capitalism without a Chinese entrepreneurial class; no Chinese entrepreneurial class without *market failures, state activism,* efficient networks, and *commercial strategy;* and no Chinese network with\ut religious moral character and a long history of repression" (emphasis added).

Heng's essay complements Harianto's by providing an in-depth case study of the entrepreneurial practice of Robert Kuok, one of Southeast Asia's most successful Sino-capitalists. Robert Kuok's entrepreneurial career spans the British colonial era in Malaysia, the import-substitution period after Malaysia's independence, and the export-oriented growth through open trade regimes since the 1970s. Starting out in sugar and other commodities trade, Robert Kuok branched into a wide range of activities, from agricultural plantations and manufacturing to mass media and entertainment. He built an empire with holdings in sixteen countries, mainly in the Far East but also in the Americas, Europe, and Australia. Heng suggests that, although Kuok was educated in British schools and developed an excellent rapport with Malay political patrons and business partners, he still relies significantly on Chinese cultural practice both in the organization of his conglomerate and in his relations with other Sino-capitalists. In other words, Kuok's empire is still a paternalistic male-centered organization in which he as the decision maker relies on a small circle of family members and trusted friends as managers of subsidiary operations. Second, it still emphasizes harmonious relations within a trust-based social network (kinship- or dialect-based groups) to gain information and credit, among other things, via a system that extends throughout Eastern Asia. On the other hand, Kuok has also strengthened the technical and professional bases of his conglomerate in the direction of a modern and professionally managed empire. Like Harianto and Park, Heng raises open questions in her conclusion regarding the Kuok Group's ability to survive the founder's demise, given the probable incompatibility among heirs and the difficulty for such a culturally rooted organization to survive in the modern international capitalist environment.

The Mutual Constitution of Confucianism and Capitalism in South Korea

Roger L. Janelli and Dawnhee Yim

During the last few years, many companies have begun to develop more personal, long-term bonds with customers. . . . Some enterprises . . . are forging bonds that bear some traces of genuine social activity. . . . Of course, all these developments are marketing strategies at root. Their aim is not to create new sociological forces but to earn profits.

New York Times, 20 February 1994, F11

The rise of East Asian economies in recent decades has added new impetus to the quest for comprehending relationships between economy and culture. Yet this quest still contends with a formidable theoretical obstacle: a Western intellectual tradition that has sought to dichotomize explanations of human actions into the ideal and the material. Generally, research into each of these domains has been pursued independently, often in different academic disciplines, and where the domains have intersected much effort has been directed toward arguing for the greater causal power of one or the other. In our view, there is a need for better theoretical models that can accommodate both.

The inadequacies of attempts to understand the pursuit of material interests while ignoring or minimizing the importance of human ideas are multiple. Some recent work in rational choice theory, for example, offers new evidence of what most anthropologists have long known: that potential costs and benefits are not perceived unmediated (Tversky and Kahneman 1990; Bloch 1983, 135–36). Instead, the ways in which alternatives are presented affect their relative preferability. Because interests involve future benefits and their attendant uncertainties, moreover, estimating their relative values and choosing between alternative means of pursuing those interests are also informed by attitudes toward risk and other subjective understandings. These include expectations regarding responses of others and what is known or assumed to be feasible or potentially successful (Douglas and Wildavsky 1982; Bourdieu 1977, 4–9). And, finally, each individual's interests are multiple, requiring further choices not only between various forms of capital but also between potential allies from among the multiplicity of persons with whom an individual shares common interests on the basis of such attributes as gender, class, age, nationality, and ethnicity (Bourdieu 1990b, 110–11; Callinicos 1988, 156, 205). Thus, it was not irrational for many middle-class South Koreans to oppose the opening of their nation's rice market to American imports, even though a continued prohibition on such imports would have required them to pay a higher price for rice. The cost of rice was outweighed by other political-economic stakes involved in the dispute, such as increasing South Korea's dependence on foreign food supplies, projecting an image of national weakness, and exacerbating domestic inequalities of wealth.

No less inadequate are efforts to comprehend ideas espoused by individuals or groups without looking to material considerations, particularly when those ideas relate to economic change or reproduction. First of all, ignoring material motivations implies that economic outcomes are largely unintended. Second, emphasizing the ways in which individual actions are outcomes of value systems or other ideas inculcated through socialization and enculturation gives inadequate attention to human choices and strategies (Giddens 1979, 1984) and to the malleability that abstract values and ideas often exhibit when they are applied to concrete cases. Moreover, such cultural determinism fails to acknowledge creativity and reformulations of cultural understandings in light of new circumstances and experiences. And, finally, such approaches give too little recognition to the ways in which cultural rules and meanings are contested, the outcome often depending on who can elicit or demand assent at the moment from whom.

The goal of this chapter is to explore relationships between cultural ideas and material gain without privileging either. By looking to the development of Confucianism and capitalism in South Korea, we seek to understand how transformations and reformulations of the Confucian heritage have been informed by a sense of material interests while the pursuit of material advantage has simultaneously been informed and reshaped by understandings of Confucianism. Though Confucian-derived ideals and the pursuit of material interests through capitalism can on occasion urge opposing actions, such oppositions seem to tend toward resolution through an ongoing dialectic by means of which cultural ideals and methods of pursuing profits are continually refashioned and reconciled though individual choices, reinterpretations, constructions, and attempts at persuasion.

Our examination of relationships between contemporary Confucianism and capitalism in South Korea recognizes both "isms" as comprised of ideas and practices that have centuries-old histories and are complex enough to exist in multiple versions (de Bary 1991, xi; Tu 1993, 141–59). The adoption of Confucianism as the official state ideology of the Chosŏn dynasty, for example, was closely tied to changes in family and lineage organization (Deuchler 1992), including a patrilineal descent system. One ultimate result was that entire local lineages (or at least those of their members who were legitimate descendants) claimed political privilege (Janelli and Janelli 1978). In other words, besides asserting one's own moral cultivation and right to rule, whole lineages could point to the morality of an ancestor to claim local political advantages. Alternatively, a lineage could point to alleged moral deficiencies of a rival lineage's ancestors and thereby attempt to deny its adversaries the privileges claimed for its own members. In the local practice of Korean Confucianism, memorials to virtuous widows and filial sons and, conversely, descent from a concubine, even after several generations, were major weapons in contests for political power (e.g., Kim Taik-Kyoo 1964).

In this chapter, we explore popular versions of Confucianism and capitalist practices in present-day South Korea and try to show how these common understandings have been and continue to be mutually reformulated. Such popular understandings have by no means been autonomous of elite discourse, but neither have they been entirely determined by it.

In view of the multiple versions of both Confucianism and capitalism, we are inclined to follow the urging of some postmodernists (e.g., Rorty 1979; Lyotard 1984; Marcus and Fischer 1986) and avoid choosing any single interpretation or "totalizing" representation of all—or the essence—of either popular Confucianism or capitalism in South Korea. Instead, we prefer to regard such summarizing interpretations as "constructions": they are not total falsehoods, complete fabrications, or inventions of whole cloth but are "partial" (Marcus and Fischer 1986) or "selective" (Williams 1977, 115) accounts that highlight some features while adumbrating others. Competing versions of each ideology differ from each other by differentially choosing texts and actions and thereby constructing different principles and interpretations. This is not an assertion that any construction is as good as any other but only the more modest claim that Confucianism and capitalism have multiple truths and can be (and have been) understood in several ways.

Pursuing this postmodernist line of thought one step further, we attempt to view all ideas and practices as having Foucauldian genealogies. Elaborating on this concept of genealogy, Foucault says:

> Genealogy does not pretend to go back in time to restore an unbroken continuity that operates beyond the dispersion of forgotten things; its duty is not to demonstrate that the past actively exists in the present, [nor] that it continues secretly to animate the present, having imposed a predetermined form on all its vicissitudes. Genealogy does not resemble the evolution of a species and does not map the destiny of a people. On the contrary, to follow the complex course of descent is to maintain passing events in their proper dispersion; it is to identify the accidents, the minute deviations—or conversely the complete reversals—the errors, the false appraisals, and the faulty calculations that gave birth to those things that continue to exist and have value for us; it is to discover that truth or being does not lie at the root of what we know and what we are, but the exteriority of accidents. (1986, 81)

Because versions of both capitalism and Confucianism have genealogies (and different genealogies in different societies), we avoid trying to essentialize popular Confucianism or capitalism by pointing to allegedly fundamental features or offering timeless definitions. We also avoid trying to define particular ideas and practices as essentially Confucian or capitalistic, looking instead to their genealogies to find Confucian and capitalist contributions.

In the case of capitalism, moreover, we do not regard the version that happened to develop in any particular society as an authoritative standard against which to judge all others.[1] Just as the South Korean version of this political-economic system has been shaped by Korean cultural understandings, so European and American versions have been no less informed by Western cultural ideas. Forms of capitalism in different societies, however, are not entirely independent of each other (Wolf 1982; Comaroff 1986). As the epigraph of our chapter indicates, Western capitalist industries now seem to be experimenting with ideas about customer relations developed largely in East Asia, just as capitalists in South Korea have been affected by commercial practices found elsewhere in the world (Cumings 1987; McNamara 1990; Eckert 1991). Our implicit comparisons of South Korean and Western, especially American, capitalism are offered not as a device for constructing otherness but as a means for identifying areas for consideration.

Given our open-ended conceptions of Confucianism and capitalism, we have not attempted to survey all of the ways in which they have interacted and continue to interact in South Korea. Instead, we have sought to demonstrate the ongoing process of genealogical development and construction that appeared among the representations, practices, and choices of those who have been at the forefront of transforming South Korea's economy in recent decades: white-collar workers and managers at one of South Korea's huge *chaebŏl* or conglomerates. Our examples are taken from Roger Janelli's experiences during eight months of anthropological fieldwork at one of South Korea's four largest conglomerates. With about eighty thousand employees and reported sales of fifteen billion (U.S.) dollars, it was one of the *Fortune* magazine's International 500 at the time. (It has subsequently grown even larger.) To the enterprise that served as the site of this research we have given a pseudonym, Taesŏng, with little hope of completely protecting its anonymity but with the goal of minimizing adverse publicity to its owners and employees, who were kind enough to make the fieldwork possible in 1986 and 1987.[2]

Ethnography

Confucianism was a term seldom heard in the offices of Taesŏng. A managing director once acknowledged in a private conversation that he thought Confucianism was the basis of Taesŏng's managerial style, but he did not elaborate that acknowledgment.[3] And a younger manager, while lamenting the authoritarianism of the conglomerate's managerial style, once muttered "Confucian ideology" (*yugyo sasang*) in tones of disgust. But otherwise "Confucianism" was evoked rather than invoked, as tacitly Confucian ideas informed many of the claims and actions of the company's white-collar workers and managers.

This implicit rather than explicit use of Confucian ideals in South Korea is not unique to the world of capitalist industry. Michael Robinson points to a similar phenomenon among state officials:

> Although the modern South Korean state is willing to indirectly use Confucian values of loyalty and service, it is reluctant to endorse the tradition itself. This is because there is a tremendous antipathy to the Confucian tradition, which is seen as an obstacle to economic development. (1991, 218–19)

One example of a modern practice that appeared to have an implicitly Confucian contribution to its genealogy was South Korean managers' insistence on a moral dimension to relations between parties to a commercial transaction. Rather than represent such relations primarily in terms of competing self-interests, they maintained that the more privileged party to a transaction had an obligation to consider the plight of the other. The term they most often used for this consideration was *injŏng* (loosely, "sympathy for the plight of others"), but rather than view *injŏng* purely as an emotion, they portrayed it as a moral imperative.

The invocation of *injŏng* was part of Taesŏng managers' frequent critiques of Western, and especially American, business practices that aimed at extracting the maximum advantage in each transaction. These included pushing for the very lowest prices during negotiations, switching orders from one company to another for the sake of any economic advantage, and insisting on strict adherence to contractual terms even when conditions had changed since the formulation of the agreement. They maintained that it was far better to establish a long-term relationship with customers by being a little less grasping and resolving to mutual satisfaction whatever problems arose. Ronald Dore (1987, 169–92) has already explored the economic rationality of such "goodwill" and suggested a connection with Confucian notions of benevolence. Here, however, we wish to explore how South Korean managers advanced a moral critique of American practices while simultaneously advancing some of their own material interests.

Our attention was first drawn to *injŏng* in a casual conversation about card playing. While teaching Roger Janelli to play Go-stop, a popular South Korean card game at the time of the fieldwork, a young manager explained that when one player thoroughly cleaned out another the winner returned some of the loser's money rather than leave him completely broke. Having recently seen an American movie that portrayed the same action, Janelli noted that the same practice could also be found sometimes in the United States. To this remark, the young manager responded with mused surprise: "So Americans too have *injŏng!*"

The surprise that the manager expressed apparently reflected a general understanding among Taesŏng office workers that Americans lacked any sympathy for, or understanding of, others less fortunate than themselves. Indeed, in several subsequent conversations and in a variety of other contexts, white-collar workers pointed to this moral deficiency of Americans. As South Korea's trade balance with the United States continued to mount and American trade representatives spoke increasingly of "level playing fields" or "playing by the same rules" in order to obtain a further opening of South Korea's domestic market, for example, several young workers maintained that it was unfair of the United States to insist that the two countries follow the same rules, for such a demand failed to consider South Korea's special circumstances. Whereas the United States was the "wealthiest nation on earth," they contended, South Korea had few natural resources, was handicapped by a high population density, had to export in order to survive, and was burdened by enormous foreign debt. South Korean markets needed protection until their companies were strong enough to compete with those of the United States, some added. All expressed agreement with the view that the United States had an obligation to understand the plight of less fortunate nations.

Older managers shared the views of their subordinates. One such manager said irately of American demands to open South Korea's agricultural market: "They don't consider the poor Korean farmers." Another noted:

> We have a proverb that says "A person who has 99 underskirts and plans to make it a round 100 asks the person who has only one for hers." But we really don't do that. If we have 99, we let the other person keep one. Americans, on the other hand, will go after even that last item.

Injŏng could also be used as a counterclaim against the morality that many Westerners apparently attribute to "honoring" contractual obligations. One manager noted that American businessmen were too rigid, pointing out that when customers reneged on their promises, pleading "please understand my situation," American businessmen were stone hearted, inhuman, and selfish. He also noted that such behavior sometimes worked to their economic disadvantage:

> Our company might sell a product for 110 *wŏn* to a Southeast Asian customer but get only 100 *wŏn* from an American buyer. However, if there were a sudden price increase of 50 *wŏn*, it would be passed along immediately to the American. If the Southeast Asian customer said he couldn't absorb such a large price increase all at once, we might sell to him at 130 *wŏn* for a while before passing on the whole price hike. Or, if there was a rise in demand, and our company couldn't satisfy all its customers, we would satisfy the needs of the Southeast Asian firm rather than those of the American.

South Korean managers saw through the alleged morality of contracts in ways that are difficult for those to whom Western business practices have become "natural." They knew full well that consent to contractual agreements, especially between parties of unequal power, is often attained through a measure of coercion. One group of managers who had recently been assigned to a newly formed joint venture with an American firm resisted formulating written agreements with their South Korean customers, persons with whom they had formerly dealt on an informal basis. The agreements were supposed to specify what services those customers would agree to accept in the future; but, the managers noted, the contracts said nothing about prices, and their potential customers would refuse to affix their seals to such agreements out of fear that the agreements might later be used as coercive instruments to force them to buy the agreed services.

We surmise that office workers' views of Americans as inhumane, rule enforcing, and *injŏng* lacking informed several of the enthusiastic responses that Roger Janelli received to his comparison of American and South Korean driving habits. As he drove to and from the research site each morning and evening, he was struck by some differences in the informal rules of the road and shared his impressions with Taesŏng office workers in casual conversations. Whereas Americans seemed to insist on the right of way, he pointed out, South Korean drivers appeared more tolerant of someone who cuts them off (not too abruptly) and then gives a slight wave of the hand to indicate "I'm sorry" or "Thanks." Most of those who enthusiastically agreed with this contrast had no experience driving in the United States, but it evidently fit their perceptions of American practices.

Though pointing to the lack of *injŏng* among Americans was a moral claim, Taesŏng office workers and managers made no effort to hide their view that keeping *injŏng* in mind was materially advantageous. In other words, their commitment to ideals and the pursuit of material interests had been brought into alignment. One manager acknowledged that American businessmen were far better skilled than their South Korean counterparts in formulating contracts, and thus having to follow such procedures disadvantaged them in dealings with Americans. And the manager who contrasted Southeast Asian and American buyers also maintained that establishing a long-term relationship was an economically rational strategy: buyers who always insisted on the lowest price worked to their own long-term disadvantage, as sudden price increases or worldwide shortages of the seller's products put such buyers in especially difficult straits.

Advancing the concept of *injŏng* as a counterclaim to "keeping one's word" was not the result of an unreflective Confucian compulsion but rather a choice of a cultural concept that was informed by Confucian understandings of how social relationships ought to be conducted and was simultaneously serviceable as a political-economic resource. Moreover, contracts were not as alien to South Korea as these managers implied. Agreements regarding rice lending, moneylending, housing, and rotating credit societies have been in use in rural and urban South Korea for decades. But the recognition that contracts often work to the disadvantage of the already disadvantaged is part of the cultural repertory of many in South Korea. A short story by Yun Heung-gil (1977

[1989]), for example, points to the dilemma confronting a middle-class couple who had agreed to rent out a room of their house to a very poor family. The latter arrive with their belongings four days early and able to pay only half of the agreed rental deposit.

Injŏng is not a concept that was usually associated with Confucianism in Korea. Song (1987, 94) maintains that *injŏng* is none other than the seven feelings (*ch'ilchŏng*), a term found in elite Confucian intellectual discourse; but most Confucian intellectuals appear to have regarded such feelings with a measure of distrust, preferring to rely on reason rather than emotion.[4] Yet in the offices of Taesŏng the concept of *injŏng* was injected into capitalist transactions and portrayed not as a naturally arising feeling but as an obligatory guide to dealing with others who are less advantaged than oneself. Taesŏng white-collar workers and managers insisted that everyone ought to empathize with or sympathetically understand the situation of others and regulate one's actions accordingly, and this insistence appears to be at least partially informed by understandings often associated with Confucianism. In their examinations of Confucian thought, both Theodore de Bary (1991, 32) and Wei-ming Tu (1986, 179) have pointed to the importance attached to empathy, reciprocity, and consideration of how one's actions affect others.

Another example of the interplay between Confucianism and capitalism appeared in managers' appeals to Confucian ideals to legitimize their control of subordinates and in the effects of these appeals on subordinates' understandings of Confucianism. Perhaps it is ironic that owners (who were also the highest managers) of the large conglomerates should attempt to use Confucian ideas as a major means of legitimating their rule. Carter Eckert has argued that the frailty of the bourgeoisie's legitimacy in South Korea stems from Confucian ideas (1993, 117–18). Capitalism was given a Confucian interpretation when first introduced into Korea, Eckert maintains, and made morally justifiable in terms of the benefits it was supposed to bring to the nation. The quest for personal gain, on the other hand, was not made morally justifiable, and even the modern bourgeoisie is still hard pressed to legitimate their accumulated wealth in the eyes of the public (Koo 1989; Choi Jang-Jip 1983, 21; Janelli and Yim 1993, 81-106).

To some degree, Taesŏng's white-collar workers, particularly those at the lowest ranks and in the earliest stages of their careers, shared the general public's critique of the conglomerate owners. Until a few years earlier, these younger employees had been college students, who comprise one of the groups that had been at the forefront of criticizing the conglomerates, their owners, and the state policies that allowed them to accumulate their vast wealth. But most subordinates seemed more concerned with challenging the control of their more immediate managers than with the legitimacy of the *chaebŏl*'s owner-managers.

Like most South Korean conglomerates in 1986–87, Taesŏng was managed in what is often called a "top-down" or "authoritarian" manner. Subordinates at all levels of the organization were given little room to exercise their own judgment or contribute to decision making. Nearly everyone at Taesŏng acknowledged that this style of management prevailed.[5] One director, for example, justified his unwillingness to grant greater autonomy to his section chiefs by pointing to their alleged immaturity (Janelli and Yim 1993, 217).

Though company training and official slogans often emphasized creativity, new employees soon learned that their creativity was expected to be restricted to finding better ways of implementing rather specific instructions given to them by superiors or of carrying out their company's standard procedures. Indeed, younger men (roughly, those under the age of forty) often complained that their opinions were disregarded by superiors, that they were treated as if they were children, that they were severely scolded for mistakes, and that their superiors gave them little autonomy. Our attention here, however, is directed not toward their evaluations of this method of management but rather on how it was legitimated by Confucian family ideals and in turn shaped subordinates' understandings of Confucianism.

Though attempts to portray the conglomerate as a family were aimed at legitimating the conglomerate's authoritarian system of management and overcoming younger men's resistance by making that kind of management more palatable, one need not infer great pretense on the part of the owner-managers or other senior managers. Indeed, their willingness to permit our research testifies to the genuineness of their convictions that their actions were justified. We think rather that they too had managed to bring their ideals into congruity with their sense of self-interest.

Statements by senior managers as well as company-produced publications, such as the conglomerate's monthly magazine, often represented Taesŏng's top-down style of management as similar to the style of control and supervision that Korean fathers exert over their offspring, especially their sons. Such representations implied that the control of subordinates was Confucian and a "Korean style" of management because it derived from national traditions of the family. To appeal to the traditional Korean family, and to the father-son relationship in particular, is to appeal tacitly to Confucianism, for it is understood that Confucian norms, and especially filial piety, were supposed to govern family relationships. The following example, taken from the conglomerate's monthly magazine issued in March of 1987, portrays the father/manager as an entirely benevolent figure who has the best interests of subordinates at heart.[6]

The managers have warm human affection, like a parent's devotion, toward the *sawŏn* [premanagerial white-collar worker], cultivate the knowledge and abilities of each, and guide their talents and ability to evaluate [their own] work. The *sawŏn,* too, like sons and daughters toward parents, have faith in and respect for them.

Similarities between family and firm, and between fathers and managers, were alleged by the owners and older managers in a seemingly endless variety of ways. A section of the conglomerate's monthly magazine was entitled "We Are One Family" and spotlighted a different member company or franchisee each month. On one occasion, the group's chairman addressed a gathering of its directors as "Taesŏng family members." And a symbolic assertion that relationships in the office resembled those of the family could be seen in the placement of flowers on the desks of section chiefs on Parents' Day of 1987.

Many of the expressions that equated the conglomerate with a family gave particular attention to authority. A managing director, for example, wrote an article for the November 1986 issue of the conglomerate's magazine in which he stated that the proper management of subordinates was like the proper education of children: severe but human. Another older manager explained in a conversation the style of the weekly managers' meeting, at which each of the young section chiefs presented a formal report on his activities during the previous week and received his superior's comments. As the older manager explained, these meetings constituted a form of training (*hullyŏnŭl sik'inda*) like that given by a Korean father to his son:

> The training is very severe. Americans would be shocked by the severity of it. It's because we Koreans are all one people (*minjok*). . . . We're not made up of several different kinds of people like Americans. We are like one family, so a person can train his subordinates like a father trains his son, pointing out mistakes rather than giving praise for things done correctly.

In all of these attempts to use the family metaphor to legitimate the conglomerate's authoritarian managerial style, the control of subordinates was represented as benevolent. Even the older manager's choice of words to describe the activities at the weekly manager's meeting, *hullyŏnŭl sik'inda,* represented these meetings as sessions aimed at improving employees' abilities. Similarly, in their public addresses to employees, members of the *chaebŏl*'s controlling kin group and other top managers often spoke of external dangers threatening the organization, especially foreign competition and trade pressure, and appealed for greater efforts on behalf of the company. Superiors did not threaten employees with firing, slower promotion, or other such punishments. This seemed to evoke cultural understandings of Korean styles of child rearing noted by several observers (Hahn Dongse 1972; Dix 1977, 84; Janelli and Janelli 1982, 35). Rather than threaten their own punishment, Korean parents often choose to control children by warning them of external dangers, such as tigers, thereby avoiding an explicit opposition of wills.[7] This method of parental control is represented in the popular Korean story about a tiger and a persimmon in which a mother attempts to stop her child's crying by warning him that a tiger will appear if his crying persists (Choi In-hak 1979, 21–22).

Statements equating the company with a family were further reinforced by claims that the company was a group whose members, including owner-managers and lower-level white-collar employees alike, all shared a common set of interests. This theme was subtly reaffirmed through a system of internal promotion that generally provided younger employees with greater opportunities for advancement when the company earned larger profits and could expand more rapidly. Other ways of implicitly representing the company as a family whose members shared common interests included gifts of company products to employees at major holidays and a whole host of other fringe benefits.

Of course, it is arguable whether or not the authoritarian or top-down managerial style found in the conglomerate is a continuation of Korean Confucian family traditions. During our own fieldwork in a Korean village, we noted that sons never disagreed with their fathers in public and were often reticent about their own opinions in their fathers' presence. We also noticed that few sons seemed to be relaxed in the presence of their fathers. Instead, their behavior was often stiff and formal. A son could not smoke or drink openly in his father's presence, for example. At the time, we were inclined to interpret all this behavior as manifestations of filial piety, a cardinal virtue in rural Korean society. Because sons owed great deference to their fathers, we reasoned, they could not openly argue with them or feel completely at ease in their presence. Thus, the claim that the managerial style prevailing at Taesŏng is a continuation of Confucian tradition is not a pure fantasy. Shin Yoo-Keun (1984) and others (e.g., Lee Hak-Chong 1989; Rhee 1981, 53–54) have sought to demonstrate this thesis in a variety of other managerial practices of South Korean enterprises. The difficulty with identifying specific Confucian traditions in modern office settings is not that such identifications are entirely wrong but rather that they are predicated on only a partial or selective view of past practices, present-day managerial control, and the relationship between them. Just as the older managers could point to similarities or continuities between their methods of control and a Korean father's manner of controlling his sons, so one could point to other interpretations of the father's role and to a variety of dissimilarities or discontinuities between his authority and that of a Taesŏng manager. Here we briefly explore some of the alternative possible interpretations of the father-son and manager-subordinate relationship.

At Taesŏng, the authority attributed to Korean fathers seems to have been stressed at the expense of acknowledging the constraints under which that authority operated. Commenting on the role of the father in Korean society, anthropologist Lee Kwang-Kyu has observed:

When we speak of our traditional culture the first thing mentioned is the ordering of vertical relationships between superiors and subordinates based on Confucian morality and the conservatism of the patriarchal family. From an anthropological perspective, however, one cannot speak so simply. (1990, 198)

Lee further added: "In our nation, the power of the housewife acted to constrain patriarchal authority" (204). There was, of course, no one at Taesŏng who played the role of a mother.

One can also point to other constraints that limited a father's authority, such as strategies available to sons for reducing or blunting the effectiveness of paternal control. One of these strategies was evasion: sons often avoided their fathers. On one occasion, for example, we were talking with a middle-aged man in our rented room in the village when his father came to visit us. The son quickly excused himself, giving as the only reason that his father had arrived. Some of this avoidance was even institutionalized, as in the practice of having only one person represent each household at village meetings. At one meeting we attended, a villager politely asked an elderly man to leave so that his son could attend.

Other strategies available to sons were linked to local interpretations of filial piety, which emphasized not *obeying* but *repaying* parents. Offspring were eternally indebted to their parents not only for the gift of life but also, as Korean funeral chants point out, for the pains taken by parents in raising them (Janelli and Janelli 1982, 66–69). This indebtedness required offspring to ensure their parents' comfort, not to cause them distress, and to attend to their needs. In many ways, filial piety imposed on offspring a higher standard than simply obeying parents' commands. As popular oral narratives of filial piety show (Choi In-hak 1979, 163–76), a filial offspring was supposed to exercise his or her own judgment and initiative in caring for parents and deciding what is in their best interests. A truly filial son did not wait to be told what to do.

This understanding of filial piety paradoxically gave offspring a measure of autonomy. When parents become elderly, for example, offspring could justify avoiding carrying out parents' wishes if that avoidance could be successfully represented as in the parents' best interest. This seemed to be not only the prevalent interpretation of this moral norm in rural villages, but it can evidently also be justified by a reading of the classical Confucian texts.

> The popular description of the father-son relationship as fixed one-dimensional subjugation in Confucian ethics in which the authority of the father is never questioned and that the obedience of the son is assumed is a limited understanding of Confucian ethics . . . . A son can never disown his father. This, however, does not mean that the son must unquestionably obey his father's commands. On the contrary, the son has a moral obligation to see to it that his father acts in accordance with the norms of fatherhood. (W. M. Tu 1986, 181)

A similar interpretation of Confucian ethics seems to underlie the case of an elderly villager who gave us the following anecdote about how he resisted his father's demands.

> Because the father seemed very lonely after his wife died, his sons found another woman to provide him with companionship in his old age. Unfortunately, the woman turned out to be a schemer with whom their father became helplessly infatuated. She soon began to persuade him to transfer all the property of his household to her name. When he finally consented, our informant moved out of the house and refused to return until his father had rid himself of the woman. The old man eventually yielded, for he knew he could not live without the help of his eldest son. (Janelli and Janelli 1982, 49)

The eldest son's action in this case can be seen as morally justifiable if it is interpreted as undertaken for the sake of the parent, but it can also be viewed cynically as a son's attempt to preserve his inheritance. The more charitable interpretation appears to have prevailed locally. The son's reputation in the community did not seem to have been seriously impaired by his act of defiance. Indeed, he happened to be a recipient of an award for filial piety from the township office, the only villager we knew to be so honored.

Understandings of filial piety gave sons autonomy in yet another way. As anthropologist Kang Shin-pyo (1987, 98) has observed, lying to a father could also be justified if it were viewed as motivated by a desire to avoid unnecessary worry on the part of a father. Though lying itself wasn't seen as morally good, it was preferable to causing distress to parents.[8]

Just as the representation of the authoritarian father is a selective interpretation, so is the representation of the manager as benevolent. The older managers' portrayal of themselves as acting in the best interests of employees was another partial representation. In a variety of ways, managers and their subordinates did not share the same interests, and what interests they did share seemed to be far less than those shared by members of a family. Since the highest managers of the conglomerate were also its principle owners, their subordinates' salaries reduced the profits available to them. Even in the case of lower-level managers, their performance was heavily affected by the activities of their subordinates. In other words, the harder the subordinates worked, the greater the advantages accruing to their managers. In addition to complaints about the conglomerate's authoritarian system of management, employees' other major complaints pertained to all the work that their superiors demanded of them and the resulting long hours they had to spend in the office.

The analogy between the father and the manager was not easily accepted by many young workers. Perhaps two reasons were that, unlike the Japanese family, the Korean family was not open to the adoption of outsiders and was seldom used as a model for other social relationships. Kinship and nonkinship relations seemed to have formed rather discontinuous realms in Korea. Even within the kinship realm, moreover, the deference owed fathers attenuated rapidly as it extended to increasingly distant agnates. Nor were sons expelled from families as readily as subordinates were dismissed (formally encouraged to resign). Nor could a son suffer the indignity of falling behind his siblings in the way a slowly promoted manager could suffer from falling behind his coworkers or being surpassed by a former subordinate. Moreover, subordinates were not entirely unaware that their own interests were sometimes antithetical to those of their immediate or higher managers. One man pointed out that he was not allowed to have his own water boiler and had to buy his coffee in the hallway from a conglomerate-owned vending machine that charged more than coffee-vending machines on university campuses. Another claimed that his manager was reluctant to give a high evaluation to one of his subordinates out of fear that the subordinate would replace him. In several other instances as well, a man's failure to be promoted along with his cohorts was attributed to a manager's evaluation. None ever spoke of a manager as helpful or supportive of subordinates.

The young workers expressed their reluctance to accept the father-son analogy in a variety of ways. Almost no one openly challenged the alleged continuity, but rarely did they volunteer it either. Often their choice of words implied their resistance to this legitimation of managerial control. Whereas older managers spoke of the weekly meetings as "training," younger managers and *sawŏn* spoke of them as "getting a scolding" (*yadanŭl matda*). Most often, however, the subordinates resisted the company-family metaphor with a countermetaphor of their own: they portrayed the company in an almost endless variety of ways as analogous to the army (Janelli and Yim 1993, 225–28).

However much we might challenge the alleged Confucianism of top-down management, subordinates generally did not. Only one man attacked the father-manager analogy head on, contrasting the scolding of a father with that of a manager by focusing on the issue of benevolence: a father's scolding is given for the benefit of a son, he maintained, whereas a manager's scolding of a subordinate was not. Yet even this man, on other occasions, complained that the managerial style was Confucian; indeed, it was he who had muttered "Confucian ideology" in tones of disgust. Thus, employees generally accepted the interpretation of the managerial style as Confucian and decided they wanted nothing to do with this "Confucian" managerial style. In the village, by contrast, we had never heard anyone attack filial piety or Confucianism per se. Instead, different courses of action were debated in terms of how well they conformed to such norms.

Capitalism contributed to the genealogy of white-collar workers' and managers' practical knowledge of Confucianism in two ways. Not only did capitalism prompt the managers to advance a particular construction of Confucianism, but also capitalist industrialization in South Korea subjected increasing numbers of the population directly to that construction. Until a few decades ago, the majority of the South Korean population lived in rural villages and engaged in farming as their primary mode of subsistence; and the overwhelming majority of Taesŏng's white-collar workers or their parents had been born in rural towns and villages. What had been a critique of Confucianism limited to urban intellectuals had become widespread by 1986.

Of course, there is more than capitalism in the genealogy of this new popular understanding of Confucianism. Neither the owner-managers nor the white-collar workers originated the understanding of Confucianism as authoritarian, nor did the younger workers limit their criticism to the company where they worked. Many expressed strong antipathy to authoritarianism throughout South Korean society, especially in its political system. The blaming of Confucianism for authoritarianism in Korea seems to have first blossomed among urban intellectuals of the 1920s, who sought to accuse this ideology and other Korean cultural traditions of causing the nation's loss of sovereignty. Their views, perhaps influenced by similar trends emerging out of the May Fourth Movement in China, were later spread among the educated by Hyŏn Sangyun's influential work (1949; cited in Robinson 1991, 212).

Conclusions

As one of South Korea's largest conglomerates, Taesŏng is at the vanguard of South Korean capitalism. Yet its managerial and other white-collar personnel are hardly profit maximizers unconcerned with cultural ideals. Neither are they pure idealists, inattentive to their personal, corporate, or national interests.

Our exploration of individual choices, strategies, and representations in Taesŏng offices points to a variety of mutually supportive relationships between cultural understandings and the defense or pursuit of material gain. Ideas related to Confucianism informed choices of strategies for attaining political-economic goals, while perceptions of material well-being in turn helped to shape cultural meanings. A popular interpretation of Confucianism that stressed authority offered older managers a device to strengthen their control over subordinates, a control that the older managers considered as serving their own and their firm's material advantage. Their adoption of it helped to spread this idea even further. Similarly, the notion that profits ought to be pursued with due consideration for others and long-term relationships presented white-collar workers with a moral counterclaim for fending off the demands of contractual obligations. It also had consequences for pricing strategies and participation in world markets.

The mutual constitution of capitalism and Confucianism now appears to have extended beyond the arena of Eastern Asia. Though future developments will depend on a host of contingencies and yet unmade choices, the current worldwide trend toward placing greater emphasis on long-term customer relations is partly rooted in an awareness of marketing successes achieved by enterprises based in Eastern Asia. And it would be difficult to assert that such approaches to marketing are entirely unrelated to ideas largely cultivated in Eastern Asian about the importance of human relationships. Yet it could also be argued that part of the genealogy of this trend lies elsewhere. Evidently Adam Smith also was aware of the material benefits to be obtained from considering the needs of other parties when conducting business transactions:

> It is not from the benevolence of the butcher, the brewer, or the baker that we expect our dinner but from their regard for their own interests. We address ourselves not to their humanity but to their self-love, and we talk to them not of our own necessities but of their advantages. (1936, 56)

NOTES

1. For an economist's discussion of the difficulties of defining capitalism relative to South Korea's political economy, see Yoon 1989.

2. For an account of the research, see Janelli and Yim 1993.

3. For varying academic interpretations of Confucian influence on South Korean firms, see Shin 1984 and Choong Soon Kim 1992.

4. We are indebted to Donald Baker for aiding our understanding of this point. Any misconceptions, however, are our own.

5. A few persons, on occasion, maintained the opposite (Janelli and Yim 1993, 9).

6. Subordination to benevolent authority, Michael Robinson (1991, 218) suggests, is itself a Confucian theme.

7. George De Vos (1986, 365) has made a similar observation about child rearing in Japan.

8. Perhaps parents could have appealed to local understandings of filial piety to bolster their control by claiming that an act of disobedience would cause them distress, but managers at Taesŏng attempted to elicit obedience per se and gave no hint of feeling distress.

Confucian Values and Contemporary Economic Development in Korea

Tae-Kyu Park

South Korea's success in economic development through the thirty-year period from the early 1960s to the late 1980s has been embraced as a model for late-developing countries such as Vietnam and Indonesia. Today, however, the Korean economy faces serious problems in maintaining its growth rate in the face of a drastically changed economic environment. Economic development has also brought Korean society such undesirable phenomena as the concentration of wealth and discrepancies in development between urban and rural areas and between agricultural and nonagricultural sectors. Analyzing how Korea was able to achieve fast economic growth within a relatively short period of time is important for finding solutions to the current problems that deter continued economic growth.

Many economists studying the economic development of the Asian Dragons—Singapore, Taiwan, Hong Kong, and Korea—have sought to explain these countries' economic development from a cultural perspective, centering on the Confucianism[1] that is common to all four. In Korea, Confucianism formed the backbone of the spiritual and moral principles that regulated the traditional society and, to a great degree, has influenced modern society. Korean Confucianism emphasizes faith, loyalty, filial piety, harmony, and intellectualism as its primary virtues. With these virtues, the Confucian value system has provided a social ethic that the ruling class used to achieve political and social stability. Characteristic of this value system is the attitude of regarding members of the civilian bureaucracy as superior. Because of this spirit, the elite bureaucrat group, reared through education accessible only members of the upper class, enjoyed the role of ruling and enlightening the general public. By emphasizing the virtue of loyalty to monarch and filial piety to parents, the ruling class centralized political power and maintained social stability. Another aspect of the Confucian value system in Korea was intellectualism through education, for education was regarded as an important and necessary process producing the elite bureaucrats who ruled traditional Korean society. In addition to these elements, the Korean Confucian value system taught that human relationships should be formed and pursued through the family unit and guided by the cherished virtues of benevolence on the part of the family head, filial piety toward family seniors, and harmony among family members.

Believing that economic factors alone cannot explain the economic development process in Asian countries, this chapter will use the concept of the Confucian value system to identify the main factors of success and failure in Korea's economic development in contrast with Western countries. More specifically, this chapter evaluates the impact of traditional cultural values on economic development, focusing on how Confucian values have characterized the three economic institutions of Korean society—government, business, and labor—that have made leading contributions to Korea's economic development during the past thirty years. The analysis herein assumes that the developmental characteristics of the Korean economy can be found in the properties of the three institutions and in their interrelationships in the process of economic development.[2] This chapter also suggestions the limitations that the Confucian value system might pose for the Korean economy as it strives to maintain growth in newly developing social and economic environments.

Government, Bureaucrats, and Economic Development

The unprecedented growth of the Korean economy since the early 1960s is attributable to the three economic institutions: government, business, and labor. Of these three, the government has played the most active role in the economic development process, and its role has been judged to be very successful (Mason et al. 1980). The government began to be active in the economy with the first economic development plan, which was launched in 1961 by the military government after its coup and continued until the 1980s. In an attempt to gain the support of the Korean people, the military government paid close attention to economic prosperity. It prepared the first economic development plan to stimulate economic development in a society still poverty-stricken after Japanese colonialism and the civil war less than a decade earlier. Small-scale production capacity inherited from Japanese colonial days had been heavily destroyed during the civil war,[3] and at the time of the coup the Korean economy was dependent on foreign aid.

To facilitate the first economic development plan, the government established the Economic Planning Board (EPB), the governmental agency that was merged with the Ministry of Finance to become the Ministry of Finance and Economy in the 1994 reform of governmental organization and still controls the overall economic development planning process. This meant that government bureaucrats actively participated in the development process from the beginning. The role of the government and its bureaucrats in the development process was much greater than that in an ordinary market economy. During the first five-year economic development plan period, the Korean government became involved in a variety of national economy-related matters such as exit and entry to markets and control of wages and market prices, as well as basic economic policy formulation. Government leaders and bureaucrats initially lacked the knowledge and experience necessary for performing these roles in economic development, yet they were quickly able to acquire it and, despite errors made while learning, managed to play the central role during the first plan period. Lack of experience meant that bureaucrats were only able to plan and execute the first plan with the help of foreign experts, however. In the second five-year development plan period, experienced bureaucrats from the first plan could more successfully manage their roles with limited help from domestic and foreign experts. As bureaucrats learned from the first two five-year economic development plans, their experience increased the importance of their role and kept them in a central position in succeeding development plans.

During these early stages of economic development, the Park Chung-hee regime considered strong leadership by the central government as necessary for successful development and therefore entrusted decision-making powers to the bureaucrats under the auspices of the president himself. All important matters of economic policy, especially development, were made through discussions among high-ranking government officials at the Economic Ministers' Meeting or the informal Economic Ministers' Roundtable. Under the Park regime, a Monthly Trade Promotion Meeting, chaired by the president himself, worked to encourage exports, as that was considered the chief route to Korean economic growth. At such meetings, the president's prime concern was whether export targets were being met; if not, he blamed the authorities concerned. If exporters mentioned barriers, the president called for policies to eliminate them. Under the office of the prime minister, an Advisory Committee of University Professors was organized to meet with the president regularly to advise on economic policy. From this brain pool, the president filled cabinet posts and other important governmental positions.[4] The late President Park's character, educational background, and personal experiences affected his sense of the role of government and its relationship with business during the early period of economic development. His training in Japanese educational and military institutions and his service in the Japanese army until 1945 influenced him to think in Japanese ways about how to manage government policies, agencies, and the government-business relationship during the development period.

The upper bureaucrats who participated in economic decision making were able, by virtue of that participation, to maintain the status they had enjoyed under the Confucian value system. Having been central historically to politics in traditional Korean society on the strength of their education, they again used education to qualify for continuing membership in the highest social class. This education was not necessarily intended to contribute to improving the economic life of the people, but it did serve to qualify them to receive the respect they had had in traditional Confucian society. Even during the colonial period, only a small fraction of the Korean people had the access to higher education needed to become colonial government officials.[5] Their monopoly on education meant that the Rhee Syng-man regime, the first Republic established after Korea's independence from Japan, had no choice but to fill important government positions with those few highly educated and experienced bureaucrats who had worked for the Japanese during the colonial period, despite harsh criticism from nationalists.[6] The same bureaucrats continued to play major roles in economic development until the 1961 military coup and beyond.

After independence, under the strong influence of the United States, many young Koreans began to go abroad for study and to learn a Western style of rational thinking that was different from the thinking of mainstream government officials in the 1950s and 1960s. Why did these young Koreans want to join the government upon their return? Did they hope to become public administrators in order to join the upper class of modern Korean society as their ancestors had in traditional Confucian society? If they did, their decisions cannot be explained by the Confucian-value argument alone. Becoming a bureaucrat was still the best investment of human resources with a high rate of return, from both economic and sociopolitical points of view. These young, talented bureaucrats, by exercising influence on the private business sector and wielding policy-making power in their favor, could expect to receive financial and other benefits from their counterparts in private business.[7] Even after retiring, former bureaucrats were effectively guaranteed important positions in semigovernmental agencies or public enterprises. From an economic point of view, it was reasonable for families to invest their limited financial resources in their children's education in the hope that their children would become bureaucrats.[8]

Business and Labor in Economic Development

Emphasizing the role of government is not intended to undervalue the role of the business sector in Korean economic development. Following government

policy direction, private enterprise has been at the forefront of that development, directly and indirectly influencing the planning process. Enterprise prosperity may be taken as a reflection of Korea's economic development, for it has
been growing as the nation's economy grows. Right after taking power in 1961,
General Park was strongly antibusiness; he imprisoned owners of large business firms and confiscated their wealth based on the assumption that they
could only have accumulated it illegally. Later, however, in an effort to gain
political popularity with the Korean people, who had long suffered from economic hardship, Park had to seek cooperation from these same businessmen to
formulate and implement the first development plan. As long as a capitalist
economic system was to be maintained in Korea and economic "modernization" was the target, he had to accept the role of business firms and leaders in
the national economy. To gain the support of business leaders, the government
granted them immunity from criminal liability for past wrongdoings,
respected their property rights and ownership shares (with the exception of
commercial banks), and rewarded firms that participated in the development
of basic industries and contributed a share of ownership to the government
(Mason et al. 1980). As a result of these offers, business leaders began to participate actively in the government's development schemes.

In the early 1960s, Korean business consisted mainly of light industry producing only basic necessities. Most firms were founded during colonial days. At
the beginning of the Park era, firms were small scale, relatively short lived, and
family managed. Even though Korean firms have grown rapidly over the last
thirty years, they are still owned and managed by the founder and his family,
who had accumulated their industrial capital over a relatively short period of
time and were acquainted with Japanese-style management because of their
training in Japanese educational institutions. In traditional Korean society,
earning an income through business activities was little respected. It was ownership of productive capital in the form of land that distinguished the upper
class. During colonial days, the established upper class broke down and a new
merchant class emerged (Cho 1991), yet the newly established industrialists
were still accustomed to Confucian values even though they were operating in
a modernized economic environment. Business founders thus were accustomed to the Confucian value system in conducting business and formulating
management-labor relationships.

Korean business leaders were progovernment and maintained a familiar
and smooth relationship with government officials and influential politicians
of the ruling party who controlled economic decisions vital to their activities.
This is as true today and can be attributed to the continuing influence of Confucian values, including respect for bureaucrats. Business leaders educated
under the traditional value system but living in a modern industrial society

realized that maintaining a close relationship with government was the best way to survive and maintain maximum growth in a business environment that was still surrounded by traditional values. Under the government's development policy target of "growth first," which meant concentrating on quantity rather than quality, they were willing to enter into any profitable undertaking to encourage the growth of their businesses. As a result, Korean firms lacked business specialization and pursued management for quantity that had little consideration for customers' needs, creating an economy led by big business firms and groups that were under highly centralized family control.

The organizational culture of Korean business is shaped by three influences: Confucian values, large-scale family systems, and communal living. Together these characteristics have produced a patriarchal business environment in which business leaders adopt authoritarian methods to manage their business activities and their relationships with labor. Some argue that authoritarian styles of management have contributed to the achievement of growth targets by inducing employees to follow their employers' directions. Traditional Confucian values have contributed to a business culture in which more value is given to personal character than to efficiency or individual ability. The absolute patriarchal authority of owner-managers, which is modeled on kinship practices maintained throughout the transitional period from premodern to modern society, is supported by the values of hierarchy, deference to the collective, and personalism. In contrast to Western business culture, the authority of superiors in Korean business firms is not limited to the workplace but extends to personal matters.

As price advantage was Korea's main strategy in international trade, Korean businesses, which lacked sufficient capital formation, had to depend on low-cost labor to compete in foreign markets. The government helped business by structuring the labor market in such a way as to limit labor mobility (Shin 1993). For their part, business firms, well aware that they had to make efficient use of the abundant oversupply of labor to meet the government's "growth first" target, mobilized human resources by taking advantage of workers' traditional Confucian values such as self-sacrifice and job loyalty. The abundance of unskilled labor, a segmented labor market, and government suppression of labor unions limited labor's power to negotiate, obliging Korean workers to adapt themselves to the Korean business culture (Park 1987). By emphasizing personal ties and nurturing family spirit, firms were able to mobilize labor even under poor working conditions. The coercive industrialization policies of government gave firms no choice but to set wage levels much lower than the workers deserved but still demand high productivity, diligence, and loyalty. This development strategy was feasible only because firms had recourse to traditional social values. Thus, during the period of transition from traditional family-type to modern businesses, traditional social values helped Korean business firms form a unique business culture characterized by respect for authority, fidelity to the firm, and unity among workers.

The Confucian cultural inheritance meant that the authority and benevolence of a business leader could be anticipated on the basis of the authority and benevolence traditionally expected of the head of a family. Similarly, cultural expectations anticipated that employees would perform their jobs at the direction of their superiors without question or debate. The reliance on cultural values in the business environment has meant that Korea's economic success came about at the expense of workers, for workers could attain job security only by showing fidelity to their firms and devotion to their employers, which in turn further strengthened the patriarchal business culture.[9] Confucian values governing husband-wife relations also contributed to the ability of the breadwinning husband to devote himself to his work and comply with the demands of an exacting employer. It may be argued that traditional family values enabled employees to adapt to the demands of business without inciting serious conflict among family members or with their business organizations. At the same time, the cultural ideal of the traditional family was appropriated as a model for regulating workers' attitudes toward their employers. Fidelity and filial piety, transcribed from the family to the firm, strengthened vertical organization. Without this business culture, Korean firms could not have contributed as they did to government-led economic development. The Korean business sector has thus formed a "Confucian capitalism" by combining Confucian values with a capitalistic economic framework.

Along with the strong influence of Confucian values, the quality of human resources in Korea has been cited as an important explanatory factor in its economic development. Korea's national educational system, which grew quickly, efficiently, and within contained costs, was allegedly able to produce a productive and disciplined labor force. Before Korea had achieved economic development, the government could not afford the burden of high educational costs. Educational development was achieved instead by relying on households themselves to make financial sacrifices to see their children educated. Almost two-thirds of the cost of education was covered in this way. This method was the only way to introduce a modern educational system at low cost to the government.[10] It was not their financial ability, but their long-standing understanding of the positive benefits of education, that induced families to bear heavy costs of education.[11] But the creation of a system of mass education meant that there were difficulties in achieving quality.[12] The incentive for investment in education has resulted in a tendency to value a diploma more than the quality or substance of education, resulting sometimes in overinvestment in children's education. Despite such criticisms of the Korean educational system, it cannot be denied that the strong emphasis on education and willingness to bear its cost have contributed much to making it possible for the Korean economy to achieve fast growth through a labor-intensive strategy.

The Government-Business Relationship and Economic Development

Government and business have played the leading roles in economic development, but this development has been achieved at the expense of Korean workers, who have taken a passive rather than active role in the process. It is important to consider the relationship between government and business not only to gain an accurate understanding of factors influencing Korean economic development but, more importantly, to help understand the economy's growth in the future.

Government and business relate vertically rather than horizontally (Shin 1993; Lee Kwang-kyu 1993). President Park's authoritarian approach to economic development meant relying on the comparative advantage of low labor costs to industrialize through foreign trade. The government adopted an "unbalanced development strategy," selecting strategic industries for top priority and relying on them to drive national development. The business sector had to accept and follow this policy. How should we evaluate the leader-follower relationship of government and business? Why did this relationship between them come into being?

The relationship between government and business, which allowed for efficient resource allocation and produced successful consequences, must also be traced to the Confucian value system with its respect for bureaucrats. The brightest manpower was eager to work for the government and thus joined the policy-making process. By contrast, the private sector lacked the qualifications needed to deal with modern economic matters, nor was it developed enough to challenge the traditional government-business relationship. Furthermore, the government at the early stages of economic development was dependent on military power; the business sector realized that complying with government directions was necessary to survive and keep its businesses intact.

Although the government-business relationship may be understood in relation to Confucian values, it was not sustained only by cultural means; nor, for that matter, can its cultural basis guarantee that the verticality between government and business will continue much longer. In fact, the Korean government has had recourse to means other than cultural values, notably economic incentives and disincentives. In order effectively to maintain a vertical relationship with business, the government created policies to favor business, notably by limiting workers' rights to organize and negotiate and thus keep wages low. The government also allocated scarce resources favorably, and at more favorable interest rates, to companies that complied with its policies, thus creating an economic incentive for business compliance. Advancing into the areas selected by the government as strategic industries and achieving targets set by the government enabled businesses to obtain scarce raw materials and financial resources at a time when the national economy lacked productive resources other than unskilled labor. The extent of the powers the government arrogated to itself to guide the economy meant additionally that it could favor compliant firms through tax policy, limits on exit and entry into certain industries, and the conferral of monopolistic or oligopolistic power. At the same time, the government did not hesitate to punish or intimidate firms or business leaders through special tax audits, disruptions of special financial resources, and surveillance of business by its intelligence agency. Only those companies that followed policy and maintained close relationships with the government could succeed in business; those that did not follow this policy perished. The government also skewed the environment for business by monopolizing all important business information, such that firms with early access to this information could make excessive economic profits at the expense of competitors (Kang 1987). This pattern in the relationship between government and business has brought about the concentration of economic power that threatens the Korean economy today and has to be resolved for the economy to advance.

The Role of Confucian Values and Their Limitations on Korea's Economic Development

The success of Korea's economic development has been due to three factors. First of all, the government formulated a specific development plan to mobilize all strategies that would enable the business sector to achieve its economic goals. Authoritarian control and the involvement of talented policy-making bureaucrats helped significantly to achieve those goals efficiently within the targeted period of time. Second, business leaders were able to meet government targets by helping their businesses grow as fast as the national economy, which they did by relying on a patriarchal business culture. Last, despite limited financial ability, the Korean people themselves paid for the human resource development that education provided. Accordingly, I regard Confucianism as having contributed to Korea's economic development through its influence on the three economic institutions of government, business, and labor and their inter-relationships.

Yet Korea's success cannot be attributed in a simple fashion to the cultural factor alone. Rather, it may be more accurate to say that the three economic institutions that have had the major roles in the development process have made use not of Confucianism but of the system of traditional values governing society, which were formed under the strong influence of Confucianism. The three institutions exploited the social environment that Confucianism has patterned in Korea. It is now being argued, moreover, that the structure of economic institutions in Korea and their reliance on the traditional system of social values are no longer adequate to the more complex economic situation at present and will not be able to sustain economic growth under the current economic and social environment. Confucian values may have exerted a positive influence in the past, yet the recent dramatic growth of the Korean economy has resulted in the weakening of the traditional value system that supported Korean society for so long a time.

As the economy grows, Korean society faces social and economic problems that have arisen as by-products of development. The government's intervention in the market economy, ranging from selective resource allocation down to interference in the internal business activities of individual firms, has resulted in business growth through oligopoly rather than competitiveness based on technological innovation and cost reduction. The "growth first, income distribution later" policy has meant that firms have competed in export markets mainly on the basis of price, by producing low-technology commodities, and have done so at the expense of labor. This was possible in a Confucian-influenced social environment and in the days when economic prosperity was the first aim. But, as economic development advances, people's perceptions of society and the economic system have changed and their expectations of both have increased. Labor union activism since 1988 has encouraged workers to regard as unendurable the conditions under which they worked during the quantity-oriented phase of economic development and to ask for their economic share and decent working conditions. We can no longer expect low wages and labor suppression to maintain economic competitiveness and growth, especially now that late-developing countries are encroaching on Korea's export market.

But Korean firms do not possess the ability to develop the technology required to produce high-technology, high-price products largely because their organizational structure does not allow for the creativity needed to meet the challenges of a changing environment. Within business firms, owner-managers are no longer able to control management efficiently by relying on patriarchal authority. The top-to-bottom, unidirectional management style is not making efficient use of resources nor creating innovative ideas for business activity. Furthermore, employees of the younger generation, who are not so strongly influenced by traditional values, no longer regard this management style as acceptable. Unless firms can meet the demands for decent working conditions, wages appropriate to production levels, and consumer satisfaction, they cannot survive or compete with competition from abroad now that the old monopolistic-oligopolistic conditions are gone.

The Korean government can no longer manage the sizable and complex national economy in opening markets in competition with foreign countries. Government intervention in the business sector no longer contributes to the efficient management of the national economy but instead reduces the efficiency and competitiveness of the business sector, and consequently it has become a major barrier to the growth both of the national economy and the business sector. Regulations initiated when the economy was small and the business sector underdeveloped have become anachronistic. Furthermore, the private sector is obtaining high-quality human resources equal to those of the government. Thus, social conditions and the private sector's awareness of the new climate will not allow government to play the same role as before, even though the tendency still exists among some bureaucrats to maintain traditional values. But the system of Confucian values that honors the government and those who serve it is no longer persuasive.

Furthermore, in education, the traditional teacher-student relationship has been weakened considerably. The previous emphasis on rote learning was successful in getting students to digest a large amount of knowledge within a short period of time, but it is now failing to foster the sort of creative and original thinking demanded for the production of high-technology commodities and the efficient and innovative management of business. To cope with the new world of high technology, information, and globalization, the educational system must produce human resources with creative abilities through quality education and innovative educational methods. In this renovation, Confucian values may prove to have no role.

NOTES

1. Confucianism is difficult to define in a word because of the many different interpretations attached to it. Confucian values regard benevolence, justice, ceremony, knowledge, and faith to be the most important virtues in the attempt to find a form of

order for people in accord with the order perceived in nature. Korea, Japan, and China have common factors in their Confucianisms, but each has maintained a different version of Confucian values (Morishima 1982; Redding 1990).

2. On the contributions of the three institutions of the Korean economy to successful economic development during the past thirty years, see Mason et al.1980; Song 1981; and *The Economist* March 1979. These analyses emphasize the importance of Confucian values in shaping the institutions and the relationships among them.

3. During the first two civil war years of 1950 and 1951, Korea's GNP declined by 15.1 percent and 6.1 percent respectively due to the destruction of production capacity (Kwon 1991).

4. Some maintain that Park's military government contributed to the success of economic development because the military was the first group in Korean society to be exposed to Western-style education. It would be more accurate to say that Park, as a strong leader, devoted himself to economic development in collaboration with the established elite bureaucrat group. Bureaucrats rather than the military played the central role in economic development.

5. In 1945, when Korea regained her independence from Japan, only 7,817 students were enrolled at higher-educational institutions, including two-year colleges.

6. During the twelve years of the first Republic led by President Rhee, more than forty of the highest administrative positions, including prime minister and minister, were filled by elite bureaucrats who had worked and cooperated with the colonial government during the Japanese occupation period (Lim Chong-Luk 1991).

7. The strong connection between bureaucrat and business has been pointed out as a major factor deterring the continued development of Korean society as well as the economy. This connection is said to be a major source of government corruption, which goes against the Confucian emphasis on the moral role of government.

8. Even in the 1990s, higher-education institutions are evaluated mainly on the basis of how successfully their graduates advance into higher government positions.

9. The average work week of Korean manufacturing workers was more than fifty-five hours in the 1960s and more than fifty hours in the 1970s, longer than the work week of any other newly industrialized country (Park 1987). The frequency rate of industrial accidents was over twenty accidents per million hours in the 1960s and over fifteen in the 1970s.

10. It should also be pointed out that large-scale American aid for investment in educational facilities made public education widely available.

11. In 1984, Korea spent 3.4 percent of GNP on education, which is not high by international standards. On the other hand, average household expenditure on education was more than 5 percent, which shows that the burden of education on the family is much higher than in most developing or developed countries.

12. Student-teacher ratios even in the mid-1980s were high in comparison with those of developed countries and even with those of many developing countries. As of 1985, the ratio for primary school was 42:1, for secondary school 35:1, and for college 36:1.

Business Linkages and Chinese Entrepreneurs in Southeast Asia

Farid Harianto

As the newly industrialized and emerging economies of Eastern Asia boom, some of the world's fastest growing business groups have emerged there. A new generation of billion-dollar companies are now to be found everywhere in the region. The striking, recognizable, common denominator among them is the ethnic identity of the owner-entrepreneurs behind these companies; they are almost entirely overseas Chinese.[1]

The dominance of overseas Chinese in local economies has been widely analyzed and speculated on elsewhere (see, e.g., Redding 1990; Harianto 1993; and, for a critical survey, Mackie 1992b). The role of overseas Chinese businesses can be gauged by the statistics of outward foreign direct investments (FDI) from the region. Since the mid-1980s, Taiwan, Hong Kong, China, and Singapore—apart from Japan and South Korea—have become the major players in Asia in terms of their outflows of foreign direct investment, with each cumulative stock of outward FDI ranging from U.S.$3.3 billion to U.S.$19.4 billion. Thailand and Malaysia are next with about U.S.$800 million and U.S.$570 million, respectively. As of 1991, the aggregate stock of foreign investment in the ASEAN economies from Taiwan (17.6 percent) surpassed that of the European Community (14.2 percent) and the United States (6.7 percent). Although such investments are understandably induced by the need to cope with rising labor costs and exchange rates, one can also see them as an indicator of the ever increasing prominence of overseas Chinese in the region.

This chapter surveys Chinese entrepreneurs in the region and attempts to describe various business linkages as the key ingredients of their success. Although using studies from Thailand and Indonesia to illustrate some of the points, it will also touch upon the general features of overseas Chinese entre-preneurs in Southeast Asia. The chapter will start with a succinct survey of three perspectives on business linkages: cultural-historical, economic, and political-economic. Besides the business-government linkages, three particular linkages (family and intrafirm, interfamily and intersectoral, and foreign) are further elaborated to show their interplay in promoting capital accumulation and business acumen among the overseas Chinese. The survey is not meant to be exhaustive. The three perspectives outlined here, nevertheless, do represent the dominant contemporary debate about the origin and nature of overseas Chinese entrepreneurs.

Perspectives on Business Linkages

The prevailing hazard in explaining the success of overseas Chinese businesses is to attribute the root of their success to one predominant set of ideas embed-ded in their traditional value systems, which go under the convenient label of "Confucianism" or "neo-Confucianism." This *cultural-historical argument*, fol-lowing the Weberian thesis, can be succinctly summarized as follows: "no capi-talist development without entrepreneurial class, no entrepreneurial class with-out moral charter, and no moral charter without religious premises" (Poggi 1983, 83; quoted in Redding 1990, 8). Confucianism becomes handy in supply-ing the religious premises necessary for the development of Chinese entrepre-neurs. However, if indeed neo-Confucianism is the moral charter that provides the foundation for overseas Chinese entrepreneurs, why then did they emerge as world-class capitalists only a few decades ago rather than much earlier in the long history of Confucianism? Why has this group been manifest in Southeast Asia but not in mainland China—or not in Australia or North America, where the history of their immigration is almost as old as their sojourn to Southeast Asia? Suffice it to say that cultural heritage has a certain role and importance but is not the only one. It is a necessary but insufficient condition. Further analyses are needed, particularly on the economic and structural conditions that enabled such latent entrepreneurship to blossom.

Historically, Chinese traders were known as victims of ruthless rulers—both in their own homeland and in their adopted countries. China was ruled for most of its history by a patrimonial bureaucracy, consisting of mandarins representing the personal power of the emperor. The influence of the man-darins was exercised through taxes, licensing fees, and travel and trade restric-tions. Civil laws, if ever codified, were subject to the interpretation of the man-darins, and traders were at the mercy of the system. In tandem with the inaccessibility of political power, these factors put the Chinese businessmen in a very difficult, if not overtly hostile, environment. In their adopted lands, Chinese have often been excluded from many more desirable statuses. In the pre- and postwar period of the 1940s, overseas Chinese in the region still experienced harsh treatment from the governments there (see, e.g., Purcell 1965 for a good account of the history of overseas Chinese in the region). Such hostile environments forced the Chinese to rely on their resources and culture: they developed a strong bond and cohesiveness among themselves, worked harder, and accumulated capital patiently. Interestingly, this line of argument has also been applied to other communities such as the Jewish in Europe and other marginal trading minorities (e.g., Hagen 1968). Such an internal cohesion also brought with it wariness toward outsiders and a need to co-opt the powerful ones. Trust—or distrust—and personal networks, in essence, became necessary for survival.

The emergence of this ethnic network provided a competitive edge for the overseas Chinese businessmen vis-à-vis their indigenous counterparts and hence a basis for capital accumulation and business expansion. At this juncture, the emergence of overseas Chinese networks will be more meaningful if it is examined within an *economic perspective,* which frames networks as an alternative to market institutions.

The standard neoclassical perspective on business linkages assumes that latent entrepreneurs are randomly distributed in an economy and their rise is dependent only on the price signal of the market. As an economy advances, household income increases and so does the demand for income-elastic goods and services, which in turn stimulates latent entrepreneurs to supply such goods and the whole arrays of their derived demand (i.e., backward linkages). Price signal, in this view, is sufficient for activating market coordination and, more importantly, entrepreneurial endeavor. In a competitive market—characterized by a large number of suppliers and buyers, relatively free entry and exit, and costless information—there is no need to bypass the market and create supplementary linkages (i.e., "extramarket linkages") among economic agents. Certainly such a caricature does not fit nicely with the real world. Entrepreneurs are not randomly distributed, and certain groups in the society, such as overseas Chinese, Jews, and Armenians, are more entrepreneurial than others. Also, the costs of transactions can be substantial, as certain information is neither free nor readily available. Writing a formal contract under conditions of uncertainty and opportunism can be prohibitive; there is no way that all parties can stipulate all contingencies to curtail opportunistic behavior. In a developing economy, the problems of uncertainty and opportunism can be particularly severe.

Continuing relationships or business linkages can serve to replace legal contracts in promoting cooperative behavior. Business relationships may exhibit a feature of what is called the "prisoner's dilemma": the pursuit of immediate gain by one party can harm everybody. Repeated interactions, fortunately, allow all parties to escape this dilemma. Anticipation of future benefits, appropriately appraised, prevents a party from pursuing short-term gain by squeezing all profit out of its transacting partner or from outright cheating. Arguably, the Japanese production structure with its complex extra-market exchanges (e.g., subcontracting schemes) is often quoted as an example of the benefits gained from ongoing, long-term, trading relations: "goodwill" and the "give and take" tradition work effectively to temper the pursuit of self-interest and short-term gain (Dore 1983).

Looking at Southeast Asia, there are two significant and interrelated characteristics of the economies: the prevalence of market failures and the central role of government in economic and business affairs. The infrastructure and institutions to support markets were, and in many cases still are, at their primitive stage of development. Prices of products and commodities are hard to appraise, and, if known, arbitraging is also difficult because of the costs and difficulties of transporting goods. It is under such structural conditions that the Chinese commercial organization—with extensive networks and access to information and capital—becomes very fitting. It is no accident that Chinese businessmen become effective intermediaries in local economies. Later, Chinese intermediation would expand from retailing to wholesaling and then to importing foreign goods. As they developed links between their urban bases and rural areas, it became only natural for them to gravitate into the other intermediary field, banking. A prominent Sino-Indonesian businessman put it aptly: "My whole business is basically . . . intermediating between places [i.e., trading] and time [i.e., banking]."

Economically speaking, the market and information imperfections prevailing in the region engender nontrivial transaction costs. Information search (e.g., finding reliable suppliers, assessing creditworthiness, and locating potential partners) is costly. Monitoring and reinforcing contracts are very difficult and expensive. The Chinese commercial network, in this regard, has been able to supplant the functioning of the (imperfect) markets and internalize the economic exchanges. Such an internalization of economic exchanges is made possible as access to information—about price, the source of traded goods, and the track records of individual transacting partners—is readily made available through the network. So are access to capital and the discipline mechanism for cheaters. Breach of contract, if it occurs, is solved through communal punishment rather than deliberation in courtrooms. Economic exchanges, as a result, are more efficiently done through the networks. It should be noted, as argued in the next section, that the networks are a more efficient alternative for coordinating economic exchanges, due not only to market failure but to hierarchical or organizational failure as well.

Apart from their networks, Chinese traders have been found for decades practicing a "low margin, high turnover" scheme for their operations, and they are very stringent in terms of controlling their cash flows (see Hicks and Redding 1982; see Limlingan 1986 for a fuller exposition). They also carefully build their reputations as reliable, trustworthy, low-cost suppliers and intermediaries. In essence, it is the efficient functioning of the Chinese business network, in tandem with the rock-bottom approach to trading, that has been very effective under the region's structural conditions. This combination set the initial basis for Chinese business expansion. At this point, the second characteristic of the region, the deep involvement of government in economic development, provided an opportunity for Chinese businesses to rapidly accumulate capital. This brings us to the third view of business linkages, the *political-economic perspective*.

Our discussion on the topic of government-business linkages will focus on Indonesia, although some parallels can be drawn for other countries in the region. As recently as 1973, Indonesia was perhaps the least industrialized among the large developing countries. Its share of non-oil manufacturing in GDP, at 9 percent, was the second smallest, and its manufacturing value added per capita (about U.S.$10) was the second lowest in East and Southeast Asian countries, only slightly ahead of Burma (McCawley 1981). Since then, however, industrialization has taken place very rapidly. Indonesia's industrial development can be categorized into four distinct phases (Hill 1992): (1) stabilization and recovery, 1966–73; (2) the oil boom, 1973–81; (3) retrenchment, 1981–85; and (4) deregulation and outward-looking reorientation, post–1986.

During the stabilization and recovery period of 1966–73, the focus of economic policy was to stabilize the macroeconomy as a countermeasure to the excesses of the previous regime (the Sukarno era). This macroeconomic policy has since become the hallmark of Indonesia's economic development, while the micropolicy (trade and industrial) could swing from liberal in the late 1960s to protectionist (import substitution) during the oil boom, and swing back to export-oriented since the mid-1980s. The 1973-74 oil boom resulted in a sharp increase in incomes and domestic demand, whereas the government pursued policies and interventions to accelerate the scope and speed of industrial development. Sizable investments in capital-intensive, resource-dependent industries (e.g., oil refining, liquified natural gas, petrochemicals, and fertilizers) were embarked upon by the government. A massive injection of subsidized capital to private firms was made possible by the revenue from the oil boom. In the retrenchment period of 1981–85, the Indonesian economy experienced strong growth but with an increasing concern over external imbalances (as evident in difficulties in its balance of payments) and the fragility of growth based on a single, volatile oil sector. In this phase, it was clear that Indonesia needed to diversify its economy away from such a dependency, leading to a rethinking of the inward-looking, protectionist industrial policy after the oil boom. The last phase of industrialization, deregulation and outward-looking reorientation, has been characterized by continued sensible macroeconomic management (steady exchange rates, inflation coming under control) as well as the introduction of a series of reform packages that have increased export incentives, eased investment licensing requirements, significantly reduced tariff and nontariff distortions, and promoted the efficiency of private sectors through international competition.

It was no coincidence that Sino-Indonesian entrepreneurs were blossoming during the second phase of Indonesia's industrial development, the oil boom period. As a natural corollary to the import-substitution regime in that period, three items became the centerpiece of Indonesian trade and industrial policy: tariff and nontariff protection, a complex system of investment approval and licensing, and the deletion program. These interrelated regimes gave rise to a high-cost economy along the following lines (from Lewis 1994, 7):

1. Certain Indonesian firm(s), often in collaboration with foreign partner(s), would identify a new activity in which profitable investment might occur.
2. These firms would then approach the Investment Licensing Board (BKPM) with the proposed project, taking pains to ensure that once there were definite plans to build sufficient domestic capacity, the activity would be declared "closed" to further investment and removed from the "Investment Priority List."
3. In the meantime, the firms would lobby for protection for imports and often managed to obtain a mixture of tariff and surcharge protection along with quantitative restrictions that provided them with the sole authority to import the competing goods.
4. Once the domestic facilities were up and running and had sufficient capacity to supply the domestic market, they would petition again for the tariff protection to be converted into an outright ban in the name of "industrial self-sufficiency."

The deletion program worked along the same lines. In a typical sector (e.g., specific machinery or electrical equipment), the Ministry of Industry would draw up a schedule for the deletion of its various parts/components and then specify a high tariff, or outright ban, to enforce the deletion. The argument for such a program was to steadily increase domestic content by nurturing domestic suppliers. The closure of the investment sector from both domestic and foreign competition, however, resulted only in the emergence of very inefficient, oligopolistic domestic industries. Clearly, once the government has erected protection from foreign (through prohibitive tariff and nontariff barriers) and domestic (through investment restrictions) competition, then powerful vested interests are created with a strong stake in ensuring that such protective measures remain in place. In essence, protectionist policies are easy to introduce but hard to eliminate. Cutting down or eliminating the protection requires strong political will and ample resources.

During the oil boom period, the government was also involved directly in various sectors of the economy; some of these activities were carried out by state enterprises and some were channeled through state monopolies such as the National Logistics Board (Badan Uruson Logistik or BULOG) which handled the local purchase, import, and distribution of basic food commodities. BULOG, as did the state oil company Pertamina, played a critical role in promoting a domestic capitalist class, particularly Sino-Indonesian, by way of granting monopolies to them. Not surprisingly, BULOG has been deeply penetrated by Chinese businessmen as recipients of such monopoly power. It should be noted, nevertheless, that similar patterns also emerged in Thailand and the Philippines, where the Chinese carefully built their networks with the government and military rulers and grew their businesses from there (see Robinson 1986; and Yoshihara 1988). Although there were no apparent discriminatory measures against indigenous businessmen, if not the contrary, it is interesting to observe that Sino-Indonesian businessmen were the ones who were most ready to take full advantage of such a protectionist regime. The victims, of course, were the domestic users of these goods who had no alternative but to buy high-cost and often inferior domestic products.

In all fairness, the Chinese are not singularly to blame. During the independence struggle, Chinese traders actively supplied the Indonesian army in Central Java with food, clothing, and supplies. In North Sumatra, the local government once prohibited the Chinese from trading, and yet consumers preferred to deal with the Chinese rather than with the retailers of their own ethnic group (for price and reliability), and soon the rule was forgotten. Similarly, in Malaysia, Thailand, and the Philippines, Chinese businesses blossomed despite the various discriminations they encountered. As noted previously, it is the way they conducted their businesses—above and beyond the government favor they enjoyed through their carefully built networks—that led them to be valued by their consumers. It is only fair to say that their access to government connections was also earned through their reputation and consistency in doing business.

The Nature of Linkages

Four types of linkage are crucial for the development of overseas Chinese businesses: government-business, family and intrafirm, interfamily and inter-sectoral, and foreign and technological. The first type of linkage, the government-business links, was elaborated in the previous section and will not be repeated here.

The industrial structure of Chinese businesses is strongly characterized by their *family and intrafirm linkages*. A typical Chinese business can reasonably be represented by the following characteristics (Redding 1990; see also Heng in this volume): (1) a close overlap of ownership, control, and family; (2) a paternalistic organizational climate with centralized decision making and overreliance upon one dominant entrepreneur cum executive; (3) relatively simple organizational structuring with an identifiable "inner circle" around the entrepreneur, consisting of a small number of entrusted family members and personal friends; (4) external links to suppliers, distributors/buyers, financial providers, and others through personalistic networks; and (5) an overriding concern over costs and financial matters.

At a glance, it may appear that such characteristics are not unique to the Chinese but are commonly shared by traditional family businesses in many parts of the world. Nevertheless, the nature of Chinese society, where trust and personal networks are a necessity for survival, strongly accentuates hierarchy and personalism as everyday facts of life in Chinese businesses. The "inner circle" personnel provide stability for the whole organization; it oversees "old retainers" in certain positions—the cashier, chief accountant, plant manager, sales manager, and even mundane jobs such as personal driver and security guards. This entrenched network within the organization gives the top executive access to information on "what is going on, how people feel, and what to watch out for" (Redding 1990, 209). This also provides a sense of security to both sides. For members of the inner circle, the secure feeling comes from the recognition that the top man will personally take care of them (e.g., annual bonus of nine to twelve months' salary, family-related protection, unexpected gratuities, and the like are common practices). For the top man, this arrangement provides an "extra mile" of resources to fall back upon: when special labor or sacrifice is needed, there is always somebody on whom to rely.

In many cases, overseas Chinese entrepreneurs also employ their personal network outside the firm—notably family members, relatives, and friends— to function as their private eyes, giving them feedback about the behavior of their own organizational members and an outsider's perspective about what is happening within the firm in general. This brings a very significant insight about the structure of overseas Chinese businesses: their ethnic network thrives not only as a result of the prevalent market failures in the region but also because of organizational or hierarchical failures within their own family businesses. In essence, networks become an efficient coordinating mechanism to supplant *both* market mechanism and hierarchy.

The benefits and costs of such internal linkages and cohesion are manifold. The whole organization can be very flexible: the simple decision-making process within the firm allows it to adapt quickly and smoothly to new situations and emerging opportunities. In Indonesia and other parts of the region, this flexibility is reflected in the growth of firms, which expand horizontally as easy as vertically. In line with that, the core people and the entrenched network within the firm allow the personal vision of the top man to be operationalized and implemented rather smoothly. The danger is that the firms can be locked into "tunnel vision" and are not open to creative tension and debates on key issues such as the future of the firm. In addition, the flexibility of the system also brings with it the danger of the firm's taking a nonrational, opportunistic expansion path. The collapse of the Summa Group of Indonesia (owned by the second son of tycoon William Suryajaya—the owner of Astra Group, the second largest industrial firm in Indonesia) in 1992 and of the empire of Sir Kenneth Fung of Hong Kong in 1987—both because of opportunistic overexpansion—are cases in point. Interestingly, in both cases, the father-founders of the firms "saved" their billion-dollar empires through their reputations and personal networks in the region. This brings us to the second type of network, *interfamily linkages,* which usually run across business sectors.

The internal structure of the firm—shaped by personal trust and suspicion toward outsiders—inherently limits the size of the organization. The complex structure of a large bureaucracy is foreign, and complex integration is avoided as much as possible. When the business grows, the organization subdivides into a federation of small units of organization. Each unit usually has its own products and markets; the units also develop their own external linkages, capitalizing on the existing linkages of the parent firm as much as possible. These various units are coordinated largely through the trusted personnel assigned to head each unit. Control and coordination across sectors are thus achieved through a web of personal networks.

It has been alluded to earlier that many economic transactions with other agents (suppliers, distributors, labor) are carried out through extramarket exchanges. The Chinese have been able to internalize economic transactions through their personal networks, and such transactions are efficient under conditions of market imperfection. Rather than relying on an army of lawyers and accountants or third-party opinions, Chinese businessmen make deals through a handshake, a telephone call, or over a cup of tea. Contracts often are represented by illegible handwriting on a corner of newspaper. Breach of contract, if it occurs, is effectively handled through communal punishment.

A random inspection of the structure of public companies in the region[2] will show how pervasive the interfirm linkages are, through both ownership interests and interlocking directorships. Joint ventures—as a special form of linkage involving equity participation—are often motivated by the desire to share risks associated with an investment project. Many large-scale property projects in Southeast Asia and China, for example, are embarked upon through a joint venture of the leading Chinese firms in the region. Certainly, such an approach is hardly unique to Chinese.

A typical case of intersectoral, inter-Chinese family linkage is the Bangkok Bank of Thailand. Its founder, Chin Sophonpanich, has been credited as a successful banker catering to Sino-Thai merchants. Through his personal network, the bank grew rapidly, tapping foreign capital, particularly from Hong Kong, for domestic loan distribution. In the process, Chin also helped his friends and relatives to obtain credit, often acting as personal guarantor. In return, many of those relatives and friends asked Chin to take an interest in their businesses. These mutual trust relationships resulted in the Sophonpanich family holding hundreds of diverse business interests. This model of interlinkages, awarding equity interest to the patron, is quite common in Chinese business practice.

The personal network of Chinese businessmen provides not only an efficient means of carrying out economic transactions, particularly under conditions of severe market imperfections, but also a means of conveying information about new business opportunities. As we will discuss shortly, this results in one dominant pattern of opportunistic expansion of the Chinese firms in the region.

The growth of Chinese businesses has also been facilitated by another type of network, *foreign and technological linkages.* In general, as industrialization in the Southeast Asian economies advances, there has been a common tendency toward economic liberalization. Domestic firms are more and more exposed to international competition. Under such pressure, the domestic firms face the challenge not only of becoming internationally efficient and competitive but also of mastering all phases of production activities (R&D, design and engineering, manufacturing and distribution). Traditionally, domestic firms possessed comparative advantage based on their country's factor endowment, notably unskilled and skilled labor, and natural resources. One thus naturally finds that Southeast Asian domestic firms tend to be strong in manufacturing (particularly labor-intensive assembly) and local distribution but weak in terms of R&D and design and engineering. It is imperative, then, for these firms to attempt to compensate for their weaknesses in technological capabilities by linking themselves to foreign firms that possess the technology.

Multinational companies have long seen the potential of the region as a production platform for reexport markets and, more importantly, as one of the fastest growing markets in the world. These firms, however, face enormous barriers to entering the region: an alien regulatory environment, cultural distance, and unfamiliar business practices. Joint venturing with local firms, therefore, has become the logical choice for expansion into the region. Nynex of the United States was able to win a multibillion dollar contract in Thailand through its local partner, Charoen-Pokphand, largely known as an agro-based conglomerate. Procter & Gamble tried for three years to set up a manufacturing operation in China to no avail until they teamed up with Hong Kong financier Li Ka-Shing. So did Motorola, Lockheed and MTV. Texas Instruments has long entrusted its computer chip production to partners in Singapore and Taiwan. In the early 1970s, when the Japanese multinationals were looking for local partners, they preferred to deal with Chinese businessmen; almost all Japanese joint ventures in Singapore and Malaysia were with local Chinese, and about 90 percent of Japanese joint ventures in Indonesia and Thailand were made through Chinese middlemen (*The Economist*, 1 June 1974).

One estimate indicates that between 1985 and 1988, 40 percent of the arm's length alliances reported in the mass media between Japanese and East Asian firms took the form of technological agreements. Current statistics show that East Asian firms are indeed a large user of Japanese technology. In 1990, these technological linkages represented 44 percent of the Japanese firms' total number of technological exchanges in the world and about 40 percent of their total value. Among the ASEAN countries, Indonesia and Thailand are the largest recipients of Japanese technologies.

Almost all leading companies in Indonesia have developed technological linkages with foreign firms. The Sinar Mas Group of Indonesia (Tachiki 1993) provides a typical case of how domestic firms expand their businesses, both domestically and internationally, through alliances with foreign firms and technologies. Founded about fifty years ago, it started business in coffee and rubber plantations and as a biscuit maker; it has now become the largest pulp and paper manufacturer in Indonesia, commanding about 60 percent of the domestic market. Its three listed subsidiaries were capitalized at about U.S.$3 billion in 1993, making Sinar Mas as one of the top three private companies in

Indonesia (after Salim Group and Astra Group). Using Indonesia's vast forestry resources, the firm built its technological capability through technical agreements with Chung Hwa Pulp and Paper (Taiwan), Yuen Foong Yue Paper (Taiwan), and Hokuetsu Pulp and Paper (Japan). In addition, the two Taiwanese firms also took equity interests (23 percent and 10 percent each) in one of the subsidiaries specializing in writing and printing paper. This equity participation, in tandem with the exchange of high-ranking personnel, reflects the high degree of commitment of the two partners in the venture.

The company runs integrated pulp and paper production plants in Java and Riau. Its paper plant in Riau, which was constructed by Mitsubishi Heavy Industries of Japan in 1990, became the largest plant in Asia, with an installed capacity of 200,000 tons per year. It also built its own port facility in Riau as a distributing point for its thirty sales offices around the world. The basic elements of Sinar Mas's strategy can be summarized as: capitalizing on Indonesia's abundant natural resources and cheap labor, exploiting economies of scale and vertical integration, developing a domestic distribution network, and building technology through foreign linkages. In the early 1990s, the firm also started to expand into new products (downstream, higher value added paper products) and a new market (China). The China venture is to produce quality paper using pulp imported from its Riau plant. The firm bought a Chinese plant in Ningbo and refurbished it. Interestingly, with a small modification based on its experience in Indonesia, the firm has been able to increase the Chinese plant's productivity very dramatically. This represents a typical example of many firms from developing countries that have been able to develop low-cost products and specific production processes or technologies to suit local inputs and conditions. Given the opportunity, firms like Sinar Mas are pushed to expand internationally, particularly under conditions of limited and/or volatile domestic demand.

Expansion Patterns of Chinese Firms: Outcomes of Business Linkages

The leading Chinese firms in the Southeast Asian countries (e.g., Salim, Astra, and Sinar Mas of Indonesia; Charoen Pokphand and Bangkok Bank of Thailand; Kuok Group of Malaysia; and Cojuangco Group of the Philippines) generally have developed dominant positions in their home markets. Many are engaged in activities involving relatively low technical skills (e.g., property, plantation, local distribution, or trading); those in more advanced manufacturing and service sectors often rely on foreign technology and management.

Some of them have also expanded regionally, and a few have become truly regional companies (e.g., Charoen Pokphand).

Two patterns of growth can be observed among these Chinese firms. The first is opportunity-driven growth, capitalizing particularly on their ability to secure business franchises from the government, as was described in the previous section on business-government linkages. In Indonesia, Salim Group obtained monopolies or quasimonopolies in the distribution of flour (and later noodles), cement, and steel. Astra did the same in the automotive industry and Sinar Mas in palm oil distribution. The Cojuangco Group of the Philippines amassed wealth by obtaining the long-distance telephone franchise in the country. Charoen Pokphand just got a multibillion dollar telephone contract in Thailand. In Hong Kong, Li Ka Shing, through his Cheung Kong Holding, has the territory's license for television and electricity and is its leading seaport operator, and the Swire Group has the airport-related franchise. Stanley Ho's monopolies on ferry and gambling licenses in Macau are widely known. Profiting from their far-reaching personal networks, these firms are very adept at exploiting business opportunities in other parts of the region. The Riady family of Lippo Group, Indonesia, has established a strong foothold in China, followed by Salim Group. Similarly, Charoen Pokphand has entered Indonesia, Malaysia, and China through its business and political connections.

The second emerging pattern is an attempt to build a strong industrial firm focusing on a limited set of markets, products and technology. Firms in this category tend to expand their businesses by developing technology mostly with the help of foreign firms and leveraging their technological and managerial skills in a limited number of closely related industries. The President Group of Taiwan is growing through specialization in food processing and retailing and is now entering the U.S. market through the acquisition of two candy manufacturers (Wyndham Foods and Famous Amos). Astra Group of Indonesia has for two decades built an impressive chain of automotive parts, components, and final assembly plants with the help of Toyota Group. Hong Kong's Sun Hung Kai has excelled in the supercompetitive Hong Kong property and construction markets, while Syme Darby of Malaysia shines in agro-based industries.

A further look at Charoen Pokphand's business evolution reveals these expansion patterns of Chinese firms. Charoen is known for its chicken farming and animal feed mills. Founded in 1921, the firm has now an integrated operation of chicken raising, hatcheries, slaughter houses, feed mills, pesticides, and export and domestic distribution of frozen chicken. The technologies for these operations (chicken breeding, agriculture, and animal feed technologies) were obtained through joint venture and licensing agreements with the U.S.-based Arbor Acres Farm, Inc., and DeKalb. After mastering these technologies,[3] Charoen then expanded geographically into Indonesia, China, Malaysia, Singapore, Taiwan, Hong Kong, Mexico, and Turkey. Also, leveraging its technology base, the company has ventured into the new, related products of shrimp farming (joint venturing with Mitsubishi) and hog farming. Recently, the company also expanded into downstream activities: food processing (i.e., TV dinners, joint venturing with Oscar Meyer of the United States) and fast-food restauranteuring (with Kentucky Fried Chicken).

Using its business and political clout, Charoen has also expanded opportunistically. In Thailand, it has entered into telecommunications (with Nynex of the United States), chemicals (with Solvay of Belgium), and retailing (with Makro of Holland, Meiji of Japan, and 7–11 of the United States). In China, it has invested in motorcycle assembly (with Honda of Japan), automotive spare parts, brewing (with Heineken of Holland) and retailing. Table 1 summarizes Charoen Pokphand's two patterns of expansion: systematic and opportunity driven.

TABLE 1.   Charoen Pokphand's Expansion Programs

Systematic Expansion			
Geographical-International Expansion			
	Chicken Farming	Hog Farming	Shrimp Farming	Feed mills
China	X	X	X	X
Indonesia	X		X	X
Malaysia	X			
Mexico			X (fishing)	
Singapore		X		
Taiwan	X			X
Turkey	X			
Product Expansion: Food Processing, Fast-Food Restaurants			

Opportunistic, Unrelated Expansion
Telecommunications (Thailand)
Retailing (Thailand, China)
Petrochemicals (Thailand, China)
Cement (China)
Brewing (China)
Motorcycle assembly (China)
Automotive parts (China)

Several observations can be made regarding Charoen Pokphand's expansion program. First, foreign linkages have been used extensively as an integral part of its expansion program. Second, until 1990, the firm seemed to focus on its core business, namely, animal stock breeding and feed mills, and systematically expanded into related businesses. Third, Charoen has invested significantly in building networks and linkages. In the case of its Chinese operations, for example, Charoen spent its first six or seven years just building connections, without any fixed idea about pursuing any particular business. This patience has paid off impressively. Charoen Pokphand has in the 1990s embarked upon various unrelated diversifications, particularly driven by its far-reaching personal connections, with both the government and business sectors, in China and Thailand. Such expansion, however, has also resulted in strain on its financial resources, and the company has been forced to actively secure additional capital in the world financial markets.

Generally speaking, the above pertinent characteristics of corporate expansion yield another interesting pattern. As opportunity in an economy is generally not evenly distributed, large firms such as Charoen Pokphand, Salim Group, and Whampoa—which are well endowed with good networks and access to information, capital, and markets—have been enjoying fantastic growth. In a period of several years, the firms will amass business holdings through a series of unrelated diversifications, driven particularly by their dense networks with other business firms as well as with government officials. It is not unusual for firms such as Charoen, Salim, and Astra to hold at one time hundreds of subsidiaries spread out in various sectors, from primary to tertiary. After a while, however, this conglomeration will absorb all cash generated by the firms and put a strain on key managerial talents and skills. Pressure for profit will then force the firms to restructure: rationalizing the businesses through reorganizing and often financial restructuring. If the firms survive, after a while they will be trapped back into the pattern of rapid, opportunistic expansion. Consolidation should then follow again.

This description reveals the challenges faced by Chinese entrepreneurs in the 1990s. In the past, it has been notoriously well known that not many Chinese businesses could survive for more than three generations because of overdependence upon the founder. An additional hazard now also prevails with respect to the various opportunities they enjoy in the region. The combination of vast opportunities and the quick, entrepreneurial decision making of the Chinese can result in overexpansion of the firm. As the organization of Chinese businesses is usually very small in nature and depends heavily on a personal network, it will experience heavy anxiety. Decline then may set in.

Concluding Remarks

This chapter argues that overseas Chinese business networks, as a product of their long history of oppression, have thrived under conditions of prevalent market failures in the region. The network has also flourished to overcome the distrust toward outsiders and the rigidity of overreliance on a small circle of trusted employees within their family business organizations. In short, Chinese networks become an efficient institution that supersedes *both* market mechanisms and organizational hierarchy in Southeast Asia. This efficient functioning of Chinese business networks, in tandem with their rock-bottom approach of trading, has been effective given the region's structural conditions. This combination set the initial basis for the Chinese business expansion. The deep involvement of government in economic development has provided an opportunity for the Chinese businesses to rapidly accumulate capital. To summarize, we can rephrase Poggi (1983): "No overseas Chinese capitalism without a Chinese entrepreneurial class; no Chinese entrepreneurial class without market failures, state activism, efficient networks, and commercial strategies, and no Chinese networks without a religious moral charter and a long history of repression."[4]

It is widely known that the giant Chinese conglomerates in the region are laggard in terms of technological competence and marketing savvy, but they are cash rich, endowed with extensive government and business connections, and aspiring to become world-class multinationals. There has been speculation that Chinese entrepreneurs are poised to take on the world as the Japanese multinationals did in the 1980s. Hong Kong and Taiwanese firms have actively invested abroad, followed by other Southeast Asian firms. Limited cases have emerged, however, indicating that the international expansion of Chinese firms— beyond the Southeast Asia and China markets—is not that easy. The acquisition of Van Kemp, the largest tuna processing and distribution firm in the United States, by a Thai firm has proven to be a failure. Even the tycoon Li Ka Shing has had to withdraw from his telecommunications venture in the United Kingdom. These instances seem to indicate that Chinese businesses and their networks can only work well under the prevailing market imperfections of Southeast Asia and China, not in the developed markets of North America and Europe.

Many regional firms have attempted, and succeeded, in building their technological competencies through foreign linkages, as indicated by the Charoen Pokphand case. This particular pattern requires commitments in terms of time and financial and managerial resources, and it can usually be achieved best if the firm focuses on a limited set of interrelated businesses. As the Charoen Pokphand case has shown, however, such an approach is not well suited to the basic characteristics of Chinese businesses.

The core strength of the overseas Chinese businesses is their instinct to co-opt political support for getting their business done. Their cozy government-business relationship has also enabled them to accumulate capital rapidly through the granting of monopolies and business franchises. As has been said earlier, it is doubtful that this strategy will work well in developed markets outside Asia. In addition, given the tendency of continuing economic liberalization in the region, the old cozy government-business relations may also diminish over time. It remains to be seen whether Chinese businesses will be able to develop themselves, technologically as well as organizationally, to compete with the Japanese and Western firms that are now considering seriously the emerging China and Southeast Asia markets.

NOTES

Support from the Canadian International Development Agency and the Centre for International Studies, University of Toronto, is gratefully acknowledged. The author wishes to thank Janet Landa, Sylvia Ostry, Richard Stubb, conference participants, and particularly Timothy Brook and Hy V. Luong for their constructive and helpful comments.

1. The term "overseas Chinese" broadly refers to people of Chinese descent outside China, regardless of their nationality, status, or length of sojourn abroad. Admittedly, they are not necessarily a homogenous group. Sino-Indonesians are quite distinct from Sino-Thai, as Cantonese origin is different from Hokkien origin.

2. It should be realized, however, that tracking down the ownership structure of Chinese firms requires detective work; ownership is invariably buried under a maze of intricate business links and subsidiaries.

3. Bear in mind that the chicken farming business is characterised by sensitivity to local weather and epidemic patterns, knowledge intensity (agriculture based), and sensitivity to social issues (involving hundreds of thousands of farmers).

4. See Harianto 1993 for elaboration.

Robert Kuok and the Chinese Business Network in Eastern Asia: A Study in Sino-Capitalism

Heng Pek Koon

This chapter seeks to explore the role played by ethnic Chinese entrepreneurs in Eastern Asia's economic development in recent decades by examining the history of Robert Kuok Hock Nien, one of the region's most successful Sino-capitalists. This close-up study is intended to supplement more generalized treatments of the broader political, economic, and social factors that have been cited to explain the role of state institutions, public policies, physical and human capital, foreign investments, and technology transfers that have contributed to the economic rise of Eastern Asia (Deyo 1987; Hughes 1988; Chan 1990; K. Lee 1993).

In those Eastern Asian countries where Chinese form majority or minority communities, private sector growth has been fueled largely by Chinese entrepreneurship. Several recent studies have focused on the salience of Chinese ethnicity and culture in explaining this growth (Lim and Gosling 1983; Menkhoff 1993; Landa 1994; M. Chen 1995). Gordon Redding (1990, 143), for example, argues that Confucian values have substantially shaped present day Chinese business behavior and practices: the Chinese family firm itself can be regarded as a cultural artifact and "a creature of Chinese tradition." These studies likewise argue that an informal Chinese business network has emerged in the region, held together by ethnic and cultural bonds (Sender 1991, 29; Hamilton 1991, 5–6). The liquid assets of the Chinese entrepreneurs who make up this network were conservatively estimated in 1994 to be worth some U.S.$2 trillion, making it the largest one of its kind in the world (Kraar 1994, 41). In the same year, *Forbes* magazine estimated that 86 percent of Southeast Asia's billionaires are ethnic Chinese. Malaysia's Robert Kuok ranks among the top ten.[1]

A recent study by James Mittelman on international division of labor theories has likewise drawn attention to Chinese culture and ethnicity as a significant factor behind the global economic transformation now under way, which "not only slices across former divisions of labor and geographically reorganizes economic activities, but also limits state autonomy and infringes upon sovereignty." He has argued that a new theory, one that gives due emphasis to the role of culture, is called for, since the classical theory and its neovariant, the New International Division of Labor (NIDL), is too narrowly focused on economic determinants (1995, 273, 290). Capital and labor flows are caused not only by considerations such as wage levels and foreign investment incentives but also by the pull of common culture and ethnicity. He sees Chinese culture as having created a Chinese transnational division of labor in Eastern Asia, a phenomenon that originated in the flow of migration from mainland China to neighboring territories and Southeast Asia. The dispersion of an immigrant Chinese population in the region has since been vital to the remarkable growth of Eastern Asian economies.

The empirical evidence on Kuok's business activities presented in this essay reinforces the major conclusions reached in other works on the nature of Chinese entrepreneurship (or Sino-capitalism) in Eastern Asia: (1) its organizing principles are derived from Confucian values; (2) its synergy and dynamism come from family-owned businesses; (3) it grows more rapidly with political patronage; and (4) the most successful Chinese companies have become transnational corporations that are currently upgrading their technological and management bases, mainly through joint ventures with Western and Japanese partners. The impact of transnational Chinese business activities on state autonomy and sovereignty is evaluated in the concluding section of this study.

Three main explanatory themes help trace the trajectory of Kuok's career: the roles played by culture, the state, and the marketplace.[2] It is argued here that in Robert Kuok's case, while Chinese culture has been important, the factor is by itself insufficient in explaining his business success. Kuok has displayed far greater cross-cultural skills than any other Sino-capitalist of his generation. In addition, the role played by the Malaysian state and opportunities offered by a fast-changing regional environment have been equally important to his success. Before discussing these three factors, I will begin by describing the scope and nature of Kuok's corporate empire and then turn to an analysis of how it has been established.

Robert Kuok's remarkable career was, like that of many Southeast Asian Chinese entrepreneurs, launched by capitalizing on economic opportunities provided by imperialist structures in the region centered on Europe. In the case of Peninsular Malaysia (Malaya before 1963), the development of the tin and rubber industries under British colonial auspices both laid the foundations of the country's modern economy and served as a magnet for large-scale Chinese immigration. Kuok's early business success stemmed in large part from effectively straddling the cultural interstices of the colonial British, immigrant Chinese, and indigenous Malay communities. Fluent in his mother tongue of the Fuzhou dialect (a variant of Hokkien), literate in both Mandarin and Malay, but most articulate in English, Kuok early in his career established a reputation for being among the most urbane and cosmopolitan of Sino-capitalists in Eastern Asia.

Kuok's skillful manipulation of a complex multicultural environment to develop his business empire has been matched by equally deft exploitation of opportunities thrown up by fast-changing economic and political regimes in the region. His long business career has spanned some of the most dramatic political and economic changes in Southeast Asia: World War II, decolonization, independence, transformation from agrarian-based to industrial economies, and integration of the region into the world capitalist economy. Consistently exploiting the vicissitudes inevitably associated with changing times, he has found commercial advantage in a wide variety of political and economic institutional settings. For example, he secured dominant stakes in commodity monopolies offered by newly independent protectionist Southeast Asian states, he adapted through offshore diversification to the more open trade regimes of the 1970s, and he extended his reach into the world's largest emerging market when China began its transformation in the 1980s to a "socialist market economy." Skillfully combining opportunities available to him as an insider in the world of overseas Chinese commerce with new ones secured as early as the 1950s in the realm of international business, Kuok by the mid-1980s had built up a robust regional empire with outposts as far flung as Paris, Vancouver, and Santiago.

The Kuok Group of Companies

At the time of writing, Robert Kuok has business holdings in sixteen countries (see appendix). The majority of companies in the Kuok Group are based in Eastern Asia (Malaysia, Singapore, Hong Kong, Indonesia, Philippines, Thailand, China, and Taiwan) with smaller enterprises in Fiji, Canada, France, Germany, Mexico, Chile, Australia, and New Zealand. The Kuok Group is engaged in a widely diverse range of activities: commodity trading, financial services (especially insurance and securities brokering), hotel ownership and management, property development, plantations and vegetable oil refining, shipping, manufacturing (primarily packaging of its food products), retail sales, mass media, and entertainment.

While the Shangri-La chain of hotels and other commercial and residential property development projects in the region have become the most conspicuous part of Kuok's corporate activities, his globally based commodities-trading operations remain the group's mainstay revenue earner. After securing a near monopoly in sugar trading and refining in Malaysia in the early 1960s, Kuok went on to acquire international fame as the "Sugar King." By the early 1970s, Kuok controlled around 10 percent of the world's freely traded sugar. By 1991, the group's 30-percent-owned Sucden Kerry International (SKI) handled 60 percent of the world sugar market (Friedland 1991, 49). Kuok is also presently a significant presence in other commodity markets, in particular wheat flour, soybeans, rice, palm oil, and animal feed. His sugar and palm oil operations are vertically integrated industries. For example, sugar and palm oil grown in Kuok-owned plantations in Malaysia are processed in company mills and transported to buyers in company ships. Outside Malaysia, Kuok has a joint venture with Liem Sioe Liong's Salim Group in Indonesia to grow and refine sugar and with Hong Kong and Shenzen partners to process vegetable oils and tallow in China.

Mass media, supermarket retailing, financial services, and beverage bottling represent the group's most recent diversification activities. In 1988, Kuok acquired a Malaysian-based chain of thirty-three cinemas, as well as a controlling stake in Television Broadcasts Ltd. (TVB), a major Hong Kong television company, from movie magnate Run Run Shaw (Friedman 1991, 48). In late 1993, Kuok diversified from electronic media into print media when he became the major shareholder of the *South China Morning Post,* Hong Kong's leading English-language newspaper. The group's retail activities were launched in 1991 through a joint venture with Japan's Chujitsu Group to operate a supermarket chain called Kerry's. At present, three stores in Malaysia and one in China (Beijing) have been opened. Kuok's most recent enterprises include a joint venture with Coca-Cola to establish bottling plants in the Chinese cities of Chongqing, Shenyang, Wuhan, Dalian, Qingdao, and Nanning (De Weaver 1994, 3) and the establishment of the Myanmar Fund to invest in the tourism and agribusiness sectors in Myanmar (Burma).[3]

The Path to Success: The Cultural Dimension

Robert Kuok's family history epitomizes a general trend in the career paths of many successful Chinese in Southeast Asia. Of meager means, ancestors left impoverished households in China around the turn of the century to build businesses in their new homelands. In this last decade of the century, their descendents, holding undreamed-of wealth, are investing in their original homeland and enjoying the fruits of its economic liberalization. Whatever explains this remarkable turnabout? Clearly, the cultural dimension is an essential explanatory element. It has often been argued that Chinese business practices and management styles are shaped by the Chinese civilizing system generally known as Confucianism. The term refers to the set of social and moral values that have determined Chinese family patterns, educational practices, attitudes toward the state, and other fundamental features of Chinese life through the centuries. As Gordon Redding (1990, 2) has argued: "Directly Confucian ideals, and especially familism as a central tenet, are still well enough embedded in the minds of most Overseas Chinese to make Confucianism the most apposite single-word label for the values which govern most of their social behavior."

The efficacy of the Chinese family business as a cultural artifact is commonly explained in terms of organizational structures and business practices influenced by the Confucian heritage. The former pertains both to patrilineal and patrilocal kinship structures bound together by a set of strict relationship rules and to social networks beyond the family, represented by voluntary associations based on kinship, common dialect origins, or other shared interests such as occupation. Voluntary associations have been particularly important as instruments of social networking within overseas Chinese communities, particularly since extensive kinship groups were not widely replicated outside of China (Freedman 1960). This framework for commercial organization and interaction originated in China, where state-provided protection of private property, provision of infrastructure, and creation and enforcement of a legal code were largely absent at the grassroots level. Private institutions evolved to provide for welfare and security needs as well as to regulate business activity (Hamilton 1991, 48–62; Redding 1990, 45). Among the most highly prized Confucian moral values are *xiao* (filial piety), *jen* (human heartedness or benevolence), and *li* (propriety or gentlemanly conduct). These moral virtues are expected to bind the parties in each of the primary sets of relationships that in theory comprise the ideal Confucian social and political entity.

Confucian traditions in the Chinese business world are evident in many ways. Kinship groups and voluntary associations, for example, have served as networking instruments for their members to gather and exchange information about market conditions as well as sources of start-up capital and other forms of credit. Confucian emphasis on morality and propriety, which underpins the concept of *xinyong* (trustworthiness and creditworthiness, i.e., one's ability to meet business and financial obligations), and stress on maintaining harmonious relationships, which buttresses the concept of *guanxi* (social relationships, i.e., networks of useful personal relationships), undergird business activities based on personal obligations and trust.[4]

Trust and personal ties are by no means uniquely Chinese business values, and they are as vital to non-Chinese as to Chinese entrepreneurs. However, Chinese business relationships are based more on personalistic ties than are Western ones, which are governed mainly by contractual agreements. Consequently, *xinyong* and *guanxi* have become an intangible Chinese factor of production, that is "cultural capital," which is as essential as capital, labor, and other inputs for running a Chinese business. If a Chinese entrepreneur breaks his word or defaults on his loans, he loses his reputation and creditworthiness within the business network.

The Beginnings of the Kuok Family Business

An examination of Robert Kuok's business endeavors reveals the significance of Chinese, as well as non-Chinese, cultural determinants behind his success. A second generation Malaysian born in 1923, Kuok inherited a medium-sized family business. His father, Kuok Keng Kang, had emigrated to British Malaya from Fuzhou in Fujian Province with an older brother toward the end of the nineteenth century.[5] By the outbreak of World War II, the company established by the brothers, Tong Seng & Co., had grown into a modest business wholesaling and retailing rice, sugar, and flour.

Having risen to middle-class status, Kuok Keng Kang spared no expense in obtaining the best education possible for his children. He chose English rather than Chinese formal schooling, since the former offered not only advantages of literacy in English in colonial Malaya but opportunities for forming personal ties with Malay establishment families whose children attended the same schools. At the same time, private tutors were employed to give the Kuok children instruction in Mandarin and the Confucian classics. Kuok recalled his childhood socialization in Confucian values and business ethics in the following words: "As children, we learned about moral values— mainly Confucian. As father was a businessman, terms such as "business integrity," "honor," "your word's your bond" were often used by the elders and sank into our minds" (Studwell 1994, 30).

Kuok and his two brothers[6] graduated from the best school in Johore Baru, the English College (since renamed Sultan Abu Bakar College), the alumni of which included the present Sultan of Johore; Datuk Onn bin Jaafar, founder of the United Malays National Organization (UMNO); Datuk Onn's son and later prime minister, Tun Hussein Onn; and two deputy prime ministers, Tun Dr. Ismail and Datuk Musa Hitam; as well as countless other top-ranking members of the Malaysian political, bureaucratic, and military elite. In 1939, Kuok continued with his tertiary education at the prestigious Raffles College in Singapore, the institution that has produced two of Malaysia's prime ministers, Tun Hussein Onn and Datuk Seri Dr. Mahathir Mohamad, as well as Singapore's former prime minister, Lee Kuan Yew. As will be shown, the opportunities provided by the old boy network, especially from the English College, enabled Kuok to transform his business from a run-of-the-mill Chinese family enterprise into a global conglomerate.

Kuok's multicultural educational experience gave him the social and psychological skills to operate effectively in the non-Chinese world, including that of the Japanese occupiers during World War II. In that period he found employment as a clerk in the Rice Department of Mitsubishi Shoji Kaisha in Singapore. Knowledge and contacts honed during his apprenticeship at one of Japan's leading *zaibatsu* were later put to good use when he reorganized the family business. In addition, firsthand exposure to Japanese business practices at Mitsubishi sharpened his entrepreneurial instincts and guided him to the Japanese economic lodestone years ahead of Malaysia's "Look East" policy initiated by Prime Minister Mahathir Mohamad in 1982. When he established his first large-scale enterprise in 1959 (Malayan Sugar Manufacturing Company Ltd.), he turned to two Japanese partners, Nissin Sugar Manufacturing Company Ltd. and Mitsui Bussan Kaisha Ltd., for joint venture capital and technical assistance. Japanese companies, for their part, seeking to reestablish their presence in the region after the war, were keen to have Chinese businessmen as joint venture partners. They recognized that, having served as intermediaries between Western big business and the local economy, the Sino-capitalists had the best insights into local market conditions as well as the necessary knowledge of modern trade and manufacturing techniques (Yoshihara 1988, 49–50). An estimated 90 percent of private sector joint venture Japanese projects in Southeast Asia today are formed with local Sino-capitalists (Australia, Department of Foreign Affairs and Trade 1995, 245). The Japanese were, however, neither the first of Kuok's non-Chinese business partners nor ultimately his most important ones. Instead, it was through deals with Western, particularly British, companies that the foundations of the Kuok Group were laid.

With the death of Kuok Keng Kang in 1949, Robert became the effective head of the family business. Employing the professional services of an Austrialian accounting firm, Harry Tooks, he liquidated Tong Seng and transferred its most lucrative parts, those involved in the rice and sugar trade, to a new company named Kuok Brothers Private Ltd., which laid the foundations for the Kuok Group. The company initially concentrated on expanding its rice and sugar local distribution operations, while Robert Kuok searched for other opportunities to diversify the family business.

In 1955, Robert Kuok made his first offensive into international trading activities with the acquisition of a Singapore-based British agency house (i.e., a trading company that held import and export licenses), Rickwood and Company. Among other activities, the company shipped machinery from Singapore to refineries owned by major oil companies based in Port Dickson, including the American giant, Esso. The company's shipping arm laid the foundations for the Kuok Group's subsequent majority ownership of the largest dry-bulk shipping line in Southeast Asia (Pacific Carriers) as well as minority ownership of a leisure watercraft and cruiser construction business in Singapore (GB Holdings).

The retreat of British agency houses, such as Edward Boustead and Company and Harper Gilfillan, and the loosening of their monopoly over Malaysia's export-import trade had paved the way for Kuok's entry into a niche in international trade that had been unavailable to Chinese entrepreneurs in the prewar period. Thus, when independence finally came to Malaya in 1957, Kuok and other enterprising local businessmen stood to reap rich rewards in markets previously dominated by the British.

Kuok's greatest success in international markets has been in the sugar trade. In fact, it was sugar trading that fueled his meteoric rise. Thanks to exceptional entrepreneurial skills and sheer good luck—world prices for sugar rose steadily during the 1960s and 1970s—he gained the necessary capital to expand and diversify dramatically. Kuok's entry into the sugar market in the early 1950s vividly demonstrated his ability not only to function effectively in a Western-dominated market but also to beat the British at their own game. Sugar transactions in Malaya before independence were monopolized by British agency houses, particularly Guthrie, Harrison, and Crosfield. Britain was the source of refined sugar for the Malayan market, and the industry there was controlled by a small number of companies, especially Tate and Lyle, E. D. & F. Mann, and M. Golodetz.

Realizing that decolonization in Malaya had brought in its wake a unique opportunity for non-British firms to enter the sugar industry, Kuok went to London to familiarize himself with the workings of the London Commodities Exchange, the nerve center of the international sugar trade. In an unprecedentedly innovative move for a Southeast Asian entrepreneur of the 1950s, he bought a seat on the London Sugar Terminal. He then concluded deals with Tate and Lyle, and E. D. & F. Mann, to act as their major sugar distributor for Malaya and Singapore. With his foothold in the international sugar trade, Kuok was strategically positioned to embark on a series of business moves that greatly expanded and diversified the scale of the family business operations. Over the next two decades, the Kuok Group became Malaysia's largest Chinese-owned multinational corporation.

While Kuok's cosmopolitan style has been instrumental in giving him the personal resources to work effectively with non-Chinese in the Malaysian and international markets, more uniquely "Chinese" factors account for the success of business operations elsewhere in Eastern Asia. The connections that his father had previously established with Sino-Thai rice millers and exporters in Thailand were instrumental in cementing Kuok's relationship with rice trader and Bangkok Bank founder Chin Sophonpanich. During the 1950s and 1960s, a period when the regional banking system was in its infancy, Bangkok Bank served as one of the biggest sources of venture capital for Southeast Asia's up and coming Sino-capitalists. Chin became Kuok's first major godfather, giving him access to credit to expand his business, especially in the international sugar trade. Kuok's business ties with the Sophonpanich family continue today; Chin's son, Chatri, participated as joint venture partner in the Shangri-La Hotel in Bangkok. Apart from the Sophonpanich family, Kuok's other major Sino-Thai business partners include the Techapaiboon (Bangkok Metropolitan Bank) and Srifeungfung (Thai-Asahi Glass) families, who are shareholders in Kuok's Don Muang Tollway project, as well as the Assadathorn family (Thai Roong Rueng) with whom Kuok has had long-standing business dealings in sugar.

Kuok's business operations in Indonesia have similarly grown out of the Chinese business network. Liem Sioe Liong (Salim Group), Kuok's partner in PT Gunung Madu, Indonesia's largest sugar-growing and milling enterprise, is a Fuzhou compatriot as well as another early favored client of Chin's Bangkok Bank. Liem and Kuok are colleagues, not competitors, in several ventures in the region. One of their most recent joint projects is the development of a large tract of land adjacent to Manila's Makati business district. Filipino Sino-capitalists Henry Sy, George Ty, Lucio Tan, and Andrew Gotianum are local partners in this undertaking (*Asian Wall Street Journal* 9 January 1995).

Kuok's major partners in Hong Kong include Li Ka Shing (Hutchison Whampoa), Frank Tsao (International Maritime Carriers), and Sir Run Run Shaw (Shaw Group). As discussed further on, Kuok has become a major force in Hong Kong in his own right, having used his operations there to expand into China.

The fact that Chinese investments into China from Hong Kong, Taiwan, and Southeast Asia have dramatically outstripped other foreign investments—accounting for 80 percent of total cumulative investments for the period 1979–93—is strong evidence that common culture and ethnicity are determining factors in capital flows (*The Economist* 27 November 1993). Several decades of Communist rule, grassroots political resocialization, and a central command economy have failed to destroy China's Confucian legacy, particularly the values governing family ties and social relationships. Foreign Sino-capitalist investors with ancestral ties to China, who have access to Chinese political and economic regulatory bodies through relatives or family friends, have dominated investments in the special economic zones in Guangdong and Fujian, creating what is commonly referred to today as "Greater China" or the "Greater China Economic Area" (Yamaguchi 1993, 3–4; Australia, Department of Foreign Affairs and International Trade 1995, 194–217).

Western investors have concluded that "it is the rule of relationships, not the rule of law" that governs business interactions in China (*Japan Times* 24 September 1995). Former Singapore Prime Minister Lee Kuan Yew has observed: "*Guanxi* capability will be of value for the next twenty years at least, until China develops a system based on the rule of law, with sufficient transparency and certainty to satisfy foreign investors" (Australia, Department of Foreign Affairs and Trade 1995, 195). While it remains moot whether Chinese entrepreneurs will lose their cultural advantage when China develops stronger legal institutions, the important point made here is that Chinese entrepreneurs fare best in economic regimes with poorly developed legal, administrative, and institutional infrastructures.

The Economic Environment

When Kuok embarked on his business career, Southeast Asian legal, administrative, financial, and other institutional infrastructures were not well developed. Chinese entrepreneurs in the region used their domestic and transnational business networks to mobilize capital, tap into the latest market intelligence, and occupy market niches where profits could be made. In this manner, they successfully competed against indigenous business rivals. In 1993, in the five ASEAN countries of Singapore, Malaysia, Thailand, the Philippines, and Indonesia, ethnic Chinese formed 6 percent of the population but accounted for 70 percent of the capitalization of listed companies not controlled by governments or foreigners (Yamaguchi 1993, 3).

Chinese business success, however, has not been achieved solely through cultural determinants. Changes in economic regimes and governmental development policies are also important variables. Stressing the central role of government and private sector cooperation in the "East Asian miracle," a 1993 World Bank report argued that only those authoritarian and paternalistic governments that were willing "to grant a voice and genuine authority to a technocratic elite and key segments in the private sector" had achieved impressive growth rates in the region (World Bank 1993, 17). Robert Kuok's relationship with the Malaysian state reflects precisely this kind of symbiosis: he relied on state patronage to further his business ambitions as much as the state relied on his entrepreneurial talent to achieve economic growth.

Kuok adapted his business strategies to exploit new opportunities in Malaysia brought by independence. For the first decade after 1957, his domestic operations benefited greatly from a trade regime that offered local industries protection from foreign competition, thus giving Chinese enterprises unrestrained opportunities for growth. During the 1970s, when protectionism gave way to a more liberal trade regime, and when Chinese enterprises were handicapped by the heavily pro-Malay bias of the New Economic Policy (NEP), he adapted by putting priority on his offshore operations.

Like most other rapidly developing countries, Malaysia embarked on a two-step process based on import-substituting industrialization (ISI) and export-oriented industrialization (EOI) to modernize its agrarian-based economy (Snodgrass 1980; Spinanger 1986). After the mid-1980s, an accelerated and intensified EOI program resulted in Malaysia achieving some of the most impressive growth rates in the postwar period (8.1 percent in 1991–93). Kuok's business strategies were tailored to take advantage of the different priorities and emphases of the two policies. Behind the protectionist wall of ISI, Kuok moved to capture the domestic sugar and flour market. He established vertically integrated operations in both these industries targeted for government encouragement under the First Malaysia Plan (1966–70). Making use of pioneer status which granted income tax relief for up to ten years for eligible industries, Kuok constructed the country's first sugar refinery, Malayan Sugar Manufacturing, in 1959. Three years later, Kuok diversified his commodities operations by building Federal Flour Mills to process wheat imported from North America.

The introduction of the EOI regime, represented by the Investment Incentives Act and the introduction of free trade zones into the country, widened the scope of incentives granted to local and foreign investors. Kuok utilized the opportunities provided during this early phase of EOI to establish another company, Perlis Plantation, to cultivate sugar in the state of Perlis. His success in controlling the domestic sugar and flour markets is reflected in his current virtual monopoly share in the former and his 45 percent share in the latter (Friedland 1991, 50).

However, instead of establishing a greater presence in the export manufacturing sector in Malaysia under the liberal trade regime created by EOI, Kuok began after the late 1960s to divert a major portion of his new investments to offshore locations. This move was prompted not only by the introduction of the NEP, which imposed restraints on Chinese enterprises in the country, but also by the availability of new investment options in the region as more and more countries began to put emphasis on stimulating foreign investments and technology transfers.

The NEP, a far-reaching pro-*Bumiputera* (Malay) affirmative action program, which lasted from 1970 to 1991, sought to increase the Malay share of national wealth and employment in the urban economic sector.[7] To achieve these economic restructuring objectives, the UMNO-controlled National Front government passed the 1973 Industrial Coordination Act, which required non-Malay businesses to apportion 30-percent equity participation for Malay shareholders.[8] At the same time, numerous state agencies and enterprises were established to conduct business and acquire economic assets on behalf of Malays. The Chinese family-based businesses that most successfully surmounted the NEP's handicaps were those that established political connections with the ruling Malay elites, converted family firms into family-controlled corporations, and broadened their international operations (Heng 1992, 123–44). Indeed, NEP-fostered Chinese business strategies have been so effective that the majority of Malaysian Sino-capitalists are post-NEP success stories.

Although Kuok could easily expand his domestic operations under the NEP, as he already possessed an effective business network of top-ranking Malay patrons and partners (discussed further on), he saw that greater profits were to be reaped by the increasingly favorable climate for foreign investments in other Southeast Asian countries, especially Thailand, Indonesia, Hong Kong, and China. In order to facilitate the expansion of his offshore activities, a third main office (besides those in Kuala Lumpur and Singapore) was opened in Hong Kong.

The bulk of Kuok's offshore operations since the mid-1970s have been initiated and managed out of his office in Hong Kong, where he has been living for the last several years. While Singapore's status as a free port and entrepôt center had initially served Kuok's needs, he felt increasingly constrained by the interventionist role of the People's Action Party (PAP) government. After Singapore seceded from Malaysia in 1965, Lee Kuan Yew's government made the decision to achieve economic growth through foreign investment and foreign technology-driven industrialization, with state-owned companies participating as joint venture partners whenever possible (Tan 1991, 201–13). Feeling that the shift in Singapore's economic regime, which gave priority to the economic symbiosis between public sector bodies and foreign multinationals, would disadvantage private sector family-based entrepreneurial initiative, Kuok chose Hong Kong as his new springboard for business expansion. Not only will Hong

Kong remain, at least until 1997, the regional haven for freewheeling capitalist deal makers in Eastern Asia, even more importantly it offers the lowest corporate taxation rates in the region (17.5 percent compared with Singapore's 27 percent) as well as no taxation of offshore operations of locally incorporated companies.

Kuok's timely relocation to Hong Kong, the financial gateway to China, several years before Beijing embraced the concept of a "socialist market economy" gave him a competitive edge over other China-bound investors. Long-term residence has given him the "insider status" necessary for cultivating contacts within circles representing Chinese official interests. By the early 1970s, in his capacity as a major supplier of sugar to the Chinese government, Kuok successfully established *guanxi* ties with Chinese state officials, thus laying the foundation for his subsequent expansion and diversification of business activities in the country.[9]

Drawn by the enormous potential of that market, Kuok currently gives top priority to his operations in China, where several of his most ambitious and costliest hotel projects are located. At the end of 1993, he had seven hotels in the country, including the China World Hotel in the Beijing World Trade Center and the Portman Shangri-La in Shanghai. By 1998, eleven more hotels will be opened in China. Elsewhere in the region, his five-star Shangri-La chain owns twenty-two hotels in Malaysia, Singapore, Indonesia, Thailand, the Philippines, Taiwan, Hong Kong, Fiji, and Canada (*Asian Wall Street Journal* 1 February 1994).

Kuok's current emphasis on luxury hotels, securities brokerage and insurance services, mass communications, and supermarket retailing reflects his confidence that Eastern Asia's rapidly growing middle class—itself a product of the region's fast-growing economy—would offer unprecedented opportunities in consumer service industries. Taking advantage of changing trends in income levels and consumption patterns, he has moved beyond businesses that address basic consumption needs (such as his sugar and flour operations) to those that provide goods and services for increasingly affluent consumers.

A recent pattern in Kuok's diversification into securities brokerage exemplifies an innovative application of Chinese culture as a business input. In 1994, he set up the Marco Polo Dynasty Fund to invest only in publicly listed, family-controlled companies in the region, the biggest of which are owned by his business partners or friends in the Chinese business network. A survey carried out by Kuok's Kerry Investment Management found that, between 1986 and 1991, average growth in the earnings per share for the top ten family-controlled, publicly listed companies in Singapore, Malaysia, Thailand, and Hong Kong outstripped the earnings for the top ten general stocks and top ten government-linked stocks by factors of three or more (Australia, Department of Foreign Affairs and Trade 1995, 138). Whether this capitalization on his insider's knowledge of the Chinese business network will succeed in attracting investors remains to be seen. Although Kuok is reported to have little ambition to become a media mogul, he has nonetheless established a secure presence in an industry that will see dramatic growth as the region becomes increasingly integrated into the global information superhighway. In 1988, he bought a majority stake in Hong Kong's TVB at the behest of Run Run Shaw, who has remained as company chairman. TVB has recently acquired rights to operate in eleven countries in and outside the region (Keenan 1996, 43). Together with international frontrunners such as Rupert Murdoch's Star TV and Ted Turner's CNN, Kuok's TVB will help pioneer the revolution in Eastern Asia's satellite broadcasting.

When Kuok established his presence in the print media with his purchase of the *South China Morning Post* in 1993. This unexpected move was a response to Beijing's request that the Hong Kong English daily not fall under "outsider" control during the final and most politically sensitive phase of the colony's reversion to Chinese control.[10] As the sinews of reciprocal *guanxi* relationships were strengthened by the performance of such favors, Kuok's standing among his Beijing patrons doubtless became stronger than ever. Such accommodation to the wishes of real or potential patrons has been a central feature of Kuok's modus operandi since his earliest days.

The Political Environment

In Southeast Asia, small and medium-sized Chinese family businesses cannot transform themselves into large conglomerates in the absence of political patronage. The most successful Southeast Asian Sino-capitalists have forged strong links with indigenous political, military, and bureaucratic patrons and have rapidly accumulated capital based on business monopolies or near monopolies granted by such patrons. Through the patronage of President Suharto, Liem Sioe Liong in Indonesia has built up his family business into Southeast Asia's largest Chinese-owned multinational corporation.[11] When Sino-capitalists lack channels of political access outside their domestic bases of operations, they form joint ventures with colleagues who have well-established connections to local power holders. For example, Kuok's business ties with Liem in Indonesia have enabled him to establish a strong presence in the country's sugar and flour industries.

Kuok's understanding of the importance of political patronage is nowhere better illustrated than in the different public images he cultivates to accommodate governments with widely contrasting political leanings. He carries himself like a Confucian businessman in Hong Kong and China, becomes the Etonian to the British, and behaves like an accommodating Baba (Straits Chinese) with the Malays. His upbringing as an English-educated, politically disadvantaged Chinese in British-ruled Malaya, and subsequently in Malay-dominated Malaysia, has taught him valuable skills in the art of political accommodation.

At the time of Malayan independence in 1957, it was clear that any Chinese business entrepreneur who wished to rise above the ranks of mediocrity would need to deal effectively with Malay-dominated state institutions. This skill was particularly essential after the 1957–69 period of relatively open political and economic competition abruptly ended with the eruption of racial rioting in May 1969. The NEP was implemented in 1970 to redress the problem of Malay economic backwardness, universally regarded as a root cause of the race riots.

Kuok demonstrated a knack for political networking among the Malay power elite at least ten years before the rest of the Chinese business community was compelled by the NEP to establish similar linkages with Malay political patrons. The old boy network from his English College school days in Johore Baru, discussed earlier, gave him ready access to the highest circles of the country's new Malay ruling class. From this elite core group, Kuok gained entry into other segments of the Malay power center. Individuals from top-echelon Malay aristocratic, bureaucratic, and military circles were carefully embraced within his network.

Kuok's relationship with his Malay mentors, while in outward forms exemplifying the usual "Ali Baba" linkage between Chinese businessmen and their Malay political patrons/protectors differs from that pattern in one fundamental aspect: his Malay business associates have always played meaningful roles in his companies. Ali Baba partnerships, like the Indonesian *cukong* relationship, developed from the requirement that the "Baba" (businessmen) employ influential Malays as directors on their boards. The "Ali" (Malays) benefit financially, while the Baba gain access to licenses, inside information, and assistance from state institutions. Until the 1980s, when significant numbers of NEP-spawned Malay businessmen began to enter the marketplace, virtually all Ali partners in Chinese family businesses tended to be quite passive partners.[12]

Kuok's Malay patrons, playing much more active roles in advancing the fortunes of the companies with which they were associated, were selected primarily for their ability to facilitate business dealings with state institutions. A typical example was his former English College schoolmate, Tan Sri Taib Andak, who had a successful bureaucratic and banking career as chairman of the Federal Land Development Agency (FELDA) and Malayan Banking, before serving as a director of Federal Flour Mills (Sia 1993, 66). When Kuok established Perlis Plantations, Andak's patronage was evident in the role played by FELDA in facilitating the purchase of public land for cane sugar cultivation, an enterprise that involved the Perlis state government as Kuok's major business partner. In addition, FELDA became Kuok's partner in the sugar refinery built next to the plantation.

Other equally well qualified and talented Malay ex-bureaucrats who currently serve on Kuok's boards of directors include the former chairman of Lembaga Urusan dan Tabung Haji (LUTH, Pilgrims's Management and Fund Board), Datuk Haji Mohamed Shamsuddin, who is the chairman of Federal Flour Mills and a director of Perlis Plantation; and former Trade and Industry Ministry secretary-general, Tan Sri Nasruddin bin Mohamed, who is a director of Federal Flour Mills.

Members of the Perlis and Johore royal families are also represented in Kuok's companies. Tunku Osman Ahmad, cousin and brother-in-law of the Sultan of Johore, is chairman of Pelangi Berhad, one of the largest housing and real estate development companies in Johore. Tengku Suleiman ibni Tengku Abu Bakar, cousin of the Sultan of Johore and son-in-law of the Raja of Perlis, is general manager of Perlis Plantation. The importance of royal patronage for Chinese businesses stems from the sultans' position as constitutional heads of the governments in the nine Malay states. As state governments have jurisdiction over land matters in their own states, and since royal patrons can influence state legislatures' decisions regarding land use and land transactions, it is not surprising that Kuok's royal patrons hold key positions in his sugar-growing and real estate development companies. Although royal prerogatives have been curbed by legislation passed by the Mahathir administration in 1993, the sultans continue to wield more than nominal authority. While some intellectuals within the growing ranks of the NEP-fostered Malay urbanized middle class have begun to question the traditional role of their rulers, large segments of the Malay population, especially in the rural areas, remain hierarchy conscious and deferential toward their hereditary rulers (Means 1991, 289–91).

The most striking difference between Kuok's business practices and those of other Chinese family businesses of the early postindependence period was his inclusion of Malays as significant shareholders in his companies. Tan Sri Geh Ik Cheong, chairman of Perlis Plantation, observed that "Robert Kuok was one of the first people to bring in Malay shareholders long, long before there was even a New Economic Policy" (*Malaysian Business* 16–23 February 1993). Back in 1949, when Kuok reorganized the family business and sold off one of Tong Seng's subsidiary distribution businesses, Pengedar Bekalan, he made the unusual move of making both Chinese and Malay former employees the company's new shareholders.

Malay investors continue to form an important constituency in Kuok's Malaysia-based operations, both as substantial shareholders represented by state or quasi-state institutions and as individual small shareholders. Kuok's present-day leading Malay corporate partners include Permodalan Nasional Berhad (the PNB, or National Equity Corporation, a major NEP vehicle set up to acquire and hold equity on behalf of the Malay community), LUTH, and the Johore Economic State Development Corporation.

Kuok's fair-minded treatment of Malay partners and investors since the early 1950s has earned him much goodwill within Malay official and political circles. The high regard that the Malaysian government has for his entrepreneurial talent and judgment is demonstrated by the various occasions when the state has relied on his services in establishing state-owned enterprises. For example, he served as chairman of Malaysia Singapore Airlines in 1968 before its split into the present two international carriers, Malaysian Airlines System and Singapore International Airlines. He was asked to help establish Malaysia's national shipping line, Malaysian International Shipping Corporation (MISC), established in 1968. He was also a founder-director of the state-affiliated Bank Bumiputera, the country's second largest financial institution. Kuok's long-standing ties with the UMNO-dominated official establishment have also been augmented with generous donations to UMNO coffers at election times.

Kuok's linkages to Chinese political circles have not been as widespread and well cultivated as his connections to the Malay power elites have been, even during the pre-NEP period when Malaysian Chinese Association (MCA) cabinet ministers held the powerful portfolios of finance and trade and industry. Kuok realized much earlier than the rest of the Chinese community that Chinese political parties in Malaysia could play, at best, only a secondary role in a Malay-dominated political system (Heng 1988, chap. 9). Therefore, the steady demise of Chinese political fortunes since the 1960s has had little, if any, appreciable impact on his business activities.

Kuok, nonetheless, has certainly not neglected the welfare of his own political and cultural community. In the late 1980s, he performed an outstanding public service to the Malaysian Chinese community: the investments of thousands of small shareholders who had invested in the MCA-sponsored Multi-Purpose Holdings Ltd. were saved as a result of Kuok's successful bailout and reorganization of the deeply troubled company.[13] He has long contributed generously to MCA party campaigns as well as key party-sponsored projects aimed at benefiting the Chinese community. For example, he has been an

important donor of Tengku Abdul Rahman College, an MCA-sponsored institution built with equal funding from Chinese private sector donations and state
subsidies to provide tertiary education opportunities for Chinese high school
graduates disadvantaged by the NEP's pro-Malay educational bias. In addition,
the Kuok Foundation was established to provide scholarships and financial aid
to needy students.

Kuok's ability to cultivate political relationships of every hue in his
domestic base is also palpably evident in his international business dealings. He
has never been known to express publicly any opinion about the political environment in which he conducts business, whether it is one that champions
democracy and human rights or abuses them.

Kuok is among the handful of Sino-capitalists who have invested heavily
in China to have unusually close relations with top-ranking Chinese national
leaders. He was selling sugar to the government before Deng Xiaoping's market
reforms of the 1980s and earned their gratitude and trust, especially by showing
consideration when the latter were late in fulfilling scheduled payments.[14]
When the Tiananmen Massacre occurred in 1989, Kuok stood by the Chinese
government by pushing ahead with his World Trade Center project in Beijing.
The Chinese authorities have amply reciprocated such favors by supporting
and expediting his projects. Kuok's clout within Chinese official circles has, in
turn, made him an attractive partner for major foreign investors in China. As
pointed out earlier, Coca Cola chose Kuok to be its joint venture partner to produce their bottles in six cities.

The Cosmopolitan "Merchant Mandarin"

Kuok stands out as one of the most cosmopolitan, urbane, and Westernized
Sino-capitalists in Eastern Asia. His highly successful penetration of the international sugar market during the 1960s, a period when the market was still a
bastion of Western big business interests, was achieved through superlative
cross-cultural networking skills. He is as at home cutting deals in the hermetic
world of the Southeast Asian *sinkeh* ("new guest," i.e., first-generation Chinese
immigrant) capitalists as he is in the cosmopolitan boardrooms of New York,
London, and Paris.

Still, for all of Kuok's cosmopolitan qualities, at base the Kuok Group is
unmistakably a traditional Chinese family business, sharing many characteristics of other Chinese family businesses in the region.[15] It is a paternalistic organization with decision-making powers concentrated in Kuok, who relies on a
carefully selected small "inner circle" of loyal family members and trusted
friends to oversee day-to-day management of the conglomerate's many sub-

sidiary operations. The group's corporate culture also reflects Kuok's traditional Chinese upbringing: Western management techniques are buttressed with *feng shui* (geomancy) and astrological beliefs to ensure corporate success. When Kuok-owned buildings are constructed, geomancer specialists in the harmonious alignment of architectural details with the forces of nature share equal billing with Western-trained architects. When his Hong Kong operations moved to new company headquarters, Kuok retained his personal office in the old building on the advice of his geomancer. Predictions of Chinese astrologers influence business decisions as much as do risk analysis reports. When the group's first Kerry Supermarket commenced business in Johore Baru, the opening ceremony was held at 5:00 A.M. in compliance with advice from his mother's astrologer regarding the most auspicious time for launching a new business.[16] While opening a store at 5:00 A.M. could be read as a showy piece of public relations guaranteed to draw people's attention, it would also be understood within traditional Chinese business circles as a prudent move to obtain heaven's blessings for mortal undertakings.

Kuok is widely regarded in Chinese business circles as the Confucian embodiment of the superior man, the *junzi,* or gentleman, who conducts his business dealings with integrity, dignity, and fairness.[17] His reputation stems from the fact that neither in the earlier days nor today has he given the appearance of succumbing to the temptation of using morally compromising "sharp practices." When a leading investigative agency took an in-depth look at the Kuok Group a few years ago, it found no skeletons in the cupboard: "Adversaries: none identified. Litigation: nothing known" (Studwell 1994, 29).

It is difficult to gauge the extent to which Kuok's reputation as an ideal type of Confucian businessman and filial son entirely reflects reality or has been inflated by skillful manipulation of popular perceptions. Certainly, he has played the public role to the hilt, but appropriate role-playing is itself in keeping with the Confucian ideal. As for his successes in the marketplace, what is clear is that business acumen (laced with good luck) has been the most important factor. In addition, his impressive cross-cultural skills have been used to build political capital for his undertakings—and these in turn have reaped great financial capital. In short, Kuok is a "man for all seasons" who knows how to change with the times and find the right camouflage for every shift in his surroundings.

Now in his early seventies, Kuok's mind is focused on the future of his empire. He appears anxious to leave a business that will last well into the next century. It has often been observed that firms based on familistic Confucian values are ill adapted to survive the founding entrepreneur's demise, an observation that is aptly expressed by the Chinese saying: "Wealth won't last for three generations." The family firm may falter due to internal fissures caused by incompatible heirs or because the cultural characteristics that facilitated economic success in the early stage are ill suited for ensuring survival in a more competitive capitalist environment marked by greater legal and administrative transparency.

Kuok has adopted some strategies to provide for the group's survival after he leaves the scene. First, his diversification from commodities trading into lower risk, less volatile ventures such as hotel development will provide his heirs with more stable profit margins. A well-capitalized business based primarily on hotel and real estate development has greater chances for continued survival than one based on commodities trading, an area where fortunes are determined by the individual's risk-taking ability. Second, he has strengthened the technological, professional, and management base of his conglomerate in order to survive competition in the international market.[18] Third, until he designates a principal heir, he is grooming a collective leadership to succeed him. The day-to-day running of his business is entrusted to two sons (Kuok Khoon Cheng, better known as Beau Kuok, and Kuok Khoon Ean) and two nephews (brother Philip's sons, Kuok Khoon Ho and Kuok Khoon Loong). While these third-generation Kuoks are being trained to work together, whether the collective spirit of leadership now in evidence can survive Kuok's demise is anybody's guess. Still, by creating a modern, efficient, and professionally managed conglomerate, Kuok has raised the odds for his group's long-term success.

Conclusion

The trajectory of Robert Kuok's business career exemplifies some typical patterns and characteristics of Chinese business activities in Eastern Asia during the last five decades. First, it is clear that Chinese businesses in the region owe much of their success to a well-established network that spans the entire region, one run exclusively for the benefit of the Sino-capitalist community. The network, by circulating market intelligence, linking up business partners, and providing lines of credit and other kinds of services and information, has given Chinese entrepreneurs an enviable competitive edge in domestic and regional markets. From a cultural perspective, this network is built on shared Chinese ethnicity and a Confucian value system.

Although Kuok is English educated, he grew up in a Chinese-speaking family that upheld Confucian values, learning from his father the centrality of such values to Chinese business ethics. At the same time, his Westernized schooling gave him the cross-cultural skills to succeed in international markets. No other top-ranking Sino-capitalist in the region has surpassed Kuok's capacity for using Chinese culture in such an adaptive, flexible, and dynamic manner. However, such cross-cultural skills are now increasingly evident among the second-generation Sino-capitalists, many of whom have received Western schooling and will inherit their family businesses in the coming years. How then will the shift in cultural perspective of these Westernized entrepreneurs transform current patterns of Chinese business activities? Will the Chinese business network continue to function as cohesively and effectively? Will individual businesses continue to be paternalistic organizations with centralized decision making and heavy reliance on one dominant executive? Will ownership, control, and family membership continue to closely overlap? At the same time, as political regimes and economic environments in the region become more institutionalized and transparent, and as competition from newly emerging groups of indigenous entrepreneurs becomes stiffer, will Sino-capitalism continue to retain its predominant private sector position? While these questions cannot be answered with any certainty at the present time, it is clear that those among the next generation of Sino-capitalists who aspire to create a transnational conglomerate as impressive as the one Kuok has established will need to be as successful as he has been in acquiring political patrons throughout the region.

The modus operandi of the Sino-capitalists is to accommodate local power holders in countries where their business operations are located. On the other hand, they can also circumscribe state autonomy, for they are esssentially "stateless" in that they and their families are domiciled in different countries. Their business empires are "borderless" in that their enterprises are headquartered in several countries. Different members of Robert Kuok's family are domiciled in Malaysia, Singapore, and Hong Kong. His corporate headquarters are located in Kuala Lumpur, Singapore, and Hong Kong, and his companies are listed on the stock exchanges of Malaysia, Singapore, Hong Kong, the Philippines, Thailand, and Chile. Although cultivating political patronage and accommodating the whims of local power centers is central to the personalistic business culture of the Sino-capitalists, their business empires are so diversified and they have spread their risks so widely in the region and globally that they are not vulnerable to the authority of individual states, even one as imposing as China.

Kuok and his fellow Sino-capitalists are establishing a legacy in Southeast Asia that has contributed markedly to strengthening the management and economic integration of that region both intraregionally and within the global economy. Similarly, in China their contribution is one not only of using *guanxi* connections, Chinese language and social skills, and astute political dealings to enhance their personal fortunes. Just as importantly, these successful Sino-capitalists, working at the interstices between the modern, contract-based, global economy and China's idiosyncratic "socialist market economy," have played a critical role in China's rapid emergence as a major economic force on the international stage through joint ventures with Western and Japanese partners.[19] At the same time, Chinese investment flows from Taiwan, Hong Kong, and Southeast Asia into Guangdong and Fujian have had integrative effects resulting in the emergence of a Greater China Economic Area.

The business activities of foreign Sino-capitalists have contributed to increasingly centrifugal forces in China: sharply rising income inequalities, massive and uncontrolled migration of labor from impoverished inland provinces to coastal special economic zones (SEZ), and Beijing's apparent inability to impose fiscal discipline over newly-affluent provinces (Chang 1995, 967). National leaders fearful of the challenge posed by such developments to the Communist state, and with the apparent support of President Jiang Zemin and Premier Li Peng, have recently reasserted the supremacy of politics by attacking Deng's market-oriented policies on "quasi privatization" and "letting one sector of the population get rich ahead of the others" as well as his pro-Western, pro-foreign investment, open door policy (*Japan Times* 23 February 1996). Carefully hedging their investments to respond to a broad range of political and business risks in China, as well as elsewhere in the region, Sino-capitalists such as Kuok have positioned themselves to minimize losses should conditions deteriorate in any one economy. Yet, should Deng's opening to international capitalism continue and economic growth in the region maintain its present momentum, Sino-capitalism will remain a dynamic force in Eastern Asia.

APPENDIX: MEMBER COMPANIES OF THE KOUK GROUP

The codes used for the appendix are as follows:

A	Listed company	G	Financial services
B	Property development	H	Food processing
C	Plantations and refining	I	Mass media
D	Hotels	J	Retailing
E	Trading	K	Shipping
F	Holdings and investments	L	Other, including manufacturing

Australia
    E   Charlick Operations
    E   KNZ Australia

Canada

    B   Abbey Woods Development
    D   Pacific Palisades Hotel

Chile

    A,C IANSA

China

    B,D China World Trade Center (two hotels)
    D   Shangri-La Hotels (Beijing, Hangzhou, Shanghai, Shenzen, Xi'an)
    H   Southseas Oils and Fats Industrial

Fiji

    D   Fiji Resorts (two hotels)

France

    E   Sucden Kerry International
    E   SKIP

Germany

    E   Marimpex

Hong Kong

    F   Sligo Holdings
    E   Kerry Trading
    E   Kerry Foodstuffs
    B   Kerry Properties (Citibank Plaza, Wing On Square, Nanyang Center, Heng Fa Chuen)
    F   Kerry Industrial
    G   Kerry Securities
    G   Kerry Insurance
    E   Kerry Godown Holdings
    E   Kerry Glory Commodities
    I   Sligo Communications
    A,D Shangri-La International Hotels (two hotels)
    D   Shangri-La International Hotels Management
    L   Aberdeen Marina Holdings
    E   Ban Thong Co
    E   Masuma Trading

Indonesia
  C   Gunung Madu
  C   TKA
  E   Swadharma Kerry Satya
  D   Shangri-La Jakarta, Shangri-La Surabaya, Bali Dynasty Resort
  E   Broderick Trading

Malaysia
  F   Kuok Brothers
  A,C   Perlis Plantations
  A,H   Federal Flour Mills
  D   Rasa Sayang Beach Hotels (four hotels)
  D   Tanjung Aru Hotel
  C   Malayan Sugar Manufacturing
  A,B   Pelangi
  C   Kilang Gula Perlis
  B   Minsec Properties (Cheras Heights)
  A,B   UBN Holdings (Shangri-La Hotel and UBN Towers)
  G   Jerneh Insurance
  L   Federal Computer Services
  L   Tego
  L   Malayan Adhesives and Chemicals
  C   Pasir Gudang Edible Oils
  H   Johore Bahru Flour Mill
  C   Sapi Plantations
  C   Saremas
  J   Chujitsu Superstore
  I   Golden Communications
  I   Cathay Cinemas
  L   Minsec Engineering Services
  L   Bintulu Adhesives and Chemicals
  K   Pari Shipping
  E   Malaysian Food Agencies
  E   Bulk Chemicals Terminal
  L   Pelangi Concrete Industries
  L   Tanjung Bintang
  L   Intan Karang
  E   Pengedar Bahan Pertanian
  E   JB Distripark
  L   Seraya Sawmill (Fourseas)

Mexico
    L   Pacnav

New Zealand
    E   Kerry (New Zealand)

Philippines
    A,F   Kuok Philippines Properties
    E   Kerry Philippines
    B,D   EDSA Plaza, EDSA Shangri-La
    D   Makati Shangri-La
    D   Mactan Shangri-La Hotel and Resort
    H   Jimenez Oil Mills
    B   KSA Realty

Singapore
    F   Kuok (Singapore)
    A,D   Shangri-La Hotel
    A,K   Pacific Carriers
    A,K   GB Holdings
    B   Allgreen Properties (Handicraft Center site)
    B   Leo Properties (Great World site)
    E   Kuok Oils and Grains
    L   Camswald
    K   Leo Shipping
    L   Singapore Adhesives and Chemicals
    L   MTK Chemicals
    B   Wyndham Construction
    B   Regency Park
    B   Dairy Farm Estates
    B   Tanglin Mall Development
    B   Midpoint Properties
    D   Sentosa Beach Resort
    L   Posty
    K   Josindo Container Services

Thailand
    A,D   Shangri-La Hotel
    E   Kerry (Thailand)
    C   Thai Rung Rueng Trust

B   Wattanathani

L   Don Muang Tollway

Taiwan

D   Far Eastern Plaza Hotel

Data for this appendix are from Friedland 1991, 47; Jordan 1994; and *Kuok Group* 1991.

NOTES

1. "Billionaires in the Making," *Forbes* 18 July 1994. In the 1992 September issue of *Fortune* magazine, Kuok was listed as the third richest man in Southeast Asia, with an estimated personal fortune of U.S.$2.1 billion. *Asiaweek* (24 August 1994) ranked him as the sixth wealthiest man in the region.

2. In her study on capitalism in Southeast Asia, McVey (1992, 9) draws attention to the significance of three explanatory themes: Confucian culture, the magic of the marketplace, and the strong state.

3. Kuok plans to build several hotels, including a Shangri-La Hotel, and to develop a container port in Yangon (Rangoon) (Australia, Department of Foreign Affairs and Trade 1995, 185–86).

4. For a discussion of the importance of *xinyong* and *guanxi* in Chinese business relationships, see Menkhoff 1993, 131–47; and Barton 1983, 46–64 (using the term *sunyung*, the Cantonese form for *xinyong*).

5. The account of the Kuok family business, as well as Robert Kuok's business activities in the rest of the essay, are based on interviews conducted on several occasions, most recently in September 1994, with family members and close family friends living in Malaysia. Due to Kuok's deep aversion to publicity, they have, with the exception of older brother Tan Sri Philip Kuok, requested anonymity. Sia 1993 is a useful source on Kuok's business activities.

6. Philip Kuok worked for a few years with Robert in the family business before embarking on a distinguished public service career, which, at one time, saw him serve as Malaysian ambassador to the Benelux countries. Younger brother William did not get involved in the family business. Taking a very different route, he joined the Malayan Communist Party after working for a short spell as a journalist with the *Straits Times*, a Singapore-based English-language daily. He died in 1952 during the Emergency but the circumstances of his death have never been revealed. The Emergency was the period of Communist insurgency in the country. It began in June 1948 and was effectively contained by the time of independence in 1957.

7. The NEP's success was to be measured principally in terms of achieving the following numerical targets in equity ownership: between 1970 and 1990, the Malay share was to increase from 2.44 to 30 percent, the non-Malay (mainly Chinese) share from

34.4 percent to 40 percent, and the foreign share to drop from 63.3 to 30 percent (*Third Malaysian Plan* 1976, 85–90).

8. Small companies that are capitalized under $2.5 million Malaysian ringgits or have less than seventy-five full-time employees and large companies producing for the export market are currently exempt from the Industrialization Coordination Act.

9. Kuok's business operations in China date back to 1971 when he packaged a deal with E. D. & F. Mann and Tate & Lyle to sell one million tons of sugar to China (Studwell 1994, 31).

10. The Kuok purchase occurred shortly after the *South China Morning Post* ran a sensational article on 22 August 1993 reporting that $28 billion Hong Kong dollars of state funds had gone missing in the preceding eighteen months, siphoned off by Bank of China officials. It took a full week before the Chinese government responded with a denial in the *People's Daily* on 28 August. Concerned to put the paper into friendly hands, Beijing asked Kuok to take over control of the paper (interview with a family member, 22 December 1993).

11. For a study of the Liem Sioe Liong's Salim Group, see Sato 1993. Many Salim Group ventures have one or more of Suharto's children as partners .

12. See McVey 1992 for a discussion of recent changes in the relationship between the Chinese "pariah entrepreneur" and the indigenous political "patron/protector/parasite."

13. Multi-Purpose Holdings was the MCA's failed attempt to corporatize Chinese business holdings on a communal basis to meet the NEP challenge (Heng 1992, 137–41).

14. Interview with Philip Kuok, 1 September 1994.

15. For a description of the standard characteristics of the Chinese family business, see Redding 1990, 205–6.

16. Interview with a family member, 22 December 1993.

17. Personal communication with Tan Siok Choo, investments manager, Southern Bank, Kuala Lumpur, as well as Jonathan Friedman, Henny Sender, and Raphael Pura, who have written on the Kuok Group for the *Far Eastern Economic Review* and the *Asian Wall Street Journal.*

18. A recent report has indicated that Robert Kuok and Li Ka Shing in Hong Kong employ the best management staff available, regardless of their ethnicity (Australia, Department of Foreign Affairs and Trade 1995, 146).

19. Western and Japanese multinational corporations that have formed joint ventures with leading Sino-capitalists, apart from Kuok's Coca Cola partner, to facilitate their operations in China include Heineken and Honda with Dhanin Chearavanont, Procter & Gamble with Li Ka Shing, and Mitsubishi Heavy Industries with Eka Cipta Widjaja (Heng 1994, 24–28).

Part 3
CULTURES OF LABOR

All the chapters in part 3 examine the cultures of labor in general and of the nonagricultural workplace in particular, paying close attention to gender. Having a common empirical focus on the Sinic sphere of influence in Eastern Asia (China, Korea, and Vietnam), these essays share a thematic emphasis on how labor is not a free commodity and how it is deeply embedded in the historical and power-laden (re)construction of cultures and economies.

Luong's chapter focuses on the twentieth-century transformation of firm organization in a major North Vietnamese center of ceramics production. In the French colonial era, none of these firms was structured by the Confucian ideology. They were organized neither with a clear-cut male-centered hierarchy nor with an emphasis on stable and multistranded interdependence. Interfirm mobility was far from uncommon, while the majority of workers received few benefits other than piece-rate wages. Women were also quite prominent in the ownership and management of these firms. However, the transmission of skills was strongly shaped by both kinship ideology and village boundaries. The male-dominated gender hierarchy and stable interdependence within the production unit did not become the norm until the Marxist-instituted industrial reform in 1959 that de facto abolished private firms and marked the ascendancy of state and cooperative enterprises. Luong suggests that the structure of ceramics firms in this Vietnamese manufacturing center in the French period and its transformation in the socialist era can be explained only with reference to the *multiplicity* of ideological voices (including Confucianism and capitalism), their contradictions, and the larger political-economic framework.

Ellen R. Judd analyzes the gender dimension of village enterprises in three communities in the northern Chinese province of Shandong in the 1980s and 1990s. The social organization of these enterprises was pervasively structured by a localized androcentric hierarchy. Women as well as workers from other communities were paid lower salaries and not assigned to significant manager-ial positions. These practices were entrenched in patrilocal postmarital resi-dence, patrilineal descent, and patriarchal authority patterns. These local prac-tices, reinforced by Confucianism, enabled and culturally characterized a process of capital accumulation that benefited the local, agnatically related men in each of these three villages. However, cultural and economic relations are not wholly determined by that central relationship, and practices reflecting con-cepts of gender and other forms of equity (associated with a residual socialist vision) can also be seen within each of these villages. In one of the enterprises in one community, managers decided to move toward pay equity for women and men in 1990. In another village, where the labor is more skilled and the community places a particularly high value on education, both men and women are required to have achieved lower middle school graduation in order to be hired, and there are no piecework differentials between village and extra-village laborers. In the third village, mature women and the local Women's Fed-eration cadres preferred household-based enterprises to rural industry, which they saw as run by men and not benefiting women. Although capital accumu-lation from women's labor was not threatened in any of these villages, there are indications of alternative constructions of the workplace.

Lary and Kim focus on the cultures of labor in socioeconomic environ-ments with which workers were not familiar. Lary examines the reemergence of mobile, docile, cheap, and benefit-deprived labor in China. This form of con-tract labor, organized by labor gang bosses, was rooted in traditional systems in which labor was recruited on the basis of family or local connections, in which there was no reliance on legal rules and regulations, and in which the individual deferred to the family. Lary argues that such a system benefits the state, employ-ers, and workers' families in their alliances with one another but not necessarily the workers themselves. The state could offer inexpensive and docile labor to employers for their capital accumulation and to fuel economic growth. Employ-ers could minimize the risks of workers' dishonesty, poor capacities, or unrelia-bility by working through labor gang bosses who were personally connected to workers. They received short-term and inexpensive labor without offering any significant benefits. Workers' families received income to meet various needs, ranging from paying for a wedding to purchasing land. To the workers, this form of labor organization also provided social comfort and mutual protection in unfamiliar surroundings. However, they toiled in miserable conditions, for long hours, and under a strict labor discipline. Lary's chapter, like Judd's, highlights how in China tradition has been used to fuel economic growth but not neces-sarily to benefit the numerous workers in the system.

Kim examines the organization of labor in the Masan export-processing zone in South Korea with a special focus on electronics firms. A gender hierarchy structured the organization of these firms and others within the zone at large. The workplace was gender segregated. Usually working under male supervision, women laborers worked longer hours and for lower wages than did their male counterparts. They were seldom able to stay for even ten years because in electronics firms managers believed that women above the age of twenty-two did not have the requisite manual dexterity. Kim suggests that, on the one hand, culturally embedded traditions of gender and age hierarchy made the subordination of women within the workplace seem natural. The conservative tendency among many workers was also reinforced by the relatively high prestige and remuneration of some jobs within the zone in comparison with other possibilities, the aspiration of women workers to join the middle class, and political repression by the government in alliance with management. Kim argues, however, that women workers occupied a volatile structural and ideological position because they were young and not offered any long-term stakes in the system. The family metaphor used by management seemed hollow to women workers who could not expect to find a permanent place there. Kim suggests: "The institutionalized subordination of women workers produces a public passivity and fatalism that conceals an inner, private rebellion, much like the colonized people discussed by Frantz Fanon." It is through this hypothesis on the source of ideological and organizational contestation that Kim seeks to explain the 1987 labor unrest and subsequent events within the zone, events that led to concessions by the state and management on the issue of union organization. The impact of labor unrest and unions on the culture of labor in the Masan export-processing zone, however, was limited by the mobility of capital, as many foreign firms closed down their operations in the zone. This limited impact highlights the power imbalance between labor and international capital in the ideological and organizational contestation in the workplace and in the construction of the culture of labor in the Masan export-processing zone in South Korea.

All four chapters in this section thus share a common focus on how the construction of labor regimes is shaped by traditional social practices and long-standing ideologies in Eastern Asia as well as, to various extents, by the state's coercive measures. The authors also share the premise that the cultural shaping of labor practices will not necessarily end when Eastern Asia catches up with "capitalist modernity." At least in the case of China and Korea, the increasing engagement with global capitalism is facilitated by, and as well favors, the cultural shaping of labor practices, the costs to women and individual workers notwithstanding.

Capitalism and Noncapitalist Ideologies in the Structure of Northern Vietnamese Ceramics Enterprises

Hy V. Luong

In the past three decades, the strength of many economies in Eastern Asia, first in Japan and later in many other parts of the region, has led to a sharpened focus on whether native ideologies might have facilitated economic development from a macroscopic perspective and, from a microscopic one, structured particular enterprise organizational forms supportive of growth. In other words, social scientists have examined in greater depth not only the extent to which the spread of capitalism from the West has restructured indigenous sociocultural formations in Eastern Asia but also the extent to which the latter have shaped capitalism into new forms and strengthened the competitiveness of Eastern Asian economies in the process. In post–World War II social science, the heightened attention to the possibility that capitalism may be restructured in its dynamic interplay with Eastern Asian sociocultural landscapes takes place in the context of the two-decade dominance of modernization theory, which postulates an East-West convergence in structure and ideology as a result of the spread of capitalist modernism from its Western core to formerly peripheral areas.

Within the framework of the aforementioned debate, a growing social science literature on Eastern Asia focuses on the extent to which and how economic organization has been shaped by the Confucian ideology once dominant in China, Japan, and Korea as well as in certain parts of Southeast Asia such as Vietnam and Singapore. Many researchers on Japanese organizational structure have suggested that relations of production in *large* firms are shaped by the sociocultural emphases of the Japanese on stable interdependence, as well as on gender and age hierarchy, and that this has promoted employee loyalty and cooperation, among other factors.[1]

In this chapter, it is in relation to the debate on the relation between capitalism and indigenous sociocultural landscapes that I examine the interplay of ideologies, political economy, and the organization of production in the ceramics enterprises of Bat Trang, a northern Vietnamese village located fifteen kilometers from Hanoi. With little agricultural land, this village was well known for its pottery as early as the fifteenth century. In Bat Trang, the male-dominated hierarchy and the multistranded interdependence within the production units were characteristic not of the small and medium ceramics firms (from 10 to over 100 employees) of the French colonial period (1883–1954) but of state-organized and larger firms in the socialist era (1954 to date). I would suggest that we cannot fully explain the organization of the ceramics firms in Bat Trang in the French colonial period and its transformation in the socialist era without a full consideration of the multiplicity of ideological voices and the ideologically structured and larger political-economic framework.

Ideologies and the Organization of Production in the Capitalist Ceramics Industry of Bat Trang

Historical records suggest the strong possibility that Bat Trang's export of ceramics to Southeast Asia dates back at least to the seventeenth century. As documented in the archives of the Dutch East Indian Company (Volker 1954, 193–222), the Dutch alone exported 1,450,000 pieces of porcelain (an average of 72,500 pieces a year) from Tonkin (North Vietnam) to other parts of Southeast Asia in a twenty-year period from 1663 to 1682, when Bat Trang had already achieved its fame as a major center of ceramics production in Vietnam (184). Those figures compare favorably with an average of 63,300 pieces a year exported from Japan from 1653 to 1683 (a total of 1.9 million) and 114,700 pieces a year from China for the 1608–82 period (a total of 8.6 million pieces) (193–222).[2] With the decline of foreign trade in the following centuries, the Tonkinese ceramics industry entered a long period of stagnation.

At least from the nineteenth century to the Marxist-inspired industrial reform of 1959, the ceramics firms of Bat Trang were well incorporated into the capitalist system. Production was oriented toward profit optimization, and it involved a clear differentiation of labor and capital. In 1907, for example, for a village with approximately 2,000 inhabitants and relying little on agriculture, there were only seventeen kilns in Bat Trang, which produced approximately 350,000 products a month, mostly inexpensive and coarse earthenware bowls (*bat dan*), for the entire northern market (Nguyen Cong Binh 1959, 56).[3] Sold cheaply for forty-five cents for 100 (Barbotin 1912, 831), these products of Bat Trang were contrasted with the higher-priced *bat su* (porcelain bowls) or *bat ngo* (Chinese bowls), coarse porcelain bowls that were sold for eighty cents to one piaster for 100, and manufactured in the Chinese-owned kilns set up at the turn of the century in Mong Cay (Barbotin 1912, 834–35; Vedrenne 1939).[4] Fired in partially partitioned cannon kilns (called *lo ca sop* [fish-shaped kiln] or *lo bat dan* [earthenware bowl kiln]), the earthenware bowls of Bat Trang were preferred by rural landowners to feed their laborers during the harvest season because of their low cost of replacement if broken.[5]

Capital was heavily concentrated in Bat Trang at the turn of the century. Village oral histories mention three large kilns at the time, all operated by a small cluster of relatives (one man and two women) who inherited their kilns from their industrialist parents and had either membership in or close linkages to the Tran patrilineage.[6] In the next generation, the three largest cannon kilns belonged to the male kiln owner's son, a Mr. Tran van (*Cuu*) Khai, and the sons of one of these two women, all of whom were related either consanguineally or affinally, as is shown in figure 1.

We do not know how many of the owners of the other fourteen kilns in the first decade of the twentieth century accumulated capital from other fields for ceramic production and how many inherited their wealth. However, the opportunities for kiln ownership were limited by the large capital requirements for the construction and operation of a kiln due to the initial risk-laden operation and the cyclical demand for ceramic products. The demand for ceramic products peaked in the second half of the year, when the costs of both labor and raw materials tended to increase. For a novice ceramics kiln owner, the risk of failure during the initial period of operation was also unusually high, as is amply illustrated in the narrative of a grandson of the first Bat Trang entrepreneur, who adopted the Mong Cay chamber kiln design in the late 1920s in order to increase the competitive edge of Bat Trang products in the high-price categories:

When I was a child, my family was poor. At the turn of the century, my paternal grandfather worked in a kiln himself. At that time, the kilns here, also called Tieochiu kilns, produced only coarse earthenware bowls [*bat dan*]. . . . My paternal grandfather, Tran van Tan, went to work in Mong Cay. He returned to the area in 1920 and built . . . a family kiln at the end of the village. . . . But we lost everything. The chamber kilns of Mong Cay had steep slopes at 13 degrees. The fire was strong [as a result]. In Bat Trang, we used red clay [at the time]. The wares cracked because of the high heat. He labored again as a worker until 1930 when he constructed another kiln, an eight-chamber one, and found a white clay in Truc Thon [district of Dong

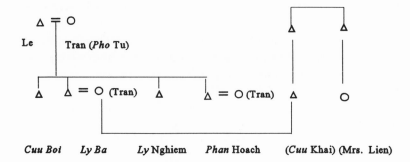

Fig. 1.   Relations among the largest kiln owners in Bat Trang

Trieu, Hai Duong province]. He was the first person to introduce the chamber kiln to Bat Trang. . . . At the beginning, we were not completely confident of a profit. We used a lot of family labor. We had only a few workers. My grandfather had to mold things himself on a potter's wheel. . . . Around 1937–38, a new source of clay was found in Tu Lac and Mao Khe [Hai Duong Province]. Tu Lac also had Ha Chieu feldspar, which my grandfather monopolized. Thanks to the new source of clay, our factory prospered. The clay was vital. Our products were the most beautiful, although our kiln was among the smallest. The porcelain was transparent. The glaze was pure white. Our products are well known among elderly people.

As a result of a native son's experiment and the discovery of kaolin, the chamber kiln design was gradually adopted by other Bat Trang industrialists in the 1930s and 1940s in order to upgrade their earthenware bowls to coarse porcelain ones and diversify their product lines to include electric porcelain devices as well as more decorative items (including statues and miniature animals).[7] Of the four additional chamber kilns in Bat Trang by 1945, one was owned by a former male worker, one by a woman merchant branching into ceramics production, and two by traditional kiln-owning families.[8] By 1954, of the twelve chamber kiln owners, six came from traditional kiln-owning and capitalist families, three rose from the workers' ranks, one had accumulated considerable mercantile wealth, while the owners of two other are of unknown backgrounds. Most of them did not engage in the production process, although some owners, especially those rising from workers' ranks, had a technical knowledge of some aspects of production.[9] Given the large quantity of exported products as early as the seventeenth century, the ceramics industry was probably among the very first in the Vietnamese social formation in which the capitalist mode of production and the market orientation developed.

In the French colonial period, unlike their counterparts in the southern center of Bien Hoa, the capitalist ceramics firms of Bat Trang were organized with neither a clear-cut male-centered hierarchy nor an emphasis on stable and multistranded interdependence (cf. Luong and Diep-Dinh-Hoa 1991). Interfirm mobility was far from uncommon, while the majority of workers received few benefits other than piece-rate wages. Their comfortable incomes during the production period were also offset by seasonal unemployment.

Pottery workers were paid by piece rates, with the exception of menial laborers who were paid daily wages. The majority of workers received payments directly from kiln owners twice a month, one as advances and the other as monthly wages with deductions for advances. In contrast, loaders and kiln firemen got paid by their team leaders at the end of each kiln firing. As a reflection of the commodification of labor, piece rates varied as a function of market supply and demand, as elaborated by a worker:

> Owners were smart. Earlier in the year, when the production had not picked up, they paid only 2 cents for a hundred bowls. The rate was increased to 2.5 cents later in the year in order to keep the worker. It dropped back to 2 cents after the New Year.

Workers had few benefits except for interest free cash advances in time of need and occasional write-offs of loans. Interest free cash advances constituted a common practice at the approach of the lunar New Year due to workers' financial needs for the festivities and owners' desires to keep good workers. The advances were vital to workers because firms closed down for three months at the beginning of the lunar year, and some were not opened until the summer due to the relatively slower demand for ceramic products in the first half of the year and the limited operating capital of most kiln owners. In other words, most workers were seasonally unemployed because few firms in Bat Trang operated for the whole year during the colonial period. In fact, only the kiln of the largest Bat Trang industrialist in the 1930s and 1940s, that of Mr. Tran Quang (*Cuu*) Khai, operated on a year-round basis. A worker elaborated:

> The production was not on a year-round basis at most kilns. We had the first lunar month off with the New Year celebration. The next two months were also off because of slow sales. In the summer, production also ceased for one month because of flooding. Production peaked between the eighth and the twelfth lunar month. At some firms, production did not

resume until the second half of the year. The laid-off workers engaged in petty trade [*di cho*], or in menial labor [*ganh thue*]. [How did you live during the laid-off period?] We scraped by, doing odd jobs in the village and relying on the family. Men did not engage in trade. They usually transported goods [for the female merchants] in the village. But they did it only after the first two months of the year. Those two months were leisure time, spent mainly on gambling. If we worked for *Cuu* Khai, we could work the full year, but the work and piece rates were less. His firm operated year-round, built up a large inventory, and sold its products at higher prices at the approach of the New Year. The quality of its products, however, was low because many workers were without much experience.

A former kiln owner explained on the wage advance system:

> There were many ways to tie workers to the jobs. At the beginning of the year, we advanced ten piasters, to be deducted over a ten-month period. If a worker was good, I might not deduct the loan for a while and forgive the remainder at the end of the year. If there was a death in the family, we lent money. Some lost money in gambling and did not even have a mosquito net. Losing sleep, they quarreled or fought with their wives in the morning. We then made the advance so that they could get back their mosquito nets. If it was a cousin, we might just give the money as a gift.

Kiln owners provided housing only to resident aliens in makeshift quarters or their ancestral hall areas. The meal benefits were limited to the rotating loading and firing teams, who played critical roles in ensuring the success of the production in its final stage. However, these meals were provided as much because of the regular offerings to the Fire God at the time of firing as for the benefit of workers as such. Training was provided not by the firm but strictly through dyadic and relatively short-term relations between master artisans and apprentices. Typically apprenticing with relatives and family acquaintances, the youngest workers received minimal pay. The latter had to take care of the various needs of master artisans, as a male potter elaborated:

> I began working as an apprentice at the kiln of Mr. Tran van De [the first chamber kiln in Bat Trang] at the age of eleven [1938]. I had to take care of the various needs of the master, including boiling water or bringing tobacco. I was paid according to piecework by the master, around three to four piasters a month. When I became a regular worker, the payment came directly from the kiln owner at a higher rate.

For more technical jobs such as kiln loading and firing, the apprenticeship lasted for a considerably longer period:

> My husband started working at eight as an apprentice. He served the bowl-sorting and loading team [*lua bat*] by bringing them tobacco and water or doing menial jobs. He learned from the master artisan [*tho chinh*] on the side, half an hour one day, one hour the next. The teacher was cruel, using a ruler to beat him on the head for any mistake. [How long did he learn before he became an independent artisan?] For ten years, until he was eighteen.

A few selected male workers with some French education also gained diverse skills in a formal training program, an opportunity not available to women at the time:

> My father was the secretary of the village administration. When I was young, I studied at the small Bat Trang branch of the École des Beaux Arts directed by Mr. Bui Tuong Vien. I learned molding [*vuot* and *nam*] and painting. Around 1945, I started working, performing all kinds of production tasks and learning on the job in the process. . . . I was on a painting contract, finishing the job at one house and moving on to the next, although I also polished the wares at times.

For numerous reasons, employment was far from stable. Workers in the rotating labor force, which included kiln loaders, firemen, bowl carriers, and woodchoppers, were contracted only for specific tasks and moved from one kiln to another. Among regular workers, comprising the rest of the pottery labor force, there were few upward mobility opportunities within a firm since, due to the small size of most firms, owners and their family members directly supervised the production process. The more ambitious workers moved on to trade (female workers) or to more financially rewarding jobs in new firms (e.g., molding of electrical porcelain devices, male workers). Even when workers did not desire mobility, the fortunes of a firm might suffer significant vicissitudes due to the strong competition not only of other enterprises in Bat Trang but also of Chinese-owned kilns in Mong Cay. The declining fortunes of the firm due to competitive market pressures, the 1946–54 Franco-Vietnamese war, and owners' lifestyles (opium addiction in one case) might lead to the delay in the operation of a firm in a calendar year, late wage payments, fewer emergency loans, temporary layoffs, or even firm closure and the termination of employment. The pattern of lifelong careers at one firm seems to have been restricted primarily to the stabler firms and to resident aliens in menial labor positions or the less ambitious workers from Bat Trang in these enterprises. Interfirm mobility and career changes were far from uncommon in the French colonial period.

To the extent that a hierarchy and multistranded and long-term interdependence existed, they were limited to rotating work teams (*phuong*). The members of a team normally came from the same community: workers from the neighboring Giang Cao, for example, specialized in building kilns and moving tree trunks floated down the river; those from Nam Du, on the other side of the Red River, in chopping wood; and those from Sai Son (Son Tay Province) and Van Dinh (Ha Dong Province) in loading and firing kilns (Do thi Hao et al. 1989, 68–72). Each of the teams was supervised by a master (*su ca*) whose share of the team payment ranged from 20 to 25 percent in the case of the loading team to 45 percent in the case of firemen (respectively, 1.5 piasters and 4 piasters at the turn of the century). Depending on their skills and experiences, other loaders' payments ranged from 27 to 80 percent of the team head's income, and those of the remaining members of the firing team ranged from 12.5 to 37.5 percent (0.5 to 1.5 piaster) of the wage of the master fireman (Nguyen Viet 1962; cf. Phan Gia Ben 1957, 170).[10]

Outside of rotating labor teams, the ceramics firms of Bat Trang did not have any formal organizational structure because, due to the relatively small size of the firms, owners or their family members directly supervised the production. This was especially the case in the cannon kiln era before the 1930s. Among workers native to Bat Trang, there was not even an informal gender stratification: at the turn of the century, the female molders (*vuot*) and male polishers (*tien*) earned slightly less than 0.20 piaster each a day on the average in the piecework system.[11]

To the extent that there was a gender hierarchy, the oral histories of Bat Trang in the cannon kiln period indicate that women were quite prominent in the ownership and management of ceramics firms. Toward the end of the nineteenth century and at the beginning of the twentieth, as earlier reported, two of the three largest industrialists in the ceramics industry were women (Mrs. *Nhieu* Huyen and Mrs. *Pho* Tu). In the next generation, two of the three largest kiln owners were also women (Mrs. *Cuu* Boi and Mrs. *Ly* Ba).

Women achieved their ownership positions in the capitalist ceramics firms of Bat Trang either through inheritance or through their own entrepreneurial activities. For example, one female chamber kiln owner in the 1940s received considerable wealth from her mother because her father had passed away in her childhood and her widowed mother had only two daughters. Most daughters, however, inherited little. Some acquired kiln ownership through marriages into wealthy families, as in the case of Mrs. Cuu Boi and Mrs. *Ly* Ba (fig. 1). Others accumulated considerable wealth through their trading activities, which constituted the exclusive domain of Bat Trang women. In the wholesale trade of ceramics, for example, female villagers joined woman merchants from elsewhere in the distribution of Bat Trang products throughout northern Vietnam. They also distributed in large quantities the areca nuts and fish sauce that merchants from Thanh Hoa and Nghe An Provinces in northern central Vietnam brought to Bat Trang to obtain cash for the wholesale purchase of Bat Trang ceramics. In the retail trade, the petty traders from Bat Trang sold the wares in nearby rural markets, although a few also served the needs of the Bat Trang population by purchasing commodities from major regional markets for daily retailing in Bat Trang. A few also opened ceramics retail outlets in the Earthenware Bowl Street (Pho Bat Dan) in Hanoi and other towns. Female villagers who considered themselves fortunate started trading in their youth and never engaged in ceramics production:

> I worked as a petty trader, selling fruits and vegetables. My husband prescribed native medicine. . . . Wealthy female villagers engaged in wholesale trade. Poorer people like myself were petty traders. The poorest people worked for capitalist firms. The lives of workers were hard. About two-thirds of village women engaged in trade. No men. [At what age did you begin to engage in trade?] I began at the age of thirteen or fourteen, helping my mother, who had earlier worked in a kiln. I operated independently after marriage, in my late twenties. [Did you carry the goods?] No, we had carriers, people from other villages who worked for us during slack agricultural seasons. A smaller trader usually had one laborer, and bigger ones had two or three. It was impossible for us to carry the goods for a distance of fifteen or twenty kilometers. [Where did you get the bowls for trade?] From the kilns of Messrs. Cuu Khai, De, Nghia, and Ly Thao. It was the manufacturers who were wealthy. [Did you pay up front or after selling the wares?] After. [How many were carried each time?] Three hundred to five hundred bowls. [How much profit did you make?] About 10 percent after expenses and the damage to the wares during transportation.

The most successful merchants accumulated sufficient wealth to move into ceramics production, as in the case of a Mrs. Lien, who was a first patrilateral cousin of the wealthy Tran Quang Khai. This female owner of one of the first five chamber kilns in Bat Trang elaborated on her entrepreneurial career path:

I did not have a cannon kiln because only extremely wealthy people could own one. I actually started out molding *bat dan* [earthenware bowls] for Mrs. Ly Ba, a patrilateral first cousin of mine. I started working early because my parents had passed away when I was only six or seven. Each day, I molded about 450 bowls. But I switched to trade because of the higher earning potential and the less arduous work. . . . I sold bowls, fish sauce, and areca nuts at local markets. . . . I later bought bowls from female kiln owners, who were all sisters and cousins. I had them transported by water and sold them wholesale to shops in Nam Dinh, Hanoi, and Hai Phong. Because I knew the boat owners, I entrusted the cargo to them and took a ship to those cities. When I reached those cities, I took pedicabs to the shops. Many of the store owners in those places were Bat Trang natives. [Did you deliver always on request?] No. Whatever I took from the kilns, I could sell them because the bowls were in demand. The shops took a few *mo* [tens of thousands of bowls] at a time. If the price of rice there was reasonable, I also bought a large quantity and had it transported by boat back to Bat Trang. I even traveled to Thanh Hoa on one occasion because a junior relative lived in Cau Bo. . . . I was a trader for a long time before we began ceramics production. Initially, we sold unfired wares to other people. Or, if they could not be sold, we rented kiln space. We hired only a few workers: clay processors, molders, and loaders. . . . I still engaged in trade at the time. Later on, we owned a chamber kiln, of which we used only four chambers and which we fired only once a month. [Did you sell the wares of your own kiln, too?] No. The wares were of high quality. The wholesalers had to come here to buy them. Our wares were either bought by traders from other places or by village traders who brought them to Hanoi or Nam Dinh.

The successful career path of Mrs. Lien, from ceramics worker, to trader, to kiln owner, reinforced a long-existing model for many female workers.

As kiln managers, despite their illiteracy during the French colonial period, the women of Bat Trang were noted for their managerial skills. A grandson of Mrs. *Nhieu* Huyen, a major kiln owner at the turn of the century, related a family legend about the latter:

Over one hundred years ago [toward the end of the nineteenth century], my maternal grandparents' firm was already a big one [*Nhieu Huyen* firm], making up about half the production in this village. She had three to four kilns, each producing forty to fifty thousand bowls with each firing. My maternal grandfather was a Confucian scholar, leaving the management of hundreds of workers to his wife. . . . Although my maternal grandmother was illiterate, she did not make mistakes. When a thousand products were received, she would put a cross on a piece of clay.

Even when a kiln was owned by a male entrepreneur, his wife or sister usually played an important managerial role. Legends abound about the tightfisted female owners and managers. At a chamber kiln factory owned by a Mr. *Cuu* Huynh, his sister as the firm manager normally accepted only 70 percent of the semiproducts, thus depriving workers of 30 percent of their incomes due to the piece-rate system. It stood in contrast to the management style of Mr. *Cuu* Khai, the biggest kiln owner in Bat Trang in the same period, who accepted virtually all products but paid lower piece rates. A molder from the neighboring village of Kim Lan reported on the management styles of the female kiln owners for whom she worked:

[How do you compare the three kiln owners, Mme. Cuu Boi, Mme. Ly Ba, and Mr. Cuu Khai?] Only the son of Mrs. Ly Ba and Mrs. Cuu Khai treated me well. Mr. Cuu Khai, who calculated the wages, was firm. I was scared of him, both of his appearance and his firm decisions. He did not say much of anything, but he did not change his mind. It was impossible to plead with him. Uncle Khanh, the son of Mrs. Ly Ba, was impulsively generous [*xoi*]. If the mother went into the kitchen, he lowered the debt figure and even burnt the piece of debt paper. When the mother asked: "How much did she [*chi*] owe?" he answered: "She [*chi*] owed ten piasters" when I actually owed more. Mr. Cuu Khai and Mrs. Ly Ba were tightfisted. As to Mrs. Cuu Boi, she yelled a lot, using obscene language [*noi tuc*]. She would fire people right away. The whole family was addicted to opium.

The major roles of Bat Trang women in the ownership and management of ceramics enterprises notwithstanding, during the French colonial period, subtle shifts took place in the gender hierarchy both at the management level and within worker ranks. In the post-1930 chamber kiln period, of the eleven kiln owners by 1954, only four (36.7 percent) were women who directly managed their firms.[12] Among the *major* kiln owners of Bat Trang, the percentage of women therefore declined from approximately 66.7 percent (two out of three) at the turn of the century to 36.7 percent in 1954.

Among workers, the change that took place with the initiation of electrical porcelain production in the 1930s and 1940s signaled a new trend: as Bat Trang expanded its product lines to include fuses, switches, and plugs and began using wooden and gypsum molds in the production process, it was male potters who specialized in the modern techniques and newer products. They received considerably higher wages than did their female coworkers. A specialized male artisan elaborated on the engendered division of labor within a new firm:

> It was nicer to work on porcelain electric items. The work was less arduous, although it required utmost attention. The quality control was strict. ... The pay was higher. Best paid were the mold specialists who made the molds. The workers who moved here from the Thanh Tri porcelain electric factory had better technical knowledge and also had more leverage with the owner. As molders, we received lower pay. We were paid piece rates. Our daily wage came to about one piaster, while we spent only one dime to feed our family. [Were there a lot of female workers?] Very few. Women specialized in grinding stone into powder in a mortar for glaze preparation or in preparing the glaze. They were paid about a dime a day. The molders were virtually all male.

The shift in gender hierarchy notwithstanding, the capitalist firms of Bat Trang were organized neither with clear-cut male dominance nor with the emphasis on stable and multistranded interdependence. I would like to suggest that these organizational features reflect not the absence of noncapitalist ideological impact but the tension between capitalist and other ideological voices, all of which played a role in structuring the organization of the firm and the local community.

At the level of the firm, despite the strong commodification of labor under French colonial capitalism, the recruitment and organization of labor were far from being immune to precapitalist ideologies. The technical knowledge of molding, polishing, or glaze preparation was transmitted only to relatives. Technology transfer was therefore stopped at the village boundary because few Bat Trang families in the old days allowed the marriages of their daughters to either resident aliens (*ngu cu*) or members of neighboring villages, even though Bat Trang men could marry female villagers from surrounding communities (Do thi Hao et al. 1989, 342–43). It was also standard practice that close relatives of employees were given hiring preferences. The prohibition on technical knowledge transmission to outsiders constituted an integral part of Bat Trang's rigid boundaries between its native members and others, as reflected in its three impossibilities (*tam bat kha*) for resident aliens: no transmission of technical knowledge to aliens, no admission of aliens to villager status, and no sale of residential land to aliens.

Within the Vietnamese ideological formation, even into the French colonial period, Confucianism played a major role in structuring the role of women in Bat Trang ceramics firms, both directly and indirectly through its ideological support for the construction of a male-centered hierarchy of public power. In the dominant Confucian conception of social order at the time, hierarchy was constructed on the basis of both gender and moral cultivation. Scholars were ranked at the top because they were supposed to transcend narrow self-interest and maintain exemplary moral behavior for larger social causes. Merchants were at the bottom among the four social categories (scholar, peasant, artisan, and merchant) because mercantile activities, unless on behalf of the state, were considered essentially self-interested and amoral pursuits. The dominant Confucian tradition also engendered female subordination. It structured the public roles of men and the domestic orientation of women. To the extent that women had to participate in the labor force, their roles were restricted to the occupations at the lower rungs of the status ladder (peasant, artisan, and especially merchant). The high status of Confucian-educated men in the local arena was codified in the 1931 village regulations, which granted honor seats to the Confucian and mandarin male elite at the communal house. More specifically, the inner seats, the most honored in the communal house, were de facto reserved for the ritual master (the highest degree holder or the highest ranked mandarin) and the village president (*tien chi*), who had to be either a Confucian doctorate degree holder or a military mandarin with duke status (*quan cong*) (Bat Trang 1931, 30–31). Women who had no access to education had no formal positions in the communal house system.

However, the organization of ceramics firms and the formal structure of Bat Trang at large were also shaped on one level by the alternative bilateral and non-Confucian model of kinship and gender relations and on another by the capitalist ideology that opposed both Confucianism and the non-Confucian bilateral model of social structure. As I have discussed elsewhere (Luong 1989), the bilateral model emphasized the unity of men and women and not their segregration and formal hierarchy as postulated by Confucianism. This model centered on the household, the social unit of greatest significance to women, over whose budgets women had considerable control. As a result, women did not simply participate in the labor force as a last resort but actively pursued household-strengthening economic activities. Constrained by the Confucian ideological framework, these activities of Bat Trang women were restricted to commercial and industrial entrepreneurship. I would like to suggest that the prominent positions of women in the labor force and in the management of the ceramics industry in Bat Trang before 1954 involved a modus vivendi between Confucian-structured female subordination and women's enhanced responsibility framed within an alternative household-centered framework.

The organization of Bat Trang ceramics firms was thus shaped by a multiplicity of ideological voices, both capitalist and other, although the capitalist ideology gained dominance in the political-economic context of strong market competition by Chinese enterprises: the ceramics firms of Bat Trang faced serious threats to their own survival and had no alternative but to engage in high-risk and organizationally destabilizing technological innovation. The impact of strong market competition on the strength of capitalist voices in the local arena can be seen most clearly through a contrast between the pottery firms of Bat Trang and those in Tan Van, a major center of ceramics production in southern Vietnam. In Tan Van, as firms enjoyed an oligopolistic position and a strong demand for their large water jars, workers received generous housing and meal benefits, among others, labor mobility was far from frequent, and noncapitalist ideological voices were strengthened in enterprise organization (Luong and Diep-Dinh-Hoa 1991). In the context of strong market competition in Bat Trang, the strengthened capitalist voice not only powerfully shaped enterprise organization but also heightened ideological tension in the structure of the community at large. In a concession to capitalist wealth, the 1931 village regulations specified that villagers who donated three thousand dongs were granted the (honorary) status of village president and those with a donation of two thousand dongs the status of village vice-president (*thu chi*). In a major departure from a long-existing tradition, other male and *female* villagers who donated funds to village coffers were entitled to seats at the communal house (Bat Trang 1931, 32). The organization of the ceramics firms of Bat Trang in the French colonial period was thus underlain both by the multiplicity of capitalist and noncapitalist voices and the larger political economic framework that structured their relative strengths in the local arena.

The Socialist Transformation

Ironically, in the ceramics industry of Bat Trang, male-dominated gender hierarchy and stable interdependence within the production unit did not become the norm until the Marxist-instituted industrial reform in 1959 that de facto abolished private firms and marked the ascendancy of state and cooperative enterprises. In 1959, all fourteen private firms were merged into a nominally joint state-private enterprise. The latter functioned de facto as a state firm because the former private owners had little input in the management of the enterprise and the production of ceramic products. A pottery cooperative was established in 1962, followed by four others in the 1980s. Under the control of the provincial government, the Bat Trang state enterprise received capital, labor, and materials from the state and produced for the state commercial network according to administrative guidelines. The cooperatives were established on the basis of members' capital and labor contributions. Although the state commercial network purchased most of the cooperatives' products, it did not have monopoly over them.

Under the influence of Marxism-Leninism, a command economy was constructed in which the state's tight control of production and trade under soft budget constraints reduced market pressure on state and cooperative firms (Kornai 1989; de Vylder and Fforde 1988; see also Luong 1993). The medium and large firms of the socialist era achieved an oligopolistic control of the production and distribution processes within the framework of bureaucratic socialism. In this context, in Bat Trang, the state firm increased in size from 556 employees at the time of its establishment to approximately 1,800 in 1978. With thirteen plants and eight offices, it instituted an elaborate organizational hierarchy of director, deputy director, office head, deputy head, and plant supervisor and organized a labor union, youth and women's associations, and party cells. The state firm offered retirement incomes, seventeen paid holidays a year, health benefits and paid maternity leave, greater employment security, upward mobility opportunities, preferential hirings of children and close relatives, and such fringe benefits as subsidized transportation for workers from Hanoi or subsidized housing to single workers from other communities as well as a work-study program up to the university level for its qualified employees—a program with two months of paid educational leave each year (Vu Quy Vy 1980, 148). Under the close supervision of a state-organized union of ceramics cooperatives (*lien hiep xa*), labor relations in the cooperatives of Bat Trang closely resembled those in state firms, although cooperative members' retirement incomes averaged only 25 percent of state workers' and their rice subsidy was only at 30 percent, in contrast to 90 percent among state employees.[13] The relations between workers and the firms became multistranded, as workers depended on their production units not simply for wages but also for a whole variety of goods and services ranging from such basic commodities as rice to housing and education. Each major firm had a senior official specifically in charge of the provision of goods and services. Among state employees in general, in the 1960–75 period, 65 to 77 percent of household expenditures involved goods and services provided by the state, primarily through its production units (Vietnam, General Statistical Office 1978, 178).

Through the process of socialist reforms, despite the socialist ideology of gender equality, women also became less visible at the top level than in the first half of the twentieth century. In the entire ceramics industry of Bat Trang, by the end of the 1980s, among the six major firms only one woman reached the top management position and served for three years (1985–88) as the president of a handicraft cooperative. If we include cooperative vice-presidents, only two out of fourteen senior cooperative managers (14.3 percent) were women at the time of my in-depth field research in 1988, although female workers comprised 52.5 percent of the labor force in the five cooperatives of Bat Trang at the time. In 1996, of the seventeen major raw materials, production, and marketing firms, only one was headed by a woman.[14]

The aforementioned conditions of women at the top level in Bat Trang during the period of socialist reforms were far from unique. According to the 1989 census, women made up only 17.32 percent of top enterprise managers in the state and cooperative firms in two urban areas of the north (Hanoi and Haiphong) and 9.02 percent of those in three predominantly rural northern provinces (Vinh Phu, Quang Ninh, and Ha Son Binh), while female workers comprised 29.39 percent of the industrial work force in the former areas and 43.23 percent in the latter (Vietnam, 1989 Population Census 1991 5:29, 33, 41, 45, 89, 101, 105, 107, 111, 312, 316, 324, 328, 372, 376, 384, 388, 390, 394).[15] Even when we include small and medium firms, (both private and nonprivate and both industrial and commercial), only 23 percent of the owners or top managers of the 256 small urban enterprises surveyed in 1991 in the north were female, in comparison with 10 percent among the 255 small rural ones (Vietnam, Institute of Labor and Social Affairs 1993, 42, 95, 116).[16]

In Bat Trang, the male-dominated gender hierarchy and stable interdependence that had eluded the ceramics firms in the French colonial era came to characterize the state and cooperative firms in the socialist period. I would like to suggest that the restructured organizational form was rooted in a multiplicity of ideologies in the local arena as well as in the Marxist-inspired and reconstructed larger political economy (cf. Walder 1986).

In the Vietnamese ideological formation, from a macroscopic perspective, the introduction of Marxism-Leninism as an anticapitalist ideology and the nationalization and collectivization programs were not hindered by the century-old and Confucian-based suspicion of, if not antipathy toward, *private* wealth accumulation. However, in seeking to break down gender and class inequality, Marxism-Leninism entered into conflict with the formerly dominant Confucian ideology. I would like to suggest that the gender hierarchy within Bat Trang firms in the socialist era was inextricably linked to *both* Marxism and other noncapitalist ideologies. On the one hand, as careers within state and cooperative enterprises were defined under the influence of Marxism within a socialist bureaucratic hierarchy and in terms of the national cause of industrial development, they became more attractive to the male and educated elite on the basis of the Confucian-based equation of maleness and public cause (cf. McVey 1992, 26). On the other hand, the dominant role of men in the ceramics firms of Bat Trang and the Vietnamese industrial organization in general was also facilitated by the persistently strong noncapitalist ideology that continued to structure the domestic orientation of women. Female managers with younger children or older sons would have encountered the problem of domestic chore arrangements both for regular daily work and for network expansion in order to obtain favorable resource allocation decisions from a male-dominated bureaucracy and within the structure of the command economy. Similarly, I would suggest that the stable and multistranded relations between the firms and their employees were constructed with relative ease in the Vietnamese context not only because of Marxist emphasis on the protection of workers' interests but because their seeds had been nurtured in the precapitalist ideology of the indigenous social formation. My interviews suggest that workers were supportive, at least initially, of the new organizational system as they won higher wages, company benefits, and security of employment. In a departure from previous practice in the private sector, state workers received retirement incomes ranging from 45 to 75 percent of their regular pay, depending on their length of service, while contractual workers received severance pay of half a month of salary for each year of service. As one worker observed:

> Although the production technology remained the same after the formation of the joint state-private enterprise, productivity and product quality increased because of workers' greater enthusiasm. Their position had been changed from hired laborers to co-owners despite the fact that . . . their incomes were still based on piecework as in the old days. They received higher incomes and were entitled to retirement pensions, among other things. All workers in the nationalized firms became state employees, while those hired after the nationalization went through a probationary period of up to six months.

The organization of production in the ceramics enterprises of Bat Trang thus had multiple genealogies, both in the French colonial period and in the socialist era (Foucault 1986; Janelli and Kim, this volume). The greater organizational emphasis on stable interdependence was also facilitated by the lack of threat to the survival of state and cooperative firms until 1988 due to the soft budget constraints and the strong reliance on administrative guidelines within the structure of the Marxist-inspired command economy.

Both the structure of Bat Trang ceramics firms in the French colonial period and its transformation in the socialist era can thus be explained only in reference to the multiplicity of ideological voices, their contradictions, and the larger political economic framework. We cannot underestimate the contradictions within the local ideological field. For example, the capitalist ideology on labor as a commodity conflicts with the precapitalist emphasis on multi-stranded interdependence within the socioeconomic unit. For another example, the ideology of gender equality of the Marxist state directly contradicts the century-old framework that justifies the domestic orientation of women in the same way that Confucian-engendered inequality is in perpetual ideological tension with the non-male-oriented model in Vietnam that postulates the unity of the sexes and the considerable role of women in household budgetary decisions. The resolution of these conflicts is shaped by the larger political economic framework, which is, however, also ideologically embedded. In the French colonial period, as the ceramics firms of Bat Trang faced serious threats to their own survival under the strong market competition of Chinese enterprises within the political economy of capitalism, their owners had no alternative but to engage in high-risk and organizationally unstabilizing technological innovation. The ideological emphasis on stable interdependence within the firm as a socioeconomic unit came under serious strain. Similarly, it was within the command economic structure that the male-dominated national bureaucracy made resource allocation decisions often in favor of male enterprise managers and could indirectly shape the gender hierarchy in Vietnamese industrial firms. The organization of ceramics enterprises in Bat Trang in both the colonial and socialist eras can only be understood in terms of the interplay of multiple ideologies within a larger political-economic framework.[17]

NOTES

1. See Rohlen 1974; Vogel 1975; Cole 1979; Gordon 1985; Dore 1973; Pelzel 1979; and Kondo 1990. The thesis on the relation between Confucianism and firm organization has also been examined in studies of the organization of production in Chinese and Korean enterprises (Ward 1972; Walder 1986; Kim 1992; Janelli and Yim 1993, among others).

2. Tonkinese porcelain did not fare as well beyond Southeast Asia as did the products of China and Japan.

3. According to Ngo Vi Lien (1928, 96), the population of Bat Trang reached 2,377 in the mid-1920s. The livelihood of villagers was sustained primarily through non-agricultural activities because in the first half of the twentieth century, the village owned only 70–80 *mau* (62.3 to 71.2 acres) of alluvial fields besides the densely populated 38 *mau* (33.8 acres) of residential land, and because a significant part of Bat Trang's alluvial fields was not obtained until the early part of the twentieth century (Archives of Vietnam, Res-

idence Supérieur du Tonkin M3–66266, Phan Gia Ben 1957, 79). In the first decade of the century, besides coarse earthernware bowls, Bat Trang also manufactured other utilitarian pottery items as well as decorative ceramics. The former included a more expensive line of bowls (*bat yeu* or *bat chiet yeu*) at eight cents a dozen, different kinds of cups and saucers, tea pots, steamed rice containers, lime pots, wine decanters, smoking waterpipes, and floor tiles. Among decorative ceramic products were incense burners, ceramic stools, vases and pots of different sizes (Barbotin 1912, 675, 831–33).

4. Initially established just across from the Chinese-Vietnamese border in order to avoid French tariffs on Chinese ceramics imports at the turn of the century, six Chinese firms had been established by 1910, employing about three hundred Chinese workers and only Chinese ones, and producing annually over two million kilograms of goods (Vedrenne 1939, 939; Barbotin 1912, 818).

5. Barbotin (1912, 681) describes a typical fish-shaped kiln whose singular inner chamber is 12 meters long, 2.6 high, and 3.6 wide; the total structure is 16.44 meters long, 4 high, and 6.8 wide (see also Nguyen Viet 1962, 32–33). It has a slightly curving floor. The floor-level heat vents between the singular chamber and the two-chimney compartment at the end force the naturally rising heat to move toward the floor to get out, resulting in a more even distribution of heat within the kiln (Barbotin 1912, 681). The cannon kilns of Bat Trang at the turn of the century are usually contrasted with Chinese-owned chamber kilns in Mong Cay. A seven-chamber kiln is approximately 17 meters long, 1.6 high, and 4 wide. These kilns had steep slopes, which I estimate at 12 to 20 degrees. Chamber depth increases in ascending order, from 1.5 meters for the first to approximately 2.9 meters for the last. Chambers are connected by vents in interstitial walls located near the floor of the next ascending chamber. Except for the fire mouth at the beginning with 40 by 50 centimeter stoke holes, each chamber had two smaller stoke holes on the sides for adding firewood and its own loading port. The firing team had to fire the fire mouth for approximately eight hours in order to warm the kiln and eliminate moisture. The firing time for each chamber is reduced as one moves upward since the flame already moves to the ascending chambers when the lower ones are fired.

6. The female owners of two of the three largest kilns around the turn of the century were Mrs. *Pho* Tu, a member of the Tran lineage (fig. 1), and a Mrs. *Nhieu* Huyen whose daughter married into the Tran lineage.

7. The firms of Bat Trang were to some extent differentiated on the basis of their products. One was well known for its fake Chinese porcelain and specialized in artistic products for exhibition. Another, built in 1941, specialized in electrical devices and such decorative ceramic items as vases, coffeepots and cups. Two others regularly manufactured some high-quality items (six to seven-thousand fine porcelain bowls with each firing at one of the kilns), while the largest factory produced low-quality pottery en masse.

8. The female merchant, Mrs. Lien, was a member of the Tran lineage and a patrilateral first cousin of Mr. Tran Quang Khai (fig. 1). The two sons of wealthy kiln owners were Mr. Tran Quang Khai and a grandson of Mrs. *Pho* Tu.

9. In both the cannon and chamber kiln eras, some ceramics manufacturers did not own kilns. They either leased kiln space for firing their products or inherited a chamber from parents (thus co-owning a kiln with siblings). An entrepreneur emerging from the

workers' ranks might start as a small-scale manufacturer leasing kiln space and build his or her own kiln after a successful period of operation.

10. The more remunerative position of fireman was left to outsiders because of the hazards of kiln collapse as the heat reached its peak.

11. During the *bat dan* period, a wheel worker molded an average of three hundred bowls a day, while a polisher worked on an average of six to seven hundred bowls (Barbotin 1912, 678). In contrast to native workers, nonnative women specialized in menial and low-paying jobs such as preparing clay, carrying ashes and limestone for glaze preparation, and assisting male kiln loaders. Male alien workers worked in more remunerative positions, primarily as kiln loaders and firemen.

12. There were three women among the four other producers (75 percent) who were classified as small capitalists (entrepreneurs without kilns) during the Marxist-initiated industrial reform in 1959.

13. The union was supposed to represent the production units in their relations with the state, but it played such a large role in enforcing state guidelines on labor and finances that even the expansion of a cooperative's labor force required union authorization.

14. Among workers, the data from the five Bat Trang cooperatives in 1988 indicate that women were heavily concentrated in painting (98.4 percent), polishing (85 percent), and molding (63.6 percent), in contrast to male workers' relative specialization in mechanics (100 percent) and firing (74.3 percent). I did not have access to enough income data to calculate gender-based income differentials, if any existed.

15. The figures from the north can be compared with those from the south: women made up 21.06 percent of the top managers in state and cooperative firms in Ho Chi Minh City, and 15.41 percent in two predominantly rural provinces (Long An and Cuu Long) (Vietnam, 1989 Population Census 1991, 5:35, 39, 233, 237, 263, 267), while female workers comprised 45.26 percent of the industrial work force in the former area and 44.06 percent in the latter (318, 322, 516, 520, 546, 550).

16. For comparative purposes, women made up 17.6 percent of the owners or top managers of the 252 small enterprises in Ho Chi Minh City and 18 percent in the 250 southern rural provinces in the 1991 survey. The 1991 survey of 1,008 small firms included 434 household ones (43.06 percent, using mostly household labor), 305 private enterprises (30.26 percent), 118 joint private-state ones (11.71 percent), 100 cooperatives (9.92 percent), and 51 state firms (5.06 percent). Women comprised, respectively, 34.9 percent and 37.8 percent of the labor force in these enterprises (201, 227, 40).

17. Cf. Laclau and Mouffe 1985; and Janelli and Yim, this volume.

Gender and Capital Accumulation in Chinese Village Enterprises

Ellen R. Judd

Land may be at the heart of rural China's economy and culture, but prosperity in agrarian China has long depended on seeking more profitable avenues in handicrafts, commerce, or labor migration. In more recent years, and especially as part of the socialist initiatives of the late Cultural Revolution period, these alternative avenues became transformed by the promotion of what was earlier termed rural industry. In the postsocialist reform era, these activities have now become subsumed within the more inclusive concept of township and village enterprises (*xiangcun qiye*) and in this form have generated the enormous quantities of capital that have funded China's rapid economic growth during the 1980s and 1990s. In addition to being a major economic force in the countryside, village enterprises combine new features of the market-oriented economy with more established features of the rural political economy centered upon the village.

In this essay I address a central issue in this intersection of global economy and local culture: the underlying structure of gender relations that conditions the relations between village enterprises and village communities. This relationship is one based on the culturally legitimate (if contested) appropriation of women's labor by androcentric communities of agnatically related men directly for the benefit of those communities, and indirectly for the benefit of higher levels of the state and more encompassing layers of the global economy. These living village communities are the primary vehicle of capital accumulation internal to rural social life in contemporary rural China. The appropriation of women's labor is universal within global capitalism, which can deny cultural difference even while using it. It is in the culturally specific mechanics of how labor is appropriated at the local level, however, that one discerns how this process determines the shape of everyday life and, in doing so, shapes contemporary Chinese culture.

Context

As the anthropologist heading for the village makes the descent through the levels of bureaucracy between capital and village, she is presented with a variety of ideological discourses on the state of the contemporary countryside: as steeped in Confucian tradition (particularly apposite for Confucius's home province of Shandong), as representing a socialist path of shared prosperity, or as demonstrating the success of Deng Xiaoping's "socialism [capitalism] with Chinese characteristics." Little of this is to be heard in the villages themselves, where the vitality of any of these discourses is best measured through the relations embedded in everyday life.

These relations are explored in this chapter through an examination of three geographically separate villages in the northern coastal province of Shandong. The three villages were studied individually at separate times in the late 1980s, and all three were revisited in 1992.[1] Zhangjiachedao is a single-surname village of about 175 households located not far from the coastal salt flats in the north of Weifang Municipality. In 1986, its economy was dominated by a large and successful village-level weaving and dyeing factory, which employed 249 staff and generated approximately 70 percent of the village's total income. Zhangjiachedao also had some smaller enterprises, including an orchard and a small clothing factory, and it was planning expansion in the form of a hotel and service complex and a canning factory to process the produce of the orchard. In 1992, Zhangjiachedao was continuing to thrive. Its weaving and dyeing factory had restructured and adjusted successfully to the difficult economic years at the turn of the decade—approximately three million rural enterprises were closed in 1989 alone—and the village was moving toward diversification. The hotel and service complex had been in operation for some years, the orchard had expanded (although the canning factory remained in the planning stage), and the buildings for a new joint enterprise producing garments for export were approaching completion. Zhangjiachedao was a village that had successfully accommodated to the economic reforms of the 1980s. It had moved from the long-term poverty of an economy centered upon agriculture, where the small amount of land available was of very poor quality, to a prosperity built upon rural industry. The key to this transition had been village-level leadership and enterprise. The new administrative village (formerly, production brigade) of

Zhangjiachedao has remained a strongly united corporate entity throughout the transition.

Qianrulin in the south of Weifang Municipality resembles Zhangjiachedao in its emphasis upon rural industry and also in being a small, single-surname village of about 140 households. In 1987, Qianrulin had built a diversified set of rural industries on the basis of accumulation originally generated through its large felt mat factory. This factory was still the largest and most important in the village, but Qianrulin was actively developing several other factories, including an aluminum furnishing enterprise jointly run with a large urban factory in the Northeast, and a factory producing high-quality packing materials for chemical goods. In 1992, the felt mat factory was much reduced in size and importance, the aluminum furnishing factory was flourishing and newly independent of its parent factory, the chemical packaging factory had divided into two enterprises, and new avenues for investment and growth were being actively sought. Qianrulin had also continued its rise to prominence in agricultural productivity despite a small land base, and years of recognition for its path-breaking achievements culminated in a national agricultural meeting held on-site in Qianrulin in 1990. Qianrulin's high unit yields were not its only source of national renown in the conservative years of the early 1990s. Qianrulin is one of the small minority of villages that remains firmly and openly collective more than a decade after decollectivization began its sweep of rural China, and its long-term village Party branch secretary was honored as a national labor model during the National Day celebrations of 1 October 1989. Qianrulin had, like Zhangjiachedao, suffered poverty prior to the rural economic reforms when its economy was essentially restricted to agriculture on a small amount of land. Successful as Qianrulin has been in raising yields—in 1982 it was the first village north of the Yangtze River to achieve grain yields over 1,000 kilograms per *mu*—agriculture has not been its road to the prosperity it is increasingly enjoying. Instead, Qianrulin has successfully accommodated itself to the opportunities offered by economic growth and markets outside the village, while making more limited changes in the political economy of the village itself. The former production brigade has become an administrative village as far as the outside world is concerned, but it continues to use a workpoint system and to own resources and allocate labor on a centralized, village level. The village maintains a strong sense of distinctiveness and cohesion based partly upon its sense of itself as a single-lineage community but also reinforced by its unusual political economy. The appearance of a high degree of village boundary maintenance was even stronger in 1992 than in 1987.

The third village to be examined in this essay is Huaili in the much less affluent Dezhou Prefecture (later Municipality). Huaili is a multisurname village of about 230 households, with a diversified and relatively successful agriculture (grain and cotton) and widespread household-based enterprises. There has been little development of rural industry in Huaili. In 1988, Huaili began running a small weaving factory. It experienced difficulties and closed for part of 1989, restructured and tried to provide some employment, if no profits, in 1990, but was closed by 1992. During the same period of time some of the youth and a few of the mature men of Huaili had contract employment in a paper factory in a nearby township and in various rural enterprises outside the village. These were not viewed as especially desirable avenues for employment, but they were used when available in 1988 and 1989. By 1990, few Huaili residents could be found involved in rural industry, which seemed to have retrenched much more severely here than in Weifang Municipality, where the first village in this study was located. This situation showed no sign of recovery in 1992. The residents of Huaili continued throughout these years to pursue prosperity primarily through household-based productive and especially commercial enterprises. Huaili will figure briefly in the present discussion for purposes of contrast. Even when employment in rural industry was available to the residents of Huaili as an alternative, it was not their preferred route. Their reasons for rejecting this path aid in illuminating the reasons why it was so attractive and profitable for Zhangjiachedao and Qianrulin.

In China as a whole, rural industry, which had been present on a smaller scale in earlier years, mushroomed in 1975 (Song 1984), restructured during the transition years to reform in 1979–81 (Perkins and Yusuf 1984), and grew dramatically in the 1980s (Tu 1986; C. Wong 1988). The rural reform program initiated at the beginning of the decade facilitated this growth by increasing rural incomes, opening private markets, and decentralizing control over production. By the mid-1980s, rural industry employed roughly 20 percent of the rural labor force. About half of this number, or thirty-seven million people, were women (Tu 1986, 33; Guan 1986, 5). At the end of the decade, Shandong Province reported that 45 percent of the total staff in its rural industry were women (Yang 1989, 8). In 1986, the total rural product of the province was officially reported to have increased 16.2 percent over the previous year, but the increase in output value of the rural industry, building, transport, and commerce sectors was 34.8 percent over the previous year. These sectors accounted for 47.7 percent of Shandong's rural output in 1986, compared with 41.8 percent only one year earlier. If rural industry is compared with other industrial sectors, the increase is even more dramatic. In 1986, Shandong's total industrial output value rose 16.4 percent over 1985, but the same increase for industrial units at or below the village level was 63.8 percent, compared with 37 percent for township-run enterprises and 7.6 percent for state-owned enterprises. The rapid growth continued in the following years[2] until the political and economic crisis of 1989. During the late 1980s, rural industry in Shandong, especially at the village level, was a major contributor to the prosperity of local rural communities and to the industrial growth of the province. This development was not unique to Shandong but characteristic of trends in the national economy. Shandong neither led nor lagged behind China's economic development during the 1980s (see Walker 1989). It similarly represented the range of possible responses to the state-enforced cooling of the economy in 1989–90, which resulted in the closure of millions of rural enterprises. This economic development was closely connected with the political events of 1989, being part of the strategy of the central state to reassert firm control over the national political economy. By 1992, those enterprises and regions that had weathered the crisis well were in a strong position for further growth. In 1992, in China as a whole, the non-agricultural sectors of the rural economy (rural industry, construction, transportation, commerce, and catering) grew at an annual rate of 36.9 percent and continued to increase their share of the rural economy (Statistical Communiqué 1993).

From Production Brigade to Administrative Village

Toward the end of the protracted Cultural Revolution period, Zhang Chunqiao and Yao Wenyuan proposed changes in the rural political economy designed to generate economic growth and, contingent upon achieving that growth, narrow the marked inequities between neighboring collectives in the countryside. The key element in their proposal was the strengthening of rural industry at the middle level of the three-tier collective structure. Expanding rural industry at the commune level (now often equivalent to the township level of the administrative structure) was not excluded, but the immediate goal was the more modest one of seeking to reduce or eliminate differences between the various production teams into which local communities were commonly divided and which had an economic base in the effective control of agricultural land and labor. If the middle-level production brigades could expand their rural industrial enterprises, it was argued, the income generated at the brigade level would be sufficient to override the differences in agricultural income between teams within a brigade. Teams could then join their economies and raise the level of the "accounting unit" (*hesuan danwei*) to the brigade without any team taking an economic loss as a consequence, although the poorer teams would experience a greater gain than others. Moves in this direction were taken, for the most part on an experimental basis, in the brief period remaining in the Cultural

Revolution but did not become widespread. This initiative coincides with the initial takeoff of rural industry in 1975, although the consequences have been more widely felt as the growth has been sustained, however unevenly, through the nearly twenty years since that time. In the reform era it has not been politically acceptable to refer to economic achievements of the Cultural Revolution period or even to observe significant continuities. It remains a paradox that moves toward a village (brigade) based prosperity driven largely by rural industry has been one of the marked developments of the reform era's changes in rural political economy.

All three of the villages examined here were formerly production brigades. Even though the existence of the production team as a level of rural social organization has been in question, the existence and boundaries of the brigades/villages have been unaltered in these and neighboring villages. Qianrulin reports an early history of modest initiatives in rural industry, all at the brigade level, prior to the Cultural Revolution (making felt hats, carpentry, and dyeing local cloth). None of these played a major role in village's later development of larger scale rural industry, although the felt hat factory did provide occasion for the contacts that later led to the felt mat factory. The first decisive development in Qianrulin occurred in 1973 with the establishment of a brigade-run chicken farm. This farm subsequently became linked with the county export bureau and grew to become a large-scale operation based on village land but only partly within the framework of the village political economy in existence since the mid-1980s. Its chief contribution to the village was in generating the capital that allowed for the establishment in 1976 of the felt mat factory, which then became the main vehicle of capital accumulation in Qianrulin. After considerable initial reluctance and evasion, Qianrulin's leadership identified 1976 as the year that Qianrulin moved its accounting unit to the brigade level.

Apart from the role of the brigade in rural industry and its political and economic management, it is important to note that other levels of the former collective system weakened. Qianrulin had initially established mutual aid groups in the 1950s on the basis of genealogical principles with agnates within the five mourning grades in the same group. These groups later formed the basis for production teams, but the number of these teams has ranged from one to four and has been a matter of continual readjustment from 1958 to 1992. In 1987, there were three "agricultural teams," as they had then been renamed (they kept most of the functions of production teams), and by 1992 there were two. Whatever nonadministrative social unit might have been reflected at one time or another in these units, they were not able to maintain a stable structure or prevent their resources from being amalgamated in 1976.

The higher level of the commune was abolished nationally by governmental decision and replaced with the specifically administrative unit of the township. Rural people still commonly refer to the township level of government as the "commune" (*gongshe*), but what was formerly a fusion of informal social and formal political roles at the commune level has been officially abandoned in the reform process.

The brigade is in quite the opposite situation. Qianrulin exemplifies an extreme point on the continuum, but brigades have largely continued their existence in the form of administrative villages. These partially coincide with natural village settlements, but, even where villages are imperceptibly separated, as is the case for Qianrulin and its closest neighboring village, the decades of living in separate collective units combined with the continuing political and economic divisions between administrative villages make these living communities as well as formal political realities. In this respect Qianrulin is less exceptional than its continuing collective form might indicate, as will be seen from comparisons with villages that have decollectivized.

Zhangjiachedao is a formally decollectivized brigade/village that has no remaining traces of its former production teams. This village had a relatively weak basis in rural industry, its only early factory at the brigade level having been a small enterprise that processed silk for a nearby factory in Liutan. This small factory was in operation during the 1960s and 1970s and closed in 1976. Although the village's subsequent success has been centred on a synthetic cloth weaving and dyeing factory, extensive discussions with those involved in both the previous and the current enterprises have not indicated any contribution made by the earlier factory to the more recent success. Indeed, on the eve of Zhangjiachedao's move into rural industry in 1979, it was the third poorest of the seventy brigades in its commune. Rural communities in severe poverty are commonly identified as targets for special assistance by higher levels of the state, often in the form of an infusion of leadership and the provision of opportunities through official channels. In 1974, a promising young official who was a native son of the village returned to take over its leadership. He has served continuously as brigade/village Party branch secretary and, since its founding, as head of its weaving and dyeing enterprise.

The village's decisive step came in 1979 with the founding of its weaving and dyeing factory, with the benefit of some outside technical assistance and a substantial loan. The brigade and its new leadership were essential in making this step possible. This factory was one of the earlier rural factories to enter this dynamic area, and it experienced rapid rates of growth throughout the 1980s. The profits generated repaid the loan by 1983, funded high levels of egalitarian social services for the village as a whole, and provided the capital for expansion and diversification. The weaving and dyeing factory continues to dominate

Zhangjiachedao's economy; it successfully weathered the 1989–90 economic crisis and was able to provide the capital for the village's new joint enterprise. Zhangjiachedao's impressive prosperity is dependent upon the success of one large-scale village-level enterprise built through the channel of the brigade/village's political leadership. The village and its leadership appear content with the rural economic reforms and, accurately or not, identify the threshold Third Plenum of the Eleventh Central Committee in December 1978 as the decisive opening of their road to prosperity. But, while Zhangjiachedao has benefitted from opening itself to market-oriented growth, it is also a village with a strong commitment to shared prosperity and a generous level of community social services reminiscent of what the earlier collective system advocated but could not achieve.

The rural economic reform was directed in the first instance toward collectives that had remained poor throughout the collective era. For most of these rural communities, the road taken was one of decollectivization, with collectives being retained longest in areas where they had been relatively successful or where there were significant collective assets that could not readily be divided. Zhangjiachedao exemplifies the utility of the brigade/village level of the polity in the mixed economic milieu of reform China. Zhangjiachedao also highlights the importance of the role of this level after decollectivization. The administrative village has definitely decollectivized, but this has not prevented it from realizing in practice many of the ideals of both brigade and village community.

Huaili shows the marks of its location in a much less affluent region of Shandong Province. Although it has a history of being somewhat more prosperous than its neighbors, this is a relative matter and one based only on success in agriculture—grain, cotton, and market vegetables. The latter allowed Huaili to do relatively well despite a lack of rural industry within the village and few such opportunities in the immediate vicinity. Huaili was classed as an "advanced" (*xianjin*) unit from 1967 to the end of the collective era, but it never made the move to a brigade-level accounting system, presumably because the brigade lacked the income from rural industry that would have been needed to overcome the substantial disparities between its five production teams. Despite the lack of brigade-run industry or any other brigade assets, Huaili resisted decollectivization until 1984. When decollectivization did occur, it was combined with equalization of assets among the five teams in the village. A complex mechanism for the assessment of the value of the assets of each team was arranged, a mechanism involving the participation of all village cadres (but not the women's head) and many of the village's mature men (but no women). The value of the assets of the poorest team (actually the two poorest were at the same level) was taken as a base, and this amount was transferred by each team to the new administrative village of Huaili (which coincided exactly with the previous brigade of Huaili). The three better-endowed teams each enjoyed a dividend of the value of the remaining assets, 15, 32, or 36 *yuan* per capita. Following this adjustment the land was allocated to households in all of Huaili on the same per capita basis. The five production teams were reorganized into three agricultural groups, and these continue to serve as a conduit for land allocation and a variety of administrative functions, though they no longer effectively serve as entities controlling land or labor. In effect, in the process of decollectivization most of the remaining suprahousehold political and economic authority in the village was transferred to the level of the administrative village.

The village also acquired some modest assets in the process. Some of these were used to purchase vehicles, essentially for consumption and service, and the rest were used to construct some commercial facilities to be contracted out. The village has since relied on its income from these facilities to meet its expenses and has declined to collect additional revenue from villagers or to take out loans for investment purposes. Instead, Huaili has for the most part relied upon encouraging households in the village to take up small-scale household-based productive and commercial enterprises. The village's only efforts at larger-scale activity are aimed directly at generating modest incomes for unemployed or underemployed villagers. One such effort is a labor-contracting organization, which procures work in manual transport and loading for some of Huaili's less skilled and less affluent men. Its other effort has been a small weaving factory run in association with the township supply and marketing society. This factory was founded later than many others in Shandong, in 1988, was faltering in 1989, made another scaled-down effort early in 1990, and closed later that year. It was still closed in 1992, and there were no attempts being made at that time to start any new village-level enterprises. It was, perhaps, a good thing for Huaili that it did not attempt to enter rural industry on a larger scale, especially at that time. During the period of my field trips to Huaili, there was a sharp decline not only in employment in rural industry within Huaili but also on the part of Huaili residents in rural industry nearby. Huaili and the county as a whole, and perhaps even the prefecture, had been hit hard by the economic crisis at the turn of the decade, when approximately 3 million out of 21.7 million rural enterprises closed (Quarterly Chronicle 1990, 768) and many others were left struggling. The contrast between Huaili and the other two villages is a dramatic reminder of the increasing economic differentiation in the countryside that the rural reform program produced in its years of growth and its years of crisis. Fortunately, the residents of Huaili have had a degree of success with their household-based enterprises. Some of their reasons for preferring these to employment in rural industry are addressed later in this essay.

The Administrative Village

The end of the commune required its replacement with a set of structures for local government. At least nominally, these were not intended to replace completely the comprehensive social, economic, and political functions of the various levels of the collective system. Formally, each of the administrative villages examined here replaced brigades in a specific governmental sense. This governmental role includes controlling access to land, as land is ultimately considered to be owned by the state and merely allocated to villages, households, and other units. The village is also responsible for collecting taxes and other levies of money, goods, and labor and for enforcing or administering a variety of economic as well as other governmental regulations. In effect, it remains an important economic entity as the local level of the state in a mixed economy.

To the extent that the village level of the state is controlled or managed from within the village, the critical organs are what are together abbreviated as the "two committees" (*liangwei*), the Party Branch Committee (*dang zhibu*) and the Village Committee (*cunmin weiyuanhui*). Nominally, the Village Committee is the site of local government, but by openly acknowledged practice the Party Branch Committee is the senior of the two. In each of these villages, it was always clear that the ranking local official was the Party branch secretary, as is usual. In each case, there was also considerable overlap between the membership of the two committees, and it is valid to examine them together as jointly forming the ruling arm of the state at the village level.

The three villages examined here show minor variations on a common theme. The simplest case is that of Zhangjiachedao, which in 1986 had five men on its Party Branch Committee and five men on its Village Committee, and these were exactly the same men. The woman in the village in the most responsible position was the village women's head, who also served as the paramedic responsible for women's health and the implementation of the birth limitation program. She was not a member of either committee and had not been accepted into the Party, although she was in the application process. By 1992, there had been some changes in membership, and only the village head served on both committees, but the structure was essentially the same. The only interesting change was that the women's head was one of the five members of the Village Committee, and she was now also a Party member. This was not an entirely unusual arrangement for 1992, as the Women's Federation with some support from leading official circles, had been promoting the entry of village women's heads to the two committees since the beginning of the decade. In many cases this was accomplished by adding one more member to the Village Committee. In the case of Zhangjiachedao, a village relatively open to and supportive of women, this able woman has entered the Village Committee without requiring that a special place be provided for her. She continues, however, to have the same responsibilities as in the past, ones that do not imply political or economic decision making or leadership in relation to men. Woman-work in Zhangjiachedao has been cited for its success and the women's head is a capable and experienced person. She was as firm in 1992 as in 1986 that her work begins and ends with women's health, the birth limitation campaign, and family education. Woman-work in this village does not directly address economic issues.

Qianrulin in 1987 had a Party Branch Committee of five men and a Village Committee of six men and one woman. There was considerable overlap in membership between the two committees among the men involved. The one woman was the village women's head, who was also a Party member and married into the cluster of agnates that provided most of the leadership of the village. She was one of the two teachers in the village-run kindergarten. Her role on the Village Committee was specifically that of doing woman-work and did not imply more general political responsibilities. In 1992, there had again been considerable personnel changes but a rough continuity in structure. There were then six men on the Party Branch Committee and five men and one woman on the Village Committee. The one woman was again the women's head and on the committee specifically in this role. This position has not been stably occupied. The middle-aged Party member who filled it in 1987 has been ill and stopped doing woman-work in 1989. The current incumbent is a young unmarried woman who has recently been a birth limitation worker in the township on a contract basis. She was then the object of some encouragement and was being prepared for Party membership, and it was unlikely that she would return to the village. In effect, her position on the Village Committee was empty and in transition. The nominally existing Women's Committee, which in 1987 had consisted of women in a variety of age cohorts, in 1992 consisted entirely of young unmarried women in the village. It will most likely be from this body that the new women's head is selected, but her term will necessarily be brief— Qianrulin is a single-lineage village in which intravillage marriage is nearly unknown[3] and uxorilocal marriage relatively rare. Qianrulin took steps between 1987 and 1992 to increase its level of activity in woman-work, but there were no claims from any quarter that Qianrulin was particularly active or successful in this respect.

Huaili had a number of changes in the personnel of its leadership bodies during the period of fieldwork, but the structure remained stable, with five men in the Party Branch Committee and five men in the Village Committee, the village head being the vice-secretary of the Party branch. The village had a succession of women's heads during this period, as two left the village for residence elsewhere. Earlier women's heads had not served on either committee, but the young married woman occupying the position in 1992 was on her way to such a position and also to Party membership. This able and energetic woman was receiving active support from the village Party branch secretary and from the township Women's Federation.

This summary of leadership structures and gender relations is cursory, but it is adequately indicative of gender representation in formal political leadership in the villages. Some aspects of the informal political structure and economic life in the village will be addressed in the following sections. In conducting investigations in each of these villages, I actively searched for women who were playing a role in village political and economic life or who had at any time held a role of public prominence. I am reasonably confident that I have identified and interviewed all such women in these three villages on at least one occasion and in some cases on each field trip. There are relatively few such women, and almost all will be included in the present discussion. The exceptions are an elderly woman who was a wartime village head and has long been retired from public life, an elderly and respected midwife (who had also once served as a village women's head), a few women Party members who are comparatively inactive in public life, and some women who have been successful in running household-based enterprises in Huaili (their voices will be heard indirectly). The role of women in the public structures of the state at the village level are important because of the enhanced role of the village and because these structures are the ones through which state policy (including policies with important implications for women and gender relations) are introduced into village life, actively or with elements of local resistance.

Village Communities

Each of these villages is simultaneously an administrative unit of the larger state and a living community. In some respects the shape of the living community is itself drawn from the political realities of decades of a political order that established deep and clear boundaries between the members of different collective units, through separating their economic interests and establishing separate lines of political authority in each collective unit.

In some respects the villages have also grown around lines of community structured less by administrative fiat than by the generative power of customary relations of gender and kinship. Here the classic considerations are those of patrilineality and patrilocal postmarital residence (see Diamond 1975). Patrilineal descent is an efficacious structuring principle in everyday life in these villages, although the descent groups standard in the literature regarding Southeast China are not to be found (see Cohen 1990). Qianrulin and Zhang-jiachedao are both single-lineage villages and Huaili is a multisurname village in which one lineage clearly predominates and at least claims to have settled the village prior to the arrival of the other lineages.[4] The founding lineages in each case arrived during the period of officially forced settlement of Shandong during the Ming dynasty, and their current descendants are concentrated around the twentieth generation from the founders. Although some descendants have since left and founded other branches, for example, in the Northeast, each community retains a core of agnatically related men who have at least an approximate sense of their genealogical relation to each other.[5] Apart from their formal genealogical connection, the men in each community—unless they leave as migrants—live in communities composed of related men throughout their lifetimes. Women, in contrast, typically marry out of their own villages early in adulthood and, although they usually do not go a great distance, almost always cross the boundary into another administrative village. Each village has a small number of uxorilocal and intravillage marriages, but the overwhelmingly predominant pattern in each case is patrilocal postmarital residence. Each village also demonstrates the usual pattern for marriage in rural China, which is that marriage matches are made through intermediaries known to the families of both parties with a view to making an appropriate match, but there is no pattern of arranging that women will marry into villages in which they have close (or even remote) relatives. In other words, women are removed from their natal communities and divided among a diversity of marital communities, while men remain for a lifetime within a community composed of a large number, and in many cases an overwhelming majority, of agnatic relatives. As I have argued elsewhere (Judd 1994), the genealogical principles are probably secondary, and the primary distinction here is one of gender difference in residence practices sustained over generations, with resulting communities that are profoundly androcentric in structure.

These lived androcentric communities are ones whose depth of experience and whose boundaries have been substantially reinforced by the shared interests generated by the vesting of local political and economic interests in localized collectives during the collective era. The importance of these communities in shaping the implementation of policy and the everyday relations of gender in rural communities has been well established for the collective era (see

Croll 1981; and Parish and Whyte 1978). The strengthening of the administrative village in the reform era has contributed to the persistence of this landed androcentry.

Village Enterprises

Within the village as the critical site for the intersection of state and community in the rural political economy, village-run enterprises are assuming an increasingly important role. This might partly be viewed as a direct consequence of its rate of growth and contribution to rural living standards and rates of accumulation. It is also the case because rural enterprises are profoundly gendered in all dimensions of their social organization and economic activity. The growth of rural enterprises is a significant arena for the contemporary reformulation of gender relations in rural China.

Village-run enterprises are able to retain part of their profit as incentives to management and workers and part as funds for further investment, but much of the capital accumulated through these enterprises is transferred to the village. The village has been the channel in each case for the original investment, whether through direct investment of village resources, through acquiring loans from outside the village, or through allocating capital accumulated from other village enterprises. The village ultimately owns these enterprises, although they may be managed under a contract system that allows each enterprise's management a degree of managerial control and material incentive.

Control at the village level resides in the village's two committees. Responsibility within these committees is divided in such a way that each area of economic importance (such as agriculture or enterprises) as well as of general public concern (such as mediation) has one committee member assigned to it. The Party branch secretary and the village head each have overall responsibility for their respective committees. As indicated in the previous discussion, these positions are entirely occupied by men. Even where women may have entered one of the committees (usually the less powerful Village Committee), she will only have responsibility for woman-work or, at most, some additional public service work. None of these villages has had women in any positions of responsibility in economic or general political roles at the village level during the period of this study. This is not unusual and is in fact the recognized norm and customary practice. There is a similar pattern of exclusion of women from economic management within village enterprises, but this issue may be better approached through a more detailed examination of the specifics of gender roles in the workplace in these villages.

Three major categories of person are to be considered in analyzing the structure of the labor force in village enterprises. The first of these consists simply of the men of the village that runs the enterprise. These may be of any age and will include ordinary workers as well as managerial and technical personnel. This category includes the overwhelming majority of men involved in village enterprises—male migrants from other communities may not be preferred employees and are themselves more likely to seek employment in urban centers than in neighboring villages. The chief exception to this is the occasional, temporary hiring of men with skills not immediately available within the village. The second major category consists of married women within the village running the enterprise. The extent to which these women are involved in village enterprises is critical in understanding the significance of these enterprises in the lives of rural women. The third major category is that of unmarried young women.[6] These women often form a very large portion of the work force in rural enterprises, and this is the case in all three of the villages examined here. These women may come from the village running an enterprise or from other villages. In either case, their relation to the enterprise is clearly understood to be temporary. It is rarely possible for a young woman working in an enterprise in her own village to continue doing so after marrying out of the village, and marriage for young women migrant workers typically also presents demands incompatible with their continuing to work as they did prior to marriage.

In Qianrulin in 1987, nonagricultural enterprises in the village provided 96 percent of the village's gross collective income and 90 percent of its net collective income according to official village figures. The same source reports that 84 percent of the village's work force was engaged in nonagricultural work. The village enjoyed full employment, as socially understood within the village. The particularly interesting feature of Qianrulin's work force is the early retirement of women in recent years. Women in Qianrulin typically retire from work outside the home between the ages of forty and forty-five. This is described by many in the village as being related to the first arrival in a household of a daughter-in-law, who can then replace her mother-in-law in the work force, commonly (in 1987) in agricultural labor. Although the arrival of a daughter-in-law was generally accompanied by household division, retirement did still occur when economic circumstances permitted. Whether or not the household had divided, close relations were maintained and the mother-in-law was available to care for grandchildren and the members of her own and closely related households. This pattern is closely related to that of Daqiuzhuang, the village that became a subject of intense debate in China in the late 1980s when many of its women chose to leave the public work force to care for other family members who remained in the work force (Zhang and Ma 1988). Although not mentioned in these public debates, Daqiuzhuang was characterized by a large complement of workers from outside the village working in its village enterprises. This was evidently part of the economic base, which allowed women to retire early as well as to contribute to high living standards and continuous investment. In 1992, a village leader who had been involved in this research during both field trips related women's lower rate of participation in the village work force to the strength of the village and its enterprises—these provided attractive opportunities within the village for men, so that men did not migrate to other locations in search of better employment. Consequently, women were less needed in the village's work force.

The critically important enterprise in 1987 was the felt mat factory. In a village with only 326 people in its labor force, the felt mat factory was large enough to employ 200 people on a year-round basis. The village's requirements for agricultural labor (58 people on a year-round basis), its determination to diversify into other enterprises (especially aluminum furnishings and chemical packaging), and the undesirable character of the work in the felt mat factory contributed to opening employment opportunities in this factory to workers from outside the village. Except where there was a temporary need for technical expertise, such opportunities were not provided in the village's preferred factories (aluminum furnishings and chemical packaging), which offered cleaner and healthier working conditions and required more skilled work. Sixty of the 99 positions held by women in the felt mat factory were held by young unmarried women from outside the village; 19 of the 101 positions held by men were held by young men from other villages.

The felt mat factory exemplifies patterns of gender division of labor that are shared with the other enterprises in the village, with the only significant differences being those connected with the scale and pattern of use of labor from outside the village. In 1988, the felt mat factory had eighteen managerial personnel at or above the workshop level, all of whom were Qianrulin men. It had eight sales and procurement personnel who played critical roles in the economic success of the enterprise and who worked on a commission basis. All of these were also Qianrulin men. The only woman in the factory who could be described as having any managerial responsibility was the woman who managed the small unit that turns some of the factory's waste products into utilitarian sofas; this unit consists of one male carpenter and three women seamstresses in addition to the head of the unit herself. This woman is one of the three women Party members in the village, a daughter of a leader in the adjacent village and a daughter-in-law of Qianrulin's Party branch secretary. There are two other women in the village who occupy comparable positions of junior management in other enterprises, and none is in a position of economic accountability or decision making.

Among the production workers in the felt mat factory there is a clear, and typical, division of labor along lines of gender and age. Women over the age of forty (who appear to be those women in the village in greatest economic need; one was over seventy years of age) cut up large pieces of raw material by hand, while young men run machines that shred smaller pieces of material. Men between the ages of eighteen and thirty-five run the simple machines that press the material into mats. The youngest women in the factory (under the age of twenty and perhaps far under that age) remove the pressed material and deliver it to the largest work group, where teams of three young women and one young man soak and press the mats, a particularly dirty and damp part of the process. Young men work in the packing workshop, women in their thirties sew the mats into bundles, and an unmarried woman in her twenties weighs the bundles. There appears to be a pattern of giving the more desirable women's work to mature married women, assigning the least desirable work to young unmarried women (most of whom are not from Qianrulin), and reserving at least some minimal employment for elderly women who are unable to retire.

Wages earned by workers from outside the village are significantly lower than wages earned by the people of Qianrulin. Remuneration is different in each factory, but the felt mat factory, as the largest employer of outside workers, is the best example. The standard daily rate for Qianrulin people working in this factory in 1987 was 6.5 *yuan*, while for outside workers it was 4.0 *yuan*. The factory leadership explained the differential as justified because the investment for the factory had come from Qianrulin; they did not observe that the capital accumulated through their work in the factory would be held by the village and that they would never enjoy the benefit of this portion of their labor. This applies to both men and women from outside the village. Here the village boundaries and village ownership of rural enterprises operate to deepen village boundaries and consolidate the landed androcentry of the village political economy (see Judd 1992). Similarly, young unmarried women of Qianrulin enjoy full employment in Qianrulin's enterprises and earn the Qianrulin wage, but they will not receive long-term benefits from the products of their labor, as marriage out of the village will terminate their rights to Qianrulin resources.

In 1992, Qianrulin had successfully weathered the economic crisis and shakeout of vulnerable rural enterprises of 1989–90; in 1991 alone, Qianrulin's enterprises had provided 600,000 *yuan* to the village. By 1992, Qianrulin had proceeded further in restructuring its village enterprises toward more capital intensive and skill intensive processes offering better working conditions. This restructuring also made Qianrulin's economy more secure, as it kept pace with shifts in China's rapidly developing rural industry. The felt mat factory was still in existence in 1992 but was in decline. The oil fields are reducing their use of industrial felt mats, and this was the sole market for these products. Although there have been some modest efforts to move the factory toward the clothing industry, the major change has been the reduction of the staff to a total of 102. No Qianrulin people are entering work in the factory, and the village intends to find alternative employment in its other enterprises for Qianrulin people who are still working at the felt mat factory. Most of the reduction in staff has been accomplished through laying off or not replacing workers from outside the village; Qianrulin has not assumed any responsibility for providing these people with alternative employment. Of the remaining 12 managerial workers, 4 are women employed at the workshop level; the 6 sales and procurement workers are all men. Women predominate among the workers in the factory—they are 64 percent of the 70 staff loosely designated as technicians and half of the 14 described as ordinary workers. The managerial and sales and procurement staff is composed of all Qianrulin people, but the majority of the workers are from outside the village—their proportions are between 50 and 70 percent in the two technical and the ordinary worker categories—and workers from outside the village comprise 55 percent of the total staff of the factory. Qianrulin leaders state that the reason for this imbalance is that work in this factory is unattractive and Qianrulin people, with more attractive alternatives in other village enterprises, are playing a reduced role in this factory.

The felt mat factory remains the village's main employer of outside workers, and the wage differential between Qianrulin and other workers also continues. It is now described as a ratio of 6:5 for the village as a whole, and benefits are provided to Qianrulin workers but not to outside workers. Prevailing opinion in Qianrulin continues to view these differences as appropriate. In three cases, young women have been able to continue their employment in Qianrulin enterprises after marriage.

Qianrulin's restructuring has moved it toward less labor intensive and more capital intensive enterprises. The leading enterprise in 1992 was the aluminum furnishing factory, which had concluded its five-year joint contract with a plant in Shenyang and from the end of 1991 had been wholly a Qianrulin enterprise. After starting with investment funds provided through the village from the profits of the felt mat factory, funds from the Shenyang factory, and some loans, the aluminum furnishing factory has been able to return increasing amounts of profit to the village since its second year of operation. Qianrulin expected to receive 400,000 *yuan* in profit from this factory in 1992, part of which would be used to fund the village's further initiatives in diversification (another furnishing enterprise was the immediate priority). All but 10 (7 men and 3 women) of the 108 staff (92 men and 16 women) are Qianrulin people. The factory leadership (all men except for one workshop head) considers itself responsible for providing employment in this factory, the village's most attractive and profitable enterprise, to Qianrulin people and hires a few outside workers only on the basis of personal connections (*guanxi*).

In 1990, the management of the aluminum furnishing factory, in consultation with the village leadership, decided to move toward pay equity for women and men employees. Previously the male to female wage differential was 8:7 in this factory. The change met with some resistance, although the difference was not enormous and occurred when the staff of the factory was experiencing increasing income. This initiative has not been carried into other factories, and the leadership of the new paper packaging factory, another important enterprise in the village, maintains women workers' wages at 85 to 90 percent of men workers' wages. The factory head in that enterprise objects to women on staff on the conventional grounds that it is a waste to train unmarried women, who will leave (a concern voiced for some technical roles in the aluminum furnishing factory as well), and that married women allow their work to suffer in giving their primary concern to their families.

The initiative of the aluminum furnishing factory in gender equity in wages has not been matched in the area of wages for workers from outside the village. The wage ratio for Qianrulin and outside workers in this factory is 4:3, and there were no efforts to change this. The factory leadership reported that the village supports this differential as one that provides more profit for the village.

Qianrulin might be viewed as making a shift from an early stage of capital accumulation dependent on appropriating the labor of young women workers from outside the village to a slightly more mature stage of enterprise development where profits and a long-term favorable position were being sought from more capital intensive and high wage enterprises. The unquestionable preference here was to generate desirable opportunities for the people of Qianrulin. It also appears that this shift was accompanied by a reduction in the employment of women. The main employer of women in the village, the felt mat factory, had reduced its staff and, because they were outsiders, these workers were not reallocated. Older women in Qianrulin retire at an early age, and the village has had a continuing preference to place young mothers in agricultural work on the grounds that this is more compatible with child care demands (although much child care is actually done by grandmothers). In 1992, Qianrulin's Women's Committee reported that only 208 of the village's 354 women were currently in the work force. Of these, 112 were assigned to the two small agricultural teams and were working less than full time. This is in line with widely observed trends toward the feminization of agricultural labor in reform era China (also see Judd 1990a, 1994).

Qianrulin also shows signs of moving in the direction of Daqiuzhuang. Boserup (1970) observed long ago that women's labor and hired labor might be alternatives within peasant households and that there were class implications to this distinction. The situation exemplified by Qianrulin suggests that villages may make similar calculations between the labor of village women and the hiring of outside labor. The outside labor in this case has been largely, although not exclusively, female, and in this sense the interests of different categories of women are placed in opposition by the structure of the deep boundaries of corporate village communities. To the extent that Qianrulin employs its own women in its enterprises, by 1992 it was able to offer these women, both unmarried and married, positions in the preferred enterprises. Young unmarried women from outside the village remained available to fill the less preferred positions, and the only effective avenues for these young women were labor market-strategies of seeking the best available employment.

Zhangjiachedao has pursued a somewhat similar path of developing village prosperity through enterprises relying heavily upon women workers and especially upon women workers from outside the village. There are, however, some illuminating contrasts that indicate the latitude individual villages have, within common economic constraints, to make differing decisions regarding the structure of their local political economy—including its gendered dimensions. Zhangjiachedao has relied overwhelmingly upon a weaving and dyeing complex while also maintaining a few smaller enterprises (such as a local construction group and an orchard). Together these have generated 90 to 92 percent of the village's total output value since 1985. Only the governmental requirement that rural communities continue to cultivate staple foods has prevented this proportion from rising still higher.

In 1986, Zhangjiachedao had 280 village people in its work force but 249 in the weaving and dyeing factory alone. The village's need for excess labor was met by hiring 99 workers for the weaving factory from outside the village, the majority of whom are young unmarried women doing shift work on the looms. In 1992, this factory had grown to become a three-factory (plus a workshop on the way to factory status) complex employing 587 people, 60 percent of whom were hired from outside the village. The majority of these were still young women working the looms. The village had nearly completed construction of a new factory building to house a joint enterprise factory to produce garments for export to Southeast Asia through the Hong Kong partner in the venture. Most of the work in this factory will require sewing and 80 of the 100 workers to be employed at the beginning will be women. The leadership does not intend to reallocate workers from its existing factories, and as only a few recent school leavers will be available from within Zhangjiachedao, the remainder will be employed from outside the village.

Management in Zhangjiachedao's weaving and dyeing enterprise was almost entirely male in 1986. The only exceptions were a young woman who worked as an accountant, a responsible position but one that did not require her to supervise men, and the factory head's wife, who ran the dining hall as an extension of her domestic responsibilities. By 1992, the young woman accountant had married out of the village, and the factory head's wife had taken on a role in the village's commercial building. The expanded weaving and dyeing complex of 1992 still showed a nearly complete absence of women in management. The management of the complex as a whole had a staff of sixty-eight, all of whom were men. This included forty sales personnel in up to twenty other cities. Each factory had its own set of factory heads and vice-heads, financial management heads and workshop heads. These remained almost completely male. The one prominent exception was a thirty-one-year-old married woman accountant who was an upper middle school graduate and a Party member. She was described as highly competent and having a promising future. A few other women were located in minor accounting and stock management roles. The factory was preserving the conventional division of labor in which men do management, sales and procurement, driving, security, and furnace and machine repair work, while women work at the looms, inspect cloth, do some of the work in packaging, and perform some of the minor accounting roles. The high demand in a weaving factory for skilled women workers to tend the looms has ensured that Zhangjiachedao will have a high proportion of women workers in its factories, even without an attempt to hire less expensive labor.

Since the beginning of Zhangjiachedao's move into rural industry, the weaving and dyeing factory has been relatively capital intensive, by contemporary rural standards, and has required the employment of skilled workers. Maintaining a high level of quality in the products is important in this competitive area of rural production, and the need to achieve and maintain this is described by the village and enterprise leadership as a reason for recruiting only workers with a minimum lower middle school education, providing relatively good wages (largely on a piecework basis), and keeping wages for workers from within and without the village at the same levels. The village has a tradition of valuing education and was ensuring that its own young people (both women and men) received lower middle school educations in 1986, although this was not necessarily the case in surrounding villages, especially for women. Zhangjiachedao's educational requirement did not result in excluding women workers but worked instead to encourage keeping young women in school at a time when this factory was one of the most attractive local employers. This is in sharp contrast to the situation more widely reported in reform era China, including Qianrulin, of young women being removed from school early in order to maximize their earnings prior to marriage.

Zhangjiachedao primarily recruits young unmarried women but does not require that they leave the factory upon marriage. Women from other villages do find it difficult to reconcile the shift work with domestic demands after marriage, however, so few married women outside the village work in Zhangjiachedao. Married women within Zhangjiachedao, many of whom first came to the village as factory workers and later married in, do continue to work in the weaving and dyeing complex, and noticeably older women are concentrated more in inspection work than on the looms. Zhangjiachedao's goal is to provide this employment for as many of its people as possible, both women and men, but my more detailed 1986 study showed that this could only be accomplished for married women when these women were able to arrange for adequate child care, even when doing shift work. In effect, women with mothers-in-law to help in the home were able to continue to work in the factory, but many women in nuclear families were unable to resolve the conflicting demands upon their time. Zhangjiachedao's policy worked where it did not place unresolvable demands upon married women.

Following a brief experiment with concentrating agricultural work in the hands of a few households in the early years of the reform, Zhangjiachedao reallocated land so that every household would have some land and, at the same time, cut factory shifts from twelve to eight hours, with the goal of avoiding an economic division in the village between those working in agriculture and those working in the more profitable village enterprises. The policy has succeeded in preventing a division between households, although it has not entirely prevented a tendency for married women to do a disproportionate amount of agricultural labor. The combination of all of these factors has allowed Zhangjiachedao to have full employment for all its available women and men and to have additional opportunities for workers—primarily but not exclusively women—from elsewhere.

Zhangjiachedao has maintained an enlightened and benign labor policy toward its women workers, including those from outside the village. Nevertheless, certain of the structural factors identified in the discussion of Qianrulin are pertinent and significant here. Women workers from outside the village and Zhangjiachedao women who marry out of the village will have contributed to the accumulation of capital through the weaving and dyeing complex but will not enjoy the long-term benefits of the increased economic activity and generous village benefits available to the men of, and to the women married into,

Zhangjiachedao. Some young women in Zhangjiachedao have indicated a desire to marry within the village so that they will be able to continue to work in the factories and enjoy the benefits offered in Zhangjiachedao. The village permits and in some cases encourages intravillage matches, but the young men of the village feel no comparable incentive and come into constant contact with young women workers from other villages. Consequently, young women in Zhangjiachedao expect to continue to marry out of this village. The men of Zhangjiachedao continue to enjoy opportunities in the management of expanding village enterprises and the prospect of continuing to reside in a prosperous village. The corporate nature of the androcentric village community perpetuates a gender imbalance in the generation of, management of, and access to capital.

Huaili exemplifies the type of village that provides outside workers to other villages. Huaili's only attempt at developing rural industry was the initiation of a small weaving factory, which began operation in 1988. This factory entered a crowded area of production late and was never successful. At its brief peak it employed thirty-four workers, and it never generated profit for the village. The village struggled to keep it in operation in order to supply some modest employment for young people who could not be productively absorbed into either agriculture or the small enterprises characteristic of the village's reform era economy. This factory failed in the crisis of the turn of the decade, and in 1992 the entire county in which Huaili is located had still not recovered from the economic crisis. This was the first of the villages I revisited in 1992, and I went on to the others in some trepidation that their entire village economies, so dependent upon rural industry, might have totally collapsed. I might better have anticipated the actual situation: that the villages with developed rural industry in more affluent regions were able to survive, while those that were more marginal and located in poorer regions were the ones to collapse.

Prior to the end of local rural industry, Huaili had some of its residents employed outside the village, although migration was not a major factor in this village, and local people appeared to have few personal contacts that might provide them with employment elsewhere. In my sample of forty households in 1989, I found five young women (four unmarried and one married) and eleven men working outside the village. The predominance of men is typical, as men migrate elsewhere more than women do, and they may retain rural households even when they are working elsewhere on a long-term contract basis; women typically either leave rural communities (if they are able to change their household registration) or work in other communities only temporarily before marriage. The weakness of rural industry in the immediate area of Huaili, which is overwhelmingly agricultural, provided few local alternatives. Apart from the older men who had long-term positions in the county seat or in urban centers further away, the work these people could find was in nearby township and village enterprises, enterprises in the county seat, or, for two of the young men, contract work in another province.

Again, apart from the men with urban employment and urban registration whose households remained in the countryside, there were some striking patterns in the employment and the accounts of employment choices of the young people of Huaili. They did seek such employment but only as a necessary and temporary means of generating some income in an area of considerable surplus labor. The employment was not viewed as remunerative or desirable unless it was urban and showed some prospect of a change in household registration and exit from the countryside. Village enterprises, of course, can never provide this attraction. As economic conditions deteriorated, both workers and managers in these enterprises went for long periods without payment and were uncertain about when, how much, and even if they would be remunerated. For some positions in factories in the county seat, workers were asked to make a substantial cash contribution in advance of being hired to contribute to the investment needs of the enterprise. Although enterprises were known to be potentially income generating, the employees and their relatives in Huaili did not find that working in such an enterprise generated much income for them individually.

The perspective of mature women in the village, including those who were participating in county-initiated activities to involve more women in income-generating work, was one of firm opposition to any move in the direction of rural industry. They perceived rural industry as inevitably run by men and as providing limited opportunities, if any, for them. Indeed, Huaili's one effort in this direction was one with management and technical roles performed by men and looms being worked by young unmarried women. Married women—in effect the adult women resident in the community in which they could expect to spend the rest of their lives—did not see rural enterprises as either a realistic or a desirable alternative. Instead, they preferred small household-based enterprises and the household sidelines traditional for women in rural China. Elements of the working conditions within the household were implicitly attractive in the autonomy they offered, and some women in the village were visibly doing very well running their own household-based enterprises.[7] It was also strikingly apparent that this was where the greatest income-generating possibilities lay and that all of the income could be retained within the household. The more successful household enterprises ("specialized households" or *zhuanye hu*) faced some tax levies, but Huaili refrained from assessing any levies against village households. Household enterprises in Huaili were able to accumulate the capital to expand their enterprises and enter new areas of endeavor; they were also able to weather the crisis of 1989–90 with some resilience.[8]

Gender and Capital Accumulation

It is not unusual, from a cross-cultural or historical perspective, to find women's labor fueling industrial transformation (Nash and Fernandez-Kelly 1983; Fox-Genovese and Genovese 1983) and yet remaining, in other respects, marginal to the continuing life of a community, a household, or even a woman's own later life. Young women in Hong Kong (Salaff 1981) and Taiwan (Gallin 1984; Greenhalgh 1985) contribute to their households and their brothers through their labor in industry prior to their own marriages. A major element in the understanding of the role of women's labor in the industrializing economies of Asia has been this substantial contribution of women's labor to their natal families. Contributions of this character are to be found in the material summarized here, and young women's natal families benefit from their wages in rural enterprises.

In the case of rural enterprises in China, the product of women's labor is also being appropriated by a form of social entity that is both an agnatically based community and a local level of the formal political economy. In the past, much of the attention given to the implications of the rural economic reform program for women has focused upon the potential strengthening of household-based patriarchy (e.g., Davin 1988). While this may well occur, an argument focused on this level of social organization appears to underestimate the role of more inclusive levels of social organization that are also androcentric in composition and patriarchal in practice. In earlier studies of the impact of collectivization on social life in rural China, the unanticipated importance of the collective system in solidifying and incorporating local communities has been observed (see Croll 1981; and Parish and Whyte 1978). The importance of patrilocal postmarital residence practices was early identified as a major limiting factor on women's role in public life in rural China (Diamond 1975).

In reform era China the rural household has assumed increased economic importance as the site of substantial control of resources in agriculture, both of land and of labor. Some households have developed household-based enterprises into relatively large-scale farms, factories, and commercial entities. At the same time, a quantitatively large and structurally influential portion of rural economic growth has been based in township and village enterprises in a mixed economy. The village communities of China, as reinforced through the collective era, remain major suprahousehold entities in the rural political economy.

Their control of rural social life is less direct than it was during the collective era, but the new indirectness and added subtlety may be viewed as an indicator of strength and resilience (cf. Shue 1988).

The rural community in its current form as administrative village has emerged from the reform process as a vital dimension of the local state and at the same time as a deeply rooted and lived community. Whereas households have commonly been too small and economically weak to induce the economic transformation of the countryside, village enterprises have been one of the most significant vehicles for this transformation by mobilizing women's labor to contribute to capital accumulation. The principles of patrilineal descent, patrilocal marriage, and filial piety that structure the androcentric communities in which these women work make it possible to legitimize the appropriation of women's labor—not only in rural industry but also in agriculture, domestic labor, and child care—and to do so in the name of community, family, and morality. Neither the appropriation of women's labor nor the legitimation of this as natural is unique or even unusual within global capitalism, but the social articulation through which these are done ensures an extraordinarily effective accumulation of capital while maintaining a distinctive shape to social life in contemporary rural China.

NOTES

The research reported here was supported by a series of grants from the Social Sciences and Humanities Research Council of Canada: SSHRCC–Chinese Academy of Social Sciences Bilateral Exchange Grants, 1986 and 1987; a SSHRCC General Research Grant, 1986; a SSHRCC Canada Research Fellowship at the University of Western Ontario, 1987–89, and at the University of Manitoba, 1989–92; and a SSHRCC Research Grant, 1992–95. The author gratefully acknowledges the cooperation and assistance of the Shandong Academy of Social Sciences, the Shandong Women's Federation, the China Shandong International Culture Exchange Center, local authorities at various levels in Shandong, and, especially, the leadership and people of Zhangjiachedao, Qianrulin, and Huaili.

1. Zhangjiachedao was visited in 1986 and 1992, Qianrulin in 1987 and 1992, and Huaili in 1988, 1989, 1990, and 1992. A much more detailed presentation of the data from the fieldwork during 1986–90 is provided in Judd 1994.

2. For details on the following years, see Shandong's Economy 1987; also see Shandong's Performance 1988; Shandong's Economy 1989; and Shandong's Economic Performance 1990.

3. I was able to locate only one case of intravillage marriage in Qianrulin. This was a marriage between members of different surnames. There are so few households in the village with surnames other than the dominant one that intravillage marriages will not

become common in Qianrulin. Qianrulin is firmly opposed in intrasurname marriage, although some other communities, such as Zhangjiachedao, do permit it when the marital partners are only remotely related. The changing practices of some rural communities is important to note—the norm of patrilocal postmarital residence is not a simple survival from the past but a continuing practice rooted in contemporary conditions such as those outlined in this essay. Indications of receptivity toward intravillage marriage, as in Zhangjiachedao, is a significant indicator of the contemporaneity of these practices and their potential openness to change.

4. Each village does in fact have a few households of other surnames, but these are recent arrivals and the presence of a few such households is not unusual in single-surname villages. What separates Huaili from the other two in this respect is the presence of several other established surnames in the village.

5. A genealogy for the core lineage in Huaili was updated in the early 1960s, and several copies are available in the village and nearby villages settled by the same surname. Qianrulin preserved some of its genealogical records by incorporating the stone monuments on which they were carved into the foundations of irrigation stations in the Cultural Revolution. The carved characters face outward and are easily read. These, together with the records in official registration books and the memories of lineage elders, enabled me to compile a complete genealogy in 1987, record of which was kept in the village. Zhangjiachedao lost its genealogy in the Cultural Revolution and does not seem to have an interest in recording this aspect of its history. I have seen a photograph in the village of a senior lineage member living abroad that shows him standing in front of a genealogy, and I assume that genealogical information is available in some form in the village.

6. This situation raises one of the important issues regarding women in rural China— the extent to which the boundaries of households and communities divide women. The patterns described here do indicate that women married into villages with successful rural enterprises are likely to be enjoying the product of other women. This is a complex question, which will require more extensive examination elsewhere. For the purposes of the present argument, it is crucial to note that control of village resources is firmly in the hands of men. It is the gender imbalance in control of resources, control of the village polity, and lifelong residence that together characterize these communities as corporate androcentric villages.

7. For a more extensive treatment of this aspect of rural economy, see Judd 1994.

8. For a more extensive treatment of women's agency and strategies in these contexts, see Judd 1990a, 1990b, 1994.

Recycled Labor Systems: Personal Connections in the Recruitment of Labor in China

Diana Lary

In the western part of Beijing is an organization that for decades was dedicated to the international propagation of news about the glories of Chinese socialism—the Foreign Languages Press. The press published magazines and translations of Chinese literature into foreign languages. Though much of its product was turgid, it did publish many fine translations, most of them by China's best translators, Gladys Yang and Yang Xianyi. The passing of revolutionary socialism in the late 1970s and its replacement with "socialism with Chinese characteristics" promised hard times for the press. Journals such as *China Reconstructs* and *Chinese Youth* no longer fitted the times, and their circulations dropped. Many of the authors whose translations the press had published moved to publishers outside China. These losses happened at a time when the press found itself forced to become commercially viable in a world in which financial self-sufficiency was becoming the watchword.

In this new commercial world, the press has been quite successful in making money, though not by pursuing its original goals. Commercial viability turned out not to lie with the adaptation of its publications work, though some of this has been done, but with the exploitation of the press's hidden asset—its huge internal courtyard. As interest in socialism withered, the courtyard became a major money spinner. In its first tentative commercial incarnation, about a decade ago, the courtyard was metamorphosed from a rather dusty but tranquil area of paths and flower beds into a depot for building supplies. The people who lived in the press apartments had to pick their way through piles of planks and iron bars and heaps of sand and coal. Loads of building materials moved quietly in and out through the side gates. Few questions were asked about who was running the business; it was assumed that the leadership had found a discreet way to make money for the good of the unit.

The next stage was more adventurous. A glittering new "dining hall" was built in the courtyard at a time when communal eating had all but ceased. The dining hall's purpose became clear each Friday and Saturday night, when it operated as a highly profitable disco. Now residents picked their way through the building materials to the strains of disco music, their steps illuminated by strobe lights. This time the moneymaking was overt, no longer discreet, though there was not much further clarification in the destination of the profits.

The third profit-making venture has been the most intrusive. It is a scheme to house contract laborers working on construction sites in the city in sheds slapped up in the middle of the courtyard. Hundreds of men, peasants brought in from various parts of North China, live in long, low sheds built of paper-thin materials, poorly lit, without sanitary facilities. They live in isolation; there is no contact between them and the people who work and live in the press. The men are disliked and even feared by their unwilling neighbors. They live shadowy lives, dimly perceived by the other residents; they come out only to go to work and to perform unmentionable acts behind the buildings (one of the reasons they are so much disliked by the residents). Lurking in their huts, they are mute, passive, and accepting of their complete inferiority as peasants in the city.

These men are members of labor gangs, brought in by labor bosses to work on specific construction projects, staying only as long as it takes to finish a job. They arrive with their own labor contractor or boss, who handles all the details of their work and accommodation. The bosses cut deals with the press for space and pay well for it. The press sacrifices the privacy of its staff members for a good, steady income.

The press is one of innumerable state units that have diversified to make money and one of the many urban units that now house migrant laborers. In all the cities of China, units make money by renting space to labor contractors to house their workers. The living conditions are grim and makeshift, but the workers are marginally better off than other migrants, the job seekers who have no fixed place of work and doss down wherever they can in station forecourts, under flyovers or bridges, and alongside railway lines.

The old system of labor segregation between city and countryside, with urban workers in permanent jobs and peasants kept out of the cities by the cordon sanitaire of the *hukou* (population registration) system, has given way to a system that relies heavily on mobile, cheap labor that commands little in the way of benefits. Is this a new labor system, derived from the ethos of the new hybrid state, dangling somewhere between socialism and capitalism? Are the present labor systems a reflection of the influence of an impersonal international economy in which low wage and benefit levels are the key element? Or are we seeing the revival of pre-Communist labor systems, of traditional Chinese economic systems of employment based on personal ties?

Cultural Reversion

The situation of the contract workers suggests the latter: that employers of labor have reached into China's traditional social and cultural systems to find ways of recruiting and using workers. Relying on contract labor signals a reversion to a traditional system in which family and local connections determined employment and in which the individual deferred to the family. Cultural reversion is producing a labor system that suits employers and benefits families but treats the individual workers shabbily. Whether the reversion is self-conscious or not is hard to tell; but clearly the attractions to employers of a system that creates a cheap, docile, labor force are the same today as they were in the economy that came to an end with the arrival of communism in 1949.

This chapter does not deal with high culture (*wenhua*), which has been the concern of earlier chapters in this volume. Instead it looks at culture as the social and economic customs that are considered characteristic of a particular category of people (*fengsu xiguan*), in this case the unwritten rules of their game for Chinese migrant workers. The two meanings of culture are connected, in that both belong to the deep structures of society governing relations between people, but they are not always equivalent. While high culture relies on text and clearly articulated patterns of behavior, the other form of culture is best observed in action and understood from the forms its takes; there is little direct written evidence to explain its working.

The old forms of labor recruitment like contract labor are manifestations of the second form of culture. They were embedded in the social fabric of China, part of the personalistic structures that dominated rural life. It was through chains of personal ties that people went abroad, moved to the cities, migrated to Manchuria, or found jobs as miners or railway builders before the Communist revolution. These recruitment systems, which dominated the lives of the early generations of urban workers who were still close to the farm (Hershatter 1986, 4, 50), have proved to be tenacious, having been able to survive for long periods in abeyance. More than three decades of communism, which saw the traditional labor system as antiquated, feudal, and inimical to proletarian organization, sent them underground but did not destroy them. As soon as the changes in economic policies after 1978 allowed, they bounced back again.

Their durability can be explained in part by the enthusiasm of employers for the cheap, easily managed labor such systems provide, but other parts of the explanation derive from basic cultural traits of a traditional, highly localized, rural society. Local ties, once swamped by a universalist ideology that stressed class ties above all else, are now ascendant in the cultural vacuum left by the atrophy of that ideology. The new contract workers owe their ability to move to local connections, the reemergence of local identities, and the reactivation of local and personal ties. There is also the respect for talent, in this case entrepreneurial, that inspires confidence in people less bold to trust labor contractors and defer to their knowledge of the outside world. A third element in the durability of this labor system is the renewed dedication to the family. The young contract worker understands that, for the sake of his family, he must go away to work. He knows he must put his family's interests before his own and suffer to help the family—as previous generations of sojourners have done.

The elements of durability in the recruitment of labor are located in cultural norms that stress local loyalty, respect for ability, and devotion to the family. They can also be made to appear as a variant of the high cultural value of reciprocity in which all participants in the labor arrangement are seen to benefit. The worker introduced to a labor boss to work away from home lives with familiar people, keeps in touch with home, and reintegrates smoothly to his native place when the contract is over. The employer gets well-behaved labor that does not require direct management, training, or benefits. The labor contractor makes a good living by helping his fellow locals. These positive traits may also be seen as window dressing for a system whose main advantage is that it is a source of cheap and docile labor. It uses cultural constructs to supply workers who will not protest against poor working conditions, squalid living conditions, and low wages. To an outsider, it might seem that these cultural constructs underlying the new-old labor system are agents of exploitation and mistreatment. To the insider, it is a tough, unbeatable system, made even stronger by the fact that it has survived the frontal attack of communism.

Traditional Employment Patterns

In the traditional economy, the recruitment of labor reflected the governing ethos of the whole economic system, the reliance on family and personal connections. Forms of recruitment evolved within this highly personalized economy and were reinforced by traditional beliefs of a society in which the individual mattered less than the collective—within what Wei-ming Tu has termed "a network of human-relatedness" (1984, 80). The network's basic unit was the family and then extended through a widening circle of more distant ties to people from their own locality, then to people who spoke their own dialect, and finally to people from their own province. All persons knew their places, knew what their duties were and what their expectations might be (Goodman 1995). An obvious corollary of the system of personal connections was that connecting a person tightly to a number of people at the same time meant disconnecting them completely from a far larger number. The whole system has been counterpoised by its protagonists against the individualist and impersonal nature of Western systems, which are seen to be based on legal rules and regulations.

China's traditional labor system was well-articulated and developed. Young workers going into skilled trades were apprenticed to a master craftsman, laborers in the countryside were hired by the month or the year, casual help needed for short terms during the busy seasons of agriculture (*nongmang*) were hired through local labor contractors, and coolie labor hired for work abroad was recruited by similar contractors. In all these forms of labor, recruitment was based on personal ties, and discipline was enforced not by written contracts but through personal hierarchies. Even in large enterprises personal ties were the rule: workers did not deal directly with their employer but with their contractor.

This highly personal system stood just above, in the employment hierarchy, the most personal of all systems, the family. In late Qing and early Republican China, though economic modernization was under way, the family was still the basic unit of the Chinese economy and each family was the economic mainstay of its members. Each grown member of the family contributed to the family economy; all were expected to work for and share in the prosperity of the family. Economic activity outside the context of the family was inconceivable. The older family economy had been localized, tied to the land, and limited in the ability to move to seek work. From the late Qing on, however, the family economy started to become more complex. The physical range of activity increased dramatically with the growth of train and steamer travel, for now it was possible for workers to be moved around inside China and to go abroad. As the number of employment opportunities expanded, families began to diversify, with different members pursuing different occupations, all for the benefit of the larger family. This trend toward diversity was perceptible both in elite families, where some young males continued to work for degrees while others went into business, and at lower levels of society, where young peasants started to leave the farm to go abroad, work in the cities, or go into the army, a process known generically as "leaving the village" (*licun*) (Bergère 1986; Tanaka 1929; Wu 1937).

The strategy of family diversification was a reaction both to new opportunities and to political and economic uncertainty; the family spread risks by seeking opportunities to earn money away from the main family base or even by setting up branches of the family in new places. The heart of the family remained in the old home, and the economic management of the family stayed with the senior members of the family; children were expected to be obedient and to accept parental assignment to employment.

Individual migrations were not haphazard in the way they were organized or in what they were intended to accomplish. They were closely tied to the needs of the family. One need was marriage. A large number of the young men moving to Manchuria, for example, were men whose marriages had just been arranged and who had to earn money to pay for the wedding. Other needs were to buy more land or build a new house. The decision to leave was made attractive to the family by an incentive, the recruitment bonus, or *anjiafei*, paid to the family just before the new worker departed. This payment, which the worker had to work off as soon as he started work, enabled the family to make money on the migration even before it had taken place.

Distinct patterns of migration emerged during the Republic. Young people who left home to work as a service to the family engaged in what were called shuttle migrations if they were for short periods over fixed distances and recurred regularly. They were called sojourner migrations if they meant going away for a longer period on a semipermanent basis. The migrants did not create their own jobs; they were dependent on the creation of new forms of employment that required large numbers of workers. The new emerging forms of labor meshed well with family needs for new sources of income. One was coolie labor, in response to the huge demand for labor outside China for railway, canal, and harbor construction, for plantation and mine work, and even to dig the trenches during World War I. Another was heavy labor inside China in mines, on docks, and on railways. A third was factory work, especially in the new industrial centers partly or fully under foreign control. Industrialization expanded the possibilities for diversification. It allowed unmarried girls, who had seldom worked outside the home before, to earn labor wages too by leaving home for a period of time and working in the new factories. The financial contribution of unmarried daughters became important to the family: it was the only contribution they would make to the family and one that could help to pay for the expenses of a marriage. A fourth new employment opportunity was to be a soldier in the swollen armies of the warlord period (Lary 1985).

Contract Labor

Recruiting young people to fill the new positions sounds as if it should have been very easy in China, with its vast population. It was actually not straightforward at all. China had no modern labor market and no means of formally advertising for workers. It was possible to go to a marketplace and simply put up a sign with two characters on it saying "looking for workers" (*zhao gong*), but there was no guarantee that this would yield anything but the unskilled and the unreliable. Armies often recruited off the streets, but they could afford a degree of roughness in a recruit that a factory might not be able to take (Lary 1985). A better way to find reliable workers was to use traditional social patterns of association to meet the new opportunities. Contract labor, one of the main planks of the traditional labor system, was well suited to finding recruits for the new forms of work available.

In the contract labor system, personal connections were fundamental. To find new workers, enterprising men set themselves up as labor contractors and made contracts with those who needed workers. They were commonly called *batou*, *gongtou*, or *baotou*, regional variations with the same meaning, normally translated as "boss" in English. These men were sometimes in business for themselves, sometimes part of a larger organization, but always directly responsible for their own workers. The boss looked for recruits in a place where he was well known, usually his native place. The recruits came in through his network of direct personal connections and were therefore all connected to each other in some way. After being hired the recruits traveled together to the place where they were going to work; once there they lived together and worked together, their whole lives organized by the boss, who stayed with them most of the time.

Employers needing workers got in touch with a boss, either directly or through his organization, and ordered a certain amount of labor for a fixed fee. The amount could be expressed in terms of the number of workers or the work to be accomplished. The contract could be detailed or simple but it always made clear that the workers worked for the contractor not for the company. The system worked in similar ways inside China and overseas. A contract for the supply of Chinese workers for a British Columbia salmon cannery at Deas Island, south of Vancouver, stipulated that Wing Chong and Co. of Victoria should supply a "sufficient number of skilled workers" to pack 25,000 cases of salmon and a boss, to be approved by the B.C. Canning Co., whose job it was to keep the workers under control and make sure that they did not sell alcohol to the local natives.[1]

A standard product of such recruitment was the labor gang, recruited to work in a neighboring province or far away across the sea. The basis of recruitment was not the terms of service but the workers' trust in the contractor based on their personal connections. It made little difference either where they were from or where they went. They might be labor gangs from Hubei in Hankou, much of whose work force on the Yangzi river boats and the docks in the late

Qing was made up of migrant laborers organized in gangs (Rowe 1989, 43). Or they might be gangs of railway builders in Heilongjiang or stevedores in Vladivostok, both recruited in Shandong. Or they could be cannery workers in British Columbia recruited in the Pearl River Delta.

Local ties worked in many different ways within this system. They were the means of recruitment, they formed the circle of comfort within which the workers lived, and they were a refuge in time of trouble. They also divided their members from other groups. If they made the workers' lives supportable, they also ensured a divided labor force. The local ties were strongly reinforced by dialect and accent; there could be no coming together of workers who were divided from each other by barriers of dialect and accent. Nor could the newcomers blend into a new city and settle down there when they were so clearly segregated (Rowe 1989, 49). The segregation did not have to be imposed by law or force; instead it relied on local ties to keep one group together and exclude others. By a neat manipulation of traditional social patterns these ties could be used to give comfort and security to the workers, to benefit their families, and to bring convenience to their employers.

The heavy reliance on personal and local ties among migrant laborers was often disguised by the fact that there were few visible characteristics defining local affiliation—no costume or physical differences. Dialect or accent was the only clear superficial indicator of difference. The size of the movements of people from the late Qing on also gave a strong sense of vast, undifferentiated numbers. This was the case with the huge migration to Manchuria that began in the late Qing and reached its full flood in the 1920s. What looked like a blind flood of young men was actually a conglomeration of small groups of people from the same place, each made up of a boss, some experienced men, and some greenhorns. The migration depended on personal recruitment and personal trust. The bosses were connectors to webs of recruitment that stretched from Manchuria into most of Shandong Province; they made arrangements with factories, mines, or labor agencies to supply a certain quantity of labor and then went home to get it. They were regarded by their workers not as vicious exploiters or as agents of the Japanese employers, the end users, but as men who made possible something essential—the earning of extra money for the family. Some were regarded almost with affection, as people who made it possible to find employment, helped to make departure from home less traumatic, and looked after the interests of the inexperienced young men while they were away.[2]

Contract labor was not a system of naked exploitation. It is difficult to use the term *exploitation* for a system in which almost all participation was voluntary. The employers benefited from having a guaranteed unit of labor power, which could be relied on to perform a specific task and then leave, and showed no responsibility or concern for the welfare of their workers. The workers had their advocate: part of the boss's job was to make sure that the terms of employment agreed upon were met, and at this task they were often quite skilled. If they wanted to stay in business, they had to have some credibility with their workers. The workers agreed, with rare challenges, to be part of a system that treated them as impersonal cogs, paradoxically, within a situation whose whole basis was personal ties.

The sense of identity between the boss and his workers could be strong enough to put them squarely in unity. In some cities, bosses were less involved in recruitment and more concerned with labor protection, fashioning what in effect were craft unions. The role of bosses as labor organizers and protectors can be seen clearly in Beijing in the 1920s, where craft guilds were long established and the workers local and tough minded. There the bosses acted as agents for workers within the craft guild system, arranging work, fixing prices, and mediating between employers and workers; for these services they took a percentage of the workers' wages, but they were still seen as the workers' friends not their enemies (Strand 1989, 149–51). Often they were workers themselves, the master craftsmen on specific jobs (161).

The sense of fellow feeling should not be exaggerated. Quite often the bosses were closer to the employers than to the workers and little concerned with the latter's welfare. This tendency shows up in the textile industry, where the gender composition of the work force made conditions worse than elsewhere. There the selection of labor was heavily determined by gender; a heavy preponderance of workers were young women. In 1929, the percentage of women workers in Shanghai industries was 61, and it kept going up. Percentages went even higher in the Depression, as women's wages were depressed, and reached their highest levels just before 1949, when percentages of women in some factories were up to 80 (Honig 1986, 50–56). Factory owners went out of their way to increase the number of women workers, in theory because their nimble fingers were best suited for the work but also because they were seen as more docile than men and less likely to strike.

Much of the female factory work force was recruited in ways similar to those used for male workers in labor gangs. The women were brought in by labor bosses, who recruited them in their home localities. The motivation for going away to work was similar, too. The girls' parents were willing to let them go so that they could first bring immediate cash into the family, the recruitment bonus (*anjiafei*—"money to settle the family"), and then take care in advance of the expense of their own marriages. The girls worked off the costs of their dowries. Personal moral safety was stressed, for their purity had to be guaranteed if they were to marry. They remained under the tight control of the person who had recruited them during their brief working careers. The girls were confined to the factory and the dormitory and met no one while they were away from home except people from their native area. Union organization was unthinkable, and good behavior was built into the system since bad behavior or bad performance would redound to the parents' discredit and might ruin the girls' chances of marriage. In this neat, smooth system, everyone seemed to benefit. Girls could work for short periods, and the work force was always young and inexperienced. The system also made sure that the women worked long hours, under terrible conditions, for minimal wages (Honig 1986, 122–24).

Migration to Manchuria depended on similar systems of recruitment through local ties, in this case within a single province, since over 80 percent of those who moved to Manchuria were from Shandong. Little direct recruitment was done, for the system of localized recruitment proved efficient, bringing in as many as half a million new workers a year during the early decades of the Republic. The main supply of labor was again secured through contracting, though some found work through family and friends from home who were already working there. Migrants settling on the land in particular tended to be recruited by family members.

Use of local ties for recruitment seemed to take little regard for the degree of economic development of a place or of the number of people already there. In Manchuria, which had a very small population before the start of Japanese industrialization, bringing in labor from outside seemed quite natural. What is surprising is to see the same system of recruitment used to bring workers into more established urban centers, where, in spite of large populations concentrated in small areas, personal connections were still the preferred means of recruitment. In Tianjin of the 1920s, virtually none of the labor force in the textile industry was native to Tianjin. Eighty-six percent of the carpet weavers were introduced to their work by friends and people from their native place (probably the same thing) (Hershatter 1986, 49–50).

The networks of personal and local ties used in contract labor were based on a profound sense of local identity captured in the term *laoxiang,* which meant either "old home" or "people from the old home." *Laoxiang* the place was where the ancestors were buried; *laoxiang* the people were those who were more distant than immediate relations but close enough to share a common heritage, common interest, and common concern. It probably meant coming from the same village or the same district. The exact definition was imprecise, but the meaning was well understood, and people knew who was connected to them and who was not. In migration the *laoxiang* connection ensured that the workers knew their boss, thus relieving them of much of the fear and uncertainty that normally goes with migration.

The second part of the *laoxiang* connection had to do with the working experience itself. People worked together in groups from the same area and found comfort and solidarity in being together. These ties could be so close that it was perfectly possible to migrate from one village in Shandong to another in Manchuria and live always with *laoxiang,* in fact to be always in a village with the same name, only that the second was the *haiwai cun,* the "village across the sea." They managed to leave home without leaving home.

Rotating Labor

This system of labor recruitment militated against the creation of a permanent working class; the whole point of the system was that it was a means of rotating labor. The aim was for a worker to return home after a brief period away and never leave home again. His or her place would be taken by the new generations of young people. These were the short-term migrants whom Gail Hershatter called "inconstant workers" in her study of the Tianjin labor movement. She cites studies by Fang Xiangting in the late 1920s to show how short were the terms worked; well under half the handicraft workers surveyed (in the carpet and weaving industries) had been at their jobs for three years (Hershatter 1986, 58). In an arrangement that suited the short-term goals of the employers (a cheap and docile labor force) and the long-term goals of the workers' families (infusions of money) the labor force stayed temporary, fairly unskilled, and firmly rooted in the countryside.

The New Year Festival, the key family ceremony, played a major role in the perpetuation of rotating labor. All workers went home for the New Year to bring their earnings to their families and renew their family ties. From Manchuria they often came back for a longer period, leaving at the onset of the harsh winter. Arrangements for future employment were made just after the New Year. Workers might or might not go back to their work, depending on whether they were offered a new contract and whether they had fulfilled their own goals.

The stay away was extended if the original financial goals had not been met or if other factors, such as warfare, prevented return. This was more likely to happen to people who had moved abroad or to Manchuria than it was to short-distance contract laborers. For unfortunates their brief time away could extend to years. Chan Sam is one of many examples. He migrated to Vancouver in the early 1920s, intending to stay a few years and then go home. The Depression left him without enough money to go home in the 1930s, the Japanese occupation made it impossible for him to return between 1937 and 1945, the Civil War made it impossible from 1946 to 1949, and the advent of the Communists put him off so much that he was still in Canada when he died in 1957, decades after he had originally intended to return home (Chong 1994).

The industrial labor force of the Republic grew in absolute numbers, but its composition shifted constantly, largely because it was recruited on the basis of these traditional patterns. The old patterns were adapted and reinforced because of the specific composition of the work force. These patterns of employment made formation of unions very difficult, which is one of the reasons why the Chinese Communist Party made so little headway either in the cities or in Manchuria. Labor activism was almost inconceivable when workers were not committed to industrial life and were controlled by personal systems of employment.

Workers' Paradise

The newly established Communist government after 1949 tried to get away from the old labor system. A key part of the industrial reforms of the early 1950s was the development of a permanent labor force, generously provided with an iron rice bowl. Workers were the heroes of the new state, and they were rewarded with lifetime security within their units. They lived where they worked and received free medical care, day care, and even paid holidays. Their direct remuneration was low; rewards were more likely to take the form of citations than of cash. They were not pushed to work very hard and worked instead at an enjoyable, even leisurely, pace, with ample time for tea, cards, and calisthenics. Workers were required to be loyal, to loudly support the Party, and to refrain from agitation on their own account. Independent trade unions were anathema.

This system may have been politically desirable, but economically it was catastrophic. It kept China in an early stage of industrialization, producing poor quality goods in antiquated facilities in the absence of market competition, production for export, or enterprise competition. The system was eventually eroded, however, not by economic but by political pressures. The upheavals of the Great Leap Forward and the Cultural Revolution deprived China's workers of much sense of heroism or enthusiasm. By the time the economic reforms started in the late 1970s, the state sector was characterized by the "two lows'"— low productivity and low morale. It could not be the engine of economic reform.

For higher productivity and greater efficiency, the new economy had to go outside the state sector and produce through local ventures, joint ventures with foreigners, and enterprises set up by individuals. This meant hiring labor outside the state sector. In 1986 the Ministry of Labor introduced new "temporary regulations" on contract labor, labor recruitment, and the dismissal of workers. In this context "contract labor" did not mean people employed through a labor contractor but people who themselves had signed a contract with an employer for a fixed period of work—more likely to be called short-term or casual work in English (Kotzec 1992, 26–27). The workers were paid wages but were not eligible for any benefits in the way of housing, health care, or retirement. There was no guarantee here that the temporary regulations would apply to all casual workers. They were interpreted less as a sign of protecting the new type of worker than as a sign that the iron rice bowl was corroding.

Cheap Labor

Since the start of the reforms and the opening to the outside, a cheap labor regime has been one of the chief factors attracting foreign investors to China. (Another is the size of the Chinese domestic market, a topic not discussed here.) China's overseas investors are drawn by the idea of a huge pool of cheap, docile labor, not as skilled as elsewhere but guaranteed to work for low wages and not ask for health care, pensions, security of employment, or workplace safety. Domestic employers in manufacturing, construction, and the booming service industry are pleased to be able to find workers who do not demand the privileges previously associated with being a worker.

In the search for reliable labor, several forms of worker recruitment have emerged. Government agencies recruit and supply labor. Labor is exported to foreign countries by the Ministry of Foreign Economic Relations and Trade (MOFERT). When these schemes started, the authorities were careful to distance themselves from any accusations of promoting coolie labor, declaring: "Labor trade is not the cruel 'slave trade' that exported 'Chinamen' in former times. Rather it is a profitable use of excess labor." At the moment, there are more than a hundred and seventy thousand Chinese laborers working abroad under direct government contracts, all sent through MOFERT (*China Daily,* 5 Aug. 1985).

A second form of labor recruitment is ad hoc—the workers themselves come to the work. In all the developing economic areas of China there are pools of job seekers milling around, people who have taken off for the city in the hope that they will find work. They often travel long distances, most noticeably by railway. This flood of workers, which reaches its peak just after the New Year, is called the blind flood (*mangliu*). Official estimates suggest that as many as twenty million people are roaming the country looking for work (*Agence France Presse*, 5 June 1994).

Chaotic as this movement seems, there is often considerable internal cohesion and order. Though the young men and women who make up the flood usually look ill equipped to take on the industrial world, they have a sense of what they are doing. They have been sent out as part of a family strategy. The family has staked them to finance the cost of their journey and the expenses of getting started at work. The idea is that the stake will be handsomely paid back by the wages the worker earns, which will fulfill the fundamental aim of contributing to the family economy. When they arrive at a new place, they look for people from their own areas and use *laoxiang* ties to find jobs and places to live. The disadvantages of a free system of recruitment such as this are that it is fairly hit or miss for the worker and offers little security to the employer; it does provide cheap labor but in no way guarantees that the worker will be capable, honest, or reliable. For the employer the risks are greater than they are with a more traditional and reliable form of recruitment—contract labor.

Contract labor is the third major system of recruitment, bringing in gangs of workers through contractors. The employer gets a fixed quantity of labor for a fixed price and a fixed period. Though the workers have no previous experience, they are regarded as highly "trainable'"—that is, not stupid, respectful, and docile. The workers come from various origins, as time goes on from further and further inland. There are both men and women. The men are destined for work in gangs in construction or other forms of heavy labor; the women, young and unmarried, will mainly go to factories or the service sector. The young people live in segregation, by sex and by age. The young men live in sheds in temporary and precarious conditions (Woon 1993, 17). The young women live in dormitories in the plant, and they seldom leave it. The plant as a whole is not made up of people from the same area, but the working units are. The women are segregated by dialect from other people in the plant. They are deeply beholden to the contractor who arranged their work, and who has probably stayed with them, and they are equally beholden to their families, who have high hopes in terms of the money they will send home or bring back when their contract is finished.

Two recent studies of working conditions in the special economic zones, one by a young Hong Kong scholar, Lee Ching Kwan, who worked in a Shenzhen factory alongside women workers, and the other by a young Taiwan scholar, Hsing You-tien, who visited Taiwan joint ventures in Guangdong and Fujian, tell sad stories of girls living in conditions not far removed from incarceration, working up to fourteen hours a day, often on piecework, and subjected to a shop floor routine that stipulates fines for a wide range of internally defined offenses (Hsing 1993; Lee Ching Kwan 1993). These stories have an uncanny resemblance to the stories of workers in the 1920s and 1930s.

As in the earlier periods, local and personal ties are deeply embedded in the new patterns of work. They are the basis on which contract workers are hired. On the job they provide a means of communication and demarcation between groups of girls who form their own units within the impersonal factory. After work they provide social comfort and personal connection (Lee Ching Kwan 1993, 13). These ties are important for those not recruited by bosses because they are their entrée to a job. They also serve the interests of the host community by identifying the outsiders and consigning them to a lower level within the work hierarchy. Woon Yuen-fang's recent research in Kaiping shows the major role that local ties play in a new and complex labor market (Woon 1993, 17).

Employment and the Family

The revival of traditional systems of recruitment is an indicator of a revival of family authority. While local ties may be the operational way to get work, it is the family that demands that its young go off to work and seeks to accumulate capital through their labor. The economic basis for the new patterns of employment may be the boom in the Chinese economy, but there is also a social basis. The family as an economic unit is flourishing again after the battering it took from socialist political movements. Family authority has been reasserted and family ritual and ceremonials reborn. The family bears new demands that its members have to meet. The revival of traditional practices such as dowries, weddings, and funerals puts major pressure on the family economy, and young people have to help pay. Young men must earn money to contribute to the setting up of proper households for their brides. Young women have serious expectations to fulfill for their families. Before they leave their families, incurring considerable costs for their marriages as they do so, they must contribute by working.

Families used to worry about the political behavior of their members. Now they must be strategic in their economic thinking. Ideally they pursue economic diversification, getting different members to contribute in different ways. The best way for an urban family to benefit from the new economy while keeping some of the security of the old system is to keep a base in the state sector, where rewards may be low but the benefits considerable, and send other members to work outside in the private sector in the special economic zones. This often produces a generational division, with the older members staying in the state sector and thereby maintaining rights to housing and other benefits.

The fact that they have greater access to urban housing than younger members do increases their value to their families and allows them to reassert control over the younger generations lost so dramatically in the Cultural Revolution.

The new family economy based on diversification is not stable. Individual elements are insecure: private sector jobs are impermanent, contract labor is short term, and the state sector is under attack, though it is politically too costly to uproot completely. There is a pervasive sense of insecurity about the maintenance of family prosperity. Urban residents are vociferously unhappy with inflation, increased rents, and high utility charges. Though people are unlikely to repeat the great protests of 1989 attacking corruption, political arrogance, and inequity, given that the protests ended in a massacre, what they will tolerate has limits. That tolerance will depend in part on the degree to which the diversified family economy can flourish.

The rural areas vary from region to region, but here, too, there are limits to how much the family economy can adapt. The opportunities seem to be drying up. Apart from the millions who are moving around looking for work, there are tens of millions more at home who are unemployed. And the young people in the "blind flood" on the move are not well protected and are vulnerable to cheats and exploiters. Their anguish is extenisvely covered in a book published in Beijing in 1990 (Ge and Qu 1990).

The new economic family is not necessarily a family based on ties of affection and earned respect, which is the form of Chinese family being more and more celebrated in Singapore and Hong Kong. It is a hard-headed, demanding family. By law its members *have* to support each other. More and more services that were once free or subsidized are now commercialized—education, health care, recreation—and have to be paid for. Some members are likely to be much more expensive than others. Nowhere is the revival of the traditional family more obvious than at the top of society. The PRC leaders started their political careers attacking their own families. Individual attacks gave way to mass attacks by young intellectuals on the "feudal family." This stage was followed by efforts to mobilize the Chinese to break the old bonds and create new people. Their conceptions of the family have modified over time and now include a regime in which the status of child or grandchild of a high Party cadre (*gaogan zinu*) is the best guarantee of success at home and abroad.

Conclusion

The term *inconstant* was used by Hershatter to describe the workers of Tianjin during the Republican period. The undertones of disparagement in the use of the term may be misleading. The system served two compatible goals, those of the employers and of the workers. The people whom it did not suit at all, hence the use of the term *inconstant*, were those who wanted to see the growth of a permanent urban labor force. After 1949 it was thrown onto the scrap heap of history.

This scrap heap turns out not to have been a moribund place but one where old cultural systems were stored for future retrieval. In the present stage of ideological bankruptcy, the retrieval of the personal system of labor seems an obvious example. But there are winners and losers. The winners are the employers, who get reliable labor at cheap prices, and consumers, often foreign, who get cheap goods. The family system is also a winner. And the biggest winner is the state of China, home of the fastest growing economy in the world. The losers are the workers who live and work under miserable conditions, their desperate ambitions to make money leading them down the garden path.

There are embarrassing discontinuities with the ideology of socialism, not yet formally discarded. The most obvious is the failure of the state to protect its workers, to provide adequate income for those in the state sector, or to protect the rights and even the lives of contract workers. A string of industrial accidents, particularly factory fires, caused by unsafe working conditions continues. In joint ventures, accidents can be blamed on "widespread abuse of worker rights by China's new overseas capitalists," as was the case with the December 1993 fire at the Gaofu plant in Fuzhou (*South China Morning Post* 11 Dec. 1993; 29 Jan. 1994). But blaming the outsiders does not displace the fact that Chinese authorities are responsible for the lack of safety regulations and worker protection. The National People's Congress in July 1994 passed China's first labor law, which promised good things for workers, but its success or failure will depend on the willingness and ability to implement it.

It remains to be seen whether the low wage scenario itself will be stable. It pits different parts of China in competition against each other and against other bottom-wage producers such as Burma and Bangladesh while enriching entrepreneurs in China and abroad. The image of socialism, even "socialism with Chinese characteristics," may have to be scrutinized. And in an age of easy communication, it may be impossible to prevent worker organization; there have already been discussions about forming unions within foreign joint venture operations. The All China Federation of Trade Unions (ACFTU) has vowed to start organizing unions in about half of the 40,000 foreign-funded enterprises in the wake of 250,000 labor disputes since 1988, most in joint ventures (*Japan Economic Newswire* 21 Feb. 1994). The ACFTU figure is higher than one given by the Ministry of Labor, which gives 60,000 cases since 1986, most of them in private firms or foreign-owned ones (*Reuters* 17 July 1994).

Inflexibility within the former labor system makes the flexibility of new systems very attractive, certainly to the state authorities and to employers. In the new industries, especially in the special economic zones, there is no question of a permanent, secure labor force being established, as short-term cheap labor is all that is available. And in construction and other forms of unskilled labor, labor gangs are the answer. Contract labor is back, labor bosses are back, and temporary work for the young and naive is back. If workers do not get serious about workers' rights, "socialism with Chinese characteristics" may have to be redefined.

NOTES

1. Contract between the B.C. Canning Co. and Wing Chong and Co. for the 1897 salmon season, signed in 1896 in Victoria. The original is held in the Special Collections of the University of British Columbia Library.

2. All references to migration to Manchuria come from my own research on the subject, which is given in a forthcoming manuscript coauthored with Thomas Gottschang.

Foreign Investment or Foreign Exploitation: Women Workers and Unionization in a Korean Free Export Zone

Seung-kyung Kim

In April 1989, after seventeen years in operation, the Tandy Corporation closed its T.C. Electronics plant in the Masan Free Export Zone (MAFEZ)[1] in South Korea and laid off its 1,400 workers. The decision to close followed nearly two years of disputes that began during the 1987 nationwide labor uprising. The closing took place in spite of the fact that both management and workers claimed that they wanted the factory to continue to operate. When it was eventually closed, Tandy attributed its decision to loss of productivity, increased union radicalism, and rising production costs. Tandy's union workers, on the other hand, attributed Tandy's decision to close the factory to an unjustified hostility toward labor unions. Some of the labor activists who had been advising the union, however, felt the closing was structurally inevitable and were more disappointed in the way the struggle ended than by the actual departure of the factory.

"How Could They Close Our Factory?"

After the plant closing, T.C.'s union continued its struggle for over a year. During this time, the union carried out a variety of militant actions and attracted worldwide media attention, but it was unable to persuade the Tandy Corporation to reopen the plant. Throughout this period, South Korea's military regime was hostile to unions and labor organizations, and most of the union officers were arrested and imprisoned for their role in the struggle, with the president, Kim Chong-im, serving the longest term of imprisonment, eighteen months. The conflict between the workers and management at T.C. Electronics was more than just an ordinary labor dispute. Since T.C. was the subsidiary of the U.S.-based Tandy Corporation, the struggle against Tandy also had an international dimension.

This chapter, based on anthropological fieldwork (1986–88, summer 1991, winter 1994),[2] examines the struggle between the women workers' labor union and the Tandy Corporation and its aftermath. I discuss the variety of motivations and political positions of the women who formed the union and consider the implications of their sometimes contradictory agendas.

The Creation of the Masan Free Export Zone

The Masan Free Export Zone was established in 1970 as part of the export-oriented development plan. The Korean government hoped to use direct foreign investment to introduce high technology and develop new foreign markets. To accommodate investors, the government promulgated the Foreign Capital Inducement Law (1969), which included tax incentives, simplified administrative procedures, waivers of the Free Trade Union Organization Law, and other inducements for foreign investors. In other words, the government established the MAFEZ by providing land, labor, and other incentives in exchange for foreign technology, resources, and trademarks.

The Korean government set the following goals for MAFEZ: first, export promotion—Korea would earn a sizable amount of foreign exchange by exporting everything manufactured in the zone; second, employment enlargement—since all the industries in the zone are labor intensive, the zone would absorb underemployed labor from the countryside; third, technology advancement—there would be technology transfer since the zone would accommodate mostly electronics, precision equipment, and metal industries with highly advanced technologies; fourth, community development—the zone would promote the migration of the farming population to an urban area, would establish Masan as an industrial area, and would develop domestic industry to supply raw and subsidiary materials.

Companies operating in the zone were allowed to repatriate the full amount originally invested and all profits made from the operation. Foreign investors in the zone were given the same access to export financing as was Korean domestic industry. Once foreign investors brought in as little as U.S.$50,000 (the minimum amount of investment to operate in the zone), they were entitled to extensive export financing. The government also enforced regulations designed to guarantee foreign investors in the zone a compliant and inexpensive labor force so that until the nationwide labor uprising of 1987 the government prevented trade unions from operating in the zone (see Seung-kyung Kim 1992).

Until 1987, "Joint Labor-Management Councils" (Nosa Hyobuihoe) were the only venue for workers to present their views in MAFEZ.[3] In many factories, labor representatives were selected by management and did nothing except listen to management present its views at council meetings. In some cases, however, the exposure to labor issues provided by the councils inspired young women to seek a more powerful voice for workers in the subsequent labor uprising.

Initially, the Masan Free Export Zone was extremely attractive to foreign investors, and, by 1975, there were 101 companies operating factories there. Many of these companies were small (with less than U.S.$50,000 investment), since the government was not very selective about the companies it recruited for the zone (MAFEZ Administrative Office, monthly statistics, 1987). In December 1978, 33 of the 95 operating companies employed fewer than 100 workers. When a recession hit the world economy, many small companies collapsed and fled without paying severance pay or overdue wages (Young Catholic Workers' Organization 1980). By 1987, there were only 76 companies operating in the zone (MAFEZ Administrative Office, monthly statistics). However, these tended to be larger and more established firms and employment in the zone reached its peak in that year.

The major investors in the Masan Free Export Zone are Japanese electronics companies. In 1987, there were twenty-three electronics factories operating in the zone, and twenty one of these were Japanese owned. Most of the other industries were also dominated by Japanese or Japanese-Korean joint venture companies. The main industries were: electronics (twenty-three companies), metal (eighteen companies), precision equipment (seventeen companies) and garment (twelve companies) (MAFEZ Administrative Office, monthly statistics). Japanese and Japanese-Korean joint ventures comprised fifty-six out of the seventy-six companies operating in 1987. Given its geographical proximity to Japan, it was not surprising that the MAFEZ accommodated primarily Japanese firms. Although MAFEZ was set up solely for foreign firms, the law governing the zone was modified in 1981 to allow Korean-owned companies to operate within the zone, and by 1987 there were ten of these.

As of 1987, the companies in the zone employed a total of about 36,411 workers (8,389 men and 28,022 women). The electronics industry employed the largest number of female workers (over 18,000—65 percent of the total female employees), followed by precision equipment and the garment and shoe industry (with about 3,000—12 percent each). By 1990, the number of companies operating in the zone had decreased to seventy and the number of workers decreased to 20,142. The decrease in workers has taken place through plant closings, attrition (mostly resignations by women intending to get married), and voluntary resignations encouraged by severance pay. There has been no public recruitment since 1987.

The most prestigious jobs were in electronics companies, which did not accept job applications from women over twenty-two years old, arguing that older workers did not have the requisite manual dexterity. Women who leave jobs in the electronics industry for whatever reason are not able to return because of the age limit and must look for jobs in either garment companies or subcontracting factories outside the zone.

Masan is best known in Korea as the starting point of the demonstrations that led to the resignation of President Rhee Syng-man in 1960. Masan continued to be at the core of resistance against the dictatorships of the Park, Chun, and Roh regimes. It is still considered politically volatile, especially concerning labor issues, since a large number of workers are concentrated in the planned industrial estates that have been established in the area.[4]

Masan in 1987 was a busy, overcrowded, bustling city. In the morning, endless lines of women workers were going to the MAFEZ. Some women who were only fifteen or sixteen had come to work in order to go to school, and they were more optimistic and bright looking; other women were over twenty six and disillusioned by working for five to ten years without making any progress and dying to get out of the factory. Workers in the MAFEZ came mostly from poor families from the city of Masan and the surrounding rural areas. There were gradations of poverty, but all were poor and struggling to support themselves and their families.[5]

South Korean Women Workers in the Global Assembly Line

Women workers have been an integral component of South Korea's industrial development. The government's export-led industrialization policy, during the 1960s and the early 1970s, initially focused on light industry (e.g., electronics, textiles, and clothing), which employed a predominantly female work force. The contribution of women factory workers to the country's economic development received praise from the government and national media, which described them as "industrial soldiers" and "the backbone of industrialization."[6] Despite this praise, women workers received few benefits from the industrialization of the country.

Young women who work in the export processing industry throughout the world are among the most powerless and exploited of all workers.[7] Conventions regarding age and gender in many societies place a low value on their work and discourage them from asserting themselves, making it difficult for them to improve their situations. Multinational companies (predominantly Japanese electronics companies) came to Masan because an easily trained, inexpensive labor force was available there. Since assembly factories required little investment to set up, multinational companies constantly employed the threat to relocate in order to silence demands for higher wages. Cultural expectations ensured a constant turnover of cheap productive workers as young women sought employment for the time between the completion of their educations and the start of their marriages.

For Korean women, a tradition of subordination[8] translates into greater subordination in the workplace. Women employed in factories worked longer hours than men for substantially lower wages. In 1989, women's workweeks averaged 54.1 hours and "sixty-hour workweeks [were] common in many firms" (U.S. Department of Labor 1990, 102). The wage differential between men and women has been decreasing recently, but "in 1989, the average female worker's wage was still only 53 percent of that of the average male worker" (U.S. Department of Labor 1991, 6; cf. Chang 1990; Kim Kum-su 1986, 73; and Korean Association of Women Workers 1987, 32).

In most factories in Masan, the regular work day began at 8:30 A.M. and went until 5:30. Two ten-minute breaks, one in the morning and one in the afternoon, and forty minutes for lunch did not count as work time. The normal workweek was six days. Saturday is a normal working day in Korea, so Sunday was the only day workers expected to be off. The regular work week was thus forty-eight hours, but overtime work in the evenings and on Sundays could push this up to eighty hours.[9] Since the wages were so low, workers usually welcomed a moderate amount of overtime work. They needed some overtime work to support themselves, but when they had to work overnight, or for several weeks without a day off, they were unable to participate in any social activities and were physically exhausted. Excessive overtime work also created a tense working environment.

The traditional hierarchical relationships between male and female and young and old serve to make the subordination of women within the workplace seem natural or common sensical. As in many other parts of the world, cheap female labor is used for factory jobs with unskilled and repetitive tasks and minimal opportunity for advancement. Gender hierarchy structures the work environment, so that women never perform the same jobs that men do, while they are usually supervised by men. Women never supervise male workers. Within the rigidly hierarchical, gender segregated workplace, women are never seriously able to challenge men's control. Ong has described the similar use in Malaysian factories of culturally elaborated notions of gender hierarchy to control and subordinate a low-wage female labor force (1983).[10]

Work in the zone provided young women with the opportunity to earn their own living, and they therefore valued the jobs provided by the zone. Workers found their independence severely limited, however, by the long hours they were required to work and by the low wages that they were paid (cf. Kung 1983; Salaff 1981; and Sheridan and Salaff 1984). Still, women in MAFEZ, even though unhappy about their wages and working conditions, generally did not voice discontent. They were resigned to accepting the conditions that existed at the factory while they made personal plans based on getting married and leaving the factory for good.

The way workers felt about and reacted to their situation changed drastically in 1987. When I arrived in Masan in 1986, most women workers did not know anything about unions and were not interested in belonging to one. Rather than getting involved with labor activism, they aspired to become part of the middle class.[11] Most did not pay much attention to politics and were especially uncomfortable with any position that seemed too radical. There was no indication that they wanted to make major changes in the way society worked. If they felt unhappy about their situation, it was merely with their fate as individuals not as part of a class. Nevertheless, women factory workers enthusiastically participated in the wave of labor activism that began with the 1987 uprising, and their militant stance attracted worldwide press coverage.

The T.C. Labor Union

The conflicting aims of multinational corporations and Korean workers was illustrated by the events leading up to the departure of the T.C. Electronics Company from the zone. T.C. Electronics, the largest U.S.-based company in Masan, was established in 1972, 100 percent owned by the Tandy Corporation. Its main products were stereo components, computer components, and telephones. In 1987, the company had 1,800 employees. The 1,700 female employees were mostly production workers, while the 100 male employees were mostly managers and technicians.

The 1987 nationwide labor uprising began in July and reached Masan by August. Eventually more than half of the companies (forty-one out of seventy-six) operating in the zone, experienced sit-in strikes. At T.C. Electronics, the strike began on the afternoon of August 20, when about 1,000 workers stopped work and demanded higher wages. Sixty workers organized a union that evening and registered it at City Hall the following day. The company responded to the strike by announcing that the factory would be closed for two days. The women who had organized the union spoke to a crowd of 300 workers assembled outside the closed factory, and 250 more workers joined the union. Male technicians demanded that the women "stop the strike and talk to the president. . . . We will try to solve your problems if you promise to disband the union." That evening, union representatives met with the company president and presented him with a list of demands. The most important of these were for a 30 percent increase in wages and a 50 percent increase in annual bonuses, the abolishment of mandatory overtime and Sunday work, and the payment of a seniority allowance.[12]

Of these demands, management only agreed to abolish mandatory overtime work. Negotiations over wage increases broke off because the company considered the amount demanded to be too high. Male technicians later approached the union officers and demanded that they abandon the union: "Do you know anything about the Labor Law?" they questioned them. "Our parent company in the United States does not have a union, and if you start one the company will surely move the plant to another country. Then who is going to support 1,800 workers? Forget the union; we can work with the Labor-Management Council System."

The factory reopened on the twenty-fourth, with the company making some concessions to the workers. Wages and bonuses were increased by about half the amount the union had demanded; however, the company also insisted that the union be disbanded. All of the workers withdrew from the union except its three officers. The company sent these three women to a "special training program" and transferred them away from the production line.[13]

Although T.C.'s first union was crushed in less than a week, workers had learned how to organize themselves. They were able to organize quickly and effectively during the next phase of the labor disputes in 1988. During these confrontations, male technicians again supported management against the women in the union and beat up several women who were trying to recruit their coworkers.[14] Several of the union women were hospitalized, but the labor union survived the confrontation. By mid-1988, 900 of the 950 women still working at T.C. Electronics had joined the union (T.C. Former Labor Union Members 1991, 66–67). The company was disturbed by these developments and began to talk about closing down. The chairman of the Tandy Corporation in the United States threatened to move some production lines out of Korea because of the "general level of cultural change and political uncertainty" (*New York Times* 26 Aug. 1988). However, he also stated that the company did not plan to pull out of Korea.

The company warned workers that orders from the parent company were decreasing. They instituted a hiring freeze in Masan and tried to move machines to subcontracting factories outside the zone. Union members threw themselves in front of the movers in an effort to stop them from removing the machines from the factory. The company sued the union for blocking the removal of equipment and obstructing daily procedures on the shop floor in February; it announced on 6 March 1989 that the factory was closing temporarily.

Both sides hardened their positions during these confrontations. Management accused the union members of slowing down productivity and interfering with shipping deadlines. The union accused the company of hiring thugs to disrupt the operations of the factory so that it could use "declining productivity" as an excuse to close. T.C Electronics also described the confrontations at the factory as being between men and women workers and thus unrelated to management policies.

On 4 April 1989, the Tandy Corporation declared that it was closing its factory in Masan and dismissed its entire staff. They paid the wages for March, the legal retirement pay, and the legal severance payment (two months' wages) to workers, following the legal requirements for closing the factory.

The core membership of the union refused to accept the plant closing and occupied the factory building. They demanded that the company reopen the plant. When they were ignored by Tandy, the workers became desperate. About twenty formed a suicide corps (*kyolsadae*), equipped themselves with paint thinner and agricultural chemicals and went to Seoul to occupy T.C.'s research institute. They found the company president in the institute and took him hostage. They held him for four days before he escaped. Their demand for direct negotiations with the parent company in the United States indicated that they still felt that the problems that had occurred in the Masan factory were due to local mismanagement rather than being intrinsic to the structural problems of export processing zones. Perhaps if the head office understood their desperation it would be sympathetic and reopen the factory. However, the union's kidnapping of the president of its Korean subsidiary did not convince Tandy to negotiate; rather, it confirmed the company in its decision to close the factory.

Since Tandy is an American company, its conflict with Korean workers became linked to nationalist issues that were important in Korean politics. Radical nationalists objected to the presence of large numbers of American troops in Korea, to the ties between the United States and South Korea's unpopular military government, and to the presence of foreign-owned companies in Masan. Anti-Americanism was an important aspect of the ideology of the student radicals who had been helping workers to organize. In this final phase of their confrontation with Tandy, strikers incorporated anti-American sentiments in their protests. On the third day of their occupation of the research institute in Seoul, they hung a banner outside the window:

> We only want to go back to work. It is all right if the American-owned company leaves. In fact, it should leave. Foreign-owned multinational corporations will always leave Korea if they do not make enough profits. They do not care about their social responsibility. We would like to work for a Korean-owned company. (Tandy Corporation Former Labor Union Members 1991, 96–97)

Strikers walked on American flags and chanted anti-American slogans in Masan: "If you want to leave, Yankees, then go. But repay all the profits you exploited from our blood and sweat for seventeen years." In spite of these elements of anti-Americanism, the union's primary goal was always to have the factory reopen in Masan.

The more radical union activists were not surprised by Tandy's intransigence. They were interested in organizing workers as part of a larger struggle and considered the closing of factories in the Masan Free Export Zone to be inevitable, if not desirable. For radicals the problem was a much larger one than whether one factory would remain open or not. The international business community was shocked by Korean labor activism. *The Economist* reported: "A few militants have pressed absurd demands. One American company, which eventually gave up and decided to close its factory, was told by a union organizer that it should not be allowed to leave Korea until it had repaid all the profits it had ever made there" (May 1990, 33).

The police forced the workers out of T.C.'s research institute, and the women occupying the factory began to leave. However, negotiations about compensation were still continuing in December 1989 when the police invaded the factory and forced the remaining fifty union supporters out. Kim Chongim, the union president, and twenty-one workers were arrested and sent to jail. A few union members made one last attempt to reoccupy the abandoned factory in January 1990, but the police immediately expelled them. The union formally abandoned the struggle with a public evaluation forum held on 25 May 1990, and the fight with Tandy was finished.

Tandy was the first major investor to pull out of Masan, and several other companies have left or threatened to leave the zone. Sumida Electronics left MAFEZ in October 1989 without paying overdue wages or severance payments. Whereas Tandy followed "legal" procedures, Sumida simply ignored them. The owner of Sumida Electronics left Korea without any warning to workers and sent a fax announcing its bankruptcy (*AMPO* 1990, 59). After the closing, the union officers organized a negotiation team to go to Japan. They held public demonstrations, which were widely reported in both Korean and Japanese newspapers, and the resultant public outcry forced Sumida to send the overdue wages and additional compensation to workers.

Workers' Perspectives on the Struggle

Organizers from outside the factories were crucial to the formation of unions in 1987, but the labor uprising was supported by mass participation. Ordinary workers were drawn into leadership roles, and as they assumed these positions their knowledge and commitment to the labor movement intensified.

JOC: A Workers' Organization. Links between workers at different companies and other organizational supports were provided by Catholic Church organizations, especially JOC, the "Young Christian Workers" (JOC, from the French "Jeunesse Ouvrière Chrétienne"). The Masan chapter of JOC was founded in 1971, and from its inception it devoted itself to educating workers within the area. Members of JOC were factory workers but were not necessarily Catholics, although many eventually converted. Women reported that they joined JOC because they were concerned about poverty and inhuman working conditions. In 1987, most union leaders were members of JOC, which had about a hundred core members in the Masan area. During the labor uprising, these members worked around the clock to publish newsletters and organize educational programs.

In 1991, there were only a handful of members left in the JOC who had been actively involved in the 1987 struggle. Many of the old leaders were in jail. The building they used as the meeting area was undergoing reconstruction, so they did not even have space to meet. Current members appeared to be more concerned with religious matters than with labor organizing. They were no longer actively organizing unions in the zone, and left the role of organizing workers to students.

Chong-im: From Worker to Labor "Hero." Most of the women who became leaders of the labor movement came from poor families and struggled to gain their educations. They were motivated by an acute sense of injustice based on their experience in the workplace. JOC was also crucial for teaching these women about unions and workers' rights and providing them with a forum in which to develop their ideas.

Chong-im transformed herself from a weak, frightened woman to a strong-willed union leader as she organized and led the union at the T.C. Electronics factory. She was a twenty-three-year-old assembly line worker in 1987 when the labor uprising erupted in the zone. She felt that the workers at her factory should join the strike and became the union leader because no one else wanted the position. She knew little about labor organizing, but when she formed the union members of the JOC contacted her and taught her how to organize it.

She led the fight to keep the factory open when Tandy announced its decision to close. Her struggle lasted 450 days and ended with her arrest by combat police in December 1989.[15] She spent a year and half in prison, and was released in July 1991 when she was twenty-seven years old. She talked about the day she was released:

> I felt like a heroine on the day I was released from Won-ju prison in Kang Won Province. About fifty workers had come from Masan to wait for me to come out, and they brought my mother with them. Normally prisoners are released at around four or five o'clock in the morning; however, the singing and chanting from outside persuaded the authorities to let me leave earlier. I remember my mother crying and telling me that I must have done something right for this many people to come and greet me. I was warmly welcomed at my village, too. Even village people who would normally consider imprisonment to be disgraceful told me that what I had done was courageous and they were proud of me. Everyone regarded me as some kind of heroine, and that made me feel a heavy responsibility. I felt that I should continue to participate in the labor movement and lead other workers because that was what was expected of me. (personal interview, August 1991)

She got married to a fellow worker when she was released from prison and returned to Masan where she worked for the Masan-Changwon Women Workers' Association for five months until she gave birth to a daughter. When I talked to her in January 1994, although she was not currently active in the labor movement, she was still considered a hero (*tusa*) among radical workers. She firmly believed what she and other women workers had done was the right thing. She also felt bad about the comparison people made between T.C. workers' failure and Sumida workers' success.

> I feel very bad when people mention Sumida's successful case. We fought really hard and long, but people think that Sumida's union succeeded because they got compensation money. We did not get any compensation; we refused to accept whatever they paid us. I wonder why people judge the success or failure of labor unions on the basis of whether compensation

money is paid or not. I saw the president of the Sumida union on TV giving interviews discussing their success. It really hurt me to watch that and hear people talking about our failure at T.C. But I think we are closer and stronger. We still meet and make plans together. Sumida workers were paid over 10 million won [U.S.$12,000] per person, but they stopped doing any kind of public work after their success. (January 1994)

Chong-im was defensive about not being currently involved in the labor movement. She felt her private life was important and that the public expectations about her life were becoming too much for her to handle. Like Chong-im, many women workers who became leaders of the labor movement after the 1987 uprising were treated as heroes and expected to continue as leaders. Most of them, however, are now married, have children, and are busy caring for their families. Although Chong-im has shifted her loyalty to her own family, she still feels a commitment to improving workers' lives and expects to come back to the labor movement soon.

Chin-ju. Many women with less leadership skill or experience than Chong-im also participated in T.C.'s union. Although they were not leaders, their participation was essential for organizing the union. One of these participants was Chin-ju. In 1987, she was twenty-two years old and a member of JOC. Through her contact with JOC, she was exposed to ideas about labor organizing and began to be concerned about the exploitation of workers by multinational corporations in MAFEZ. She began working for T.C. in 1986 and became a member when Chong-im first organized the union in August 1987. When the management demanded that workers withdraw from the union, she obeyed the order. She talked about how she was intimidated into withdrawing from the union.

My line supervisor called me into his office and told me to sign a withdrawal form. He knew about my JOC membership and in a loud voice asked me why I wanted to become a communist. He also told me that our wages would be raised and overtime work reduced. And, finally, he told me that I would be fired if I did not withdraw from the union. I did not want to get fired, so I signed the form. (November 1987)

In May 1988, when the T.C. union was reorganized, Chin-ju again became a founding member. She learned a lot about working conditions in other factories and her own by participating in small group meetings at JOC and by talking to other workers. She thought that she was ready to fight against the company. She remained a union member throughout the struggle against the plant closing; however, she was not one of the core members who went to Seoul to occupy the T.C. research institute. After the union disbanded, she moved back to her native city, Taejon, and got married.

Hyon-suk: A Disguised Worker. Students' involvement in the struggle for workers' rights in South Korea dates back to the early 1970s. Student activists began to work in factories as "disguised workers" to help organize workers (see Kim 1994; and Ogle 1990). By the 1980s, this practice was widespread, and organized student groups became involved in the workers' struggle (see Dong 1987). The alliance of radical students and workers culminated in the July-August nationwide labor uprising in 1987.

Hyon-suk was a former college student working as a "disguised worker" to help organize workers in 1987. She was the oldest of four daughters and was a native of Inchon City. Her father, who was an army officer, died during the Vietnam War when she was only eight years old. Her mother brought four daughters up by managing a movie theater. They were not rich but did not experience extreme hardship.

In 1982, she entered the Department of French Literature at Koryo University. While she was a high school student, her dream had been to go to France to study painting, but she decided that was a romantic fantasy. Before starting college, she became a member of an underground club in her Catholic church. There, she read antigovernment, anti-American, and Marxist literature. She was already well versed in this literature when she began her first year at the college, and there she joined her college's underground club. She met her future husband at the club meetings. She eventually became unhappy about being in the French Literature Department, which she considered to be teaching "decadent" materials. She began taking other classes, such as philosophy, sociology, political science, and history, rather than classes in her own subject. She explained how she came to Masan:

> I was expelled from college when I was a junior for being involved in a "night class" movement. I had to run away from the police. My future husband . . . suggested that I come down to Masan. I started working for T.C. in 1987 and had been there for only six months before the uprising. I did not volunteer for any overt leadership since I was afraid of being discovered using false documents. I just followed others in encouraging my line friends to participate in strikes. Thus, I was not active in the attempt to organize the first union in 1987, which was crushed within a month.
>
> When we tried to reorganize the union in 1988, I got actively involved and took charge of the education section. As the head of that section, I taught union members about the Labor Law, workers' rights, and Korean

history. Not long after I started to be active, the management found out about my "disguised worker" status and started to spread rumors that I was a "communist" and had been sent to T.C. to start a "communist revolution." When I distributed flyers about the save the company corps [*kusadae*] in front of the MAFEZ on 12 July 1988, the men dragged me and five other workers into the factory and hit us over and over again. They especially targeted me at that time, saying: "Since you are a communist, it is not a crime to kill you here." However, they told each other: "Do not leave any surface injuries" and used steel helmets to hit my head. They also pulled out clumps of my hair.

When we sent our suicide corps [*kyolsadae*] to the Seoul research institute, my friends decided that I should not get involved in it because of my ex-student status. Also, around this time, my health deteriorated, and I went back to my mother's house in Inchon.... I admit that I was not at the center of the action. I was not with my comrades during the last attempt to take over the factory in January 1990. Even though I was not with them physically, my mind was always with them. (January 1994)

Conclusion

Labor unions were unfamiliar to most of the women working in MAFEZ until the uprising in 1987. In the years following the uprising, unions flourished in the zone. Large numbers of women workers joined unions and participated in strikes and demonstrations. The high level of participation did not last, however, and only four years after the nationwide uprising democratic workers' unions had virtually ceased to exist in the zone.

Before 1987, workers were effectively prevented from organizing by government policy, but after unions were permitted the factors determining their success or failure became more complicated. Several factors have inclined women workers to reject unions and accept their condition without protest. For many workers it still seems inevitable that young women will be in low-paid, low-status jobs subordinate to men. The relatively high prestige of some of the factory jobs in MAFEZ compared with other possibilities also strengthened conservative tendencies among workers (cf. Kim Chang-ki 1991). Electronics workers in the zone were indoctrinated to see themselves as part of the corporate family, and since this enhanced their status many accepted this ascription. Some of workers' frustration dissipated as wages increased. Wages more than doubled between 1987 and 1991 (although much of this gain was erased by inflation, real wages for women workers increased by 52 percent during this period [Korean Women's Development Institute 1994, 234]), and factory owners argued that since they had met the workers' principal demand they should withdraw from confrontational unions.

Political repression also continued to be important in limiting union activity in MAFEZ. Especially from 1989 to 1992, the government cooperated with the factory owners to suppress workers' organizations. Union leaders were fired, and the government systematically arrested them. Actual or threatened factory closings have also frightened workers away from union activism.

In spite of all these factors discouraging women factory workers from adopting radical positions, many did, especially between 1987 and 1989. During that period, a radical leadership also developed from within the ranks of factory workers, and these deeply committed leaders continue to be politically active. The low pay and poor working conditions of factories in MAFEZ aroused a sense of injustice that led some workers to seek radical solutions to their problems.

Young women seeking employment for the few years between the end of their educations and the beginning of their marriages are an easily exploitable labor force, but they are also a volatile one since they do not share any long-term interests with their employers. The high turnover rate also cancels out companies' efforts to indoctrinate new workers. There are no older workers to argue in favor of the benefits of selfless service to the company; there is only propaganda about company loyalty, which must sound hollow to women who cannot expect to remain at the firm for even ten years.

Company executives were surprised by the vehemence of the young women during the labor uprising, but they should not have been. The youth and inexperience of workers in the zone, which made them appear to be a capitalist's ideal labor force, cheap and easily exploited, also made them unpredictable. Women who were only twenty-one organized and led unions, and a twenty-six-year-old woman factory worker was already considered to be very senior.

The institutionalized subordination of women workers produces a public passivity and fatalism that conceals an inner, private rebellion, much like the colonized people discussed by Frantz Fanon. Like people subordinated by colonization, women factory workers have repressed their anger at their mistreatment, and when their anger emerges it leads to intense and spontaneous action (see Fanon 1969). The rigidly controlled working environment in MAFEZ factories nearly eliminated opportunities for workers to express their anger individually without risking reprisals.[16] Only in the context of widespread opposition to factory management did it become practical for workers to speak out on their own behalf. The rebellion of young women, exploited and isolated on the global assembly line, may result in expressive but unfocused activity such as the mass hysteria in the Malaysian case discussed by Ong (1987, 1988). When political organizers are present, however, as in the South Korean case, the rebellion takes a definite political form. The radicalism of workers in Masan is the result of the combination of their frustration at being excluded from power and their exposure to political ideologies that promise them power.

The government's removal of leaders among the workers, also increased the importance of outside organizers and radical ideologies. As the dominant ideology of those who are organizing workers in Masan has shifted from the Catholic JOC to more radical groups run by students from Seoul, workers' organizations have also become more radical. The government's abuse of power has not only eliminated much of the moderate opposition, but it has fostered radicalism by angering workers. However, as noted previously, conflicts between the goals of radical programs and the immediate needs of workers may lead to workers' rejection of radicalism and may have contributed to the decrease in union membership.

Between 1987 and 1991, the number of factory jobs in MAFEZ declined by almost half. While workers in Masan were successful in organizing unions to achieve higher wages and better working conditions, they were unable to stop multinational corporations from leaving Korea looking for cheaper, unorganized labor. The events at Tandy were complicated by cultural misunderstandings between workers and the parent company and contradictory objectives among the union leaders. Nevertheless, the departure of additional companies points to the need to address the structural problems inherent in multinational corporations' exploitation of women workers in export processing zones throughout the world. Workers remain vulnerable to exploitation as long as they remain unorganized in their struggle with large powerful adversaries.

NOTES

I am grateful to my husband, John Finch, for editorial assistance and conversations about various issues raised in this essay. This chapter also benefited from insightful comments by Roger Janelli and the editors of this volume, Timothy Brook and Hy V. Luong. I have used pseudonyms for women workers named in this essay, except when their roles have been well publicized.

1. Free export zones (sometimes called export processing zones or free trade zones) are specific areas set up by governments to attract foreign investment and manufacture goods, not for domestic consumption but for export. Export processing zones are expected to (1) earn foreign exchange, (2) reduce high unemployment, and (3) aid in transferring technology. Export processing zones throughout the world have similar

characteristics: they are specifically designated industrial areas where fully or partially foreign owned firms can import raw materials or semifinished goods free of duty for the purpose of manufacturing, processing, or assembling items for export. Generally, the state plays a direct role in controlling union organization so as to preclude labor disruption, and supplies land, utilities, transport facilities, and buildings within the zone at subsidized rates. Foreign firms are also offered incentives over and above those extended to investors outside the zone. For information on free export zones, see *AMPO* 1977; and Grunwald and Flamm 1985.

2. I went to Korea in December 1986 and stayed until February 1988 to conduct anthropological fieldwork. I planned to rely on participant observation to conduct my fieldwork and intended to actually work in a factory in order to better understand conditions there. This presented several problems: first, I no longer had a Korean identification card, so I could not get a job legally; second, to prevent college students from helping workers organize, the government had established laws forbidding anyone with a college degree from working in a factory; and, third, the electronics factories in the zone did not hire any women older than twenty-two years old. I was able to get around these problems with the help of a cousin, who was a middle manager in a Japanese-owned electronics factory in the Masan Free Export Zone. I worked for three months at K.T.E. For a detailed discussion of my experience as a worker, see Kim 1990, 1994. I made brief follow-up visits to Masan in 1991 and 1994.

3. Joint Labor-Management Councils were set up under the provisions of the "Labor-Management Council Act" of 1980 to control labor and limit disputes. Each firm was required to set up a Labor-Management Council, in which representatives of labor and management were to "meet regularly to discuss issues of mutual interest" (Cho 1994, 104). Naturally, these tended to become instruments of management policy rather than open forums for workers to air their grievances.

4. Adjoining Masan is the city of Changwon, where, in 1974, the government established a heavy industrial estate as part of a nationwide program to develop heavy industry. The machinery and metal industries in Changwon employ a predominantly male work force, which in 1989 consisted of approximately 70,000 workers (Kang 1990, 138).

5. Some families in Masan were much poorer than others, as their varied ability to provide their daughters with education indicates. Although many families supported their daughters through high school, others could not even afford to send them to middle school, and a few even sent their daughters out to earn money by working as housemaids when they should have been attending primary school.

6. Before factory jobs became widely available in the 1960s, becoming a factory worker was not considered a respectable course for a young woman. Young women without supervision were seen as susceptible to bad influences and in danger of becoming morally loose. Since respectability affected a woman's marriage prospects, few women were willing to work for factories. Government propaganda and mass media promoted factory work, calling women workers "industrial solders" (*sanop chonsa*). As factory work became more common, it became more respectable. Young women also began to like the idea that it offered them more control over their lives.

7. Many studies confirm this status of young women: c.f. Chapkis and Enloe 1982;

Cho 1987; Elson and Pearson 1981; Fernandez-Kelly 1983; Frobel et al. 1980; Fuentes and Ehrenrich 1983; Grossman 1979; Kung 1983; Lim 1978, 1983; Nash and Fernandez-Kelly 1983; Ong 1983, 1987; and Safa 1981.

8. For a discussion of gender relations during the Yi dynasty, see Deuchler 1977; for the contemporary period, see Cho Hye-jong 1988.

9. While I was working at a MAFEZ factory, my longest work week was seventy-six hours.

10. The relationship between patriarchy and multinational corporations has been examined by several scholars working in Southeast Asia. Economist Linda Lim (1983) argues that in Southeast Asia it is patriarchy that gives management the edge in the exploitation of workers in multinational firms. She argues that patriarchal ideology is utilized by the management of the multinational corporations for their own ends, but that what is ultimately to blame for the exploitation of female labor is the patriarchy inherent in Southeast Asian culture. On the other hand, anthropologist Aihwa Ong (1983) argues that even with preexisting ideas of patriarchy in Malaysia, Japanese management uses Japanese gender ideology to bolster power relations in the industrial system. In Southeast Asian countries and South Korea, the existing patriarchal ideology was not challenged by multinational corporations penetrating into their economies. Rather, it was perpetuated in conjunction with the capitalist goal of producing maximum profits.

11. For an excellent discussion of class identification and workers in South Korea, see Koo 1993.

12. Workers throughout the country presented their factories with similar lists of demands during the July-August labor uprising.

13. Usually, places in these special training programs were used as rewards for model workers. In this case, however, management merely wanted to remove the women from the factory.

14. In factories where all production workers are women, the union membership is all female.

15. Chong-im was charged with organizing illegal demonstrations and obstructing the company's lawful activities.

16. Workers did complain, gossip, and occasionally defy their supervisors. However, acts of individual resistance were relatively infrequent, and when typical "weapons of the weak" such as sabotage of equipment were employed against a company it was almost invariably carried out by a group rather than individuals acting alone. Close surveillance of the shop floor and other controls over workers effectively prevented most acts against authority by individual workers.

Bibliography

Alatas, Syed Hussein. 1968. "Feudalism in Malaysian Society: A Study in Historical Continuity." *Civilisations* 18, no. 4: 1–15.

AMPO *(Japan-Asia Quarterly Review)*. 1977. "Free Trade Zones and Industrialization of Asia." *AMPO* no. 8: 4, and no. 9: 1–2.

———. 1990. "Union's Struggle across the Border: Mass Dismissals at Korea Sumida." *AMPO* 21:4.

An Na'im, Abdullahi. 1986. "The Islamic Law of Apostasy and Its Modern Applicability: A Case from the Sudan." *Religion* 16:197–224.

———. 1988. "Mahmud Muhammad Taib and the Crisis in Islamic Law Reform: Implications for Religious Relations." *Journal of Ecumenical Studies* 25, no. 1: 1–21.

Anagnost, Ann. 1989. "Prosperity and Counterprosperity: The Moral Discourse on Wealth in Post-Mao China." In *Marxism and the Chinese Experience,* edited by Arif Dirlik and Maurice Meisner, pp. 210–34. Armonk, N.Y.: M. E. Sharpe.

Australia, Department of Foreign Affairs and Trade. 1995. *Overseas Chinese Business Networks in Asia.* Canberra: Australian Department of Foreign Affairs and Trade.

Balasz, Etienne. 1964. *Chinese Civilization and Bureaucracy.* New Haven: Yale University Press.

Barbotin, A. 1912. "La poterie indigene au Tonkin." *Bulletin économique de l'Indochine* 55:659–85, 815–41.

Barlow, Tani. 1993. "Colonialism's Career in Postwar China Studies." *Positions* 1, no. 1: 224–67.

Barton, Clifton A. 1983. "Trust and Credit: Some Observations regarding Business Strategies of Overseas Chinese Traders in South Vietnam." In *The Chinese in Southeast Asia.* Vol. 1, *Ethnicity and Economic Activity,* edited by Linda Y. C. Lim and L. A. Peter Gosling, pp. 46–64. Singapore: Maruzen Asia.

Bat Trang. 1931. "Huong uoc lang Bat Trang" (Regulations of Bat Trang village). Manuscript deposited in the Archives of the École Française d'Extrême-Orient, Hanoi.

Bauman, Zygmunt. 1992. *Intimations of Postmodernity.* London: Routledge.

Bergère, Marie-Claire. 1986. *L'age d'or de la bourgeoisie chinoise.* Paris: Flamarion.

Bello, Walden, and Stephanie Rosenfeld. 1990. *Dragons in Distress: Asia's Miracle Economy in Crisis.* San Francisco: Institute for Food and Development Policy.

Birch, Cyril, trans. 1958. *Stories from a Ming Collection*. New York: Grove.

Bloch, Maurice. 1983. *Marxism and Anthropology: The History of a Relationship*. Oxford: Oxford University Press.

Boserup, Ester. 1970. *Woman's Role in Economic Development*. New York: St. Martin's.

Bourdieu, Pierre. 1977. *Outline of a Theory of Practice*. Translated by Richard Nice. Cambridge: Cambridge University Press.

————. 1990a. *The Logic of Practice*. Translated by Richard Nice. Cambridge: Polity.

————. 1990b. *In Other Words: Essays towards a Reflexive Sociology*. Translated by Matthew Adamson. Stanford: Stanford University Press.

Braudel, Fernand. 1977. *Afterthoughts on Material Civilization and Capitalism*. Baltimore: Johns Hopkins University Press.

————. 1981–84. *Civilization and Capitalism, 15th-18th Century*. 3 vols. New York: Harper and Row.

Brokaw, Cynthia. 1991. *The Ledgers of Merit and Demerit: Social Change and Moral Order in Late Imperial China*. Princeton: Princeton University Press.

Brook, Timothy. 1981. "The Merchant Network in 16th Century China: A Discussion and Translation of Zhang Han's 'On Merchants.'" *Journal of the Economic and Social History of the Orient* 24, no. 2 (May): 165–214.

————. 1993. "Rethinking Syncretism: The Unity of the Three Teachings and their Joint Worship in Late-Imperial China." *Journal of Chinese Religions* 21:13–44.

————. 1995. "Weber, Mencius, and the History of Chinese Capitalism." *Asian Perspective* 19, no. 1: 79–97.

————. 1997. *The Confusions of Pleasure: Commerce and Culture in Ming China*. Berkeley: University of California Press.

Bui Xuan Dinh. 1993. "Mot vai suy nghi ve hien tuong 'tai lap huong uoc' o nong thon hien nay" (Some thoughts about the 'restoration of rural covenants' phenomenon in the villages at present). *Nha nuoc va phap luat* (State and law) 3:14–18.

Callinicos, Alex. 1988. *Making History: Agency, Structure, and Change in Social Theory*. Ithaca: Cornell University Press.

Chan, Steve. 1990. *East Asian Dynamism: Growth, Order, and Security in the Pacific Region*. Boulder: Westview.

Chandra, Muzaffar. 1979. *Protector? An Analysis of the Concept and Practice of Loyalty in Leader-Led Relationships within Malay Society*. Penang: Aliran.

Chang Ji-yon. 1990. "Hanguk sahoe jikopui songbyol punjolhwawa kyongjejok bulpyongdung" (Gender segmentation of the labor market and economic inequality in Korean society). In *Hanguk sahoeui yosongkwa kajok* (Women and family in Korean society), edited by the Korean Research Center for Social History, pp. 121–85. Seoul: Munhakkwa Chisongsa.

Chang, Maria Hsia. 1995. "Greater China and the 'Chinese Global Tribe.'" *Asian Survey* 35, no. 10 (October): 955–67.

Chapkis, W,. and C. Enloe, eds. 1982. *Of Common Cloth: Women in the Global Textile Industry*. Washington, D.C.: Transnational Institute.

Chen Feng. 1988. *Qingdai yanzheng yu yanshui* (Qing dynasty salt administration and taxation). Kaifeng: Zhongzhou Guji Chubanshe.

Chen, Min. 1995. *Asian Management Systems: Chinese, Japanese, and Korean Styles of Business*. London: Routledge.

Chen Shaoming. 1992. *Rujia de xiandai zhuanzhe* (The contemporary reorientation of Confucianism). Shenyang: Liaoning Daxue Chubanshe.

Choi, In-hak. 1979. *A Type Index of Korean Folktales*. Seoul: Myong Ji University Publishing.

Choi, Jang-Jip. 1983. "Interest Conflict and Political Control in South Korea: A Study of the Labor Unions in Manufacturing Industries, 1961–1980." Ph.D. diss., University of Chicago.

Cho Hye-jong. 1988. *Han'gukui yosonggwa namsong* (Korean women and men). Seoul: Munhakkwa Chisongsa.

Cho Ki-joon. 1991. "Han'guk Chabonjuui ui Chonsa" (Prehistory of capitalism in Korea). In *Han'guk kyongjaeui yoksajok chomyong* (The Korean economy from a historical viewpoint), edited by Koo Bon-Ho and Lee Kyu-ok, pp. 11–110. Seoul: Korea Development Institute.

Cho, Soon. 1994. *The Dynamics of Korean Economic Development*. Washington, D.C.: Institute for International Economics.

Cho, Soon-kyong. 1987. "How Cheap is 'Cheap Labor'? The Dilemmas of Export-Led Industrialization." Ph.D. diss., University of California, Berkeley.

Chong, Denise. 1994. *The Concubine's Children*. Toronto: Penguin.

Chu Van Thanh. 1991. "Mot so van de ve moi quan he giua nhan dan va nha nuoc xa hoi chu nghia o nuoc ta" (Some problems with respect to relations between the people and the socialist state in our country). *Nha nuoc va phap luat* (State and law) 1:53–56.

Clark, Rodney. 1978. *The Japanese Company*. New Haven: Yale University Press.

Cohen, Myron. 1990. "Lineage Organization in North China." *Journal of Asian Studies* 49, no. 3: 509–34.

Cole, Robert. 1979. *Work, Mobility, and Participation: A Comparative Study of American and Japanese Industry*. Berkeley: University of California Press.

Comaroff, Jean. 1986. *Body of Power, Spirit of Resistance: The Culture and History of a South African People*. Chicago: University of Chicago Press.

Cotton, James. 1994. "The State in the Asian NICS." *Asian Perspective* 18, no. 1: 39–56.

Croll, Elisabeth. 1981. *The Politics of Marriage in Contemporary China*. Cambridge: Cambridge University Press.

Cumings, Bruce. 1987. "The Origins and Development of the Northeast Asian Political Economy." In *The Political Economy of the New Asian Industrialization*, edited by Frederic C. Deyo, pp. 44–83. Ithaca: Cornell University Press.

Danh Son. 1993. "Kinh te tu nhan trong qua trinh chuyen dich co cau kinh te o Viet-Nam" (The private economy in the transformation process of economic structures in Vietnam). *Nghien cuu kinh te* (Economic research) 194 (August): 31–34.

Davin, Delia. 1988. "The Implications of Contract Agriculture for the Employment and Status of Chinese Peasant Women." In *Transforming China's Economy in the Eighties*. Vol. 1: *The Rural Sector, Welfare and Employment*, edited by Stephan Feuchtwang, Athar Hussain, and Thierry Pairault, pp. 137–46. Boulder: Westview; London: Zed.

de Bary, William Theodore. 1991. *The Trouble with Confucianism*. Cambridge: Harvard University Press.

De Vos, George. 1986. "Confucian Family Socialization: The Religion, Morality, and Aesthetics of Propriety." In *The Psycho-Cultural Dynamics of the Confucian Family: Past and Present*, edited by Walter H. Slote, pp. 327–405. Seoul: International Cultural Society of Korea.

de Vylder, Stefan, and Adam Fforde. 1988. *Vietnam: An Economy in Transition*. Stockholm: Swedish International Development Authority.

Deng, Gang. 1993. *Development versus Stagnation: Technological Continuity and Agricultural Progress in Pre-Modern China*. Greenwood.

Deuchler, Martina. 1977. "The Tradition: Women during the Yi Dynasty." In *Virtues in Conflict*, edited by Sandra Mattielli, pp. 1–47. Korea: Royal Asiatic Society.

———. 1992. *The Confucian Transformation of Korea: A Study of Society and Ideology*. Cambridge: Council on East Asian Studies, Harvard University.

DeWeaver, Mark. 1994. *Peregrine China Research*. London: Peregrine Securities.

Deyo, C. Frederic, ed. 1987. *The Political Economy of the New Asian Industrialism*. Ithaca: Cornell University Press.

Diamond, Norma. 1975. "Collectivization, Kinship, and the Status of Women in Rural China." In *Toward an Anthropology of Women*, edited by Rayna R. Reiter, pp. 372–95. New York: Monthly Review Press.

Dirks, Nicholas. 1992. "Introduction: Colonialism and Culture." In *Colonialism and Culture*, edited by Nicholas Dirks, pp. 1–23. Ann Arbor: University of Michigan Press.

Dix, M. Griffin. 1977. " 'The East Asian Country of Propriety': Confucianism in a Korean Village." Ph.D. diss., University of California, San Diego.

Do Muoi. 1993. *The hien khat vong cua nhan dan ve chan thien-my* (Realizing the aspiration of the people for the true, the good, and the beautiful). Hanoi: Nha xuat ban Van hoc.

Do thi Hao et al. 1989. *Que gom Bat Trang* (The home of ceramics: Bat Trang). Hanoi: Hanoi Publishing House.

Dong, Won-mo. 1987. "University Students in South Korean Politics: Patterns of Radicalization in the 1980s." *Journal of International Affairs* 40, no. 2: 233–55.

Dore, Ronald. 1973. *British Factory—Japanese Factory: The Origins of National Diversity in Labor Relations*. Berkeley: University of California Press.

———. 1983. "Goodwill and the Spirit of Market Capitalism." *British Journal of Sociology* 39:404–59.

———. 1987. *Taking Japan Seriously: A Confucian Perspective on Leading Economic Issues*. Stanford: Stanford University Press.

Douglas, Mary, and Aaron Wildavsky. 1982. *Risk and Culture: An Essay on the Selection of Technological and Environmental Dangers*. Berkeley: University of California Press.

Dower, John. 1986. *War without Mercy: Race and Power in the Pacific War*. London: Faber and Faber.

Du Xiaoshan. 1988. "Ya-Tai fazhanzhong guojia he diqu de nongye hezuo jingji" (The agricultural cooperative economics of the developing countries and regions of the Asia-Pacific). *Zhongguo nongcun jingji* (Chinese village economics) 2:61–62.

Eckert, Carter J. 1991. *Offspring of Empire: The Koch'ang Kims and the Colonial Origins of Korean Capitalism.* Seattle: University of Washington Press.

———. 1993. "The South Korean Bourgeoisie: A Class in Search of Hegemony." In *State and Society in Contemporary Korea,* edited by Hagen Koo, pp. 95–130. Ithaca: Cornell University Press.

Economic Planning Board. 1990. *Social Indicators in Korea.* Seoul: Economic Planning Board.

Elson, Diane, and Ruth Pearson. 1981. "Nimble Fingers Make Cheap Workers: An Analysis of Women's Employment in Third World Export Manufacturing." *Feminist Review* 7:87–107.

Fanon, Frantz. 1969. *The Wretched of the Earth.* New York: Penguin.

Farquhar, Judith B., and James L. Hevia. 1993. "Culture and Postwar American Historiography of China." *Positions* 1, no. 2: 486–525.

Fei Xiaotong. 1994. "Lüe tan Zhongguo de shehuixue" (A brief discussion of Chinese sociology). *Shehuixue yanjiu* (Sociological research) 1:2–8.

Fernandez-Kelly, Maria Patricia. 1983. *For We Are Sold, I and My People: Women and Industry in Mexico's Frontier.* Albany: State University of New York Press.

Foucault, Michel. 1986. "Nietzsche, Genealogy, History." In *The Foucault Reader,* edited by Paul Rainbow, pp. 76–100. New York: Pantheon.

Fox-Genovese, Elizabeth, and Eugene D. Genovese. 1983. "The Ideological Bases of Domestic Economy." In *Fruits of Merchant Capital,* edited by E. Fox-Genovese and E. D. Genovese, pp. 299–336. New York: Oxford University Press.

Freedman, Maurice. 1960. "Immigrants and Associations: Chinese in Nineteenth Century Singapore." *Comparative Studies in Society and History* 3, no. 1 (October): 25–48.

Friedland, Jonathan. 1991. "Kuok the Kingpin." *Far Eastern Economic Review,* 7 February.

Frobel, F., J. Heinrichs, and O. Kreye. 1980. *The New International Division of Labor: Structural Unemployment in Industrialized Countries and Industrialization in Developing Countries.* Cambridge: Cambridge University Press.

Fuentes, Annette, and Barbara Ehrenrich. 1983. *Women in the Global Factory.* INC Pamphlets no. 2. New York: South End.

Gallin, Rita S. 1984. "Women, Family, and the Political Economy of Taiwan." *Journal of Peasant Studies* 12, no. 1: 76–92.

Gan Yang. 1987. "Bashi niandai wenhua taolun de jige wenti" (Several questions regarding the discussions on culture in the 1980s). In *Wenhua: Zhongguo yu shijie* (Culture: China and the world), vol. 1, edited by Gan Yang, pp. 2–37. Beijing: Sanlian Shudian.

Garon, Sheldon. 1994. "Rethinking Modernism and Modernity in Japanese History: A Focus in State-Society Relations." *Journal of Asian Studies* 53, no. 2 (May): 346–66.

Ge Xiangjian and Qu Weiying. 1990. *Zhongguo mingong chao—mangliu zhenxiang lu* (China's labor tide: An exposé of the "blind flood"). Beijing: Zhongguo Guoji Guangbo Chubanshe.

Giddens, Anthony. 1979. *Central Problems in Social Theory: Action, Structure, and Contradiction in Social Analysis.* London: Macmillan.

————. 1984. *The Constitution of Society: Outline of a Theory of Structuration.* Cambridge: Cambridge University Press.

Goodman, Bryna. 1995. *Native Place, City, and Nation: Regional Networks and Identities in Shanghai, 1853–1937.* Berkeley: University of California Press.

Gordon, Andrew. 1985. *The Evolution of Labor Relations in Japan: Heavy Industries, 1853–1955.* Cambridge: Harvard University Press.

Grant, George. 1985. *English-Speaking Justice.* Toronto: House of Anansi.

Gray, Christine. 1991. "Hegemonic Images: Languages and Silence in the Royal Thai Polity." *Man: Journal of the Royal Anthropological Institute,* n.s., 26:43–65.

Greenhalgh, Susan. 1985. "Sexual Stratification: 'Growth with Equity' in East Asia." *Population and Development Review* 11, no. 2: 265–314.

Grossman, Rachel. 1979. "Women's Place in the Integrated Circuit." *Southeast Asia Chronicle* 66:2–17.

Grunwald, Joseph, and Kenneth Flamm. 1985. *The Global Factory: Foreign Assembly in International Trade.* Washington, D.C.: Brookings Institute.

Guan, Minqian. 1986. "Agricultural Systems, Women, and Women's Organizations in Socialist China." Manuscript.

Guo Chuan et al. 1993. *Xiahai jingshang shiwu zhinan* (Practical guide for those "going out to sea" and working as merchants). Beijing: Hongqi Chubanshe.

Habermas, Jürgen. 1990. *The New Conservatism: Cultural Criticism and the Historians' Debate.* Translated by S. W. Nicholsen. Cambridge, Mass.: MIT Press.

Hagen, Everett E. 1968. *The Economics of Development.* Homewood, Ill.: Richard Irwin.

Hall, John A. 1985. *Powers and Liberties: The Causes and Consequences of the Rise of the West.* Oxford: Blackwell.

Hall, John Whitney. 1965. "Changing Conceptions of the Modernization of Japan." In *Changing Japanese Attitudes toward Modernization,* edited by Marius Jansen, pp. 7–41. Princeton: Princeton University Press.

Hamashita, Takeshi. 1994. "Economic Culture in Overseas Chinese Business Networks." Paper presented at the conference Economy and Culture in Eastern Asia, Toronto.

Hamid, Jusoh. 1991. *The Position of Islamic Law in the Malaysian Constitution with Special Reference to the Conversion Case in Family Law.* Kuala Lumpur: Dewan Bahasa dan Pustaka.

Hamilton, Gary, ed. 1991. *Business Networks and Economic Development in East and Southeast Asia.* Hong Kong: University of Hong Kong Press.

Hahn, Dongse. 1972. "Maturity in Korea and America." In *Mental Health Research in Asia and the Pacific,* vol. 2: *Transcultural Research in Mental Health,* edited by William P. Lebra, pp. 185–90. Honolulu: University of Hawaii Press.

Harianto, Farid. 1993. "Oriental Capitalism." Working paper, Centre for International Studies, University of Toronto.

Hayhoe, Ruth. 1993. "Political Texts in Chinese Universities before and after Tiananmen." *Pacific Affairs* 66, no. 1 (Spring): 21–43.

Heilbroner, Robert. 1992. *Twenty-First Century Capitalism.* Concord, Ont.: House of Anansi.

Heng Pek Koon. 1988. *Chinese Politics in Malaysia: A History of the Malaysia Chinese Association.* Kuala Lumpur: Oxford University Press.

————. 1992. "The Chinese Business Elites of Malaysia." In *Southeast Asian Capitalists*, edited by Ruth McVey, pp. 127–44. Ithaca: Cornell University Press.

————. 1994. "Asia's New Dynasty: The Sino-Capitalist Network." *Japan Scope* (Autumn): 24–28.

Hershatter, Gail. 1986. *The Workers of Tianjin*. Stanford: Stanford University Press.

Hicks, G. L., and S. G. Redding. 1982. "Culture and Corporate Performance in the Philippines: The Chinese Puzzle." In *Essays in Development Economics in Honor of Harry T. Oshima*, pp. 199–215. Manila: Philippine Institute of Development Studies.

Hill, H. 1992. "Manufacturing Industry." In *The Oil Boom and After: Indonesian Economic Policy and Performance in the Soeharto Era*, edited by A. Booth, pp. 204–57. Oxford: Oxford University Press.

Ho Chi Minh. 1980. *Ho Chi Minh toan tap* (The collected works of Ho Chi Minh). Hanoi: Nha xuat ban su that.

Hoang Chi Bao et al. 1992. *Co cau xa hoi-giai cap o nuoc ta: ly luan va thuc tien* (The class-society structure in our country: Theory and practice). Hanoi: Nha xuat ban thong tin ly luan.

Hoang Kim Giao. 1991. "Chien luoc phat trien kinh te ngoai quoc doanh" (Economic development strategy outside state management). *Nghien cuu kinh te* (Economic research) 180 (April): 27–30.

Hobsbawm, Eric, and Terence Ranger, eds. 1983. *The Invention of Tradition*. Cambridge: Cambridge University Press.

Hong Huanchun. 1983. "Ming Qing fengjian zhuanzhi zhengquan dui zibenzhuyi mengya de zuai" (The obstacles posed to incipient capitalism by Ming-Qing feudal political power). In *Zhongguo zibenzhuyi mengya wenti lunwenji* (Essays on the problem of incipient capitalism), edited by the History Department, Nanjing University, Nanjing: Jiangsu Renmin Chubanshe.

Honig, Emily. 1986. *Sisters and Strangers: Women in the Shanghai Cotton Mills, 1911-1949*. Stanford: Stanford University Press.

How Tan Tarn. 1993. *The Lady of Soul and Her Ultimate "S" Machine*. Singapore: Sirius.

Hsing, You-tien. 1993. "Transnational Networks of Taiwan's Small Business and China's Local Government." Ph.D. diss, University of California, Berkeley.

Hughes, Helen, ed. 1988. *Achieving Industrialization in Asia*. Cambridge: Cambridge University Press.

Hussin, Mutalib. 1990. *Islam and Ethnicity in Malay Politics*. Singapore: Oxford University Press.

Hyŏn Sangyun. 1949. *Chosŏn yuhaksa* (A history of Korean Confucianism). Seoul: Minjung Sŏgwan.

Janelli, Roger L., and Dawnhee Yim Janelli. 1978. "Lineage Organisation and Social Differentiation in Korea." *Man: Journal of the Royal Anthropological Institute*, n.s., 13: 272–89.

————. 1982. *Ancestor Worship and Korean Society*. Stanford: Stanford University Press.

————. 1993. *Making Capitalism: The Social and Cultural Construction of a South Korean Conglomerate*. Stanford: Stanford University Press.

Jesudason, James V. 1989. *Ethnicity and the Economy: The State, Chinese Business, and Multinationals in Malaysia*. Singapore: Oxford University Press.

Johnson, Chalmers. 1977. *MITI and the Japanese Miracle: The Growth of Industrial Policy, 1925–75.* Stanford: Stanford University Press.

Jones, Bryn. 1977. "Economic Action and Rational Organisation in the Sociology of Weber." In *Sociological Theories of the Economy,* edited by Barry Hindess, pp. 28–65. London: Macmillan.

Jones, Eric. 1981. *The European Miracle: Environments, Economies, and Geopolitics in the History of Europe and Asia.* Cambridge: Cambridge University Press.

———. 1988. *Growth Recurring: Economic Change in World History.* Oxford University Press.

Jordan, Miriam. 1994. "Shangri-La Revisited." *Asian Wall Street Journal,* 1 February.

Judd, Ellen R. 1990a. "Alternative Development Strategies for Women in Rural China." *Development and Change* 21, no. 1: 23–42.

———. 1990b. "'Men Are More Able': Rural Chinese Women's Conceptions of Gender and Agency." *Pacific Affairs* 63, no. 1: 40–61.

———. 1992. "Land Divided, Land United." *China Quarterly* 130:338–56.

———. 1994. *Gender and Power in Rural North China.* Stanford: Stanford University Press.

Jung, Ku-hyun. 1993. "Business-Government Relations." Mimeo.

Kahn, Joel S., and Francis Loh Kok Wah, eds. 1992. *Fragmented Vision: Culture and Politics in Contemporary Malaysia.* Kensington: Asian Studies Association of Australia.

Kang Chul-kyu, Ch'oe Chong-p'yo, and Chang Chi-sang. 1991. *Chaebŏl* (Conglomerates). Seoul: Bibong Ch'ulpansa.

———. 1987. "Kiopkwa sijangjojik" (Business enterprise and market structure). In *Han'guk kyongjae ŭi ihae* (Understanding the Korean economy), edited by Lim Won-tak et al., pp. 88–188. Seoul: Bibong Ch'ulpansa.

Kang In-sun. 1990. "Masan, Changwonui nodongja kyegupui kajoksaenghwal" (The family life of production workers in Masan and Changwon). In *Hanguk kajokron* (Essays on the Korean family), edited by the Korean Social Research Center for Women, pp. 131–57. Seoul: Kachi Sa.

Kang, Shin-pyo. 1987. "Korean Culture, the Olympics, and World Order." In *The Olympics and Cultural Exchange: The Papers of the First International Conference on the Olympics and East/West and North/South Cultural Exchange in the World System,* edited by Kang Shin-Pyo, John MacAloon, and Roberto DaMatta, pp. 85–103. Ansan, Kor.: Institute for Ethnological Studies, Hanyang University.

Karim, Wazir Jahan. 1992. *Women and Culture: Between Malay Adat and Islam.* Boulder: Westview.

Keenan, Faith. 1996. "Road Show." *Far Eastern Economic Review,* 5 January.

Kessler, Clive S. 1992. "Archaism and Modernity: Contemporary Malay Political Culture." In *Fragmented Vision: Culture and Politics in Contemporary Malaysia,* edited by Joel S. Kahn and Francis Loh Kok Wah, pp. 133–57. Kensington: Asian Studies Association of Australia.

Keyes, Charles. 1993. "Buddhist Economics and Buddhist Fundamentalism in Burma and Thailand." In *Fundamentalisms and the State: Remaking Politics, Economics, and Militance,* edited by Martin E. Marty and R. Scott Appleby, pp. 367–409. Chicago: University of Chicago Press.

Khoo Kay Jin. 1992. "The Grand Vision: Mahathir and Modernisation." In *Fragmented Vision: Culture and Politics in Contemporary Malaysia*, edited by Joel S. Kahn and Francis Loh Kok Wah, pp. 44–75. Kensington: Asian Studies Association of Australia.

Kim Chang-ki. 1991. "Largest Labor Union Collapses at Pohang Steel." *Chugan Choson*, 24 August, 34–37.

Kim, Choong-soon. 1992. *The Culture of Korean Industry: An Ethnography of Poongsan Corporation*. Tucson: University of Arizona Press.

Kim Il-kon. 1988. *Jugyō bunkaken jitsujō to keizai* (Order and economy of the Confucian cultural region). Nagoya: University of Nagoya Press.

Kim Kum-su. 1986. *Hanguk nodong munje ui sanghwang gwa insik* (The circumstances and interpretation of the Korean labor problem). Seoul: Pulbit.

Kim, Seung-kyung. 1990. "Capitalism, Patriarchy, and Autonomy: Women Factory Workers in the Korean Economic Miracle." Ph.D. diss., City University of New York.

———. 1992. "Export Processing Zones and Worker Resistance in South Korea." In *Anthropology and the Global Factory: Studies of the New Industrialization in the Late 20th Century*, edited by Frances Rothstein and Michael Blim, pp. 220–237. New York: Bergin and Garvey.

———. 1994. "Negotiated Realities: Fieldwork with a 'Disguised' Worker in the Korean Labor Movement." Paper presented at the symposium Korean Traditions: Their Impact on the Future, Washington, D.C.

Kim Taik-Kyoo [Kim T'aekkyu]. 1964. *Tongjok purak ŭi saenghwal kujo yŏn'gu* (A study of the structure of life in a single-lineage village). Taegu: Ch'ŏnggu College Press.

Kondo, Dorinne K. 1990. *Crafting Selves: Power, Gender, and Discourses of Identity in a Japanese Workplace*. Chicago: University of Chicago Press.

Koo Bon-Ho and Lee Kyu-ok, eds. 1991. *Han'guk kyongjaeui yoksajok chomyong* (The Korean economy from a historical viewpoint). Seoul: Korea Development Institute.

Koo, Hagen. 1989. "Middle Class Politics and the New East Asian Capitalism: The Korean Middle Classes." Paper presented to the American Sociological Association, San Francisco.

———. 1993. "The State, Minjung, and the Working Class in South Korea." In *State and Society in Contemporary Korea*, edited by Hagen Koo, pp. 131–62. Ithaca: Cornell University Press.

Korean Association of Women Workers. 1987. *Han'guk yosong nodongui hyonjang* (The scene of Korean women workers) Seoul: Baeksan Sodang.

Korean Women's Development Institute. 1994. *Social Statistics and Indicators on Women*. Seoul: Korean Women's Development Institute.

Korean Young Catholic Workers' Organization (JOC). 1980. *Masan Suchul Chayujiyok hyupyeope kwanhan yongu* (Masan Export Processing Zone Report on company suspension and closure). Masan: JOC.

Kornai, János. 1989. "The Hungarian Reform Process: Visions, Hopes, and Reality." In *Remaking the Economic Institutions of China and Eastern Europe*, edited by David Stark and Victor Nee, pp. 32–94. Stanford: Stanford University Press.

Kotzec, Michael. 1992. *Labour and the Failure of Reform in China.* London: St. Martin's.

Kraar, Louis. 1994. "The New Power in Asia." *Fortune,* 31 October.

Kung, Lydia. 1983. *Factory Women in Taiwan.* Ann Arbor: UMI Research Press.

Kuok Group. 1991. *The Kuok Group.* Hong Kong, Kuala Lumpur, and Singapore: Kuok Group.

Kwon, Yong-hun. 1991. "Pundanhu Han'guk kyongjae ui pyeonch'eon" (Change in the Korean economy after division). In *Han'guk kyongjaeui yoksajok chomyong* (The Korean economy from a historical viewpoint), edited by Koo Bon-ho and Lee Kyu-ok, pp. 111–68. Seoul: Korea Development Institute.

Laclau, Ernesto, and Chantal Mouffe. 1985. *Hegemony and Socialist Strategy: Towards a Radical Democratic Politics.* London: Verso.

Landa, Janet. 1994. "Culture and Entrepreneurship in Less-Developed Countries." In *The Culture of Entrepreneurship,* edited by Brigitte Berger, pp. 53–72. San Francisco: ICS Press.

Lary, Diana. 1985. *Bad Iron: Warlord Soldiers in Republican China.* Cambridge: Cambridge University Press.

Le Dinh Thu. 1993. "Moi truong dau tu, muc tieu-dinh huong cua dau tu trong nuoc o Viet-Nam" (The investment environment, objectives, and directions of domestic investment in Vietnam). *Nghien cuu kinh te* 196 (December): 3–10.

Lee Ching Kwan. 1993. "Despotism and Nepotism: The Politics and the Poetics of Production in South China's Capitalist Enclave." Paper presented at the Regional Seminar of the Center for Chinese Studies, University of California, Berkeley.

Lee Hak-Chong [Yi Hakchong]. 1989. *Kiŏp munhwa non: Iron, kipŏp, sarye yŏn'gu* (A study of corporate culture: Theories, techniques, and case studies). Seoul: Pommunsa.

Lee, Keun. 1993. *New East Asian Economic Development: Interacting Capitalism and Socialism.* Armonk, N.Y.: M. E. Sharpe.

Lee Kwang-Kyu. 1990. *Taehak e tŭrŏgan adŭl ege* (To my son who entered college). Seoul: Chiphyŏnjŏn.

———. 1993. *Han'gukui Kiopmunhwa* (Business culture in Korea). Seoul: Bakyongsa.

Le Hong Phuc. 1981. "Tu ban Hoa trong kinh tecac nuoc ASEAN" (Ethnic Chinese capital in the economies of the ASEAN countries). *Nghien cuu kinh te* 123 (October) 70–79.

Lewis, J. D. 1994. "Indonesia's Industrial and Trade Policy during and after the Oil Boom." Paper presented at the conference Managing the Oil Boom: Lessons for Colombia from the Indonesian Experience, Bogota.

Li Jinming. 1990. *Mingdai haiwai maoyishi* (A history of Ming dynasty sea trade). Beijing: Zhongguo Shehui Kexue Chubanshe.

Lim Chong-kuk. 1991. *Sillok ch'inilpa* (Documentary: Japan sympathizers). Seoul: Tolbegae.

Lim, Linda. 1978. "Women Workers in Multinational Corporations: The Case of the Electronics Industry in Malaysia and Singapore." Michigan Occasional Papers in Women's Studies, no. 9. Ann Arbor: University of Michigan.

———. 1983. "Capitalism, Imperialism, and Patriarchy: The Dilemma of Third-World Women Workers in Multinational Factories." In *Women, Men, and the International*

Division of Labor, edited by J. Nash and M. P. Fernandez-Kelly, pp. 70–91. Albany: State University of New York Press.

Lim, Linda, and L. A. Gosling, eds. 1983. *The Chinese in Southeast Asia,* vol. 1: *Ethnicity and Economic Activity.* Singapore: Maruzen Asia.

Lim Mah Hui. 1981. *Ownership and Control of the One Hundred Largest Corporations in Malaysia.* Kuala Lumpur: Oxford University Press.

Limlingan, Victor Simpao. 1986. *The Overseas Chinese in ASEAN: Business Strategies and Management Practices.* Manila: Vita Development Corp.

Lin Renchaun. 1987. *Mingmo Qingchu siren haishang maoyi* (A history of the late Ming and early Qing private sea trade). Shanghai: Huadong Shifan Daxue Chubanshe.

Lin Yongkuang and Wang Xi. 1991. *Qingdai xibei minzu maoyishi* (A history of trade among northwestern peoples in the Qing dynasty). Beijing: Zhongyang Minzu Xueyuan Chubanshe.

Liu Yunbo. 1990. *Zhongguo rujia guanli sixiang* (Confucian managerial thinking in China). Shanghai: Shanghai Renmin Chubanshe.

Lufrano, Richard. 1996. *Honorable Merchants: Commerce and Self-Cultivation in Late Imperial China.* Honolulu: University of Hawaii Press.

Luong, Hy Van. 1989. "Vietnamese Kinship: Structural Principles and the Socialist Transformation in Northern Vietnam." *Journal of Asian Studies* 48, no. 4: 741–56.

———. 1993. "The Political Economy of Vietnamese Reforms: A Microscopic Perspective from Two Ceramics-Manufacturing Centers." In *Reinventing Vietnamese Socialism: Doi moi in Comparative Perspectives,* edited by William Turley and Mark Selden, 119–48. Boulder: Westview.

Luong, Hy Van, and Diep Dinh-Hoa. 1991. "Culture and Capitalism in the Pottery Enterprises of Biên-Hòa, South Vietnam (1878–1975)." *Journal of Southeast Asian Studies* 22:16–32.

Lyotard, Jean-François. 1984. *The Postmodern Condition: A Report on Knowledge.* Translated by Geoff Bennington and Brian Massumi. Minneapolis: University of Minnesota Press.

Mackie, Jamie. 1992a. "Changing Patterns of Chinese Big Business in Southeast Asia." In *Southeast Asian Capitalists,* edited by Ruth McVey, pp. 161–90. Ithaca: Cornell University Southeast Asia Program.

———. 1992b. "Overseas Chinese Entrepreneurship." *Asian-Pacific Economic Literature* (May): 41–64.

Mahathir Mohammad. 1970. *Malaysian Dilemma.* Singapore: Asia Pacific Press.

Mann, Susan. 1992. "Household Handicrafts and State Policy in Qing Times." In *To Achieve Security and Wealth: The Qing Imperial State and the Economy, 1644–1911.* Ithaca: Cornell University East Asia Program.

Marcus, George E., and Michael M. J. Fischer. 1986. *Anthropology as Cultural Critique: An Experimental Moment in the Human Sciences.* Chicago: University of Chicago Press.

Marshall, Byron K. 1967. *Capitalism and Nationalism in Prewar Japan: The Ideology of the Business Elite.* Stanford: Stanford University Press.

Masan Free Export Zone Administrative Office. 1987. *Masan Suchul Chayujiyok 15 nyonsa* (A history of Masan Free Export Zone's fifteen years). Masan: Masan Free Export Zone Administrative Office.

Mason, E. S., et al. 1980. *The Economic and Social Modernization of the Republic of Korea.* Cambridge: Harvard University Press.

McCawley, P. 1981. "The Growth of the Industrial Sector." In *The Indonesian Economy During the Soeharto Era,* edited by A. Booth and P. McCawley, pp. 62–101. Kuala Lumpur: Oxford University Press.

McNamara, Dennis L. 1990. *The Colonial Origins of Korean Enterprise, 1910–1945.* Cambridge: Cambridge University Press.

McVey, Ruth, ed. 1992. *Southeast Asian Capitalists.* Ithaca: Cornell University Press.

Means, Gordon. 1991. *Malaysian Politics: The Second Generation.* Singapore: Oxford University Press.

Menkhoff, Thomas. 1993. *Trade Routes, Trust, and Trading Networks: Chinese Small Enterprises in Singapore.* Saarbrucken: Verlag Breitenbach.

Mittelman, James H. 1995. "Rethinking the International Division of Labour in the Context of Globalisation." *Third World Quarterly* 16, no. 2.

Mohamed Ariff, ed. 1991. *The Muslim Private Sector in Southeast Asia.* Singapore: Institute of Southeast Asian Studies.

Mohd Suffian Hashim et al. 1978. *The Constitution of Malaysia: Its Development, 1957–1977.* Kuala Lumpur: Oxford University Press.

Morishima, Michio. 1982. *Why Has Japan 'Succeeded'?* Cambridge: Cambridge University Press.

Muhammad Syukri Salleh. 1992. *An Islamic Approach to Rural Development: The Arqam Way.* London: ASOIB International.

Nagata, Judith. 1978. "The Chinese Muslims of Malaysia: New Malays or New Associates?" In *The Past in Southeast Asia's Present,* edited by Gordon Means, pp. 102–14. Hamilton, Ont.: Canadian Council for Southeast Asian Studies, McMaster University.

———. 1980. "Religious Ideology and Social Change: The Islamic Revival in Malaysia." *Pacific Affairs* 53, no. 3:405–39.

———. 1984. *The Reflowering of Malaysian Islam: Religious Radicals and Their Roots.* Vancouver: University of British Columbia Press.

———. 1992. "Alternatives to Development: Small-Scale 'Islamic Economics' in Malaysia." *Manusia dan Masyarakat* 7:45–54.

Najita, Tetsuo. 1987. *Visions of Virtue in Tokugawa Japan.* Chicago: University of Chicago Press.

Nanjing daxue lishixi (Department of History, Nanjing University), ed. 1981. *Ming-Qing zibenzhuyi mengya yanjiu lunwenji* (Studies on incipient capitalism in the Ming-Qing period). Shanghai: Shanghai Renmin Chubanshe.

———, ed. 1983. *Zhongguo zibenzhuyi mengya wenti lunwenji* (Essays on the problem of incipient capitalism). Nanjing: Jiangsu Renmin Chubanshe.

Nash, June, and Maria Patricia Fernandez-Kelly, eds. 1983. *Women, Men, and the International Division of Labor.* Albany: State University of New York Press.

Ngo Vi Lien. 1928. *Nomenclature des communes du Tonkin.* Hanoi: Le van Tan.

Nguyen Cong Binh. 1959. *Tim hieu giai cap tu san Viet Nam thoi Phap thuoi* (To understand the Vietnamese capitalist class in the French colonial period). Hanoi: Van Su Dia.

Nguyen Dong. 1993. "De xay dung mot thi truong chung khoan hoat dong co hieu qua trong dieu kien Viet-Nam" (To establish an active stock market that will be effective under Vietnamese conditions). *Tap chi truong mai Seaprodex* (The Seaprodex commercial journal) (July): 3–5.

Nguyen Q. Thang. 1993. "Kham dinh Dai Nam hoi dien su le, mot bo sach bien soan cong phu" (The "Imperially Authorized Compendium of Institutions and Institutional Cases of the Great South," a laboriously compiled work). *Nhan dan* (The people), 28 August: 3.

Nguyen Viet. 1962. "Ban ve mam mong tu ban chu nghia o Viet Nam duoi thoi phong kien" (On the origin of Vietnamese capitalism in the feudal period, pt. 1). *Nghien cuu lich su* (Historical research) 35:21–34.

Nonini, Donald. 1993. "On the Outs on the Rim: An Ethnographic Grounding of the 'Asia-Pacific' Imaginary." In *What Is in a Rim: Critical Perspectives on the Asia Pacific Idea,* edited by Arif Dirlik, pp. 161–82. Boulder: Westview.

O'Connor, David. 1994. *Managing the Environment with Rapid Industrialisation: Lessons from the East Asian Experience.* Paris: Development Centre, Organisation for Economic Co-operation and Development.

Ogle, George E. 1990. *South Korea: Dissent within the Economic Miracle.* London: Zed.

Ong, Aihwa. 1983. "Global Industries and Malay Peasants in Peninsular Malaysia." In *Women, Men and the International Division of Labor,* edited by J. Nash and M. P. Fernandez-Kelly, pp. 426–39. Albany: State University of New York Press.

———. 1987. *Spirits of Resistance and Capitalist Discipline: Factory Women in Malaysia.* Albany: State University of New York Press.

———. 1988. "The Production of Possession: Spirits and the Multinational Corporation in Malaysia." *American Ethnologist* 15, no. 1: 28–42.

———. 1991. "The Gender and Labor Politics of Postmodernity." *Annual Review of Anthropology* 20:279–309.

Ortner, Sherry. 1984. "Theory in Anthropology since the Sixties." *Comparative Studies in Society and History* 26:126–66.

Ozawa, Terutomo. 1994. "Exploring the Asian Economic Miracle: Politics, Economics, Society, Culture, and History." *Journal of Asian Studies* 53, no. 1 (February): 124–31.

Parish, William L., and Martin King Whyte. 1978. *Village and Family in Contemporary China.* Chicago: University of Chicago Press.

Park Se-il. 1987. "Koyong, Imkum mit Nosakwankye" (Employment, wages, and labor-management relations). In *Han'guk kyongjae ui ihae* (Understanding the Korean economy), edited by Lim Won-tak et al., pp. 171–250. Seoul: Bibong Ch'ulpansa.

Parsons, Talcott. 1972. "Culture and Social System Revisited." *Social Science Quarterly* 53:253–66.

———. 1977. *The Evolution of Societies.* Edited by Jackson Toby. Englewood Cliffs, N.J.: Prentice-Hall.

Pelzel, John. 1979. "Factory Life in Japan and China Today." In *Japan: A Comparative View,* edited by Albert Craig, pp. 371–432. Princeton: Princeton University Press.

Peng Yuxin. 1990. *Qingdai tudi kaikenshi* (A history of Qing dynasty land clearance and settlement). Beijing: Nongye Chubanshe.

Perkins, Dwight. 1967. "Government as an Obstacle to Industrialization: The Case of Nineteenth-Century China." *Journal of Economic History* 27, no. 4: 479–92.

Perkins, Dwight, and Shahid Yusuf. 1984. *Rural Development in China*. Baltimore: Johns Hopkins University Press.

Pham Xuan Nam et al. 1991. *Doi moi kinh te-xa hoi: thanh tuu, van de, va giai phap* (Economic and social renovation: Successes, problems, and solutions). Hanoi: Nha xuat ban khoa hoc xa hoi.

Phan Gia Ben. 1957. *So thao lich su phat trien tieu thu cong nghiep Viet Nam* (Brief history of handicraft and small industrial development in Vietnam). Hanoi: Van su dia.

Phongpaichit, Pasuk. 1995. "Gender and Industrialisation in South East Asia." Paper presented at the seminar Gender and Human Resources in Economic Development Strategy, Vietnamese National Assembly, Hanoi.

Poggi, G. 1983. *Calvinism and the Capitalist Spirit: Max Weber's Protestant Ethic*. London: Macmillan.

Purcell, Victor. 1965. *The Chinese in Southeast Asia*. New York: Oxford University Press.

Qian Xun. 1991. "Rujia yi-li, li-yu zhi bian ji xiandai yiyi" (Confucian debates between righteousness and profit, and between principle and desire, and their contemporary significance). In *Rujia sixiang yu weilai shehui* (Confucian thought and future society), edited by Fudan University History Department, pp. 49–59. Shanghai: Shanghai Renmin Chubanshe.

Qiongzhou fuzhi (Gazetteer of Qiongzhou prefecture). 1619. Edited by Ouyang Can.

"Quarterly Chronicle and Documentation." 1990. *China Quarterly* 124 (July-September): 760–81.

Rankin, Mary Backus. 1990. "The Origins of a Chinese Public Sphere: Local Elites and Community Affairs in the Late Imperial Period." *Études chinoises* 9, no. 2: 13–60.

Ratnam, K. J. 1965. *Communalism and the Political Process in Malaya*. Kuala Lumpur: University of Malaya Press.

Rawski, Thomas. 1989. *Economic Growth in Prewar China*. Berkeley: University of California Press.

———. 1994. "Social Foundations of East Asian Economic Dynamism." Paper presented at the conference Economy and Culture in Eastern Asia, Toronto.

Redding, S. G. 1990. *The Spirit of Chinese Capitalism*. Berlin: Walter de Gruyter.

Rhee Yang-soo. 1981. "A Cross-Cultural Comparison of Korean and American Managerial Styles: An Inventory of Propositions." *Journal of East and West Studies* 10, no. 2: 45–63.

Robbins, Lionel. 1952. *An Essay on the Nature and Significance of Economic Sciences*. London: Macmillan.

Robinson, Michael. 1991. "Perceptions of Confucianism in Twentieth-Century Korea." In *The East Asian Region: Confucian Heritage and Its Modern Adaptation*, edited by Gilbert Rozman, pp. 204–25. Princeton: Princeton University Press.

Robinson, R. 1986. *Indonesia: The Rise of Capitalism*. New York: Allen and Unwin.

Rohatyn, Felix. 1994. "World Capital: The Need and the Risks." *New York Review of Books* 41, no. 13 (July 13): 48–53.

Rohlen, Thomas. 1974. *For Harmony and Strength: Japanese White-Collar Organization in Anthropological Perspective.* Berkeley: University of California Press.

Rorty, Richard. 1979. *Philosophy and the Mirror of Nature.* Princeton: Princeton University Press.

Rowe, William. 1989. *Hankow: Conflict and Community in a Chinese City, 1796–1889.* Stanford: Stanford University Press.

Rozman, Gilbert. 1991. *Confucian Heritage and Its Modern Adaptation.* Princeton: Princeton University Press.

Rutten, Mario. 1994. *Asian Capitalism in the European Mirror.* Amsterdam: VU University Press.

Safa, Helen I. 1981. "Runaway Shops and Female Employment: The Search for Cheap Labor." *Signs* 7, no. 2:418–33.

Sahlins, Marshall. 1976. *Culture and Practical Reason.* Chicago: University of Chicago Press.

Salaff, Janet W. 1981. *Working Daughters of Hong Kong: Filial Piety or Power in the Family.* Cambridge: Cambridge University Press.

Sato, Yuri. 1993. "The Salim Group in Indonesia: The Development and Behaviour of the Largest Conglomerate in Southeast Asia." In *The Developing Economies,* pp. 408–41. Tokyo: Institute of Developing Economies.

Savage, Stephen P. 1977. "Talcott Parsons and the Structural-Functionalist Theory of the Economy." In *Sociological Theories of the Economy,* edited by Barry Hindess, pp. 1–27. London: Macmillan.

Sender, Henny. 1991. "Inside the Overseas Chinese Network." *Institutional Investor,* August.

"Shandong's Economic Performance in 1989." 1990. *Summary of World Broadcasts.* Pt. 3: *The Far East, Weekly Economic Report,* 25 April, FE/W0125. London: British Broadcasting Corporation.

"Shandong's Economy in 1986." 1987. *Summary of World Broadcasts.* Pt. 3: *The Far East, Weekly Economic Report,* 6 May, FE/W1439. London: British Broadcasting Corporation.

"Shandong's Economy in 1988." 1989. *Summary of World Broadcasts.* Pt. 3: *The Far East, Weekly Economic Report,* 10 May, FE/W0076. London: British Broadcasting Corporation.

"Shandong's Performance in 1987." 1988. *Summary of World Broadcasts.* Pt. 3: *The Far East, Weekly Economic Report,* 22 June, FE/W0031. London: British Broadcasting Corporation.

Shapiro, Ian. 1990. *Political Criticism.* Berkeley: University of California Press.

Sheridan, Mary, and Janet Salaff, eds. 1984. *Lives: Chinese Working Women.* Bloomington: Indiana University Press.

Shiba Yoshinobu. 1968. *Sōdai shōgyō-shi kenkyū.* Tokyo: Kazama Shobo. English abridgment: Mark Elvin, trans. 1970. *Commerce and Society in Sung China* (Ann Arbor: Center for Chinese Studies, University of Michigan).

Shimada, Haruo. 1993. "Same Game, Slightly Different Rules." *Intersect,* May.

Shin Yoo-Keun [Sin Yugŭn]. 1984. *Han'guk kiŏp ŭi t'ŭksŭng kwa kwaje* (The characteristics and issues of Korean enterprises). Seoul: Seoul National University Press.

———. 1993. *Han'gukui kyongyong* (Business management in Korea). Seoul: Pakyongsa.

Shue, Vivienne. 1988. *The Reach of the State: Sketches of the Chinese Body Politic.* Stanford: Stanford University Press.

Sia, Irene. 1993. "Robert Kuok: Taipan Incorporated." In *Formation and Restructuring of Business Groups in Malaysia,* edited by Hara Fujio, pp. 55–69. Tokyo: Institute of Developing Economies.

Skinner, G. William. 1964–65. "Marketing and Social Structure in Rural China." *Journal of Asian Studies* 24, no. 1: 3–43, and no. 2: 195–399.

Smith, Adam. 1776. [1936]. *The Wealth of Nations.* New York: Modern Library.

Smith, Paul J. 1991. *Taxing Heaven's Storehouse: Horses, Bureaucrats, and the Destruction of the Sichaun Tea Industry, 1074–1224.* Cambridge: Council on East Asian Studies, Harvard University.

Snodgrass, Donald. 1980. *Inequality and Economic Development in Malaysia.* Kuala Lumpur: Oxford University Press.

Solinger, Dorthy. 1984. *Chinese Businesses under Socialism: The Politics of Domestic Commerce, 1949–1980.* Berkeley: University of California Press.

Song Byong-nak. 1981. *Han'guk kyongjeron* (The Korean economy). Seoul: Pakyongsa.

Song Linfei. 1984. "The Present State and Future Prospects of Specialized Households in Rural China." *Social Sciences in China* 5, no. 4: 107–30.

Song Sŭk-ku. 1987. *Yulgok ŭi ch'ŏrhak sasang yŏn'gu* (A study of the philosophical thought of Yulgok). Seoul: Hyŏngsŏl Ch'ulp'ansa.

Spinanger, Dean. 1986. *Industrialization Policies and Regional Economic Growth in Malaysia.* Singapore: Oxford University Press.

"Statistical Communiqué for 1992." 1993. *Summary of World Broadcasts.* Pt. 3: *The Far East, Weekly Economic Report,* 24 February, FE/W0270. London: British Broadcasting Corporation.

Strand, David. 1989. *Rickshaw Beijing.* Berkeley: University of California Press.

Studwell, Joe. 1994. "Sweet and Sour Times for a Sugar King." *Asia, Inc.,* December: 28–35.

Su Guoxun. 1987. "Makesi Weibo yu 'zibenzhuyi jingshen'" (Max Weber and the "spirit of capitalism"). In *Wenhua: Zhongguo yu shijie* (Culture: China and the world). Vol. 1, edited by Gan Yang, pp. 161–209. Beijing: Sanlian Shudian.

T.C. Former Labor Union Members. 1991. *T.C. chonja nodongjohap undongsa* (The History of the T.C. Labor Union). Seoul: Nulbot.

Tachiki, D. S. 1993. "Striking Up Strategic Alliances: The Foreign Direct Investments of the NIEs and ASEAN Transnational Corporations." In *RIM Pacific Business and Industries,* vol. 3, pp. 3–35. Tokyo: Sakura Institute of Research.

Tan Hock. 1991. "State Capitalism, Multinational Corporations, and Chinese Entrepreneurship in Singapore." In *Business Networks and Economic Development in East and Southeast Asia,* edited by Gary Hamilton, pp. 201–16. Hong Kong: Centre of Asian Studies, University of Hong Kong.

Tanaka Tadao. 1929. "Zhongguo nongmin de licun wenti" (The problem of Chinese peasants leaving their villages). In *Zhongguo nongmin wenti yu nongmin yundong*

(China's peasant problem and the peasant movement), edited by Wang Zhongwu. Shanghai: Shangwu Yinshuguan.

Tham Seong Chee. 1983. *Malays and Modernisation*. Singapore: Singapore National University Press.

Third Malaysia Plan 1976–1980. 1976. Kuala Lumpur: Government Press.

Tran Do. 1989. "Vai tro cua cac to chuc xa hoi ve van hoa" (The role of social organizations with respect to culture). *Nhan dan* (The people), 4 March: 3.

Tu Nan. 1986. "Rural Industry: China's New Engine for Development." *FAO Review* 19, no. 6: 32–38.

Tu, Wei-ming. 1984. *Confucian Ethics Today*. Singapore: Federal Publishers.

———. 1986. "An Inquiry on the Five Relationships in Confucian Humanism." In *The Psycho-Cultural Dynamics of the Confucian Family: Past and Present*, edited by Walter H. Slote, pp. 175–90. Seoul: International Cultural Society of Korea.

———. 1988a. "Cong Zhong-Xi wenhua de bijiao kan Zhongguo wenhua fazhande qianjing" (Prospects for Chinese cultural development from a comparison of Chinese and Western culture). In *Zhong-wai wenhua bijiao yanjiu* (Comparative studies of Chinese and foreign culture), pp. 93–121. Beijing: Sanlian Shudian.

———. 1988b. "Zhongguo wenhua de rentong ji qi chuangxin" (The identity and remaking of Chinese culture). In *Zhong-wai wenhua bijiao yanjiu* (Comparative studies of Chinese and foreign culture), pp. 64–92. Beijing: Sanlian Shudian.

———. 1993. *Way, Learning, and Politics: Essays on the Confucian Intellectual*. Albany: State University of New York Press.

———. 1994 "The Confucian Dimension in the East Asian Development Model." Paper presented at the conference Economy and Culture in Eastern Asia, Toronto.

Tversky, Amos, and Daniel Kahneman. 1990. "Rational Choice and the Framing of Decisions." In *The Limits of Rationality*, edited by Karen Schweers Cook and Margaret Levi, pp. 60–89. Chicago: University of Chicago Press.

U.S. Department of Labor. 1990. *Worker Rights in Export Processing Zones: Korea*. Washington, D.C.: Bureau of International Labor Affairs.

———. 1991. *Foreign Labor Trends: Korea*. Washington, D.C.: Bureau of International Labor Affairs.

Van Tao. 1992. "Ket hop truyen thong va hien dai trong xay dung va quan ly chinh quyen" (Combining the traditional and the modern in the construction and management of political power). *Tap chi Cong san* (The communist journal) (April): 43–45.

Vedrenne, Bernard. 1939. "Les poteries de Mon-cay." *Bulletin économique de l'Indochine* 42:939–60.

Vietnam, General Statistical Office. 1978. *Tinh hinh phat trien kinh te va van hoa mien Bac xa hoi chu nghia Viet Nam, 1960–1975* (Economic and cultural developments in the socialist north of Vietnam, 1960–1975). Hanoi: Tong Cuc Thong ke.

Vietnam, Institute of Labor and Social Affairs. 1993. *Doanh nghiep nho o Viet Nam* (Small enterprises in Vietnam). Hanoi: Nha xuat ban khoa hoc va ky thuat.

Vietnam, 1989 Population Census. 1991. *Ket qua dieu tra toan dien* (Completed census results). Hanoi: Central Census Steering Committee.

Vogel, Erza, ed. 1975. *Modern Japanese Organization and Decision-Making*. Berkeley: University of California Press.

Volker, T. 1954. *Porcelain and the Dutch East India Company*. Leiden: E. J. Brill.

Vu Hanh Hien. 1993. " 'Qua bieu' lam nen doanh nghiep" ("Presents" make a basis for business). *Nhan dan chu nhat*, 25 July: 3.

Vu Huy Tu. 1993. "May y kien ve co phan hoa doanh nghiep nha nuoc hien nay" (Some opinions on the conversion to shareholding of present state enterprises). *Nhan dan* (The people), 4 February: 3.

Vu Minh Giang. 1993. "Xay dung loi song theo phap luat nhin tu goc do lich su truyen thong" (Establishing a way of life according to the law as viewed from the angle of historical tradition). *Nha nuoc va phap luat* (State and law) 3:14–18.

Vu Quy Vy. 1980. "La fabrique de ceramique de Bat Trang." In *Etudes Vietnamiennes* 62: 136–50.

Walder, Andrew. 1986. *Communist Neo-Traditionalism: Work and Authority in Chinese Industry*. Berkeley: University of California Press.

Walker, Kenneth R. 1989. "40 Years On: Provincial Contrasts in China's Rural Economic Development." *China Quarterly* 119:448–80.

Wang, Gungwu. 1991. *China and the Overseas Chinese*. Singapore: Times Academic Press.

Wang Xun. 1993. "Rujia wenhua yu jingji xiandaihua de qidong" (Confucian culture and the inspiration for economic modernization). *Shehui kexue zhanxian* (Social science frontline) 2:134–38.

Wang Yuquan, Liu Ruzhong, Guo Songyi, and Lin Yongkuang. 1991. *Zhongguo tunkenshi* (A history of Chinese land settlement). Vol. 3. Beijing: Nongye chubanshe.

Wang Zhenzhong. 1993. "Ming-Qing shiqi Hui shang shehui xingxiang de wenhua tou-shi" (A cultural perspective on the social images of Huizhou merchants in the Ming-Qing period). *Fudan xuebao* (Fudan University journal) 6:80–84, 96.

Ward, Barbara. 1972. "A Small Factory in Hong Kong: Some Aspects of Its Internal Organization." In *Economic Organization in Chinese Society*, edited by W. E. Willmott, pp. 535–85. Stanford: Stanford University Press.

Weber, Max. 1949. *The Methodology of the Social Sciences*. New York: Free Press.

———. 1958a. *The Protestant Ethic and the Spirit of Capitalism*. New York: Scribners.

———. 1958b. *The Religion of India*. New York: Macmillan.

———. 1964. *The Religion of China*. New York: Macmillan.

Wee, C. J. W.-L. 1993. "Contending with Primordialism: The 'Modern' Construction of Postcolonial Singapore." *Positions* 1, no. 3: 715–44.

Will, Pierre-Étienne, and R. Bin Wong. 1991. *Nourish the People: The State Civilian Granary System in China, 1650–1850*. Ann Arbor: Center for Chinese Studies, University of Michigan.

Williams, Raymond. 1977. *Marxism and Literature*. Oxford: Oxford University Press.

Wolf, Eric. 1982. *Europe and the People without History*. Berkeley: University of California Press.

Wong, Christine P. W. 1988. "Interpreting Rural Industrial Growth in the Post-Mao Period." *Modern China* 14, no. 1: 3–30.

Wong , R. Bin. 1982. "Food Riots in the Qing Dynasty." *Journal of Asian Studies* 41, no. 4 (August): 767–88.

————. 1983. "Les émeutes de subsistances en Chine et en Europe Occidentale." *Annales* 38, no. 2 (March April): 234–58.

————. 1988a. "Naguère et aujourd'hui: Reflexions sur l'État et l'économie en Chine." *Études Chinoises* 7, no. 1:7–28.

————. 1988b. "Rural Industry and Demographic Change in China and Western Europe: A Preliminary Sketch." *Chūgoku kindaishi kenkyū* (Studies in the history of modern China) 6:1–32.

————. 1992a. "Chinese Economic History and Development: A Note on the Myers-Huang Exchange." *Journal of Asian Studies* 51, no. 3:600–611.

————. 1992b. "Studying Republican China's Economy: What's New and What's Needed." *Republican China* 18, no. 1:77–89.

————. Forthcoming. *Worlds of Difference: States, Economics, and Social Protests in China and Europe.* Ithaca: Cornell University Press.

Woodside, Alexander. 1989. "Peasants and the State in the Aftermath of the Vietnamese Revolution." *Peasant Studies* 16, no. 4:283–97.

————. 1991. "The Contributions to Rural Change of Modern Vietnamese Village Schools." In *Reshaping Local Worlds: Formal Education and Cultural Changes in Rural Southeast Asia,* edited by C. F. Keyes, pp. 174–199. New Haven: Southeast Asia Council, Yale University.

Woon Yuen-fong. 1993. "Circulatory Mobility in Post-Mao China: The Case of Temporary Migrants in Kaiping County." Paper presented at the Regional Seminar of the Center for Chinese Studies, University of California, Berkeley.

World Bank. 1993. *The East Asian Miracle: Economic Growth and Public Policy.* Oxford: Oxford University Press.

Wu Chengming. 1985. *Zhongguo zibenzhuyi yu guonei shichang* (Chinese incipient capitalism and domestic markets). Beijing: Zhongguo Shehui Kexue Chubanshe.

Wu Zhixin. 1937. "Zhongguo nongmin licun wenti" (The problem of village leaving among Chinese peasants). *Dongfang zazhi* 34 (August 15).

Xie Xialing. 1994. "Ping 'Rujia fuxing'—jian lun 'Rujia zibenzhuyi' ji qi ta (On the "Confucian renaissance" and "Confucian capitalism"). *Fudan xuebao* (Fudan University journal) 3:34–38.

Xu Hong. 1972. *Qingdai Lianghuai yanchang de yanjiu* (Studies on the Qing dynasty Lianghuai salt yards). Taipei: Taiwan Daxue Lishi Yanjiusuo.

Yamaguchi, Masaki. 1993. *The Emerging Chinese Business Sphere.* Tokyo: Nomura Research Institute.

Yang Yanyin. 1989. "Quansheng funü tuanjie qilai wei jianshe Shandong, zhenxing Shandong er nuli fendou" (Women of the province unite to struggle hard to reconstruct and revitalize Shandong). *Funü gongzuo* (Women's work) 5:7–16.

Ye Sheng. 1991. *Shuidong riji* (Diary from east of the river). Compiled 1465–72. Reprint of Siku quanshu edition. Beijing: Zhonghua Shuju.

Yoon Suk-bum [Yun Sŏkpŏm]. 1989. "Han'guk chabonjuǔi chŏngnibǔl ǔihan mosaek" (Toward the foundation of Korean Capitalism). In *Chabonjuǔi wa sahoejuǔi: Iron kwa hyŏmsil* (Capitalism and socialism: Theory and reality), edited by Yoon Suk-bum, et al., pp. 499–564. Seoul: Segyŏngsa.

Yoshihara, Kunio. 1988. *The Rise of Ersatz Capitalism in South-east Asia.* Singapore: Oxford University Press.

———. 1993. "Economic Development, Technology, and Culture: The Case of East Asia." *Asian Perspective* 17, no. 2:247–68.

Yoshino, Michael J. 1968. *Japan's Managerial System: Tradition and Innovation.* Cambridge, Mass.: MIT Press.

Yü Ying-shih. 1984. *Cong jiazhi xitong kan Zhongguo wenhua de xiandai yiyi* (The contemporary significance of Chinese culture from the point of view of its value system). Taipei: Shibao Wenhua Chuban Qiye.

———. 1987. "Zhongguo jinshi zongjiao lunli yu shangren jingshen" (The modern Chinese religious ethic and the spirit of merchants). In *Shi yu Zhongguo wenhua* (The gentry and Chinese culture), pp. 441–579. Shanghai: Shanghai Renmin Chubanshe.

Yun Heung-gil. 1977 [1989]. "The Man Who Was Left as Nine Pairs of Shoes." In *The House of Twilight,* translated and edited by Martin Holman, pp. 96–147. London: Readers International.

Zhang Haipeng and Wang Tingyuan, eds. 1985. *Ming-Qing Hui shang ziliao xuanbian* (Selected materials on Huizhou merchants of the Ming and Qing). Hefei: Huangshan Shushe.

Zhang Jing. 1992. "Guojia zai shehui jingji fazhanzhong de zuoyong" (The functions of the state in social and economic development). *Shehuixue yanjiu* (Sociological studies) 2:53–59.

Zhang Juan and Ma Wenrong. 1988. "Daqiuzhuang 'funü huijia' de sisuo" (The thinking behind "women returning home" in Daqiuzhuang). *Zhongguo funü* (Chinese women) 1:8–10.

Zhang Liwen. 1990. *Chuantong xue yinlun* (Introduction to the study of tradition). Beijing: Renmin Daxue Chubanshe.

Contributors

Timothy Brook is Professor of History at Stanford University. A specialist in the social history of the Ming dynasty, he is the author of *Quelling the People: The Military Suppression of the Beijing Democracy Movement* (1992) and *Praying for Power: Buddhism and the Formation of Gentry Society in Late-Ming China* (1993). His current research explores Chinese collaboration with Japan during Japan's occupation of central China in 1937–45.

Farid Harianto is a faculty member of Institute PPM, Jakarta, teaches at the University of Indonesia, and edits the *Indonesian Economic Journal*. He has published extensively on the economic behavior of the firm and other topics on economy and security in Southeast Asia.

Heng Pek Koon is a faculty member at American University. Her publications include *Chinese Politics in Malaysia: A History of the Malaysian Chinese Association* (1988) and "The Chinese Business Elite of Malaysia" (1992).

Roger L. Janelli is Professor of Folklore and East Asian Languages and Cultures at Indiana University. He coauthored *Ancestor Worship and Korean Society* (1982) and *Making Capitalism* (1993) and has coedited *The Anthropology of Korea: East Asian Perspectives* (forthcoming). Together with Dawnhee Yim, he has published several articles on Korean intellectual history, lineage organization, popular religion, and women's rotating credit societies. His current research focuses on South Korea's postwar social, political, and economic transformations.

Ellen R. Judd teaches anthropology at the University of Manitoba. She has published widely on Chinese political culture and gender, most recently *Gender and Power in Rural North China* (1994).

Seung-kyung Kim is Assistant Professor of Women's Studies at the University of Maryland, College Park. Her publications include "Export Processing Zones and Worker Resistance in South Korea" (1992). She is currently completing *Individual Mobility and Collective Struggle: Lives of Women Factory Workers in South Korea.*

Diana Lary is Professor of Modern Chinese History at the University of British Columbia. She is also codirector of the Canada and Hong Kong Project of the Joint Centre for Asia Pacific Studies, Toronto. Her research interests are in warlordism and regional history in China. She is the author of *Region and Nation: The Kwangsi Clique in Chinese Politics, 1925–1937* (1974) and *Bad Iron: Warlord Soldiers in Republican China* (1985).

Hy V. Luong is Professor of Anthropology at the University of Toronto and has also taught at Hamilton College and Johns Hopkins University. In addition to numerous book chapters and journal articles on Vietnamese discourse, social organization, and political economy, he is the author of *Discursive Practices and Linguistic Meanings: The Vietnamese System of Person References* (1990); and *Revolution in the Village: Tradition and Transformation in North Vietnam, 1925–1988* (1992).

Judith Nagata is Professor of Anthropology at York University, Toronto. She is the author of several books on Malaysia, most recently *The Reflowering of Malaysian Islam* (1984), and is coeditor of *Religion, Values and Development in Southeast Asia* (1986).

Tae-Kyu Park is Professor of Economics at Yonsei University, Seoul. A specialist in public economics, his research interests include government expenditure and taxation policy, social insurance, and the economics of private nonprofit organizations and philanthropy.

R. Bin Wong teaches history at the University of California, Irvine. He is coauthor of *Nourish the People: The State Civilian Granary System in China, 1650–1850* (1991) and *Societies and Cultures in World History;* in addition, he has published articles on economic, social, and political history in American, Chinese, Japanese, Taiwanese, French, and Dutch journals. He is currently finishing a book provisionally entitled *Economic Development, Political Change, and Social Protest in Chinese and European History.*

Alexander Woodside teaches Chinese and Southeast Asian history at the University of British Columbia. He is the author of *Vietnam and the Chinese Model* (1971, 1988) and *Community and Revolution in Modern Vietnam* (1976), and a coauthor of *Education and Society in Late Imperial China* (1994).

Dawnhee Yim is Director of Women's Affairs and Professor at Dongguk University, Seoul, where she teaches anthropology, folklore, and women's studies. She is also the president of the Korean Society for Cultural Anthropology. Together with Roger L. Janelli, she coauthored *Ancestor Worship and Korean Society* (1982) and *Making Capitalism: The Social and Cultural Construction of a South Korean Conglomerate* (1993) and is currently studying South Korea's recent social and cultural changes.

Index